D1726972

European Yearbook of International Economic Law

EYIEL Monographs - Studies in European and International Economic Law

Volume 20

EYIEL Monographs is a subseries of the European Yearbook of International Economic Law (EYIEL). It contains scholarly works in the fields of European and international economic law, in particular WTO law, international investment law, international monetary law, law of regional economic integration, external trade law of the EU and EU internal market law. The series does not include edited volumes. EYIEL Monographs are peer-reviewed by the series editors and external reviewers.

More information about this subseries at http://www.springer.com/series/15744

Fabian Bickel

Customs Unions in the WTO

Problems with Anti-Dumping

 Springer

Fabian Bickel
Berlin, Germany

ISSN 2364-8392 ISSN 2364-8406 (electronic)
European Yearbook of International Economic Law
ISSN 2524-6658 ISSN 2524-6666 (electronic)
EYIEL Monographs - Studies in European and International Economic Law
ISBN 978-3-030-86311-1 ISBN 978-3-030-86312-8 (eBook)
https://doi.org/10.1007/978-3-030-86312-8

This Springer imprint is published by the registered company Springer Nature Switzerland AG.
The registered company address is: Gewerbestrasse 11, 6330 Cham, Switzerland

Meinen Eltern

Acknowledgements

In the journey leading to this monograph, I was fortunate to have enjoyed the company of my wonderful friends and colleagues. First and foremost, I am thankful for the support of Prof. Christoph Herrmann. He was always there in times of need and encouraged and challenged my ideas. I am thankful to Prof. Pauwelyn for his valuable and extremely detailed comments on earlier drafts of this book.

I am grateful to Dr. Karl Brauner and Dr. Christian Melischek without whom my research stay at the WTO would not have been possible and for being great hosts. I thank Dr. Gustav Brink, Maxim Shmelev, Sahar Hosni, Darlan Martí, Alexis Massot, Jean-Daniel Rey, Nathalie Diaz, Carina van Vuuren, and Graham Cook for their valuable comments and helpful discussions. I also thank Dr. Katharina Steinbrück for her valuable input on an earlier draft of this book and her enduring support.

This monograph is a revised version of my doctoral thesis which was written at the Universität Passau. The thesis was supervised by Prof. Christoph Herrmann, who also acted as the first examiner. Prof. Joost Pauwelyn acted as the second examiner and Prof. Hans-Georg Dederer chaired the defence, which took place in June 2021.

This thesis would not have been possible without the unconditional support and help of my loved ones and especially not without my parents and Sarah Tillmann.

.

Contents

1 Introduction 1
   1.1   Research Question 6
   1.2   Scope of This Study 7
   1.3   Structure of This Study 9
   1.4   Contribution to the Existing Body of Literature 9
   References 10

2 Why Do Customs Unions Contain Rules on Anti-Dumping? 11
   2.1   Why Are Anti-Dumping Measures Legal? 12
       2.1.1   To Counteract Predatory Pricing 12
       2.1.2   For Political Reasons 13
       2.1.3   To Counteract Injurious Exploitation of Asymmetric
              Market Access 15
   2.2   Why Are Customs Unions Entered Into? 17
       2.2.1   Why Does Regional or Bilateral Economic Integration
              Happen Generally? 17
       2.2.2   Why Specifically in the Form of Customs Unions? 19
   2.3   Why Do Customs Unions Modify Anti-Dumping Legislation
       Internally? 21
       2.3.1   Predatory Pricing: Replacement by Competition Law 21
       2.3.2   Political Necessity: Pressure Valve 23
       2.3.3   Asymmetric Market Access 23
       2.3.4   Conclusions 24
   2.4   Why Do Customs Unions Modify Anti-Dumping Measures
       Externally? 24
       2.4.1   Transaction Costs 25
       2.4.2   Transition Costs 27
       2.4.3   Conclusions 28
   References 28

3   Practice in Customs Union   33
   3.1   Categorizing the Different Modifications   39
   3.2   Methodology   43
   3.3   Internal Practice   45
         3.3.1   Prohibition of Internal Anti-Dumping Measures   47
         3.3.2   Disincentivizing Anti-Dumping Measures   49
         3.3.3   Procedural Integration   51
         3.3.4   Conclusions   59
   3.4   External Practice   59
         3.4.1   Investigation Stage   63
         3.4.2   Imposition Decision   68
         3.4.3   Scope of Investigation and Measure   73
         3.4.4   Conclusions   75
   3.5   Associated Problems   76
         3.5.1   Membership in Several RTAs   76
         3.5.2   Non-preferential Rules of Origin   82
         3.5.3   Anti-Dumping Action on Behalf of a Third Country   83
   3.6   Conclusions   85
   References   86

4   WTO Framework   89
   4.1   Breach of WTO Provisions   90
         4.1.1   Violation of Art. VI GATT, ADA   91
         4.1.2   Violation of the MFN Principle   97
         4.1.3   Conclusions 104
   4.2   Justifications According to WTO Provisions 106
         4.2.1   Sources of Law 106
         4.2.2   Art. XXIV:5 GATT 108
         4.2.3   Enabling Clause 128
   4.3   Justification According to the RTA: Resolving the Conflict of
         Laws 139
         4.3.1   Third Party Claims 139
         4.3.2   Claims by Members of the Customs Union 140
   4.4   Customs Unions with Non-WTO Members 141
   4.5   Conclusions 143
   References 144

5   Responsibility for and Attribution of Anti-Dumping Measures 149
   5.1   What Is Responsibility and What Is Attribution? 151
         5.1.1   Definitions in International Law 151
         5.1.2   Responsibility, Attribution, International Obligations and
                 Anti-Dumping Measures 152
         5.1.3   Practical Relevance of Responsibility and Attribution 155
   5.2   Applicable Law 156
         5.2.1   Special Rules of Responsibility in WTO Law 157

      5.2.2   Special Rules of Responsibility in the Internal Laws of the
             Customs Unions 158
      5.2.3   Conclusions 161
  5.3 Degrees of Centralization 161
  5.4 Attribution of Anti-Dumping Measures to Customs Unions 162
      5.4.1   International Organizations 163
      5.4.2   Art. 6 ARIO: Organs or Agent of the International
             Organization 164
      5.4.3   Art. 7 ARIO: State Organs at the Disposal of an
             International Organization 177
      5.4.4   Art. 9 ARIO: Conduct Acknowledged and Adopted by
             an International Organization 179
      5.4.5   Chapter IV: Subsidiary Responsibility 180
      5.4.6   Conclusions 183
  5.5 Attribution of Anti-Dumping Measures to the Member States
      of Customs Unions 184
      5.5.1   Art. 4 ARSWIA: Organs or Agents of a State 185
      5.5.2   Art. 11 ARSIWA: Conduct Acknowledged and Adopted
             by a State 195
      5.5.3   Part Five ARIO: Subsidiary Responsibility 196
      5.5.4   Conclusions 197
  5.6 Relationship of the Responsibilities 197
  5.7 Conclusions 199
  References 200

6 Economic Integration and Economic Disintegration 205
  6.1 Case Studies: Economic Integration 206
      6.1.1   Measures of the State That Loses Its Competences 212
      6.1.2   Interim Reviews: EU Case Law & the Commission's
             Opinion 215
      6.1.3   Conclusions 221
  6.2 Case Study: Economic Disintegration (Brexit) 222
      6.2.1   Before Leaving the EU 223
      6.2.2   During the Transition Period 224
      6.2.3   After the Transition Period 225
      6.2.4   Conclusions 232
  6.3 WTO Law Limits 232
      6.3.1   Which Measures Apply Following Economic
             Integration? 232
      6.3.2   Which Measures Apply Following Economic
             Disintegration 235
      6.3.3   Can the Territorial Scope of Anti-Dumping Measures
             Change? 236
      6.3.4   Must the Applicable Measures Be Reviewed? 243
  6.4 Conclusions 255
  References 256

7   Anti-Dumping Measures Against Customs Unions   261
  7.1   Scope of Anti-Dumping Measures Applied Against a Customs
        Union or a Member Thereof   263
        7.1.1   Member Practice   263
        7.1.2   Anti-Dumping Measures Imposed Against Member States
                of a Customs Union   264
        7.1.3   Anti-Dumping Measures Imposed Against Customs
                Unions   265
  7.2   Effects of Economic Integration and Disintegration   268
        7.2.1   Anti-Dumping Measures Against an Enlarging Customs
                Union   268
        7.2.2   Anti-Dumping Measures Following Withdrawal   269
  7.3   Conclusions   270
  References   271

8   Conclusions   273

Cited Treaties and Legislation   277
  General International Law   277
  WTO Law   277
  Regional Agreements & Customs Union Law   278
      CACM   278
      CAN   278
      CARICOM   278
      CEMAC   278
      COMESA   279
      EAC   279
      EAEU and Predecessor   279
      ECOWAS   280
      EU and Predecessor   281
      EU – Andorra   286
      EU – San Marino   286
      EU – Turkey   286
      GCC   286
      MERCOSUR   286
      SACU   287
      WAEMU   287
      Other   287
  National Law   288

Cited Cases   291
  WTO & GATT Panels   291
  Other   294

Official Documents   297
  WTO & GATT Documents   297
  Other   303

Abbreviations

AB	Appellate Body
ADM	Anti-Dumping Measure
Brexit	UK Withdrawal from the EU in 2020
CACM	Central American Common Market
CAN	Andean Community
CARICOM	Caribbean Community and Common Market
CCT	Common Customs Tariff
CEMAC	Economic and Monetary Community of Central Africa
COMESA	Common Market for Eastern and Southern Africa
CTD	Committee on Trade and Development
CU	Customs Union
DIMD	EAEU Department for Internal Market Defence
DIT	UK Department for International Trade
DSB	Dispute Settlement Body
EAC	East African Community
EAEU	Eurasian Economic Union
ECOWAS	Economic Community of West African States
EEA	European Economic Area
EEC	Eurasian Economic Commission
EU	European Union
FSVPS	Russian Federal Service for Veterinary and Phytosanitary Supervision
GCC	Gulf Cooperation Council
GSP	General System of Preferences
IO	International Organization
LDC	Least Developed Country
MERCOSUR	Southern Common Market
MFN	Most-Favoured Nation
MS	Member States
NAFTA	North American Free Trade Agreement

NME	Non-Market Economies
ORC	Other Regulations of Commerce
ORRC	Other Restrictive Regulations of Commerce
PRS	Price Range System
SACU	South African Customs Union
TRA	UK Trade Remedy Authority
UN	United Nations
USMCA	United States Mexico Canada Agreement
WAEMU	West African Economic and Monetary Union
WTO	World Trade Organization

List of Figures

Fig. 3.1 Possible modifications of anti-dumping legislation 43
Fig. 3.2 Overview of Levels of Integration and Harmonization in Customs
Unions 44

List of Tables

Table 3.1   All customs unions and total anti-dumping measures   35
Table 3.2   Overview internal modifications   60
Table 3.3   Summary of additional rights and obligations if there is a
            centralized external investigating authority   65
Table 3.4   Summary   77
Table 3.5   RTAs concluded by CUs or their MS   78
Table 3.6   Overview of membership in several customs union   81
Table 4.1   Overview Breaches of WTO Obligations   105
Table 4.2   Justifications following Art. XXIV:5 GATT   128
Table 4.3   Justification following the enabling clause   138
Table 4.4   Overview of WTO legality of modifications   144
Table 5.1   Attribution of anti-dumping measures   200
Table 6.1   Effects of economic integration on anti-dumping measures   209
Table 7.1   Anti-dumping measures against customs unions or their
            member states   263

Chapter 1
Introduction

Even though the World Trade Organization (WTO)[1] sits at the centre of international trade law today, historically economic integration has usually happened through bilateral and regional trade agreements. Their existence should therefore not be seen as an anomaly in a multilateral trade order. Rather, the reverse is more true with the WTO being an exception in a unilateral, bilateral or regional world trade order.[2]

Therefore unsurprisingly, ongoing regional or bilateral economic integration has probably been the most significant trend for international trade in goods since the creation of the WTO. Whereas in 1995, when the WTO was founded, 47 Free Trade Agreements (FTAs) and customs unions (together: RTAs) were in force, this has increased more than six-fold to 303 in 2020.[3] RTAs have not only increased quantitatively but also qualitatively, with many RTAs now including wide-ranging obligations from investment provisions, the protection of IP rights, providing effective competition laws or ensuring labour standards, human rights or environmental protection[4]—all topics that are not or only scarcely regulated multilaterally.

This trend towards more and deeper regionalism is also reflected in a proliferation of customs unions. Whereas in 1995 only eight customs unions existed, by 2020 the number has doubled to 16. Among those, more are deeply integrated with four customs unions now reporting their anti-dumping measures jointly instead of just one—the EC—in 1995.

Events until 5 July 2021 were considered.

---

[1] Agreement Establishing the World Trade Organization (WTO Agreement).

[2] Cattaneo (2018), pp. 30–34.

[3] Source: WTO RTA Database, available at: https://rtais.wto.org/ (last accessed: 5 July 2021). This only includes RTAs that have been notified to the WTO.

[4] Chauffour and Maur (2010).

© The Author(s), under exclusive license to Springer Nature Switzerland AG 2021
F. Bickel, *Customs Unions in the WTO*, European Yearbook of International
Economic Law 20, https://doi.org/10.1007/978-3-030-86312-8_1

Some attribute this trend to the fact that multilateralism has been in decline ever since the failed WTO negotiations at the 1999 Seattle Ministerial Conference[5] or 2003 Cancun Ministerial Conference—the pivotal Conference that led to the failure of the Doha Round.[6,7] There are strong indications the trend against multilateralism will persist. The US' refusal to appoint Appellate Body members and thereby effectively blocking its functioning[8] or the US' threat to withdraw from the Government Procurement Agreement (GPA)[9] and even the WTO itself[10] are just an expression of this. More fundamentally, some argue that especially the emergence of China as an economic power has led towards a more geo-economic international trade order, dominated by political interests rather than a neoliberal attempt to free trade. One consequence of this is that multilateral decisions are more difficult to be reached.[11]

The decline of multilateralism leads to a void that can either be filled by regional economic integration or by unilateralism. Somewhat in contradiction to each other, there are indications that both trends will intensify.

Signs that there will be more regional economic integration are the conclusion of "mega-regionals" such as the Comprehensive and Progressive Trans-Pacific Partnership (CPTPP),[12] the Comprehensive Economic and Trade Agreement (CETA)[13] between the EU and Canada or the EU-South Korea FTA.[14] These "mega-regional" Agreements are special in that they are the first bilateral agreements between two or more large trading partners.[15] Above that, some regions, such as Africa, show prospects of further regional integration. The Treaty of Abuja[16] sets out the goal to conclude a single customs union between the members of the African Economic

[5]Bayne (2000), p. 131.

[6]Evenett (2004), p. 1.

[7]Lester et al. (2018), p. 3.

[8]On the Appellate Body crisis, see: Pauwelyn (2019), p. 297; Hoekman and Mavroidis (2019); Mcdougall (2018), p. 867.

[9]Baschuk (2020).

[10]'Trump Threatens to Pull US out of World Trade Organization' *BBC News* (31 August 2018) <https://www.bbc.com/news/world-us-canada-45364150> accessed 5 July 2021; 'Trump Threatened Then-WTO Chief With U.S. Withdrawal, Book Says' *Bloomberg.com* (10 September 2020) <https://www.bloomberg.com/news/articles/2020-09-10/trump-threatened-then-wto-chief-with-u-s-withdrawal-book-says> accessed 5 July 2021.

[11]Roberts et al. (2019), pp. 655, 670–673.

[12]Entry into force: 30.12.2018.

[13]Comprehensive Economic and Trade Agreement (CETA) between Canada, of the one part, and the European Union and its Member States, entry into force: 21.9.2017.

[14]Free Trade Agreement between the European Union and its Member States, on the one part, and the Republic of Korea, of the other part, entry into force: 1.12.2015.

[15]Lester et al. (2018), p. 4.

[16]Treaty Establishing the African Economic Community (Treaty of Abuja), 3.6.1991, entry into force: 12.5.1994.

Community through an integration of different customs unions.[17] The conclusion of the African Continental Free Trade Area (AfCFTA) in 2019[18] may be an important steppingstone in that direction.[19]

There are also good indications that unilateralism will proliferate in the future. The most significant indicator is the UK's withdrawal from the EU[20] which constitutes the first withdrawal of a state from a closely integrated customs union.

Regardless of whether tendencies towards more unilateralism, bilateralism or regionalism, or multilateralism intensify, regional economic integration is ever evolving and changing and the relationship between the different forms of economic integration create fundamental problems in general International Law and WTO law whose importance can hardly be overstated.

As a starting point, the WTO Agreement and RTAs are international agreements. In international law—except for *jus cogens*—no hierarchy exists.[21] Rather, international agreements can define their hierarchy to other agreements themselves. Any conflict between the two thus raises fundamental questions about the relationship between multilateral Agreements—the WTO Agreement—and bilateral or regional Agreements—the RTAs. This study contributes to the task of defining that relationship by focussing on the liberties WTO law provides to accommodate for customs unions specifically in the area of anti-dumping. This is relevant from a general international law perspective, as it clarifies when a conflict between customs unions and WTO law exists.

RTAs do not only sit uneasily within the WTO legal system from an abstract international law perspective but also because substantively they undermine the WTO system. A cornerstone of the multilateral trading system is that of equal treatment between WTO members. This has found its way into WTO law *inter alia* in the most favoured nation (MFN) principle as regulated in Art. I:1 GATT for trade in goods. However, the very idea of an RTA is to give preferential treatment to some countries, thereby standing in stark contrast to the principle of equal treatment, especially as mandated in the MFN clause. The way the WTO Agreements treat RTAs therefore also demonstrates its stance towards the different forms of economic integration. This study clarifies the delicate approach chosen by the WTO for customs unions in the area of anti-dumping.

Overall, RTAs are a reality in international trade law, but they fundamentally challenge the WTO, and their proliferation and changes cause multiple practical problems in consequence. This study is situated at the forefront of these developments and analyses the problems that regionalism brings about from the perspective

---

[17] Art. 4.2 Treaty of Abuja.

[18] Agreement Establishing the African Continental Free Trade Area, 21.3.2018, entry into force: 30.5.2019.

[19] Ajibo (2019), p. 871.

[20] See below: Sect. 6.2.

[21] Some discussions exist if e.g. Art. 103 United Nations, Charter of the United Nations, 24 October 1945, 1 UNTS XVI introduces a hierarchy in international law, Liivoja (2008), p. 583.

of WTO law. It considers how WTO law reacts to one form of RTA—customs unions—by focussing on one area of law that has traditionally been heavily regulated in the WTO and its predecessor the GATT, namely anti-dumping. Both points of focus of this study—anti-dumping and customs unions—are well suited to analyse the overlap between regionalism and multilateralism.

Anti-dumping measures are well suited to illustrate how WTO law deals with regionalism as they have a special place in WTO law. Their imposition has already been regulated in Art. VI GATT 1947[22] and an Anti-Dumping Code was later added in the Kennedy Round 1967.[23] That Anti-Dumping Code was then replaced by the Anti-Dumping Agreement in the Uruguay Round.[24] The rules on anti-dumping are relatively precise, compared to other areas of law in the WTO, because they are politically extremely sensitive and often face criticism of being protectionist instruments. This also explains why they have accounted for over 20% of all disputes in the DSB.[25] Their contentious standing within the WTO is also highlighted by the fact that one core criticism of the US against the Appellate Body relates to anti-dumping measures[26] and proposals are discussed to have a special Appellate Body for trade remedy appeals alone.[27]

Customs unions are well suited to illustrate how WTO law deals with regionalism, as especially the fact that they harmonize external trade raises specific structural problems. This is because centralizing institutions up to possessing international legal personality raises fundamental questions of responsibility. Like Free Trade Agreements (FTAs) customs unions liberalize internal trade, but beyond that they also harmonize external trade by creating and applying a common external tariff.[28] Creating and applying a common external tariff requires central institutions which in turn requires the conferral of competences that member states previously held to the customs union. Through the conferral of competences and the creation of centralized institutions, customs unions may gain international legal personality themselves, thus becoming international organizations and even potentially be eligible to join the WTO.[29]

---

[22] The General Agreement on Tariffs and Trade 1947 (GATT).

[23] Sub-Committee on Non-Tariff Barriers, Group on Anti-Dumping Policies, 'Draft Report on the Group on Anti-Dumping Policies' (1967 Anti-Dumping Code), TN.64/NTB/W/19, 24.4.1967.

[24] Agreement on Implementation of Article VI of the General Agreement on Tariffs and Trade 1994 (Anti-Dumping Agreement or ADA).

[25] 134 of 596 cases have cited the ADA in their request for consultation. See: WTO, Disputes by Agreement (https://www.wto.org/english/tratop_e/dispu_e/dispu_agreements_index_e.htm), last accessed: 5 July 2021.

[26] United States Trade Representative, 'Report on the Appellate Body of the World Trade Organization', 02.2020, pp. 95–104.

[27] Hillman (2020), pp. 4–7 <https://t.co/8WeQjqFyB4?amp=1>.

[28] Compare Art. XXIV:8 GATT.

[29] Art. XII WTO Agreement speaking of "any state or *separate customs territory*". The EU is the only customs union that is a WTO member.

If customs unions may even be WTO members alongside their member states, this raises the question of the relationship to their members. An analysis of customs unions in the WTO therefore also analyses what kind of requirements or legal consequences the WTO sets for the institutional setup of customs unions. This in turn defines the relationship between multilateral and bilateral or regional economic integration in general as it clarifies the framework in which bilateral or regional economic integration is even possible. Moreover, how the WTO has accommodated customs unions is in turn relevant for other forms of regional integration, where setting up institutions gains prominence and where similar questions may arise in the future.[30]

This study analyses from a WTO perspective how anti-dumping measures change if states are in a customs union. It thereby explores and adds to the existing body of literature on questions why customs unions regulate anti-dumping at all, how they do so and what limits the WTO poses.

Beyond this, this study also considers the WTO law consequences of the different institutional setups the various customs unions have adopted in the area of anti-dumping. How a customs union has structured its anti-dumping regime becomes relevant in three situations. First, the institutional setup influences responsibility for and attribution of anti-dumping measures. This is relevant as it answers who can claim the benefits of and who is accountable for anti-dumping measures. Second, the institutional setup influences the consequences of economic integration and disintegration on anti-dumping measures. This seemingly rare situation gains prominence with the UK's withdrawal from the EU and the UK's contentious plan to copy and paste the EU's anti-dumping measures. Third, the institutional setup of a customs unions is relevant for third parties that wish to impose anti-dumping measures against the customs union or members thereof.

These issues are not only conceptually important but also bear significant practical relevance. 36–38% of all anti-dumping measures imposed since 2011 have been imposed by states in a customs union or by customs unions themselves.[31] The results are even more staggering if one accounts for the fact that where a customs union

---

[30] Steger (2012), p. 109.

[31] Committee on Anti-Dumping Practices, Report (2010) of the Committee on Anti-Dumping Practices, G/L/935, 28.10.2010; Committee on Anti-Dumping Practices, Report (2011) of the Committee on Anti-Dumping Practices G/L/966, 26.20.2011; Committee on Anti-Dumping Practices, Report (2012) of the Committee on Anti-Dumping Practices G/L/1006, 25.10.2012; Committee on Anti-Dumping Practices, Report (2013) of the Committee on Anti-Dumping Practices G/L/1053, 29.10.2013; Committee on Anti-Dumping Practices, Report (2014) of the Committee on Anti-Dumping Practices G/L/1079, 31.10.2014; Committee on Anti-Dumping Practices, Report (2015) of the Committee on Anti-Dumping Practices G/L/1134, G/ADP/22, 30.10.2015; Committee on Anti-Dumping Practices, Report (2016) of the Committee on Anti-Dumping Practices G/L/1158, G/ADP/23, 1.11.2016; Committee on Anti-Dumping Practices, Report (2017) of the Committee on Anti-Dumping Practices G/L/1193, G/ADP/24, 30.10.2017; Committee on Anti-Dumping Practices, Report (2018) of the Committee on Anti-Dumping Practices G/L/1270, G/ADP/25, 29.10.2018; Committee on Anti-Dumping Practices, Report (2019) of the Committee on Anti-Dumping Practices G/L/1344, G/ADP/26, 21.11.2019.

imposes anti-dumping measures jointly, all member states of that customs union are protected by that measure. Focussing on which states are protected by a measure (i.e. counting the EU's anti-dumping measures as 27 instead of one, as it protects 27 states), the percentage of anti-dumping measures imposed by a customs union or members thereof raises to an average of 77% in the last 10 years.

The empirical relevance of customs unions in the context of anti-dumping measures, combined with the relevance within the broader debate on the relationship between regionalism and multilateralism give the necessary relevance to a comprehensive study on the issue. Before diving into this study, the research question will be defined (under Sect. 1.1), the scope of this study justified (Under Sect. 1.2), the structure of the research explained (under Sect. 1.3) and its contributions to the existing body of literature highlighted (under Sect. 1.4).

1.1   Research Question

The typical process for states to impose and apply WTO compliant anti-dumping measures is as follows: First, the state passes legislation that allows its authorities to conduct investigations and impose anti-dumping measures. This legislation will have to comply with WTO law. Second, the national authorities will then investigate and impose measures following that legislation. The measure then applies against imports into that state. Third, insofar as third parties believe that either the legislation or the resulting measure violate WTO law, they can challenge it in the WTO's Dispute Settlement System and the state that has legislated or imposed the measure will be responsible for any violation of WTO law. Conversely and fourth, if third parties wish to apply anti-dumping measures against goods produced within the territory of that WTO member, they can do so upon adopting the necessary legislation and imposing a measure in compliance with their WTO obligations.

However, if a WTO member is a member of a customs union as well, this process differs in several key aspects. First, legislation allowing authorities to investigate and impose anti-dumping measures will have to be passed either by the member states of the customs union or by the customs union itself, depending on who is competent. That law must comply with WTO obligations as well as obligations stemming from the customs union agreement or other RTAs. Second, the respective authority conducts the investigation and imposes the measure according to that legislation. The resulting measure then normally applies against imports into the territory of the state or the entire customs union. As customs unions are not static, their composition or their competences can change. The effect of such changes on anti-dumping measures is not clear. Even though territorial changes are also problematic with states, they happen more frequently and in different forms in customs unions. Third, if third countries believe that either the legislation or the resulting measure violate WTO obligations, they may challenge them in the WTO's Dispute Settlement System. However, challenges can only be brought against WTO members and the member must be responsible for the measure. Responsibility for the anti-dumping measures could either lie with the customs union or its member states or both. Forth, if third countries wish to impose anti-dumping measures against products originating in that customs union, it is not clear whether they can impose anti-dumping measures against the entire customs union or only against the member states of the customs union.

This study examines these differences. In more abstract terms, this study explores the differences between anti-dumping regimes by states and anti-dumping regimes that apply if states are in customs unions. The aim of this is to clarify the rules and flexibilities WTO law offers for customs unions in the field of anti-dumping. This will be approached on two levels: First, how anti-dumping legislation of customs unions differs from anti-dumping legislation of states will be considered. This includes an examination of why and how anti-dumping legislation differs in customs unions and the limits WTO law sets on these modifications. Second, the effects of these differences will be explored. This includes an assessment of how the different modifications relate to notions on responsibility, how the different modifications impact anti-dumping measures in cases of economic integration and disintegration and what effects these modifications have for third parties that wish to impose anti-dumping measures against states or customs unions.

1.2 Scope of This Study

This study is limited to an examination of anti-dumping regimes in customs unions.

It is difficult to define customs unions, due to the great variance of existing regional trade agreements that call themselves a customs union. This study understands customs unions broadly following the prescriptive definition provided in Art. XXIV:8(a) GATT:

> A customs union shall be understood to mean the substitution of a single customs territory for two or more customs territories, so that
>
> (i) duties and other restrictive regulations of commerce (except, where necessary, those permitted under Art. XI, XII, XIII, XIV, XV, XX [GATT]) are eliminated with respect to substantially all the trade between the constituent territories of the union or at least with respect to substantially all the trade in products originating in such territories, and,
>
> (ii) subject to the provisions of [Art. XXIV:9 GATT], substantially the same duties and other regulations of commerce are applied by each of the members of the union to the trade of territories not included in the union.

A customs union thus has an internal element, whereby its members liberalize trade to the specified extent and an external element, whereby members must apply the same rules to trade with third countries to the specified extent.

Apart from customs unions, regional integration can also occur through Free Trade Agreements or through Generalized Systems of Preferences. These forms of regional integration do not harmonize external trade and will therefore not be considered in this study. Some parts of this study relate to trade liberalization between the member states of the customs union. Arguments in these parts could also apply to those other forms of regional economic integration. Those parts that focus on external harmonization or the consequences that derive from having shared institutions flowing from that harmonization are, however, specific to customs unions. It is also this external element that leads to specific conceptual and practical problems, which justifies that the study remains overall limited to customs unions.

Sometimes further distinctions are made between customs unions, single markets and economic unions.[32] This study will not take these further distinctions into account for several reasons. First, the precise point at which an RTA becomes a single market, or an economic union is not clear. Second, the distinguishing feature of a single market is that there is free movement of goods. Although prohibition of internal anti-dumping measures is necessary for this, it is not sufficient. Third, single markets do not have to be customs unions. The additional requirements mainly relate to internal trade liberalization, which is why the EEA is typically classified as a single market. Fourth and finally, WTO law only distinguishes between FTAs and customs unions.

This study is limited to anti-dumping measures and does not consider other trade remedy measures, namely countervailing and safeguard measures. Anti-dumping measures are trade measures that take the form of either provisional or definitive tariffs or price undertakings.[33] They are imposed following an investigation that establishes that producers or exporters conduct dumping, i.e. export products at prices below normal value[34] and this causes material injury or a threat of material injury to the domestic industry or materially retards the establishment of such industry.[35]

Compared to this, safeguard measures do not react to unfair trade practices but are justified only because of injury to domestic production that is caused by exports.[36] Due to differences in the justification of the measure, many arguments cannot apply to safeguard measures. Similarly, countervailing measures are imposed as a reaction to subsidization causing injury to the domestic production.[37] Although the reasoning in many sections of this study can also apply to countervailing measures, they have been omitted because they are significantly less relevant in practice and because some arguments developed in this study specifically relate to the justification of anti-dumping measures so that these arguments cannot necessarily apply.

---

[32] E.g. Marceau (1994), p. 168; Jovanović (1992), p. 9; Krueger (1997), pp. 169, 173–174.

[33] Art. 7, 8, 9 ADA.

[34] Art. 2 ADA.

[35] Art. 3 ADA.

[36] Art. 2.1 Agreement on Safeguards (Safeguards Agreement or SG).

[37] Art. 19.1 Agreement on Subsidies and Countervailing Measures (SCM).

1.3   Structure of This Study

The purpose of this study is to analyse how WTO law in the field of anti-dumping deals with one kind of regionalism, namely customs unions. This study considers the effects of a WTO member being in a customs union on anti-dumping legislation and measures on two levels. First, it analyses how anti-dumping legislation in customs unions differs from WTO compliant anti-dumping legislation in states. This includes an examination of why and how customs unions modify anti-dumping legislation and what limits WTO law sets on the ability of customs unions to diverge from the requirements in the ADA as applied by states. Second, it analyses the effects of these modifications. This includes an analysis on the effects on responsibility for anti-dumping measures, the consequences of the different anti-dumping regimes in situations of economic integrations and disintegrations and on third parties that wish to impose anti-dumping measures against a customs union or member states thereof. The study is structured along these lines.

Chapter 2 traces the reasons why customs unions modify anti-dumping legislation. Chapter 3 analyses how the current customs unions do so, and Chap. 4 considers the limits WTO law sets on these modifications. The institutional arrangements of anti-dumping legislation impact the responsibility for these measures. Responsibility for and attribution of anti-dumping measures will be considered in Chap. 5. The way in which the anti-dumping regime works also impacts existing anti-dumping measures in cases of economic integration and disintegration. This will be analysed in Chap. 6. Finally, certain modifications may allow that third countries do not only impose anti-dumping measures against states but against the entire customs union. This will be considered in Chap. 7.

1.4   Contribution to the Existing Body of Literature

This study adds to the existing body of literature in the field of trade defence and regionalism in several aspects. From a normative point of view, this study analyses WTO legality of changes that occur to anti-dumping legislation in customs unions as well as rationalizing why these changes occur. From a factual point of view, this study provides an overview of the different anti-dumping legislations in the various customs unions, analyses the WTO cases that raised issues relating to regionalism, and provides an overview of instances of economic integration and disintegration that have occurred in the past.

Overall, the main contribution of this study to the existing body of literature is that it considers different abstract problems that arise due to regionalism in the WTO from a different perspective. Typically, problems that arise due to regionalism have been discussed in isolation from each other: The question why customs unions modify anti-dumping provisions has been answered without reference to the actual modifications, a study on the modifications of anti-dumping provisions in RTAs has been conducted in isolation from the WTO legality of these provisions. Responsibility has typically been considered from an abstract perspective with the goal to define responsibility for all international organizations or a customs union in all cases.

The approach taken in this study is different. Instead of attempting a comprehensive study in any of these areas, this study focuses on one aspect of these studies—anti-dumping regimes in customs unions—and combines the different fields of study.

References

Academic Texts

Ajibo C (2019) African continental free trade area agreement: the euphoria, pitfalls and prospects. J World Trade 53:871

Baschuk B (2020) Trump considers withdrawing from WTO's $1.7 trillion purchasing pact. Bloomberg.com, 4 February 2020. <https://www.bloomberg.com/news/articles/2020-02-04/trump-mulls-withdrawal-from-wto-s-1-7-trillion-purchasing-pact>. Accessed 5 July 2021

Bayne N (2000) Why did Seattle fail? globalization and the politics of trade. Gov Oppos 35:131

Cattaneo O (2018) The political economy of PTAs. In: Lester S, Mercurio B, Bartels L (eds) Bilateral and regional trade agreements - commentary and analysis. Cambridge University Press

Chauffour J-P, Maur J-C (2010) Beyond market access: the new normal of preferential trade agreements. Policy Research Working Paper WPS5454, The World Bank. <http://documents.worldbank.org/curated/en/638891468326209179/Beyond-market-access-the-new-normal-of-preferential-trade-agreements>. Accessed 5 July 2021

Evenett SJ (2004) Systemic research questions raised by the failure of the WTO ministerial meeting in Cancun. Legal Iss Econ Integr 31:1

Hillman J (2020) Three approaches to fixing the World Trade Organization's appellate body: the good, the bad and the ugly? Institute of International Economic Law, Georgetown University Law Center <https://t.co/8WeQjqFyB4?amp=1>

Hoekman B, Mavroidis PC (2019) Burning Down the House? The Appellate Body in the Centre of the WTO Crisis. EUI Working Paper RSCAS 2019/56, European University Institute – Robert Schuman Centre for Advanced Studies 2019. <https://www.ssrn.com/abstract=3424856>. Accessed 5 July 2021

Jovanović MN (1992) International economic integration. Routledge

Krueger AO (1997) Free Trade Agreements versus customs Unions. J Dev Econ 54:169

Lester S, Mercurio B, Bartels L (2018) Introduction. Bilateral and regional trade agreements - commentary and analysis, 2nd edn. Cambridge University Press

Liivoja R (2008) The scope of the supremacy clause of the United Nations Charter. Int Comp Law Q 57:583

Marceau G (1994) Anti-dumping and anti-trust issues in free-trade areas. Oxford University Press

Mcdougall R (2018) The crisis in WTO dispute settlement: fixing birth defects to restore balance. J World Trade 52:867

Pauwelyn J (2019) WTO dispute settlement post 2019: what to expect? J Int Econ Law 22:297

Roberts A, Choer Moraes H, Ferguson V (2019) Toward a geoeconomic order in international trade and investment. J Int Econ Law 22:655

Steger DP (2012) Institutions for regulatory cooperation in "New Generation" economic and trade agreements. Legal Iss Econ Integr 39:109

Chapter 2
Why Do Customs Unions Contain Rules on Anti-Dumping?

If a state wishes to impose anti-dumping measures, legally the situation is straight-forward: Art. VI GATT and the ADA set out the requirements that must be fulfilled for the imposition of anti-dumping measures to be legal. This is less straight-forward if a state is in a customs union as well. The state will not only be bound by WTO law but also by customs union law. Moreover, customs union law on anti-dumping usually deviates from WTO law on two different levels. Internally, customs unions restrict or even prohibit the imposition of anti-dumping measures and externally they harmonize their imposition. Even though customs unions amend WTO rules on anti-dumping along these lines, the resulting anti-dumping systems differ greatly.

This Chapter considers why the different modifications that occur within customs unions are similar in their aim but, despite that common motivation, result in vastly different anti-dumping regulations in the various customs unions. This study adds to the debate on why customs unions modify anti-dumping regulation internally by linking existing arguments to the justification of anti-dumping measures. Moreover, this study develops arguments under which circumstances external harmonization of anti-dumping measures—an aspect that has yet to receive in depth analysis—occurs. It does so by applying strands of argumentation of the institutional analysis research field.

These arguments will be developed in two steps. The first step considers why anti-dumping measures are imposed (under Sect. 2.1) and why customs unions are formed (under Sect. 2.2). The second step then considers how forming a customs union modifies the reason why anti-dumping measures are imposed and thereby necessitates legal amendments internally (under Sect. 2.3) and externally (under Sect. 2.4).

F. Bickel, *Customs Unions in the WTO*, European Yearbook of International Economic Law 20, https://doi.org/10.1007/978-3-030-86312-8_2

2.1   Why Are Anti-Dumping Measures Legal?

The ADA does not contain a preamble or a provision that explains why anti-dumping measures are allowed or necessary.[1] Their purpose can, however, be derived from the requirements they must meet to be legal. WTO law conditions the imposition of anti-dumping measures on certain substantive requirements. These are that there must be dumping[2] causing injury to the domestic production.[3] Dumping thereby refers to a pricing practice by producers or exporters that export goods at prices below normal value.[4] The normal value of a product is usually the comparable price of the like product in the ordinary course of trade when destined for consumption in the exporting country.[5]

The lack of justification within the ADA or GATT has broadly led to three different strands of argumentation why anti-dumping measures are justified.

2.1.1   To Counteract Predatory Pricing

Historically, anti-dumping measures have been justified by focussing on the requirement that there must be dumping. The argument was that if dumping is harmful, the prevention of dumping through anti-dumping measures is justified. Dumping is harmful as its purpose is to gain market access with the aim to establish a monopoly and then raise prices above the competitive level to seek monopolist rents, leading to an overall welfare loss. This pricing strategy is referred to as "predatory pricing". Supporters of this view acknowledged that besides predatory pricing, dumping may also have other causes that are not harmful.[6] However, dumping prices are "presumptive evidence of abnormal and temporary cheapness" which in turn justifies the imposition of anti-dumping measures, even if the exporter or producer follows a different aim.[7]

Even though there is consensus that predatory pricing is harmful,[8] it cannot serve as justification for all anti-dumping measures. Empirically, cases of predatory pricing are rare and most cases of dumping even lead to overall welfare gains as

---

[1]*European Union - Anti-Dumping Measures on Biodiesel from Argentina* [2016] WTO Panel Report WT/DS473/R [7.238]; *European Union - Anti-Dumping Measures on Biodiesel from Argentina* [2016] WTO Appellate Body Report WT/DS473/AB/R [6.25].

[2]Art. 2 ADA.

[3]Art. 3 ADA.

[4]Art. 2.1 ADA.

[5]Art. 2.1 ADA.

[6]Viner (1923), pp. 145–146.

[7]Ibid 147.

[8]Morgan (1996), pp. 61, 68–69; Miranda (1996), p. 255; Hoffmeister (2018) para 18. For a Definition of the term, see: Thompson et al. (2018) para 10.078.

consumers benefit from cheaper (dumped) products with future price increases being unlikely.[9] Above that, the justification does not fit the requirements. If the purpose of anti-dumping measures is to combat predatory pricing, this cannot explain why a cross-border element and injury are necessary, why other forms of monopolization such as through mergers are not prohibited[10] and why there is no leeway to defend the dumping practice if it is motivated differently.

2.1.2 For Political Reasons

These shortcomings have led some to conclude that anti-dumping measures—except for cases of predatory pricing—cannot be explained on economic grounds. Rather, anti-dumping measures are political tools. Opinions then differ on which aims anti-dumping measures follow.

Traditionally, it has been argued that the political reason to employ anti-dumping measures are protectionist reasons,[11] without considering more specifically what these protectionist aims are and without questioning whether they may be justified. Although protectionist aims are better achieved through the imposition of tariffs, anti-dumping measures are a second-best alternative.[12] Because of the discretion offered to investigating authorities,[13] there is enough room to interpret the provisions in a way that pursues protectionist aims.[14] Anti-dumping measures are particularly well suited to achieve those aims, as the detected unfair trade practices can be used to disguise the real intent of the measures, which enables the imposing party to diffuse political costs of the decision.[15] Finally, anti-dumping measures are biased towards protection from import competition. This is because they can only address the situation in which dumping causes an injury but not the lack of import competition.[16]

---

[9] Müller et al. (2009) para I.08; Hoffmeister (2018) para 17; Depayre (2008), pp. 123, 125–126; Mankiw and Swagel (2005), pp. 107, 110–112; Kovacic (2009); Choi (2016) SSRN Scholarly Paper ID 2916049 <https://papers.ssrn.com/abstract=2916049> accessed 5 July 2021; Conway (1991) WPS782 <http://documents.worldbank.org/curated/en/872661468767079890/The-economic-effects-of-widespread-application-of-antidumping-duties-to-import-pricing> accessed 5 July 2021.

[10] Mavroidis (2012), pp. 420–422.

[11] Ibid; Michael Finger (1993), pp. 31–32; Mankiw and Swagel (2005), p. 107; Karacaovali (2011).

[12] Prusa (2016), p. 120.

[13] Tharakan (1995), p. 1550, 1556.

[14] Prusa and Teh (2011), p. 64; Depayre (2008), p. 127. Moore analyses sunset reviews in the US and concludes that the system is flawed because although reviews are formally compliant with WTO law, they always lead to the same result, namely that the measure will be kept. See: Moore (2002), p. 675.

[15] Finger et al. (1982), pp. 452, 453–455; Finger (1993), pp. 30–31.

[16] Teh et al. (2007); Prusa and Teh (2011), p. 64.

In direct response to this, some have argued that pursuing protectionist aims is a necessary evil in the process of trade liberalization. This view has been developed in the context of retaining anti-dumping measures in RTAs. The same argument can also be made generally: The WTO allows anti-dumping measures as their retention was necessary to achieve multilateral trade liberalization to the degree that has been achieved.

Some argue that anti-dumping measures are a necessary evil in trade liberalization. Anti-dumping measures can work as a pragmatic tool to deal with the political demands for protection that trade liberalization provokes.[17] This is because necessary adjustments upon trade liberalization may be cushioned by the imposition of anti-dumping measures.[18] Moreover, trade liberalization may have unintended effects on import competing sectors.[19] Anti-dumping measures anticipate the costs of adjustments and alleviate their pressure (like a pressure valve). Although it is still unclear whether this effect actually exists in practice,[20] it is at least plausible that this is a reason why the WTO allows anti-dumping measures in some cases.

Even if one follows this argument, the impacts of it are limited. It only applies to the limited case where greater trade liberalization is only achieved by retaining anti-dumping measures. It is difficult to prove this hypothesis empirically. Moreover, it only serves as an argument to cushion unintended effects for the period of adjustment, thereby setting a time limit on how long this justifies anti-dumping measures above economic necessity.

Some have then considered what kind of political motives are being followed when imposing anti-dumping measures.

Sohn has attempted to rationalise China's anti-dumping strategy by arguing that China uses anti-dumping measures to retaliate against perceived injustices. Sohn's empirical analysis shows that China rarely imposes anti-dumping measures against developing countries but frequently does so against developed countries, despite increasing trade with developing countries. Sohn reasons that this is done to retaliate against trade measures imposed by developed countries.[21]

Beyond that, anti-dumping measures may also be applied to pursue more general political aims such as environmental issues, human rights protection and ensuring higher labour standards. Examples of this are Ghana's anti-dumping law where the injury calculation also considers broader injuries to society and the environment,[22]

---

[17]Teh et al. (2007), p. 167; Prusa and Teh (2011), p. 65; Prusa (2016), p. 120; Grabitz et al. (1994), p. 20.

[18]Teh et al. (2007), p. 168; Prusa and Teh (2011), p. 65; Prusa (2016), p. 120.

[19]Prusa (2016), p. 120.

[20]Research is divided on the issue. Where a developing country is a heavy user of Anti-Dumping there is clear support for this argument. See: Moore and Zanardi (2009), p. 469; Moore and Zanardi (2011), p. 601; Bown and Tovar (2011), p. 115. These articles are, however, of using the argument beyond the scope of the research. Arguing that the argument is valid in general: Bown and Crowley (2013), p. 1071; Fischer and Prusa (2003), p. 745.

[21]Sohn (2020), p. 127.

[22]Kufuor (2013).

or examples where anti-dumping measures in the renewable energy sector have been used to promote green industrial policy.[23] This strand of argumentation accepts that anti-dumping measures lack a clear rationale and accepts that the requirements to impose anti-dumping measures are sufficiently vague to pursue political goals. However, it argues that the political goals pursued are justified as they are issues where the multilateral trade system has not produced satisfactory outcomes. Using anti-dumping thereby unilaterally advances these goals, as multilateral agreements on these issues are not in sight.

2.1.3 To Counteract Injurious Exploitation of Asymmetric Market Access

A final strand of argumentation tackles the political explanations of anti-dumping measures by attempting a different economic explanation. It draws the justification of anti-dumping measures not from their requirements but from a precondition that enables dumping, namely an asymmetry of market access.[24] The assumption is that without asymmetric market access, dumping is not possible. If goods could move freely between two states, it would not be possible to export products to another state at prices below the normal value, as importers could re-export the products to the market in which they originate at prices below normal value until the prices of the two markets align (arbitrage). Dumping is only possible if products cannot be re-exported because of some market entry barriers that exist in the country of production or export of the dumped product, i.e. in cases of asymmetric market access. Some suggest that asymmetric market access acts in a similar way as a subsidy.[25]

Asymmetric market access is a result of active government intervention or is at least acquiescence of anti-competitive behaviour by their economic operators (e.g. by not employing competition rules effectively).[26] It may result traditionally from keeping tariff and non-tariff barriers to trade in place. Beyond that, it may also result from broad government interventions that favour domestic production, such as subsidies that cannot be challenged under the SCM, export taxes or participation by the government in the economic market up to a point that calls into question whether a country is still a market economy.[27]

As asymmetric market access may result from different reasons, detecting it is challenging and it is difficult to take these considerations into account sticking purely to the methodologies provided in the ADA. The EU has attempted to take

---

[23] Espa (2019).

[24] Müller et al. (2009) para I.06; Hoffmeister (2018) para 19; Lux (2017) para 5.

[25] Depayre (2008), p. 126.

[26] Müller et al. (2009) para I.06; Mastel (1998), pp. 15–16.

[27] Wu (2016), p. 65; Geraets (2018).

these wider considerations on market access into account when it introduced a new dumping calculation methodology allowing it to construct the normal value, if there are 'significant market distortions' in the exporting country.[28] Whether anti-dumping measures can be used to address these market distortions generally[29] and whether it is possible to do it in the way the EU has proposed,[30] has been at the centre of significant academic debate.

Irrespective of which considerations can be taken into account to assess asymmetric market access, anti-dumping may be justified according to notions of fairness. Where domestic producers are injured by import competition not because they are less efficient or comparatively disadvantaged but because of behaviour enabled through market segregation, that is not fair. Put differently, not allowing competition in one's home market, yet benefitting from the openness of other markets is unfair.[31] Of course, the best way to remedy this unfairness would be to prevent market segregation altogether. Before that has been achieved, anti-dumping measures are a second-best solution, according to this view.[32]

Cases of strategic dumping may illustrate this view. Strategic dumping occurs where a monopolist or oligopolist in the home market uses the monopoly rents to lower export prices with the aim to gain market shares in foreign markets. This may drive a more efficient competitor in the foreign market out of competition, as that competitor does not have a sanctuary home market from which it can profit and possibly cannot penetrate the monopolist's or oligopolist's home market due to market entry barriers.[33] In this case the asymmetry in market access may originate from the exporting state's unwillingness to enforce competition rules or a state's involvement in the monopolist, actively hindering competition thus enabling the monopolist to secure such a position in the first place or the exporting state's tariff or non-tariff barriers, both preventing arbitrage.

However, this view has not been without criticism either. If the purpose of anti-dumping measures is to prevent unfair advantages stemming from market segregation, it is not clear why investigating authorities do not even need to test if there is market segregation.[34] Above that, asymmetric market access can also occur even if competition law is applied effectively and if there are no tariff or non-tariff barriers. It is possible that a company becomes a monopolist without violating competition law and can utilize monopoly rents to gain market shares in another market. Beyond that, certain goods have higher market entry costs for reasons that lie in the characteristic of the good. E.g., if a monopolist car producer dumps cars onto another

---

[28] Reg. (EU) 2017/2321 amending Reg. (EU) 2016/1036 and introducing a new Art. 2(6)(a).

[29] Zhou and Percival (2016), p. 863.

[30] Akritidis and Sneij (2018), p. 129; Espa and Levy (2018), p. 313; Noël and Zhou (2019); Antonini (2018), p. 79; Suse (2017), p. 951.

[31] Vermulst (2007), p. 714.

[32] Ibid; Müller et al. (2009) para I.09.

[33] Müller et al. (2009) para I.13.

[34] Hoekman and Mavroidis (1996), p. 27, 30.

market, transportation costs may prevent re-exportation of the cars at competitive prices. Anti-dumping law does not distinguish between that situation and a situation in which the exporting state acted unfairly.

2.2 Why Are Customs Unions Entered Into?

Having considered why anti-dumping measures are legal, the rationale for the other element of this study—customs unions—must be considered. Answering why customs unions are entered into consists of two parts: a general part on why bilateral or regional economic integration happens at all (under Sect. 2.2.1) and a concrete part, why it happens in the form of customs unions (under Sect. 2.2.2).

2.2.1 Why Does Regional or Bilateral Economic Integration Happen Generally?

The question why regional or bilateral economic integration happens has always been at the centre of significant academic debate. Various typologies and strands of argumentation have developed whereby a lot of the debate has centred around two main attempts to explain bilateral and regional economic integration: an economic and a political one.

The starting point of the economic argument for regional or bilateral integration is that trade liberalization is economically beneficial. Numerous trade theories have emerged to support this in general,[35] but this rationale does not apply unequivocally.[36] The crucial question is then how trade liberalization can be achieved: unilaterally, bilaterally and regionally, or multilaterally. Economic theory typically sees unilateral[37] or multilateral economic integration as superior to bilateral or regional economic integration. The reason it sees bilateral or regional economic integration with caution is because the positive effects of trade creation must be weighed against the negative effects of trade diversion[38] with numerous economic theories trying to answer how this is best done.[39] This is why generally RTAs are seen as a second-best option.[40]

---

[35] For an overview, see: Krugman et al. (2015), pp. 42–237.

[36] See e.g. on the argument to protect infant industries: Juhász (2018), p. 3339.

[37] E.g. Krugman (1997), p. 113.

[38] Viner (1950); Meade (1955).

[39] For a historical account, see: Tovias (1991), p. 5. For a general overview: Jovanovic (2016), pp. 40–207; Lyons (2018), pp. 11–13; Alan Winters (2011).

[40] Mavroidis (2006), p. 187, 190.

Even though regional and bilateral economic integration is only a second-best option, most international economic integration happens in that way. This is because regional and bilateral economic integration is politically more easily attainable compared to unilateral or multilateral economic integration. Why it is more easily attainable than unilateral economic integration can be explained by portraying economic integration as a prisoner's dilemma. As the costs of protecting the domestic industry can be passed on to foreign exporters through tariffs, this incentivises states to defect from unilateral trade liberalization. This means that each state has an incentive to engage in protectionism (to help its domestic industry at the expense of foreign industry), but all states could be better off as a group if they liberalized trade. Trade agreements neutralize the incentive to do this.[41] Why it is more easily attainable than multilateral integration can be explained by understanding trade agreements as a balance between free trade and protectionist advocates within a state. RTAs are more flexible and easier to achieve than multilateral agreements. This is because sensitive sectors can be carved out of the agreements, which may appease protectionists. Moreover, new disciplines can be pursued where multilateral consensus has not yet been reached which may generate support from groups that advocate free trade.[42]

A political explanation of why bilateral or regional integration occurs sees RTAs as a foreign policy instrument. The economic policy objectives that especially the EU and the US pursue through RTAs are imposing rules (e.g. on competition, IP) and standards on the rest of the world. Above that, some argue that RTAs also operate as foreign policy instruments to avoid military conflict through greater economic integration, as has been one of the founding reasons for the EU. Moreover, especially the EU, US and China are said to use RTAs to pursue broader political objectives. Examples of this are that the US has rewarded participation in the war against terror through the conclusion of RTAs; the EU includes provisions that exceed trade policy and encompass environmental or human rights provisions; and China is said to have become active in concluding FTAs to isolate Taiwan.[43]

Overall, for the purpose of this study it is sufficient to point out that there are some economic reasons for concluding an RTA, even though they do not unequivocally and in all instances support the conclusion of an RTA. Beyond that, RTAs must be seen as part of a complex web of international political interactions.

---

[41] Trachtman (2016), p. 353. For more detail, see: Bagwell and Staiger (2011), p. 1238.
[42] Cattaneo (2018), pp. 38–40.
[43] Ibid 42–48.

2.2.2 Why Specifically in the Form of Customs Unions?

Bilateral and regional integration generally happens for a myriad of different reasons. Why then does bilateral economic integration sometimes happen specifically in the form of customs unions and why do the customs unions differ so greatly in their setup? FTAs and customs unions share the characteristic that they liberalize internal trade, but the defining feature of customs unions is that they also harmonize external trade by employing a common external tariff. Coordinating that common external tariff requires common rules and centralized authorities that employ and regulate with varying degrees of competences—all of which are institutions in the broad sense of the term.[44] An explanation that therefore focuses on why institutions are created may also explain why external trade is harmonized.

Institutional analysis has developed to answer why institutions are created, setup and why they change. Customs unions as well as their centralized authorities are institutions.[45] Institutional analysis suggests that customs unions are designed to maximise the members' net gains equalling the transaction gains minus transaction losses, transaction costs,[46] and transition costs. This may explain why regional economic integration sometimes happens in the form of customs unions rather than FTAs.

The transaction gains and transaction losses are those gains and losses that occur in every form of bilateral or regional economic integration, plus the additional costs and gains that are specific to customs unions. A common external tariff allows for greater internal integration as it may make rules of origin checks on internal border crossings unnecessary.[47] Whereas FTAs only apply to goods originating within the members of the agreement, customs unions apply to all goods in free circulation of the customs union and goods can be imported via a single point of entry. As customs unions liberalize internal trade with respect to more products and potentially eliminate more non-tariff trade barriers such as rules of origin checks, they allow for more internal integration. This exacerbates the trade creation and trade diversion effects.[48]

If customs unions enable more trade creation, why does regional or bilateral integration then not happen more often in the form of customs unions? This may be due to the transaction costs associated with setting up the institutions necessary to ensure a common external tariff. Transaction costs are the uncertainties and risks involved in the creation and enforcement of a transaction which make it difficult or expensive for two parties to achieve a mutually beneficial exchange. According to

---

[44] See: Sect. 3.4.

[45] According to North, Institutions are "the rules of the game in a society" consisting of "formal and informal constraints that shape human interaction" (North 1990, pp. 3–4).

[46] Trachtman (1996), pp. 470, 472–473.

[47] See below at: Sect. 3.5.2.

[48] Rolf Mirus and Nataliya Rylska, 'Economic Integration: Free Trade Areas v. Customs Unions' 19.

North, this specifically refers to the "costliness of information" and the "cost of protecting rights and policing and enforcing agreements".[49] These costs are not limited to economic costs but also include political transaction costs, which are concerned with the distribution or exchange of resources or benefits between/among different interest groups.[50] In concrete, transaction costs refer to the costs of establishing and promoting cooperation to avoid uncertainties in behaviour such as defections and the complexities associated in identifying, evaluating, and negotiating a Pareto-optimal transaction.[51]

Ensuring cooperation and avoiding strategic behaviour may happen through the creation of stronger institutions. The assets traded for the creation of a central authority are assets of power i.e. competences.[52] In customs unions, the starting point is that member states have all competences. Competences are then distributed to the party to whom they are most *valuable,* i.e. who may satisfy state preferences at the lowest cost.[53] The necessary degree of institutionalization depends on the envisaged transaction gains. If deeper internal integration is aimed at, stronger institutions to ensure cooperation and avoid defection are necessary. This means that to realize the transaction gain of not needing rules of origin checks on internal border crossings, institutions are necessary to ensure that a common external tariff is applied. As the potential transaction gains vary because the degree of trade creation and diversion are uncertain and because the political costs with handing over competences vary as well, this explains why many RTAs only take on the form of FTAs and why customs unions have differing degrees of integration.

Finally, once an institutional arrangement has been setup, specific costs that go beyond limited rationality explanations of path dependency accrue to change those institutions. Traditional transaction cost analysis by North falls short of specifically explaining institutional change. Transition costs, as developed by Khan, focus on the costs associated with contesting institutions. Institutions thereby reflect the political settlement, i.e. the distribution of power across organisations. Institutional change only happens due to changes in the power balance between the actors or a change of preference by the most powerful actor.[54] Focussing more on power structures justifies, why certain institutions are setup in the way they are setup. These costs may explain why the creation of some institutions has not yet occurred despite them being envisaged in customs unions and may rationalize a divergence between the degree of institutionalization and economic integration.

---

[49] North (1990), p. 27.

[50] Ibid 49.

[51] Trachtman (2016), p. 364; Trachtman (1996).

[52] Trachtman (1996), pp. 497–499.

[53] Ibid 529–530.

[54] Mushtaq H. Khan, 'Political Settlements and the Governance of Growth-Enhancing Institutions' (2010) SOAS Working Papers <https://eprints.soas.ac.uk/9968/1/Political_Settlements_internet. pdf>.

2.3 Why Do Customs Unions Modify Anti-Dumping Legislation Internally?

The first step of analysis has focussed on the questions why anti-dumping measures are justified and why customs unions are entered into. The second step of analysis now combines these two explanations and considers how the justifications to impose anti-dumping measures changes if customs unions are formed.

This section considers how the formation of a customs union influences the decision to impose anti-dumping measures internally that is between the member states. Customs unions modify internal trade by liberalizing it. How this affects the different justifications of anti-dumping measures will be considered in turn.

2.3.1 Predatory Pricing: Replacement by Competition Law

If the only legitimate purpose of anti-dumping measures is to prevent predatory pricing, it will no longer be necessary to impose anti-dumping measures if the customs union internally contains other instruments that are capable to combat predatory pricing. Competition law could be such an instrument and could replace anti-dumping.[55]

The overlap between competition law and anti-dumping law is, however, limited as there are fundamental differences between the two. At a basic level, whereas competition law focuses on the defence of consumers and the lifting of entry barriers to markets, anti-dumping measure are more concerned with defending producers by introducing trade barriers. This leads to some differences in the requirements for them to apply. Taking EU Competition law as an example, Art. 102 TFEU requires a dominant position[56] but anti-dumping law applies to all producers or exporters in a specific territory.[57] Moreover, Art. 102 TFEU does not require a cross-national element to apply[58] but an effect on the trade between Member States suffices. Competition law focuses on overall welfare benefits instead of considering whether a domestic industry has been injured. Finally, Art. 102 TFEU requires temporary dumping with the intent to force competitors out of business and to then raise prices above a competitive level[59] but economic undertakings may defend their pricing

---

[55] Competition Law is not regulated multilaterally in the WTO yet, despite some efforts in that regard. See: Malinauskaite (2012) <http://www.elgaronline.com/view/9781849800013.00023.xml> accessed 5 July 2021.

[56] Chapeau of Art. 102 TFEU.

[57] Art. 9 (5) Regulation (EU) 2016/1036 of the European Parliament and of the Council of 8 June 2016 on protection against dumped imports from countries not members of the European Union (Reg. (EU) 2016/1036 or Basic Anti-Dumping Regulation), OJ L 176/21, 30.6.2016.

[58] Fuchs (2019) para 232.

[59] Ibid.

strategy.[60] No such intent is investigated in anti-dumping proceedings and dumping cannot be justified.

Despite these fundamental differences, at least in the EU some have argued that there is some alignment between competition law and anti-dumping practices. Competition considerations can be considered in the union interest test, the lesser duty rule and the EU's market economy test.[61] As these are not mandatory in WTO law and as they do not remove all differences, the general statement that there is no complete overlap between anti-dumping and competition law can still be made. Considering that, it is also not surprising that an OECD study has concluded that 90% of all anti-dumping measures could not be justified under competition law.[62]

This means that competition law does not apply to certain cases that are covered by anti-dumping law and *vice versa*. Nevertheless, some argue that if there is an effective Competition system in place, anti-dumping measures are no longer necessary.[63] Such a system includes harmonious competition rules as well as mechanisms that ensure that the rules are applied effectively, by e.g. having a central competition authority.[64] Supporters of this view argue in effect that the 90% of anti-dumping measures that would not have been caught under competition rules have been imposed illegitimately. Empirically, this position may be supported as certain FTAs prohibit the imposition of trade defence measures but contain competition chapters.[65]

However, if the purpose of anti-dumping measures goes beyond preventing predatory pricing competition law cannot replace anti-dumping law.[66]

---

[60] Weiß (2016) para 37.

[61] François-Charles Laprévote, 'Antitrust in Wonderland: Trade Defense through the Competition Looking-Glass' [2015] Concurrences Review <https://www.concurrences.com/en/review/issues/no-2-2015/legal-practice/antitrust-in-wonderland-trade-defense-through-the-competition-looking-glass> accessed 5 July 2021.

[62] Referring to that study: International Trade and Investment Division, 'Trade and Competition: Frictions after the Uruguay Round' (OECD 1996) OCDE/GD(96)105 17.

[63] Hoekman (1997); Fox (1995), pp. 1, 29–33; Boscheck (2000), pp. 282, 285–287; Hoekman and Mavroidis (1996), pp. 49–50. See also for an economic analysis that replacing competition law would be beneficial for consumers: Kasteng (2016).

[64] Miranda (1996), p. 267; Petter and Quick (2018), pp. 39–41.

[65] Australia – New Zealand Closer Economic Relations Trade Agreement, date of signature December 14, 1982, the Protocol to the Australia New Zealand Closer Economic Relations – Trade Agreement on Acceleration of Free Trade in Goods, date of signature August 18, 1988 ("ANZCERTA"), specifically Article 4 of the Protocol; Free Trade Agreement between the EFTA States and The Republic of Chile, date of signature June 26, 2003 ("EFTA – Chile"), Article 18; Agreement between the EFTA States and Singapore, date of signature June 26, 2002 ("EFTA – Singapore"), Article 9, 16 (2); Free Trade Agreement between Armenia and Kazakhstan, date of signature September 2, 1999 ("Armenia – Kazakhstan"), Article 1.

[66] Müller et al. (2009) para 1.17; Hoekman and Mavroidis (1996), p. 36; Morgan (1996), pp. 75–82. EU practice seems to support this criticism: Kasteng and Prawitz (2013), p. 5 9 <http://www.kommers.se/publikationer/Rapporter/2013/Eliminating-Anti-Dumping-Measures-in-Regional-Trade-Agreements/> accessed 5 July 2021.

2.3.2   Political Necessity: Pressure Valve

Political explanations of anti-dumping measures either support their use or are sceptical of them, depending on whether one supports the political justification employed. If one is sceptical of the political justification, one could still support their use by accepting them as a necessary evil in the process of trade liberalization. Anti-dumping measures may act as a pressure valve to cushion the costs of adjustments and their retention may therefore be necessary for the conclusion of the RTA.[67]

The problem with that reasoning is that it lacks specificity. This could in theory be used to justify any anti-dumping regime, even one where the imposition of internal anti-dumping measures are easier by lowering the thresholds to impose them. The argument gains specificity by considering RTAs as a result of several *quid pro quos* where one state offers market access to a sensitive market in exchange for market access to a sensitive market of the other member. Using anti-dumping measures especially in industries where trade liberalization has been sensitive may be perceived by the other members of the RTA as unfair or as undermining negotiated concessions.

This means that there is an interest in RTAs to ensure that anti-dumping measures are not used to circumvent those concessions. This may justify prohibiting internal anti-dumping measures or modifying anti-dumping measures to ensure that they are not used to circumvent negotiated concessions. Below that, this may justify procedural integration such as through a central investigating authority, additional cooperation requirements between the member states' authorities or harmonization of national legislation which also fulfils the dual purpose of increasing transparency and predictability.[68]

2.3.3   Asymmetric Market Access

The most comprehensive economic justification of anti-dumping measures sees them as preventing injury to the domestic industry resulting from dumping enabled by asymmetric market access. The justification of anti-dumping measures thereby depends on the presumption that there is asymmetric market access.

Without asymmetric market access, they are no longer justified. In that case their internal use should be prohibited. However, no common views exist of when that is the case. What is typically required is the elimination of all tariff and non-tariff

---

[67]Teh et al. (2007), p. 167; Prusa and Teh (2011), p. 65; Prusa (2016), p. 120; Grabitz et al. (1994), p. 20.

[68]On the legal costs of diverging legal systems and the non-normative advantages of harmonization: Stephan (1998), pp. 743, 747; Kozuka (2007), pp. 683, 685–686.

barriers and guaranteeing the free movement of goods as well as the operation of a harmonized and effective competition and state aid system.[69]

Even without defining the exact point at which market access is no longer asymmetric, this reasoning is already helpful because it works on a spectrum. Partial elimination of asymmetric market access, e.g. through the elimination of most tariff and non-tariff barriers but without the harmonization of State aid or competition rules, may already affect the likelihood of dumping, however. If re-exportation becomes more viable, the risk of dumping decreases respectively. A decreasing probability of dumping may be reflected by disincentivizing anti-dumping measures. This may justify including additional requirements for the imposition of anti-dumping measures.

2.3.4 Conclusions

Bilateral or regional economic integration impacts the justifications of anti-dumping measures in different ways. If one perceives that anti-dumping measures are only justified insofar as they prevent predatory pricing, a bilateral competition system may replace them. If one sees anti-dumping measures as a pressure valve to deal with legitimate concerns that arise due to economic integration, this justifies that internal anti-dumping measures are not eliminated and explains why procedural harmonization to avoid misuse of the instruments occurs. Finally, if the purpose of anti-dumping measures is to prevent injury to the domestic industry through dumping and enabled by asymmetric market access, anti-dumping legislation will have to be adapted to reflect the level of asymmetric market access. If the markets are not segregated any longer, internal anti-dumping measures should be prohibited. If asymmetric market access persists, anti-dumping legislation should be modified to reflect changes in the asymmetry, by disincentivizing the measures.

2.4 Why Do Customs Unions Modify Anti-Dumping Measures Externally?[70]

Explanations why anti-dumping provisions are included in RTAs have often only focused on the internal trade dimension. These reasons cannot apply externally, as the purpose of external modifications is to harmonize and not to liberalize trade. Imposing anti-dumping measures is still necessary but anti-dumping procedures may

---

[69]Hoekman and Mavroidis (1996), p. 30; Müller-Ibold (2018), pp. 199–200.

[70]The author would like to thank Anna Berg for the plenty fruitful discussions that formed the basis of this argumentation. All mistakes remain the author's.

have to be harmonized to ensure a common external tariff. Nevertheless, not all customs unions have completely harmonized their anti-dumping regimes.

The Institutional Analysis framework can be used to explain why external harmonization occurs in the area of anti-dumping. Harmonization occurs if the expected transaction gains are greater than the transaction losses, costs and transition costs. The transaction gains and losses of harmonizing anti-dumping measures are the same as with customs unions generally. Harmonizing external anti-dumping measures allows easier internal cross-border movements and thus exacerbates the trade creation and diversion effects. This will, however, only be achieved if the transaction costs (under Sect. 2.4.1) and transition costs (under Sect. 2.4.2) are lower than these gains.

2.4.1   Transaction Costs

According to North, transaction costs are the "costliness of information" and the "cost of protecting rights and policing and enforcing agreements".[71] The relevant transaction costs for the decision to harmonize anti-dumping measures are the costs of ensuring cooperation and avoiding strategic behaviour, which is achieved by creating central institutions. The traded assets are the competences that are centralized if state preferences are satisfied at lower costs on a customs union level.[72]

Whether state preferences are satisfied at lower costs on a customs union level depends on the state preferences. As the imposition of an anti-dumping measure ultimately depends on whether a domestic industry is injured, the aim of anti-dumping measures is to protect the domestic industry from injury that occurs through dumping. Anti-dumping measures are most effective if the scope of the measure correlates with the injured industry. If the scope of the investigation covers a larger geographical area, not the overall producing industry but only parts of it may be injured. Conversely, if the scope of the investigation covers a geographical area that is smaller than the injured industry, only parts of the producing industry are protected by the measures. Anti-dumping measures will be harmonized if it is more likely that dumping by third countries injures the entire customs union production instead of only national producers. Whether this is the case depends on the overall level of market integration that is aimed at.

If markets in the customs union are still relatively segregated, it remains possible that third party imports cause injury only to the industry of one member state. This is because importers will not be able to sell the dumped imports profitably to other national markets of the customs union and because the national producers will not be able to compensate the loss of market shares on the national market with more union-wide activity. Reasons for that are that tariff- and non-tariff barriers could increase

---

[71] North (1990), p. 27.

[72] Trachtman (1996), pp. 529–530.

the price of the imported product upon re-export to another member state so that it will not undercut prices in the other member states. In such a case, anti-dumping measures that operate on a union-wide basis would not be able to protect the injured producing industry effectively. The national industry that is hurt will have greater difficulty to reach the necessary quorum[73] to request the initiation of an investigation and the injury determination will generally focus on the entire union industry and not just that of the member state.[74]

However, if market segregation is minimal or if free movement of goods exists, it may be more effective to harmonize anti-dumping measures, i.e. to conduct investigations on a union-wide basis and to have a central investigating authority and imposition decision. The small degree of market segregation will increase the likelihood of arbitrage. If dumped products have been exported to one member state at prices below the normal value of a like product in the union, these products can be resold at profit to other member states until the prices in the union align. Even if this effect does not take place and dumped products only enter one member state, the producers of that member state will be injured less because of intra-regional exports.

If in such a situation member states had to conduct investigations, multiple investigations would need to take place instead of just one. This would cause substantive problems as the complex movement of goods within the customs union will make the causation determination more difficult. Moreover, the willingness of an authority to impose anti-dumping duties as well as its efficiency to conclude the investigations as quickly as possible will impact the injury caused to a national producing industry. If anti-dumping measures are not imposed at the same time, trade will divert towards those countries where anti-dumping measures have not (yet) been implemented. The surge of dumped products in some national markets may exacerbate the injurious effects to the producing industry there. The same effect but to a lesser degree may happen if the anti-dumping amounts differ. Even if anti-dumping measures are then imposed, rules of origin checks will have to take place on internal border-crossings which impedes trade even more.

Put simply, state preferences are to have national investigations in case a national industry is injured by dumping and a union-wide dumping regime if the industry of the entire customs union is injured by dumping. The risk of conducting anti-dumping measures on the wrong level are the transaction costs and whichever is more likely depends on overall market integration, i.e. on the overall transaction gains. If the risk of injury to the national production is greater than the risk of injury to union-wide production, the transaction costs of harmonizing anti-dumping regimes outweigh the gains and states will retain the competence in the area of anti-dumping. Conversely, if it is more likely that injury happens to the entire union industry, the transaction costs are smaller due to a lesser chance of conducting the investigation on the wrong

---

[73] Art. 5.4 ADA.

[74] Art. 4 ADA. Although it is possible that the exception of Art. 4.1 (ii) ADA is employed on a regular basis.

level and a centralized anti-dumping regime will be set up. In that scenario, the ability of the central investigating authority to exceptionally limit the investigation to certain parts of the customs union[75] further reduces transaction costs.

2.4.2   Transition Costs

A transaction cost analysis cannot explain why certain customs unions have not harmonized anti-dumping regimes, despite a generally high level of market harmonization and it cannot explain why in some customs unions some states are obliged to copy anti-dumping measures by other states without being able to participate in the investigation.

The reason these systems still exist is because of the transition costs associated with contesting them, as developed by Khan. Institutions reflect the political settlement, i.e. the distribution of power across organisations. Institutional change only happens due to changes in the power balance between the actors or a change of preference by the most powerful actor.[76]

Protectionist tendencies by a powerful actor within a customs union may prevent harmonization of anti-dumping regimes, despite transaction costs being low. Because trade is liberalized internally, there may even be a drive towards pursuing protectionism externally.[77] Some research exists to support this "protection diversion".[78] That states retain competences because a powerful partner wishes to pursue protectionist aims is particularly likely in the external dimension of anti-dumping measures, as the parties hurt by external protectionism—the exporters and producers of third countries—are not represented in discussions on the setup of the customs union.

In situations of great power asymmetry, the more powerful party may even be able to harmonize anti-dumping measures by making the weaker parties copy the stronger parties' anti-dumping measures. This may explain the Anti-Dumping setup in SACU and the EU-Andorra and EU-San Marino customs unions.[79]

Only if power dynamics shift or if the stronger party changes its policy unilaterally, may the anti-dumping regime in these customs unions be reformed.

---

[75] Art. 4.1(ii), 4.2 ADA.

[76] Khan (2010).

[77] This is an expression on the greater debate on whether bilateral liberalization can lead to multilateral liberalization ("stumbling stone"—"building block" debate). See generally: Baldwin and Venables (1995). Economic evidence of "stumbling stones": Limão (2006), p. 155. Providing evidence for the "building block" side: Estevadeordal et al. (2008), p. 1531. Including an observation on the use of Anti-Dumping in the evidence: Bown and Tovar (2016), p. 262.

[78] See for more detail: Prusa (2016), pp. 139–143; Prusa and Teh (2010); James (2000), p. 14; Bown et al. (2014) WPS6898; Tabakis and Zanardi (2018) 2018/002.

[79] See below at: Sect. 3.4.2.2).

2.4.3   Conclusions

A transaction cost analysis suggests that the external anti-dumping regime will be harmonized if generally a high level of market integration is pursued. If only a moderate amount of market integration is pursued, the transaction costs of harmonizing the external anti-dumping regime will outweigh the transaction gains. A transition cost analysis builds up on this and explains why deviations from this exist. These deviations exist because customs unions represent a political settlement of power dynamics and sometimes the individual preferences of powerful members of the customs unions are decisive for the institutional structure.

References

Academic Texts

Akritidis V, Sneij F (2018) 'The Shake-Up of the EU Institutions' dumping calculation methodology and the compatibility of a market-oriented concept of normal value with WTO law. Global Trade Cust J 13:129

Antonini R (2018) A "MES" to be adjusted: past and future treatment of Chinese imports in eu anti-dumping investigations. Global Trade Cust J 13:79

Bagwell K, Staiger RW (2011) What do trade negotiators negotiate about? Empirical evidence from the World Trade Organization. Am Econ Rev 101:1238

Baldwin R, Venables A (1995) Regional economic integration. In: Grossman G, Rogoff K (eds) Handbook of international economics, vol 3 1st edn. Elsevier

Boscheck R (2000) Trade, competition and antidumping—breaking the impasse!? Intereconomics 35:282

Bown CP, Crowley MA (2013) Self-enforcing trade agreements: evidence from time-varying trade policy. Am Econ Rev 103:1071

Bown CP, Karacaovali B, Tovar P (2014) What do we know about preferential trade agreements and temporary trade barriers? The World Bank, WPS6898

Bown CP, Tovar P (2011) Trade liberalization, antidumping, and safeguards: evidence from India's tariff reform. J Dev Econ 96:115

Bown CP, Tovar P (2016) Preferential liberalization, antidumping, and safeguards: stumbling block evidence from MERCOSUR. Econ Polit 28:262

Cattaneo O (2018) The political economy of PTAs. In: Lester S, Mercurio B, Bartels L (eds) Bilateral and regional trade agreements - commentary and analysis. Cambridge University Press

Choi N (2016) Economic effects of anti-dumping duties: protectionist measures or trade remedies? Social Science Research Network. SSRN Scholarly Paper ID 2916049 <https://papers.ssrn.com/abstract=2916049> Accessed 5 July 2021

Conway P (1991) The economic effects of widespread application of antidumping duties to import pricing. The World Bank, WPS782 <http://documents.worldbank.org/curated/en/872661468767079890/The-economic-effects-of-widespread-application-of-antidumping-duties-to-import-pricing> Accessed 5 July 2021

Depayre G (2008) Anti-dumping rules: for a predictable, transparent and coherent application - a European view. Global Trade Cust J 3:123

Espa I (2019) New features of green industrial policy and the limits of WTO rules: what options for the twenty-first century?. J World Trade 53

Espa I, Levy PI (2018) The analogue method comes unfastened - the awkward space between market and non-market economies in EC-Fasteners (Article 21.5). World Trade Rev 17:313

Estevadeordal A, Freund C, Órnelas E (2008) Does regionalism affect trade liberalization toward nonmembers? Quart J Econ 123:1531

Finger JM (1993) The origins and evolution of antidumping regulation. In: Michael Finger J, Artis NT (eds) Antidumping: how it works and who gets hurt. University of Michigan Press

Finger JM, Hall HK, Nelson DR (1982) The political economy of administered protection. Am Econ Rev 72:452

Fischer RD, Prusa TJ (2003) WTO exceptions as insurance. Rev Int Econ 11:745

Fox EM (1995) Competition law and the Agenda for the WTO: forging the links of competition and trade. Pac Rim Law Policy Assoc 4:1

Fuchs (2019) AEUV Art. 102 AEUV. In: Immenga and Mestmäcker (eds) Wettbewerbsrecht, 6th edn

Geraets D (2018) The Continued Quest for a Single Set of Rules for Two Economic Systems: Addressing "Significant Distortions" Arising from State Influence. Glob Trade Cust J, 13

Grabitz E, von Bogdandy A, Nettesheim M (eds) (1994) Europäisches Aussenwirtschaftsrecht: Der Zugang Zum Binnenmarkt: Primärrecht, Handelsschutzrecht Und Aussenaspekte Der Binnenmarktharmonisierung. CH Beck

Hoekman B (1997) Competition policy and the global trading system. The World Bank. Policy Research Working Paper WPS1735

Hoekman BM, Mavroidis PC (1996) Dumping, antidumping and antitrust. J World Trade 30:27

Hoffmeister (2018) Erwägungsgründe. In: Günter Krenzler H, Herrmann C, Niestedt M (eds) EU-Außenwirtschafts- und Zollrecht 12th edn

James WE (2000) The rise of anti-dumping: does regionalism promote administered protection? Asian-Pac Econ Liter 14:14

Jovanovic MN (2016) The economics of international integration, 2nd edn. Edward Elgar Publishing Ltd

Juhász R (2018) Temporary protection and technology adoption: evidence from the Napoleonic Blockade. Am Econ Rev 108:3339

Karacaovali B (2011) Turkey: temporary trade barriers as resistance to trade liberalisation with the European Union? In: Bown CP (ed) The great recession and import protection: the role of temporary trade barriers. World Bank

Kasteng J (2016) The abolition of antidumping measures in the EU: an example and inspiration for the TTIP. In: Bhagwati JN, Krishna P, Panagariya A (eds) The world trade system: trends and challenges. MIT Press

Kasteng J, Prawitz C (2013) Eliminating Anti-Dumping Measures in Regional Trade Agreements: The European Union Example. Kommerskollegium 2013:5 <http://www.kommersse/ publikationer/Rapporter/2013/Eliminating-Anti-Dumping-Measures-in-Regional-Trade-Agree ments/> Accessed 5 July 2021

Khan MH (2010) Political Settlements and the Governance of Growth-Enhancing Institutions. SOAS Working Papers <https://eprints.soas.ac.uk/9968/1/Political_Settlements_internet.pdf>

Kovacic WE (2009) Price differentiation in antitrust and trade instruments. In: Bagwell KW, Bermann GA, Mavroidis PC (eds) Law and economics of contingent protection in international trade. Cambridge University Press

Kozuka S (2007) The economic implications of uniformity in law. Uniform Law Rev 12:683

Krugman PR (1997) What should trade negotiators negotiate about? J Econ Lit 113

Krugman PR, Obstfeld M and Melitz MJ (2015) International economics: theory and policy, 10th edn. Pearson

Kufuor KO (2013) Reformulating material injury: the socialization of Ghana's antidumping system. Global Trade Cust J 8

Limão N (2006) Preferential vs. Multilateral Trade liberalization: evidence and open questions. World Trade Rev 5:155

Lux M (2017) AntidumpingVO: Einführung. In: Rüsken R (ed) Zollrecht: Recht des grenzüberschreitenden Warenverkehrs, vol 5 172nd edn. Stollfuß

Lyons TJ (2018) EU customs law, 3rd edn. Oxford University Press

Malinauskaite J (2012) International competition law harmonisation and the WTO: past, present and future. In: Andenas M, Andersen C (eds) Theory and practice of harmonisation. Edward Elgar Publishing. <http://www.elgaronline.com/view/9781849800013.00023.xml> Accessed 5 July 2021

Mankiw G, Swagel P (2005) Antidumping: the third rail of trade policy. Foreign Aff 84:107

Mastel G (1998) Antidumping laws and the U.S. economy. ME Sharpe

Mavroidis P (2012) Trade in goods: the GATT and other WTO agreements regulating trade in goods, 1st edn. Oxford University Press

Mavroidis PC (2006) If I Don't Do It, Somebody Else Will (Or Won't): testing the compliance of preferential trade agreements with the multilateral rules. J World Trade 40:187

Meade JE (1955) The theory of customs Unions. North-Holland Pub Co

Miranda J (1996) Should antidumping laws be dumped. Law Policy Int Bus 28:255

Moore MO (2002) Department of commerce administration of antidumping sunset reviews: a first assessment. J World Trade 36:675

Moore MO, Zanardi M (2009) Does antidumping use contribute to trade liberalization in developing countries?: Antidumping contribute to trade liberalization? Canadian J Econ/Revue canadienne d'économique 42:469

Moore MO, Zanardi M (2011) Trade liberalization and antidumping: is there a substitution effect? Rev Dev Econ 15:601

Morgan C (1996) Competition policy and anti-dumping - is it time for a reality check? J World Trade 30:61

Müller W, Khan N, Scharf T (2009) EC and WTO anti-dumping law: a handbook, 2nd edn. Oxford University Press

Müller-Ibold T (2018) EU trade defence instruments and free trade agreements: is past experience an indication for the future? Implications for Brexit? In: Bungenberg M, others (eds) The future of trade defence instruments: global policy trends and legal challenges, vol 1

Noël S, Zhou W (2019) 'EU's new anti-dumping methodology and the end of the non-market economy dispute? Global Trade Cust J 14

North DC (1990) Institutions, institutional change, and economic performance. Cambridge University Press

Petter B, Quick R (2018) The politics of TDI and the different Views in EU Member States: necessary safety-valve or luxurious rent-seeking device? In: Bungenberg M, and others (eds) The future of trade defence instruments: global policy trends and legal challenges. Springer, Berlin Heidelberg

Prusa T (2016) Antidumping provisions in preferential trade agreements. In: Bhagwati JN, Krishna P, Panagariya A (eds) The world trade system: trends and challenges, 1st edn. MIT Press Ltd

Prusa T, Teh R (2011) Contingent protection rules in regional trade agreements. In: Bagwell K, Mavroidis PC (eds) Preferential trade agreements: a law and economics analysis. Cambridge University Press

Prusa TJ, Teh R (2010) Protection reduction and diversion: PTAs and the incidence of antidumping disputes. National Bureau of Economic Research, Working Paper 16276

Sohn I (2020) Asymmetrical fairness: China's use of antidumping measures. J World Trade 54:127

Stephan B (1998) The futility of unification and harmonization in international commercial law. Virginia J Int Law 39:743

Suse A (2017) Old Wine in a new bottle: the EU's response to the Expiry of Section 15(a)(Ii) of China's WTO protocol of accession. J Int Econ Law 20:951

Tabakis C, Zanardi M (2018) Preferential trade agreements and antidumping protection. Lancaster University Management School, 2018/002

Teh R, Prusa TJ, Budetta M (2007) Trade Remedy Provisions in Regional Trade Agreements. World Trade Organization - Economic Research and Statistics Division Staff Working Paper ERSD-2007-03

Tharakan MP (1995) Political economy and contingent protection. Econ J 105:1550

Thompson R, Brown C, Gibson N (2018) Article 102. In: Bailey D, Elisbeth John L (eds) Bellamy & child: European Union law of competition. Oxford University Press

Tovias A (1991) A survey of the theory of economic integration*. J Eur Integr 15:5

Trachtman JP (1996) The theory of the firm and the theory of the international economic organization: toward comparative institutional analysis. Northwest J Int Law Bus 17:470

Trachtman JP (2016) Trade. In: Katz Cogan J, Hurd I, Johnstone I (eds) The Oxford handbook of international organizations, 1st edn. Oxford University Press

Vermulst EA (2007) Anti-dumping in the second millenium: the need to revise basic concepts. In: Vermulst EA, Graafsma F (eds) Customs and trade laws as tools of protection: selected essays. Cameron May

Viner J (1923) Dumping: a problem in international trade. The University of Chicago Press

Viner J (1950) The Customs Union issue. Carnegie Endowment for International Peace

Weiß (2016) AEUV Art. 102 (Ex-Art. 82 EGV) [Mißbrauch Marktbeherrschender Stellung]. In: EUV and AEUV (eds) Calliess/Ruffert, 5th edn

Winters LA (2011) Preferential trading agreements: friend or foe? In: Bagwell K, Mavroidis PC (eds) Preferential trade agreements: a law and economics analysis. Cambridge University Press

Wu M (2016) 'The "China, Inc." challenge to global trade governance. Harv Int Law J 2:65

Zhou W, Percival A (2016) Debunking the myth of "Particular Market Situation" in WTO antidumping law. J Int Econ Law 19:863

Chapter 3
Practice in Customs Union

The previous chapter has dealt with the reasons why customs union anti-dumping regimes differ from the WTO rules on anti-dumping as applied by states. This chapter now considers how they differ. More specifically, this chapter compares anti-dumping legislation in the various customs unions and thereby focusses on how the customs union legislation differs from the WTO obligations as applied by states.

Previous studies have already analysed modifications to anti-dumping legislation in RTAs generally. This study is limited only to customs unions. However, this study goes beyond a mere characterization of different anti-dumping regimes but categorizes every modification of anti-dumping legislation in customs unions. Going beyond previous studies, this study also categorizes and compares external anti-dumping regimes, provides an analysis of conflicts that arise due to membership in multiple customs unions and links the modifications to problems associated with rules of origin and anti-dumping action on behalf of a third country.

The main deviations correspond with the reasons why customs unions would modify anti-dumping rules: internally, customs unions disincentivize anti-dumping measures and harmonize procedures on their imposition up to the point that some customs unions have prohibited internal anti-dumping measures. Externally, harmonization happens in various degrees up to some customs unions employing a union wide investigation and the resulting measures applying to imports into the entire customs union.

To this end, this Chapter is structured as follows: The different modifications to WTO rules are categorized (under Sect. 3.1), the methodology of the comparison is explained (under Sect. 3.2) and the different internal (under Sect. 3.3) and external amendments (under Sect. 3.4) will be considered. Finally, associated problems arise if customs unions or their members are party to multiple RTAs, with regards to rules of origin or if the country of import and injury do not coincide (all under Sect. 3.5).

F. Bickel, *Customs Unions in the WTO*, European Yearbook of International Economic Law 20, https://doi.org/10.1007/978-3-030-86312-8_3

This analysis will focus on those customs unions that have been notified as such to the WTO.[1] This includes 17 customs unions,[2] of which 16 are in force today.[3] Table 3.1 lists these customs unions and provides some information on them: their members, when they came into force, the aggregate GDP of their members, whether they employ a common external tariff or are even a single market, and the number of anti-dumping measures they have imposed since 2010. Those countries with an asterisk next to them are not WTO members.

Two important caveats apply.

First, whether a customs union imposes a common external tariff or whether it is in fact a single market is difficult to assess. The table assumes that there is a common external tariff, if at least a substantial part of goods are subject to a common tariff. This means that variations between the member states on certain products remain possible. Beyond that, there is no set definition of a single market and it is not a concept employed in the WTO. Generally, a single market requires the free movement of goods, services, capital, and workforces. This is achieved through the elimination of factors not only relating to the movement of goods but also through the elimination of differences in the factors of production.[4] For the purpose of this study, I assumed that a single market exists if the customs union guarantees free movement of goods, calls itself a single market or employs a single point of entry system for customs matters.

Second, the table only lists the measures that were reported to the WTO by the members in their semi-annual reports pursuant to Art. 16.4 ADA. During that time, the EU notified the WTO of its measures jointly and the EAEU, GCC and SACU started to notify their anti-dumping measures jointly in 2015.

This table illustrates two points. First, it shows that anti-dumping measures are unevenly used with some customs unions or members of customs unions having imposed more than 200 measures since 2010 and some not even having the necessary legislation in place. It is difficult to explain exactly why that is the case.

---

[1]This is both underinclusive and overinclusive. This excludes those customs unions that are not notified to the WTO such as the customs union between France and Monaco, Customs Convention, 18.5.1963 (Journal officiel de la République Française of 27.9.1963, p. 8679) or those that notified to the WTO but not as a customs unions, such as the Southern African Development Community (SADC) established through The Treaty of the Southern African Development Community, 17.8.1992. However, it includes customs unions that do not meet the definition of a customs union, probably such as the Andean Community that has not set up an external tariff yet.

[2]WTO RTA Database, available at: https://rtais.wto.org/ (last accessed: 5 July 2021).

[3]The customs union between the Russian Federation, Belarus and Kazakhstan has now been replaced by the EAEU. For an overview of the steps of integration in the EAEU, see: Eurasian Economic Commission, 'The Eurasian Economic Union - Facts and Figures' (Library of Eurasian Integration, 2018), pp. 4–9.

[4]Marceau (1994), p. 168; Krueger (1997), p. 174; Mavroidis (2015), p. 295; Herrmann et al. (2007), p. 265, 266. Some make a distinction between common market and single market, whereby a single market guarantees completely free movement of goods and common markets only align some regulations on the factors of production: Krueger (1997), p. 174. This distinction will not be followed.

Table 3.1 All customs unions and total anti-dumping measures

Customs Union	Entered into Force	Members	Combined GDP of CU in Mio. USD[a]	All Members or the CU have notified AD leg[b]	Definitive Anti-Dumping Measures Reported in 2010–2020[c]			Actual integration	
					Internal	External	Total	CET[d]	SM[e]
Andean Community (CAN)	25.5.1988	Bolivia, Colombia, Ecuador, Peru[f]	698.981	Yes	1	30	31	−	−[g]
Caribbean Community and Common Market (CARICOM)	1.8.1973	Antigua and Barbuda, Bahamas*, Barbados, Belize, Dominica*, Grenada, Guyana, Haiti, Jamaica, Montserrat*, Saint Kitts and Nevis, Saint Lucia, Saint Vincent and the Grenadines, Suriname, Trinidad and Tobago	84.851	No	−	1	1	+	−[h]
Central American Common Market (CACM)	4.6.1961	Costa Rica, El Salvador, Guatemala, Honduras, Nicaragua, Panama	269.924	Yes	−	1	1	+	−[j]
Common Market for Eastern and Southern Africa (COMESA)	8.12.1994	Angola, Burundi, Comoros*, Egypt, Eritrea*, Eswatini, Ethiopia*, Kenya, Lesotho, Malawi, Mauritius, Rwanda, Sudan*, Somalia*[j] Tanzania, Tunisia,[k] Uganda, Zambia, Zimbabwe[l]	832.224	No	−	26	26	−	−[m]
East African Community (EAC)	7.7.2000	Burundi, Kenya, Rwanda, Tanzania, Uganda	206.202	No	−	−	−	+	+[n]
Economic and Monetary Community of Central Africa (CEMAC)	24.1.1999	Cameroon, Central African Republic, Chad, Congo (Rep), Equatorial Guinea*, Gabon	90.801	No	−	−	−	+[o]	−[p]

(continued)

Table 3.1 (continued)

Customs Union	Entered into Force	Members	Combined GDP of CU in Mio. USD[a]	All Members or the CU have notified AD leg[b]	Definitive Anti-Dumping Measures Reported in 2010–2020[c]			Actual integration	
					Internal	External	Total	CET[d]	SM[e]
Economic Community of West African States (ECOWAS)	23.8.1995	Benin, Burkina Faso, Cabo Verde, Côte d'Ivoire, Gambia, Ghana, Guinea, Guinea-Bissau, Liberia, Mali, Niger, Nigeria, Senegal, Sierra Leone*, Togo	689.197	No	–	–	–	+	–[q]
EU—Andorra[r]	1.7.1991	EU (and its Member States), Andorra*	15.595.949	No	–	74	74	+	–[s]
EU—San Marino[t]	1.4.2002	EU (and its Member States), San Marino*	15.594.433	No	–	74	74	+	–[u]
EU—Turkey[v]	1.1.1996	EU (and its Member States), Turkey	16.347.206	Yes	10	136	146	+	–[w]
Eurasian Economic Union (EAEU)[x]	1.1.2015 +	Armenia, Belarus*, Kazakhstan, Kyrgyz Republic, Russian Federation[y] +[z]	1.965.246	Yes	–	25	25		
European Union (EU)	1.1.1958	Austria, Belgium, Bulgaria, Croatia, Cyprus, Czech Republic, Denmark, Estonia, Finland, France, Germany, Greece, Hungary, Ireland, Italy, Latvia, Lithuania, Luxembourg, Malta, Netherlands, Poland, Portugal, Romania, Slovak Republic, Slovenia, Spain, Sweden[aa]	15.592.795	Yes	–	74	74	+	+[ab]

Gulf Cooperation Council (GCC)[ac]	1.1.2003	Bahrain, Kuwait, Oman, Qatar, Saudi Arabia, United Arab Emirates	1.647.893	Yes	—	5	5	+	+[ad]
Southern African Customs Union (SACU)	15.7.2004	Botswana, Eswatini, Lesotho, Namibia, South Africa	389.004	No	—	15	15	+	—[ae]
Southern Common Market (MERCOSUR)	29.11.1991	Argentina, Brazil, Paraguay, Uruguay[af]	2.383.612	Yes	16	259	275	+	—[ag]
West African Economic and Monetary Union (WAEMU)	1.1.2000	Benin, Burkina Faso, Côte d'Ivoire, Mali, Niger, Senegal, Togo	148.405	No	—	—	—	+[ah]	—[ai]

[a] Gross Domestic Product in 2019 or 2018 if not available for 2019, according to World Bank national accounts data, and OECD National Accounts data files, The World Bank, 'GDP (Current US$) | Data' https://data.worldbank.org/indicator/NY.GDP.MKTP.CD accessed 5 July 2021

[b] Committee on Anti-Dumping Practices, Report (2019) of the Committee on Anti-Dumping Practices G/L/1344, G/ADP/26, 21.11.2019

[c] Committee on Anti-Dumping Practices, Report (2010) of the Committee on Anti-Dumping Practices, G/L/935, 28.10.2010; Committee on Anti-Dumping Practices, Report (2011) of the Committee on Anti-Dumping Practices G/L/966, 26.20.2011; Committee on Anti-Dumping Practices, Report (2012) of the Committee on Anti-Dumping Practices G/L/1006, 25.10.2012; Committee on Anti-Dumping Practices, Report (2013) of the Committee on Anti-Dumping Practices G/L/1053, 29.10.2013; Committee on Anti-Dumping Practices, Report (2014) of the Committee on Anti-Dumping Practices G/L/1079, 31.10.2014; Committee on Anti-Dumping Practices, Report (2015) of the Committee on Anti-Dumping Practices G/L/1134, G/ADP/22, 30.10.2015; Committee on Anti-Dumping Practices, Report (2016) of the Committee on Anti-Dumping Practices G/L/1158, G/ADP/23, 1.11.2016; Committee on Anti-Dumping Practices, Report (2017) of the Committee on Anti-Dumping Practices G/L/1193, G/ADP/24, 30.10.2017; Committee on Anti-Dumping Practices, Report (2018) of the Committee on Anti-Dumping Practices G/L/1270, G/ADP/25, 29.10.2018; Committee on Anti-Dumping Practices, Report (2019) of the Committee on Anti-Dumping Practices G/L/1344, G/ADP/26, 21.11.2019; Committee on Anti-Dumping Practices, Report (2020) of the Committee on Anti-Dumping Practices G/L/1366, G/ADP/27, 30.10.2020

[d] Common External Tariff

[e] Single Market

[f] Until 2011: Venezuela. See: Carlos Malamud. 'Venezuela's Withdrawal from the Andean Community of Nations and the Consequences for Regional Integration' (Real Instituto Elcano 2006) Working Paper WP 28/2006; 'Chávez Withdraws Venezuela From Andean Trade Pact; Blames Colombia & Peru Free Trade Agreement With U.S.' Latin America News Dispatch (22 April 2011) https://latindispatch.com/2011/04/22/chavez-withdraws-venezuela-from-andean-trade-pact-blames-colombia-peru-free-trade-agreement-with-u-s accessed 5 July 2021

[g] Trade Policy Review Body, Trade Policy Review, Report by the Secretariat, Peru, 27.9.2019, WT/TPR/S/393, 2.22, p. 37

[h] Although the Treaty of Chaguaramas foresees the establishment of a single market and it was scheduled to be achieved by the end of 2016, this has been deferred due to "administrative, fiscal and legal issues". See: Trade Policy Review Body, Trade Policy Review, Report by the Secretariat: Trinidad and Tobago,

(continued)

Table 3.1 (continued)

27.3.2019, WT/TPR/S/388, p. 29, 2.12–2.14; Trade Policy Review Body, Trade Policy Review, Report by the Secretariat: Jamaica, Revision, 10.11.2017, WT/TPR/S/359/Rev.1, 24, 25, 2.25-2.27

[i] Trade Policy Review Body, Trade Policy Review, Report by the Secretariat: El Salvador, 10.8.2016, T/TPR/S/344, pp. 32, 33

[j] Since 2017

[k] Since 2017

[l] Lesotho and Eswatini are also members of SACU. SACU's measures appear multiple times

[m] Trade Policy Review Body, Trade Policy Review, Report by the Secretariat, Egypt, WT/TPR/S/367, 16.1.2018, p. 31

[n] Trade Policy Review Body, Trade Policy Review, Report by the Secretariat, East African Community, WT/TPR/S/384, 13.2.2019, pp. 15–17

[o] However, numerous exceptions exist

[p] Trade Policy Review Body, Trade Policy Review, Report by the Secretariat, Countries of the Central African Economic and Monetary Community, WT/TPR/S/285, 24.6.2013, pp. 18–19

[q] Trade Policy Review Body, Trade Policy Review, Report by the Secretariat, The Member Countries of the West African Economic and Monetary Union, WT/TPR/S/362, 14.9.2017, pp. 24–26. If certain members of ECOWAS (those that are in WAEMU) do not have a single market, ECOWAS cannot have a single market

[r] The EU's measures appear multiple times

[s] Trade Policy Review Body, Trade Policy Review, Report by the Secretariat, European Union, WT/TPR/S/395, 10.12.2019, p. 43

[t] The EU's measures appear multiple times

[u] Trade Policy Review Body, Trade Policy Review, Report by the Secretariat, European Union, WT/TPR/S/395, 10.12.2019, p. 43

[v] The EU's measures appear multiple times

[w] Trade Policy Review Body, Trade Policy Review, Report by the Secretariat, Turkey, WT/TPR/S/331, 9.2.2016, pp. 31, 32

[x] Since 2015. The EAEU succeeded the Belarus, Kazakhstan, Russia Customs union which harmonized its Anti-Dumping regime in 2011 (see below: F.I.1). Russia became a WTO Member in 2012. All anti-dumping measures since then are counted

[y] Russia since 2012, Armenia, Kazakhstan, and the Kyrgyz Republic since 2015

[z] Trade Policy Review Body, Trade Policy Review, Report by the Secretariat, Armenia, WT/TPR/S/379, 25.9.2018, p. 28

[aa] Croatia since 2013. The United Kingdom until 31.1.2020

[ab] Art. 28, 30 TFEU

[ac] Reported jointly since 2015

[ad] Trade Policy Review Body, Trade Policy Review, Report by the Secretariat, The Kingdom of Saudi Arabia, WT/TPR/S/333, 29.2.2016, p. 24, 25

[ae] Trade Policy Review Body, Trade Policy Review, Report by the Secretariat, Southern African Customs Union, WT/TPR/S/324, 30.9.2015, pp. 19–20

[af] Until 2016: Venezuela

[ag] Trade Policy Review Body, Trade Policy Review, Report by the Secretariat, Uruguay, WT/TPR/S/374, 23.5.2018, pp. 35, 36

[ah] This is the ECOWAS Common External Tariff. But as all WAEMU members are ECOWAS members too, the CET also applies to WAEMU

[ai] Trade Policy Review Body, Trade Policy Review, Report by the Secretariat, The Member Countries of the West African Economic and Monetary Union, WT/TPR/S/362, 14.9.2017, pp. 24, 25

One reason may be that due to the technical challenges associated with imposing anti-dumping measures, some countries may lack the expertise to conduct the investigations. The fact that in 1995 only 20 WTO Members imposed anti-dumping measures, and this rose to 43 in 2020 may support this.[5] Beyond that and especially for smaller countries, it may also be uneconomical to conduct the necessary investigations as the administrative costs of doing them—especially against a large trading partner, with many different exporters—may outweigh the advantage of the additional duty. Further, associated instruments such as subsidies, other trade defence measures or taxes may be used to compensate the effects of dumping or in case where the duty as applied is below the bound duty rates, the as applied rate may simply be raised. Lastly, not all countries believe in the economic benefits of anti-dumping measures and may therefore refrain from imposing anti-dumping measures in hope that the benefits to the consumers may outweigh the injury to domestic industry.

Second, external anti-dumping measures happen more frequently than internal anti-dumping measures. Overall, this stresses the uncertainties of this comparison. Whereas the functioning of the anti-dumping regime in some customs unions is rather straight-forward, significant uncertainties may exist with respect to other customs unions. One explanation could be that due to the increased market access the risk of arbitrage rises and the corresponding necessity for anti-dumping measures drops. Beyond that, it is also possible that other instruments such as common competition law instruments may substitute anti-dumping measures or that the negative political tensions that are created when an anti-dumping measures is imposed against a fellow member of the customs union disincentivizes their imposition.

3.1 Categorizing the Different Modifications

Anti-dumping legislation in customs unions is different from the WTO rules on anti-dumping as applied in the anti-dumping legislation by states. Although every customs union has a unique set of anti-dumping rules, the deviations can be grouped along two lines.

First, customs unions modify the WTO anti-dumping provisions differently according to the subject of investigation. If the investigation is aimed at countries within the customs union, this relates to the internal dimension of the customs union. If the investigation is aimed at countries that are not within the customs union, this concerns the external dimension of the customs union.

---

[5]Compare: Committee on Anti-Dumping Practices, Report (1995) of the Committee on Anti-Dumping Practices G/L/34, 14.11.1995; Committee on Anti-Dumping Practices, Report (2020) of the Committee on Anti-Dumping Practices G/L/1366, G/ADP/27, 30.10.2020.

Second, modifications can be categorized by their aim.[6]

The first aim of modifying the WTO rules on anti-dumping is to impact the likelihood with which an anti-dumping measure can be imposed or the severity of its effect. This can be achieved by changing the substantive requirements to impose anti-dumping measures, e.g. by changing the *de minimis* thresholds,[7] by imposing a mandatory lesser-duty-rule[8] or by modifying when an expiry review[9] must be initiated.

These requirements can either be stricter or less strict than the WTO rules. If the requirements to impose anti-dumping measures are stricter compared to the WTO rules, the imposition of an anti-dumping measure becomes less likely, the anti-dumping duty will be lower, or the duration of the measure is shorter. In that case, the modifications generally disincentivize anti-dumping measures. If the requirements are less strict than the WTO rules, the opposite is the case: the imposition of anti-dumping measures becomes more likely, the effects of the duty are more severe, and the duration of the anti-dumping measure will be longer. In that case, the modifications incentivize anti-dumping measures.

The second purpose why WTO rules on anti-dumping are modified is to integrate anti-dumping procedures. This will be achieved by modifying either substantive or procedural WTO rules on anti-dumping. Substantively, instead of conducting the investigation on a member state-wide basis and imposing the measure to apply to imports into the respective member state, some customs unions carry out the investigations and impose the measures on a union wide basis. Procedurally, the investigation and the decision to impose the measure can either be carried out by a central authority, by the members' authorities or by a combination of the two. Moreover, additional procedural requirements that define the relationship between the customs union and its member states can be introduced: this can include information or cooperation requirements between national authorities of the customs union members or additional rights and obligations of national authorities against the central authorities of customs unions.

As customs union aim to liberalize trade internally but harmonize it externally, the modifications will also differ between internal and external trade.

Internally, customs unions aim to liberalize trade.[10] To achieve this with respect to anti-dumping measures, WTO rules will be modified for two reasons: to disincentivize or even prohibit anti-dumping measures. If the possibility to impose anti-dumping measures is retained as a "pressure valve" to allow concluding the customs union, procedural modifications to minimise the risk that they are abused for

---

[6]Mainly focussing on a classification of internal modifications: Compare the classification in Prusa (2016), pp. 132–133; Prusa and Teh (2011), pp. 77–78.

[7]Art. 5.8 ADA.

[8]Art. 9.1 ADA.

[9]Art. 11.3 ADA.

[10]Art. XXIV:8(a)(i) GATT.

protectionist aims may be introduced.[11] Insofar as they are not prohibited, customs unions may disincentivize them by raising or applying additional substantive requirements. Above that, customs unions that allow internal anti-dumping measures may install additional cooperation requirements up to outsourcing the investigation to a centralized authority to minimise the risk of their abuse. If parties must consult before they can impose internal anti-dumping measures, cases in which an investigating authority uses anti-dumping measures purely for protectionist aims may be spotted more easily and deterred. Moreover, soft law mechanisms such as consultation requirements may apply to deter the imposition of anti-dumping measures in industries where market access has been won through significant concessions of the other parties. Procedural integration also serves the purpose that it constitutes an additional barrier that disincentivizes the imposition of anti-dumping measures.[12]

The reverse situation, that customs unions make the imposition of anti-dumping measures easier by lowering the respective thresholds, has not happened so far. However, it is conceivable that to counteract asymmetric market access[13] or to promote other political goals[14] states may want to make the imposition of anti-dumping measures internally easier. This could be done by lowering respective thresholds or by adding additional elements that justify the imposition of anti-dumping measures. This may include allowing for different methodologies to calculate normal values—such as importing the EU's 'significant market distortion test'—or more directly could also include taking human rights, environmental or labour law violations into account when calculating respective values. Legality of this will be considered in the next Chapter.[15]

Externally, the aim of a customs union is to establish a common external trade regime.[16] In the field of anti-dumping this can be achieved by harmonizing national anti-dumping regimes.[17] This includes conducting anti-dumping investigations and imposing measures on a union wide basis and establishing a central investigating authority tasked to do that. In that case, data is collected on a union-wide instead of a state-wide basis. Moreover, procedural requirements are modified because competences are handed to a central authority. Below that, cooperation requirements may exist between the parties.

Some customs unions may also modify WTO requirements to disincentivize the imposition of external anti-dumping measures. E.g. the EU has imposed a mandatory

---

[11] See above at: Sect. 2.3.2.

[12] Saying that there is a "theoretical presumption and some empirical evidence" of this effect: Prusa and Teh (2011), p. 63.

[13] See: Sect. 2.1.3.

[14] See: Sect. 2.1.2.

[15] See: Sect. 4.1.2.1.

[16] Art. XXIV:8(a)(ii) GATT.

[17] On harmonization: Andenas et al. (2012); Boodman (1991), p. 699; Orford (2005), p. 179.

lesser-duty rule or considers the union interest before imposing a measure[18]—both modifications that generally disincentivize anti-dumping measures. As the reason for these modifications does not stem from the formation of a customs union, but can also occur unilaterally by states, these will not be considered further.

Overall, customs unions modify anti-dumping legislations as shown in Fig. 3.1.

Although customs unions modify anti-dumping legislation with the same aims, the extent to which the modifications pursue these different aims differs greatly.

The greatest form of integration and harmonization occurs where a customs union prohibits internal anti-dumping measures and the same anti-dumping measures apply against imports into the entire customs union. The other end of the spectrum is that no modification of WTO anti-dumping legislation takes place, i.e. that anti-dumping measures are imposed internally and externally by the member states of the customs union on a state wide basis. Between these two, internal integration and harmonization and external harmonization may happen at least to some extent.

Figure 3.2 summarizes where each customs union falls on this spectrum. The x-axis depicts the different degrees of internal integration with prohibition of internal anti-dumping measures being the highest degree and no modifications the lowest. The y-axis represents the different degrees of external harmonization with no modifications being the lowest degree of harmonization and the highest level of harmonization being that the same anti-dumping measures apply to imports into the entire customs union. As it is difficult to weight the different degrees of integration and harmonization against each other, the classification of the customs unions in between these extremes is merely an approximation.

First, this figure illustrates that there are two clusters with some customs unions having completely harmonized and integrated and others without really having modified anti-dumping legislation. The EU-Turkey customs union, CARICOM and CAN fall in between as they have mechanisms to deter internal anti-dumping measures and show some degree of external harmonization yet the degree of internal liberalization and external harmonization falls short of e.g. the EU, EAEU or GCC.

Second, there is overlap between customs unions that are common markets as well and customs unions with significant harmonization and integration in anti-dumping. All common markets fall into the cluster that has a significant degree of internal integration and external harmonization. The only exception is the EAC where none of its members have ever imposed anti-dumping measures. However, this is not exclusive. Customs unions that do not have a common market, such as WAEMU,[19] SACU and the EU-Andorra and EU-San Marino customs unions also fall into the cluster of customs unions with a significant degree of integration and harmonization.

---

[18]Art. 9 (4)(2), 21 Reg. (EU) 2016/1036.

[19]For an overview of western African economic integration: Mossner (2016).

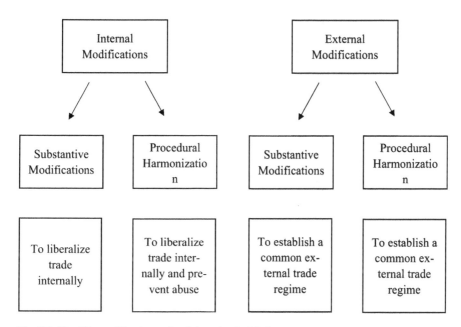

Fig. 3.1 Possible modifications of anti-dumping legislation

Third, this figure suggests that there is a correlation between internal integration and external harmonization. ECOWAS and CEMAC are outliers to this but neither have made use of their mandate to apply anti-dumping measures, so that it is difficult to see how these systems will work in practice.

3.2 Methodology

How customs unions deviate from WTO law on anti-dumping will be compared by way of a system comparison.

In a system comparison, a legal institution (here: anti-dumping regulation) is detached from its context and is compared to overall solutions concerning similar legal cases in other systems.[20]

The problem with such an approach is that functional equivalents, such as competition law will not be looked at.[21] This may create the impression that those customs unions that prohibit the internal imposition of anti-dumping measures do not have any provisions that deal with unfair trade practices. This is, however, not

---

[20] Husa (2014), p. 63.

[21] Ibid.

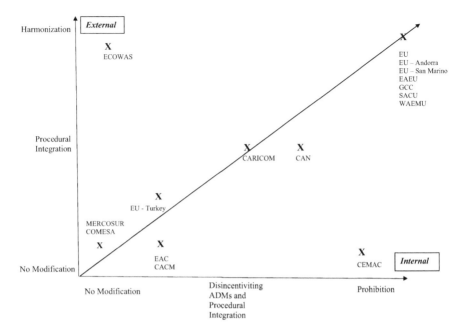

Fig. 3.2 Overview of Levels of Integration and Harmonization in Customs Unions

the case, as competition law covers some forms of dumping or their overall level of economic integration makes dumping less likely.[22]

The purpose of this chapter is to categorize the different modifications of anti-dumping regulation in customs unions. This will serve as a basis to then analyse their WTO compatibility and the effects they have concerning questions of responsibility, in situations of economic (dis-) integration and for third parties that wish to impose anti-dumping measures against customs unions or their member states. The need for comparison will therefore focus on the legislations and not on the legal practice or the general culture of the customs unions.[23] Four preliminary points are in order.

First, the following categorization deals with the legal framework employed in the different customs unions and not their actual use. Some customs unions foresee that a centralized authority should conduct the investigations even though no such authority has been set up yet.[24]

Second, no weighing between the customs unions takes place. This means that the modifications the EU makes to anti-dumping measures are as relevant for this study as the ones that COMESA makes, despite the EU's GDP being 185 times higher than COMESA's.

---

[22] See: Sect. 2.3.

[23] For the distinction: Hage (2014), pp. 49–51.

[24] For examples of differences in the legislation and how it is employed, see: Gantz (2011), p. 103.

Third, only the applicable rules that fall within the scope of the customs union are considered. E.g. the EU-Andorra customs union does not apply to a variety of goods[25] and the modified anti-dumping regime therefore does not apply to these goods. This study only considers the applicable rules on the trade in goods that fall within the scope of the customs union.

Fourth, this chapter does not distinguish between customs unions notified under Art. XXIV GATT or the Enabling Clause or between those customs unions where all of its members are WTO members and those where only some of them are. Different legal regimes apply, which will be considered in the next chapter.[26] An empirical comparison irrespective of a legal categorization of the customs union is valuable, as it demonstrates broadly, how customs unions have deviated from Art. VI GATT and the ADA.

3.3 Internal Practice

Internally, customs unions deviate from the WTO rules on anti-dumping as applied by states to liberalize trade. The strongest form in which this can be achieved is by prohibiting the internal imposition of anti-dumping measures altogether (under Sect. 3.3.1). Below that, customs unions may nevertheless disincentivize the imposition of internal anti-dumping measures and may add procedural steps to prevent the abuse of anti-dumping measures. This means that they will modify WTO provisions to disincentivize anti-dumping measures (under Sect. 3.3.2) or to procedurally integrate anti-dumping investigations (under Sect. 3.3.2.2).

A prerequisite of any internal modification is that the customs union is competent to legislate and has legislated on internal anti-dumping measures. Irrespective of the precise effect of customs unions' legislation (i.e. whether it has direct effect, has supremacy or not), 6 customs unions that allow internal anti-dumping measures have legislated and thereby harmonized or replaced the national rules at least to some

---

[25] According to Art. 11.1 Agreement between the EEC and San Marino (EU—Andorra Agreement), 28.3.2002, the agreement does not apply to Products covered by Ch. 1 to 24 of the Harmonized System.

[26] See below: Chap. 4.

extent. These are: the EAC,[27] MERCOSUR,[28] CACM,[29] the EU-Turkey customs union,[30] CARICOM,[31] and COMESA.[32] The CAN[33] has only partially harmonized its internal anti-dumping regulation and ECOWAS[34] has a mandate to harmonize but has not yet made use of it. The other eight customs unions prohibit internal anti-dumping measures altogether so that no rules had to be harmonized in that regard.

---

[27] According to Reg. 4. 2 East African Community Customs (Anti-Dumping Measures) Regulations, Annex IV Treaty for the Establishment of the East African Community, 30.11.1991, the Regulation applies in conjunction with the existing national legislation. Member states are thereby obliged to harmonise with this Regulation, Reg. 5.2. The competence is derived from Art. 16 Protocol on the Establishment of the East African Customs Union, 2.3.2004.

[28] Defensa Comercial Intrazone (Dec. N 22/02), MERCOSUR/CMC/Dec. N 22/02; Acuerdo Antidumping de la Organización Mundial de Comercio (Dec. N 13/02), MERCOSUR/CMC/Dec. N 13/02. They must be transposed into national law following Art. 38, 40 Additional Protocol to the Treaty of Asunción on the Institutional Structure of MERCOSUR (Ouro Preto Protocol), 17.12.1994. On the status of MERCOSUR Law in the Member States see generally: Fuders (2008), pp. 105–142.

[29] Art. 8 Protocolo al Tratado General de Integración Económice Controamericana (Guatemala Protocol), 29.10.1993 obliges States to harmonize their rules and gives the Executive Committee on Economic Integration (Art. 42 Guatemala Protocol) the competence to regulate inter alia on Anti-Dumping. It has done so in Art. 6-22 Resolucion No. 193-2007 (COMIECO–XLIV), 24.4.2007.

[30] Art. 12 (1) Council Decision No 1/95 of the EC-Turkey Association Council of 22.12.1995 on implementing the final phase of the Customs Union (96/142/EC) (Decision No. 1/95) requires Turkey to adopt the EU Basic Anti-Dumping Regulation.

[31] Art. 133 (5) Revised Treaty of Chaguaramas establishing the Caribbean Community including the CARICOM Single market and Economy (Revised Treaty of Chaguaramas), 5.7.2001, binds Member States to implement Art. 125–133 Revised Treaty of Charguarmas.

[32] Art. 51 Revised COMESA Treaty amended by Council Meeting 2009 (COMESA Treaty), 12.09.2012 mandates COMESA to regulate anti-dumping. This has happened in COMESA Regulations on Trade Remedy Measures, 10.2002.

[33] Within the scope of Decision 456, Normas para prevenir o corregir las distorsiones en la competencia generadas por prácticas de dumping en importaciones de productos originarios de Países Miembros de la Comunidad Andina (Decision 456), 4.5.1999. See: Sect. 3.3.2.3.

[34] Art. 42 Economic Community of East African States (ECOWAS) Revised Treaty (ECOWAS Treaty), 6.7.2005, allows internal Anti-Dumping measures. Regulation C/Reg.6/06/13 Relative to Defense Measures to be Imposed on Imports Which are Dumped from Non-Member States of the Economic Community of West African States (Regulation C/Reg.6/06/13), 21.6.2013, does not apply, as it only applies to imports by third parties. In the absence of more specific regulation, WTO Law applies to those ECOWAS Members that are WTO Members.

3.3.1 Prohibition of Internal Anti-Dumping Measures

Of the 16 customs unions considered, eight (i.e. 50%) have eliminated internal anti-dumping measures. These are: the EU,[35] the EU-Andorra[36] and EU-San Marino[37] customs unions, the EAEU,[38] GCC,[39] CEMAC,[40] SACU,[41] and WAEMU.[42]

---

[35] Art. 28 Treaty on the Functioning of the European Union (TFEU), consolidated version OJ 2012/ C 326/01, 26.10.2012.

[36] Art. 5, 6 Agreement between the EEC and Andorra (EU-Andorra Agreement), 28.6.1990. Although the Communication from the EU to the Committee on Regional Trade Agreements, 'Customs Union Between the European Community and the Principality of Andorra', WT/REG53/ 3, 12.11.1998, p. 4, does not mention that internal anti-dumping measures are prohibited, the duty to copy the EU's anti-dumping measures, Art. 7 EU-Andorra Agreement leaves no room for internal Anti-Dumping measures.

[37] Art. 5 (1), 6 Agreement between the EEC and San Marino (EU—San Marino Agreement), 28.3.2002. Although the Factual Presentation by the Committee on Regional Trade Agreements, 'The Cooperation and Customs Union Agreement between the European Union and the Republic of San Marino (Goods)', WT/REG280/1, 9.2.2018, para. 3.27 states that the Agreement does not contain provisions on anti-dumping, the similarities in the wording of Art. 5 (1) (prohibiting future tariffs and ORRC) and 6 (eliminating existing tariffs and ORRC) EU-San Marino Agreement is identical to Art. 5, 6 EU-Andorra Agreement and can thus be interpreted in the same way.

[38] Art. 28.3 Treaty on the Eurasian Economic Union (EAEU Treaty), 29.5.2014, entered into force: 1.1.2015.

[39] Art. 1 (iv) The Economic Agreement Between the GCC States (GCC Agreement), 31.12.2001. On the Interpretation: Committee on Trade and Development, Committee on Regional Trade Agreements, 'Factual Presentation, Gulf Cooperation Council Customs Union (Goods)', WT/REG276/1, 21.3.2018, para. 3.29.

[40] Art. 13 (a) Traité Instituant la Communauté Économique et monétaire de l'afrique centrale (CEMAC Agreement), 16.3.1994, entered into force: 24.6.1999, lays down the work program to establish a common market. On the status of creating that common market see: Communauté Économique et Monétaire de l'Afrique Centrale, 'Rapport Intermimaire de Surveillance Multilatérale 2017 et Perspective Port 2018', 34th Edition, 03.2018, pp. 42–46. Accordingly, a common market should have been established by now. Art. 19 CEMAC Agreement includes the mandate that anti-dumping provisions can be imposed against third countries. Because of the limited wording of Art. 19 CEMAC Agreement and because of the general interpretation of Art. 13 (a) CEMAC Agreement, internal anti-dumping measures are consequently eliminated.

[41] Art. 18.1 Southern African Customs Union Agreement 2002 (SACU Agreement), 21.10.2002, as amended on 12.4.2013 eliminates "customs duties and quantitative restrictions", which should include anti-dumping measures. Art. 41 SACU Agreement gives the Council a mandate to develop instruments and policies to address unfair trade practices. Currently, the South African legislative framework applies, and the anti-dumping measures adopted by South Africa are replicated in other SACU Members. As the investigations take place on a union-wide basis, internal anti-dumping measures are not possible. See: Report by the Secretariat, Trade Policy Review Body, 'Trade Policy Review, Southern African Customs Union', WT/TPR/S/324, 30.9.2015, para. 3.36–3.42.

[42] Art. 76 (a) Traité modifié de l'Union Economique et Monetaire Ouest Africaine (WAEMU Treaty), 29.1.2003. Whether this general provision eliminating tariffs and measures of equivalent effect also encapsulates anti-dumping measures does not become clear in the Report by the Secretariat, Trade Policy Review Body, 'Trade Policy Review, The Member Countries of the West African Economic and Monetary Union (WAEMU)', WT/TPR/S/362 of 14.9.2017, para. 3.81–3.84. Since none of the Member States have reported the imposition of anti-dumping measures and because anti-dumping measures are tariffs or have at least that effect, they are prohibited.

The elimination of anti-dumping measures is usually not explicit in the Agreements. Only the EAEU explicitly regulates that anti-dumping measures are prohibited between the parties.[43] Rather, customs unions usually regulate that all duties and measures of equivalent effect are eliminated between the parties. As anti-dumping measures are duties or at least measures of equivalent effect, they are eliminated following that provision. An exception to this may be if another provision explicitly allows them. This interpretation of these clauses also corresponds with the factual presentations of some customs unions.[44]

Interestingly, this finding differs from other studies.[45]

It differs greatly from Prusa's as well as Prusa and Teh's finding, according to which only the EU (or 6% of all customs unions) prohibit internal anti-dumping measures.[46] As these studies have analysed specifically the language discussing anti-dumping rules,[47] those customs unions that do not explicitly regulate the elimination of anti-dumping measures, but only rule generally that duties and measures of equivalent effect are prohibited, have not been classified as prohibiting the use of internal anti-dumping measures.

A discrepancy also exists to Rey's study.[48] In that study those RTAs that did not contain any specific anti-dumping provisions were classified as copying the WTO anti-dumping regime.[49] Rey thereby assumed that the absence of explicit prohibition means WTO rights and obligations remain unchanged, without critically analysing provisions that prohibit duties and measures having an equivalent effect.[50] The GCC was therefore classified as an RTA in which the WTO rules on anti-dumping apply without change[51] and CEMAC and WAEMU were classified as RTAs that do not explicitly refer to, but substantially replicate, without meaningful substantial changes, Art. VI GATT and the ADA.[52]

The findings of these studies should be rejected in that regard.

---

[43] Art. 28.3 EAEU Treaty.

[44] E.g. for the GCC: Committee on Trade and Development, Committee on Regional Trade Agreements, 'Factual Presentation, Gulf Cooperation Council Customs Union (Goods)', WT/REG276/1, 21.3.2018, para. 3.29.

[45] Sagara finds six out of ten: Sagara (2002) 02-E-013 ch 2.1. Prusa finds 1 out of 16: Prusa (2016), p. 131. Rey finds 6 out of 16: Rey (2016), pp. 214–215. Kasteng and Prawitz find 3 out of 16: Kasteng and Prawitz (2013), p. 5. Prusa and Teh find 1 out of 10: Prusa and Teh (2011), pp. 69–71.

[46] Prusa (2016), p. 131; Prusa and Teh (2011), pp. 77–78.

[47] T. Prusa (Personal Communication, 12.6.2019).

[48] Rey (2016). The same discrepancy exists to studies that are based on Rey's study: Kasteng and Prawitz (2013), p. 5.

[49] Rey (2016), pp. 174–175.

[50] Ibid. 37.

[51] Rey classifies it as Profile A1. On the definition of that profile: ibid. 175. On the classification: ibid. 208.

[52] Rey classifies it as Profile A4. On the definition of that profile: Rey (2016), p. 176. On the classification: ibid. 211–213.

3.3.2 Disincentivizing Anti-Dumping Measures

The customs unions that allow the imposition of internal anti-dumping measures are: CAN, CARICOM, CACM, COMESA, EAC, ECOWAS, MERCOSUR and the EU-Turkey customs union (50% of all customs unions). They have modified the rules on anti-dumping to disincentivize the imposition of measures and to integrate anti-dumping procedures.

There are different modifications which disincentivize or aim to reduce the impact of anti-dumping measures. First, there are rules that affect the likelihood of imposing anti-dumping duties. These include altering the *de minimis* margins or negligible volumes.[53] Second, there are rules that affect the size of the duty such as imposing a mandatory lesser duty rule.[54] Third, there are rules that shorten the duration of the duties.[55,56]

Five of the eight customs unions that allow internal anti-dumping measures (31% of all customs unions) have not modified the substantive requirements to disincentivize anti-dumping measures. These are: ECOWAS,[57] EAC,[58] COMESA,[59] CACM,[60] and CARICOM.[61]

The three other customs unions (19% of all customs unions) disincentivize internal anti-dumping measures in different ways.

3.3.2.1 EU-Turkey Customs Union

In the EU-Turkey customs union both parties apply the EU's Basic Anti-Dumping Regulation.[62] This includes some deviations from the ADA, such as a mandatory lesser-duty-rule[63] or the additional requirement that the Union interest must call for an intervention.[64] As the EU applies these modifications to all anti-dumping investigations, these modifications do not specifically disincentivize anti-dumping

---

[53] Art. 5.8 ADA.

[54] Art. 9.1 ADA.

[55] Art. 11.3 ADA.

[56] Prusa (2016), p. 132. Prusa also includes mechanisms to resolve disputes under this category. To illustrate the different forms of cooperation, these are included below at: Sect. 3.3.3.

[57] Art. 42 ECOWAS Treaty allows internal Anti-Dumping measures. Regulation C/Reg.6/06/13 does not apply, as it only applies to imports by third parties. In the absence of more specific regulation, WTO Law applies to those ECOWAS Members that are WTO Members.

[58] EAC Customs Union (Anti-Dumping Measures) Regulations replicate the ADA.

[59] The COMESA Regulation on Trade Remedy Measures replicates the ADA.

[60] Resolucion No. 193/2007 replicates the ADA.

[61] The Revised Treaty of Charguramas replicates the ADA.

[62] Art. 12 (1) Decision 1/95. The Basic Anti-Dumping Regulation is Reg. 1036/2016.

[63] Art. 9 (4)(2) Reg. (EU) 2016/1036.

[64] Art. 21 Reg. (EU) 2016/1036.

measures in the EU-Turkey relation. The EU-Turkey customs union includes one variation to anti-dumping rules, however. It foresees that interim protective measures shall not remain in force for longer than 3 months[65] as opposed to four or 6 months in the ADA.[66]

3.3.2.2   MERCOSUR

In MERCOSUR the only substantive change relates to the duration of the anti-dumping measures. An expiry review must take place after 3[67] instead of 5[68] years.

3.3.2.3   CAN

The CAN includes the most sophisticated modifications that disincentivize the internal imposition of anti-dumping measures, but this only applies to the internal anti-dumping measures within the scope of Decision 456.

Decision 456 applies, where dumping practices originate in another CAN member state and threaten to cause or cause injury to the branch of national production destined for the domestic market or intended for export to another member country.[69] If a branch of the domestic industry produces goods destined for export to a third country, Decision 456 does not apply. In that case national legislation applies.

Decision 456 includes rules that affect the likelihood of imposing anti-dumping measures. These include raising the negligible volumes to 6%[70] instead of 3%,[71] the *de minimis* margins to 5%[72] instead of 2%,[73] the requirements to determine whether an application has been made by or on behalf of the domestic production to 50%[74] as

---

[65] Art. 47 (2) Additional Protocol to the Agreement establishing the Association between the EEC and Turkey (Additional Protocol), 23.11.1970. Art. 47 Additional Protocol applies according to Art. 44.2 Decision 1/95.

[66] Art. 7.4 ADA.

[67] Annex, Nr. 5, Dec. N 13/02.

[68] Art. 11.3 ADA.

[69] Art. 2 Decision 456.

[70] Art. 27 (3) Decision 456. If more than one country is under investigation, they must combined account for 15% of import to the Member State for the amounts not to be negligible.

[71] Art. 5.8 ADA.

[72] Art. 64 Decision 456.

[73] Art. 5.8 ADA.

[74] Art. 27 (4) Decision 456. This is different from Art. 5.4 ADA which requires that 50% of the domestic production of those who have either supported or objected to the investigation and at least 25% of total production of the like product.

well as reducing the time of the investigation to 6 or 8 months[75] instead of 12 or 18 months.[76]

Decision 456 also includes rules that aim to reduce the duty level such as a compulsory lesser duty rule[77] and rules that limit the duration of the measure by requiring an expiry review after 3 years[78] instead of 5 years.[79]

3.3.3 Procedural Integration

The second type of modification that may occur internally, if internal anti-dumping measures are not prohibited, is procedural integration. The customs unions that allow internal anti-dumping measures, where this could happen are: CAN, CARICOM, CACM, COMESA, EAC, ECOWAS, MERCOSUR and the EU-Turkey customs union.

Anti-dumping procedures can be divided into investigatory steps and imposition decisions. The investigation comprises the initiation of an investigation,[80] the actual investigation[81] as well as the review process.[82] The imposition step includes the decision to impose provisional[83] or definitive[84] anti-dumping measures, to accept undertakings[85] or to decide on the results of reviews,[86] circumvention proceedings,[87] or refund requests.[88]

The regulation concerning procedural steps in customs unions either delineates competences between member states and central organs or creates additional procedural steps that the member states must consider. The scope of the investigation can only be member state wide, as otherwise there would be overlap between the territory against which the measure applies and the territory applying a measure.

---

[75] Art. 38 Decision 456.

[76] Art. 5.10 ADA.

[77] Art. 65 Decision 456.

[78] Art. 69 Decision 456.

[79] Art. 11.4 ADA.

[80] Art. 5.1 ADA.

[81] Art. 5, 6 ADA.

[82] Art. 11 ADA.

[83] Art. 7 ADA.

[84] Art. 9 ADA.

[85] Art. 8 ADA.

[86] Art. 11 ADA.

[87] They are not regulated in WTO law, the Trade Negotiations Committee, Decision on anti-circumvention, 15.12.1993, 14.4.1994 recognised circumvention as a problem and referred it to the Anti-Dumping Committee for resolution. This has not resulted in legislation yet, but some states and customs unions have regulated circumvention: e.g. Art. 13 Reg. 2016/1036. For more on anti-circumvention: Yanning (2008).

[88] Art. 9.5 ADA.

3.3.3.1 Investigation Stage

During the investigation stage, the strongest form of procedural integration is to have a central investigating authority. There is currently no customs union in which a centralized authority conducts the internal investigations in all cases but in some customs unions a centralized authority is competent in a certain set of cases or acts as a supervisory body. If the member states' authorities remain competent to investigate, additional cooperation requirements may exist.

Central Investigating Authority

The CAN, CARICOM and CACM (19% of all customs unions) have a central investigating authority that is responsible to investigate internally in some cases. The central investigating authority is not responsible in all cases but rather acts as a supplement to national investigating authorities by either being competent in some cases—as in CAN—or by being a supervisory instance—as in CARICOM and CACM.

CAN

Only the CAN (6% of all customs unions) has a central investigating authority that is competent to conduct internal investigations in a specific set of cases. The General Secretariat[89] thereby acts in cooperation with the authorities of the member states.

The General Secretariat is competent in the cases in which Decision 456 applies.[90] However, member states participate in the investigation as well. They can request the initiation of an investigation[91] and during the investigation, the General Secretariat works closely together with the member states. Although the General Secretariat has the mandate to carry out the investigations itself,[92] it can request evidence and information from the member states.[93] The General Secretariat may even include officials or experts of member states in the verification of information by the interested parties.[94]

Interestingly, the scope of the investigation is limited with regards to the injury determination to consider the influence of dumped products on the prices of the like products by the domestic industry for the domestic market or for export to another

---

[89] Being the investigating authority, according to Art. 18 Decision 456.

[90] See: Sect. 3.3.2.3.

[91] Art. 24 Decision 456.

[92] Art. 33 (2) Decision 456.

[93] Art. 33 (1) Decision 456. The Member State is obliged to deliver that information, Art. 53 Decision 456.

[94] Art. 52 Decision 456.

member country,[95] i.e. not the price of like products for export to third countries. This limitation results from the peculiar scope of Decision 456 but since there is no recent practice of a regional investigation, it is difficult to see how this will happen in practice.

CARICOM

In CARICOM, the member states' authorities are the investigating authorities in principle.[96] In certain cases, member states may, however, impose provisional anti-dumping measures and refer the investigation to the Council for Trade and Economic Development (COTED)[97]—a central authority—which then takes over as a central investigating authority. This may only be done where the country under investigation unreasonably impedes an investigation, or has not made satisfactory efforts to afford consultations.[98]

A similar system exists for reviews. If a review of the measures has been requested and the applicant is not satisfied that the competent authority has given enough consideration to the review, the applicant may refer the request to COTED which shall recommend to the member state appropriate action.[99] Whereas in the initial investigation the investigating member state may refer the investigation to COTED due to a complaint against the member under investigation, in the review process the applicant may refer the investigation to COTED because of a complaint against the investigating authority. Above that and more generally, COTED keeps all anti-dumping measures *under review*[100] and ensures that the member states observe the conditions and timetable for review and withdrawal of the measures.[101] COTED is thereby best described as a supervisory body.

CACM

The CACM system is like the CARICOM system in that the member states authorities are the principal investigating authorities[102] but the central authority, here the Secretaría de Integración Ecónomica Centroamericana (SIECA),[103] can in certain

---

[95] Art. 19 (1) Decision 456.

[96] Art. 125 Revised Treaty of Chaguaramas.

[97] Council for Trade and Economic Development, Art. 10 (2)(b) Revised Treaty of Chaguaramas.

[98] Art. 129 (9) Revised Treaty of Chaguaramas.

[99] Art. 133 (3)(e) Revised Treaty of Chaguaramas.

[100] This wording is used in the Agreement. However, it is unlikely that this grants a general competence to review Anti-Dumping measures. Rather, the use of the term review should be understood in a non-formal manner.

[101] Art. 133 (4) Revised Treaty of Chaguaramas.

[102] Art. 25 Convenio sobre el Regimen Arancelario y aduanero Centroamericano (Central American Tariff and Custom Regime), 27.12.1984.

[103] Art. 37 (3)(a) Guatemala Protocol.

circumstances, take over as the investigating authority. Unlike in CARICOM, SIECA only acts as a supervisory body in certain situations of dumping action on behalf of a third country.

The CACM system foresees that SIECA may act as the investigating authority in certain cases where the place of dumped exports and injury do not coincide.[104] In cases of anti-dumping on behalf of a third country, the injured member's government must request the initiation of a regional procedure through SIECA[105] which forwards the request to the relevant investigating authority of the member state that imports the dumped goods. The investigating authority should then initiate and conduct the investigation.[106] Only if the investigating authority fails to initiate the investigation, SIECA may initiate it[107] and operate as the investigating authority.[108]

Cooperation Requirements

Except in the limited cases just outlined, in those customs union which allow internal anti-dumping measures, authorities of the member states are exclusively competent to investigate and impose anti-dumping measures.

However, the anti-dumping procedures may have been integrated to some extent. Procedural integration may happen through the introduction of voluntary or compulsory cooperation requirements between the members of the customs union.

Of the eight customs unions that allow internal anti-dumping measures, CACM, ECOWAS, the EU-Turkey customs union and CAN—except for the cooperation foreseen in Decision 456—do not include any cooperation requirements during the investigation stage. A general reiteration that the member states should cooperate can be found in COMESA[109] and a general reiteration that there should be the possibility for consultations between the investigating member and the member under investigation can be found in the EAC.[110] Only CARICOM and MERCUSOR include detailed cooperation requirements.

CARICOM

In CARICOM a general cooperation requirement exists.[111] Above that, further additional cooperation requirements apply. The respective exporters and producers

---

[104]For an analysis of Anti-Dumping on behalf of a third party generally, see: Sect. 3.5.3.

[105]Art. 28 Resolucion 193/2007.

[106]Art. 29 Resolucion 193/2007.

[107]Art. 30 Resolucion 193/2007.

[108]Art. 31 Resolucion 193/2007.

[109]Art. 54.1 COMESA Treaty. Art. 19.4 COMESA Regulation on Trade Remedy Measures replicates Art. 6.9 ADA.

[110]Reg. 19.2 East African Community Customs (Anti-Dumping Measures) Regulations.

[111]Art. 131 (3) Revised Treaty of Chaguaramas.

as well as the member state shall cooperate with the investigating authority for the verification of information.[112] The results of the investigation shall then be disclosed to the exporting member state.[113]

Above that, where a preliminary investigation provides sufficient evidence of dumping and injury, the investigating authority may request consultations with the exporting member state and that request must be notified to COTED.[114]

MERCOSUR

In MERCUSOR, prior to the initiation of an investigation, consultations between the investigating member and the exporting member take place.[115] These consultations should, however, not prevent the competent authorities from deciding to initiate an investigation.[116]

The decision to initiate an investigation must be notified to the member state affected and the MERCUSOR Trade Commission. The notification to the member state affected must include a copy of the application[117] and the MERCUSOR Trade Commission shall be updated on the status of the investigation at each ordinary meeting.[118]

During the investigation, the exporting State party shall, upon request, assist the investigating authorities in identifying further producers.[119] The exporting State has a right to view the non-confidential file of the proceeding at any time during the investigation[120] and can request further consultations during the investigation and before a preliminary or final determination is reached as well as before the application of measures.[121]

3.3.3.2 Imposition Decision

Decisions must be made during different stages of the procedure: a decision is necessary to impose provisional[122] or definitive[123] anti-dumping duties, to accept

---

[112] Art. 132 (1) Revised Treaty of Chaguaramas.

[113] Art. 132 (2) Revised Treaty of Chaguaramas.

[114] Art. 129 (5) Revised Treaty of Chaguaramas.

[115] Para. 1.1 (3) Dec. N. 22/02.

[116] Para. 1.1 (8) Dec. N. 22/02.

[117] Para. 1.1 (3), (4) Dec. N. 22/02.

[118] Para. 6 Dec. N. 22/02.

[119] Para. 1.3(a) (3) Dec. N. 22/02.

[120] Para. 1.3 (b) Dec. N. 22/02.

[121] Para. 1.3 (c) Dec. N. 22/02.

[122] Art. 7 ADA.

[123] Art. 9 ADA.

an undertaking[124] or to decide upon the outcome of a review,[125] circumvention proceeding,[126] or refund request.[127]

These decisions can be taken at a union level instead of a national level. The central decision can thereby either bind the members of the customs union directly or can authorize the member states to act. Alternatively, the member states may be competent to make decisions that relate to anti-dumping measures.

A central imposition decision at least for certain measures is required in the EU-Turkey customs union, the EAC, CACM, CARICOM, and CAN. In the other customs unions—MERCOSUR, ECOWAS, COMESA—the member states remain competent to make decisions and no additional requirements must be met.

EU-Turkey

The EU-Turkey customs union extensively regulates how different decisions must be taken.

In case of internal dumping, an application must be made to the Council of Association.[128] Where the Council agrees with the investigating authority and finds that dumping occurs, it shall address recommendations those who dump.[129] Ultimately, the measures are imposed by the EU or Turkey so that this procedure is best seen as an authorization procedure. Only if the Council has not taken a decision within 3 months or despite its recommendations dumping still continues, may Turkey and the EU implement anti-dumping measures against each other without prior approval by the Council of Association.[130] Beyond this, where the interests of the injured party call for immediate action and where the Council of Association has been informed, one party may introduce interim measures for a maximum duration of 3 months.[131]

If measures have been imposed, the Council of Association may decide to suspend them upon issuing a recommendation if they are interim measures or if they have been imposed because the Council of Association has taken more than 3 months to reach a decision.[132] In the cases where dumping continues despite the recommendations by the Council, the Council of Association may recommend the abolition or the amendment of those measures.[133]

---

[124] Art. 8 ADA.

[125] Art. 11 ADA.

[126] They are not regulated in WTO law yet. See: Fn. 80.

[127] Art. 9.5 ADA.

[128] Art. 47 (1) Additional Protocol, Art. 44 (2) Decision 1/95.

[129] Art. 47 (1) Additional Protocol.

[130] Art. 47 (2) (1) Additional Protocol.

[131] Art. 47 (2) (2) Additional Protocol.

[132] Art. 47 (3) (1) Additional Protocol.

[133] Art. 47 (3) (2) Additional Protocol.

Moreover, Art. 44 (1) Decision 1/95 provides that the Association Council shall review existing anti-dumping measures upon the request of either Party and during that time, the Association Council can decide to suspend[134] the measures.

EAC

In the EAC only some decisions are taken centrally. The decision to impose provisional[135] or definitive[136] anti-dumping duties is taken by the Committee, a central organ of the EAC.[137] The Secretariat, another central organ of the EAC, notifies the WTO of any anti-dumping measure.[138]

The decision to apply provisional measures, accept an undertaking[139] or to determine the outcome of a review[140] is taken by the investigating authority, meaning the member states' authorities.[141]

CARICOM

The member states decide to impose provisional duties.[142] CARICOM legislation contains a unique feature if the subsequent investigation reveals that no definitive anti-dumping measures can be imposed. In that case, COTED may determine the nature and extent of compensation for damages deriving from the provisional measure.[143]

After considering the available evidence, COTED authorises the member state to impose anti-dumping measures.[144] COTED also monitors the imposition of anti-dumping measures by member states and their review.[145]

---

[134] "Provided that Turkey has implemented competition, State aid control and other relevant parts of the *acquis communautaire*", Art. 44 (1) Decision 1/95.

[135] Reg. 12.1, 12.6 East African Community Customs (Anti-Dumping Measures) Regulations.

[136] East African Community Committee on Trade Remedies, Art. 24 Protocol on the Establishment of the East African Customs Union.

[137] Reg. 14.1 East African Community Customs (Anti-Dumping Measures) Regulations.

[138] Art. 16.2 Protocol on the Establishment of the East African Customs Union.

[139] Reg. 13.3, 13.5 East African Community Customs (Anti-Dumping Measures) Regulations.

[140] Reg. 16.2, 16.3, 16.4 East African Community Customs (Anti-Dumping Measures) Regulations.

[141] See generally on the EAC: Kafeero (2009) <https://d-nb.info/99448609x/34>.

[142] Art. 130 Revised Treaty of Chaguaramas.

[143] Art. 133 (3)(g) Revised Treaty of Chaguaramas.

[144] Art. 133 (1) Revised Treaty of Chaguaramas.

[145] Art. 144 (4) Revised Treaty of Chaguaramas.

CAN

Within the scope of Decision 456, the General Secretariat,[146] a central organ, is competent to apply provisional anti-dumping measures,[147] accept undertakings[148] and conduct reviews.[149] The General Secretariat also imposes definitive anti-dumping measures.[150] Member states are then bound to implement the measures.[151]

CACM

In CACM, the decision to impose provisional[152] and definitive[153] anti-dumping duties rests with the member states. The member states' investigating authorities also take other decisions.[154] In case of a regional investigation, the Executive Committee, a central organ, will decide the actions that can be taken.[155] The members then impose the measures.[156]

Some additional procedural elements apply in cases other than the regional investigation. Following the imposition of a definitive anti-dumping measure against a CACM member, the measure must be notified to SIECA by sending a summary of the file.[157] The state party affected by the adopted measure shall present SIECA a presentation of the case[158] and SIECA will then notify the other member states and convene the Executive Committee to hear the matter.[159] The Executive Committee is able to request further information[160] and will make a recommendation to the imposing member state.[161]

---

[146] Art. 29–39 Acuerdo de Integracion Subregional Andino (Cartagana Agreement), 12.5.1987, entered into force: 25.5.1988, last amended by the Decisión 583, 26.6.2003.

[147] Art. 39 Decision 456.

[148] Art. 43 Decision 456.

[149] Art. 70, 71, 73 Decision 456.

[150] Art. 65 Decision 456.

[151] Art. 94 Cartagena Agreement.

[152] Art. 16 Resolucion 193/2007.

[153] Art. 22 Resoucion 193/2007.

[154] No specific regulation exists but according to Art. 2 Resolucion 193/2007 the purpose of the Resolucion is to implement Art. VI GATT, ADA, the general WTO rules apply. According to Art. 8.3, 11.2, 11.3 ADA the investigating authorities, which are in this case member state authorities, take the decisions.

[155] Art. 32 Resolucion 193/2007.

[156] Art. 34 Resolucion 193/2007.

[157] Art. 22, 23 Resolucion 193/2007.

[158] Art. 15 Resolcuion 193/2007.

[159] Art. 23 Resolucion 193/2007.

[160] Art. 26 Resolucion 193/2007.

[161] Art. 27 Resolucion 193/2007.

3.3.4 Conclusions

The two extremes how customs unions deal with anti-dumping rules internally is by
either prohibiting them or by not modifying them at all. The existing customs unions
make full use of that spectrum. 50% of all customs unions—the EU, EAEU, GCC,
CEMAC, SACU, WAEMU and the EU-Andorra and EU-San Marino customs
unions prohibit internal anti-dumping measures, whereas 19% of customs unions
apply the WTO rules on anti-dumping between them with only minimal changes.
These are: MERCOSUR, ECOWAS and COMESA. ECOWAS does not modify
WTO rules, COMESA only insofar as it reiterates that members should cooperate
and MERCOSUR includes some material and procedural changes but overall the
level of modification remains low.

  The remaining five customs unions have disincentivized and integrated anti-
dumping procedures to varying degrees. CAN has included the most elaborate
changes to WTO rules by changing several substantive requirements to impose
anti-dumping measures, having a central investigating authority with set competences and taking the imposition decision at a central level. CARICOM is a little less
integrated as the central investigating authority is not competent to investigate in a
certain set of cases but rather acts as a supervisory body. However, extensive
cooperation requirements exist and the decision to impose measures is taken centrally. Finally, the substantive rules on anti-dumping have not been modified. The
remaining three customs unions have integrated anti-dumping measures again to a
lesser degree. The EAC and EU-Turkey customs union have centralized the decision
to impose anti-dumping measures but—apart from shortening the duration of interim
measures in the EU-Turkey customs union—no other material integration has taken
place. Finally, CACM provides for a central investigation in a limited set of cases
and has included some cooperation requirements during the imposition decision.

  Table 3.2 summarizes the results. An asterisk next to an x means that additional
conditions apply.

3.4 External Practice

Externally, customs unions regulate anti-dumping to harmonize the imposition of
anti-dumping measures. Anti-dumping measures are harmonized if the same measures apply to imports into the entire customs union. The strongest form of harmonization is by transferring investigatory competences as well as the imposition
decision to a central authority and to conduct the investigations on a union wide
basis. Member states may retain rights and obligations during the investigation and
in the decision-making bodies to varying degrees. Below that, if member states
remain competent to investigate and impose measures, cooperation requirements can
be introduced between the members.

Table 3.2 Overview internal modifications

Customs Union	Prohibition	Substantive changes to deter ADMs	Procedural Integration		
			Central Investigating Authority	Cooperation Requirements	Central Imposition Decision
Andean Community (CAN)		x	x		x
Caribbean Community and Common Market (CARICOM)			x*		x
Central American Common Market (CACM)			x*	x	x*
Common Market for Eastern and Southern Africa (COMESA)					
East African Community (EAC)					x
Economic and Monetary Community of Central Africa (CEMAC)	x				
Economic Community of West African States (ECOWAS)					
EU—Andorra	x				
EU—San Marino	x				
EU—Turkey		x			x
Eurasian Economic Union (EAEU)	x				
European Union	x				
Gulf Cooperation Council (GCC)	x				
Southern African Customs Union (SACU)	x				
Southern Common Market (MERCOSUR)		x		x	
West African Economic and Monetary Union (WAEMU)	x				

A study on external modifications to anti-dumping measures presuppose that the customs unions have legislated in that field. The effects of the legislation may, however, differ. Customs union legislation can at least partly replace national laws. This is the case in six of the 16 (i.e. 38%) customs unions. These are: EAEU,[162] ECOWAS,[163] GCC,[164] WAEMU,[165] CAN,[166] and EU.[167] In these customs unions only customs union law applies at least to some extent. Beyond that, customs unions may also harmonize national law. This has happened in five of 16 (i.e. 31%) customs unions. These are: CACM,[168] CARICOM,[169] EU-Turkey,[170] EU-Andorra,[171] EU-San Marino.[172] No harmonization of external anti-dumping legislation has taken place in the remaining five (i.e. 31%) customs unions. These are COMESA, EAC, CEMAC, MERCOSUR and SACU. Only members of COMESA, MERCOSUR and SACU have imposed anti-dumping measures at all. SACU is a special case that will be described below.[173] COMESA[174] and EAC[175] have regulated that the WTO rules apply without modification externally. This means that member states remain competent in the area of anti-dumping. Although CEMAC is

---

[162] Art. 48.1 EAEU Treaty. The Commission is directly bound by it: Art. 277 Protocol 8 EAEU Treaty. Member States retain no Competences.

[163] Regulation C/Reg.6/06/13. Regulations are binding upon Member States following Art. 12.3 ECOWAS Treaty.

[164] Art. 7 The GCC Common Law on Antidumping, Countervailing Measures and Safeguard Measures and Its Rules of Implementation (GCC Antidumping law), 2011-1432.

[165] Art. 3 Règlement N° 09/2003/CM/UEMOA portant Code Communautaire Antidumping (Reg. N. 09/2003), 23.05.2003.

[166] Within the scope of Art. 2 (c), (d) Decision 283, Normas para prevenir o corregir las distorsiones en la competencia generadas por prácticas de dumping o subsidios (Decision 283), 31.3.1991.

[167] Reg. (EU) 2016/1036. It applies directly, Art. 288 TFEU.

[168] Art. 8 Guatemala Protocol obliges States to harmonize their rules and gives the Executive Committee on Economic Integration (Art. 42 Guatemala Protocol) the competence to regulate such provision. It has done so in Art. 6-22 Resolucion 193/2007.

[169] Art. 133.5 Revised Treaty of Chaguaramas.

[170] Following Art. 12 (1) Decision 1/95, Turkey must mirror the Basic Anti-Dumping Regulation.

[171] Art. 7 (1) EU—Andorra Agreement.

[172] Art. 7 (1) EU—San Marino Agreement.

[173] See: section "SACU".

[174] Even though the Council has a mandate to regulate these proceedings (Art. 51.6 COMESA Treaty), it regulated that externally only the WTO Agreement applies (Art. 3.6 COMESA Regulation on Trade Remedy Measures).

[175] Reg. 4.4 EAC Customs Union (Anti-Dumping Measures) Regulations.

competent,[176] no external anti-dumping regime has yet been introduced.[177] As only certain countries in CEMAC have introduced anti-dumping measures at all, it is difficult to see why this is the case. The general reasons on why anti-dumping measures are applied only by some countries[178] may apply.

Similarly, although MERCOSUR has the competence to introduce an external anti-dumping regime and external anti-dumping regulations have been proposed, this has not happened yet. The reason for this probably stems from the general reluctance also to implement the common customs code.[179]

Harmonizing external anti-dumping measures can occur on two levels. First, anti-dumping procedures may be harmonized. This includes harmonizing the investigation (under Sect. 3.4.1) or the imposition decision (under Sect. 3.4.2). Second, substantive rules on anti-dumping may be modified. This means that the scope of the investigation and the resulting measure are modified to a union wide basis (under Sect. 3.4.3).

---

[176] Art. 13 (b) Convention Régissant l'Union Économique de l'Afrique Centrale (UEAC), 16.3.1994.

[177] Trade Policy Review Body, 'Trade Policy Review, Report by the Secretariat, Countries of the Central African Economic and Monetary Community (CEMAC)', WT/TPR/S/285, 24.6.2013, p. 45. The only country that has reported Anti-Dumping legislation in CEMAC is Cameroon (Committee on Anti-Dumping Practices, 'Report (2019) of the Committee on Anti-Dumping Practices', G/L/1344, G/ADP/26, 21.11.2019, pp. 6–10). Cameroon has never initiated an anti-dumping procedure but the national law has been reported (Committee on Anti-Dumping Practices, 'Notification of Laws and Regulations under Articles 18.5, 32.6 and 12.6 of the Agreements, Cameroon' G/ADP/N/1/CMR/1, 4.7.2013; Committee on Anti-Dumping Practices, 'Notification of Laws and Regulations under Articles 18.5, 32.6 and 12.6 of the Agreements, Cameroon, Supplement' G/ADP/N/1/CMR/1/Suppl.1, 27.5.2014; Committee on Anti-Dumping Practices, 'Notification of Laws and Regulations under Articles 18.5, 32.6 and 12.6 of the Agreements, Cameroon, Corrigendum', G/ADP/N/1/Corr.1, 13.6.2014).

[178] See: Chap. 3.

[179] MERCOSUR has the competence to regulate external Anti-Dumping measures: Art. 4 Treaty Establishing a Common Market between the Argentine Republic, the Federal Republic of Brazil, the Republic of Paraguay and the Eastern Republic of Uruguay, 26.3.1991 (MERCUSOR Treaty). The MERCOSUR Trade Commission has been instructed to implement a common Anti-Dumping framework, Art. 2 Marco Normativo del Reglamento común relative a la defensa contra las importaciones objeto de dumping provenientes de países no miembros del Mercado común del sur (Dec. N. 11/97), MERCOSUR/CMC/DEC N 11/97. A common Customs Code has, however, not yet been set up and the common Anti-Dumping Regulation does, therefore, not apply yet, see: Trade Policy Review Body, 'Trade Policy Review, Report by the Secretariat, Uruguay', WT/TPR/S/374, 23.5.2018, p. 35. Until this happens, member states impose Anti-Dumping measures according to national legislation (Art. 3 Dec. N. 11/97): e.g. Definitive Anti-Dumping Measures on Ceramic, marble, travertine or glass tiles against Brazil and China, 2.7.2014, Official Journal of Argentina No. 32941 (Resolución N 309/2014).

3.4.1 Investigation Stage

The strongest form of integration during the investigation stage is if a central investigating authority is competent to investigate. If that happens, member states may still participate in the investigations by having certain rights and obligations. Alternatively, member states may remain competent to investigate and different cooperation requirements between the member states can be introduced.

3.4.1.1 Common Investigating Authority

Of the 16 customs unions, seven (i.e. 44%) require that the investigation be conducted by a central authority. The customs unions that have a competent central investigating authority are the CAN,[180] CARICOM,[181] ECOWAS,[182] EAEU,[183] EU,[184] GCC,[185] and WAEMU.[186]

Important caveats apply in CAN, CARICOM, ECOWAS, and WAEMU.

In CARICOM the central investigating authority has not acted yet[187] and Trinidad and Tobago have imposed an anti-dumping measure in 2016[188] based purely on national legislation. In ECOWAS, although the Common External Tariff is operational,[189] the central investigating authority has not acted yet. Similarly, in WAEMU the Commission has not acted as the investigating authority yet.[190] Even though the

---

[180] E.g. Art. 11 Decision 283.

[181] Art. 131 (5) Revised Treaty of Chaguaramas.

[182] The ECOWAS Commission, created by Art. 17 of the ECOWAS Treaty, is the investigating authority, Art. 22-36 Regulation C/Reg.6/06/13.

[183] According to Art. 48.1 EAEU Treaty, the EAEU has the competence to apply trade remedy measures. The investigating authority is designated by the Eurasian Economic Commission (EEC), Art. 48.4 EEU Treaty, being the Department for Internal Market Defence of the EEC (DIMD).

[184] The EU is exclusively competent, Art. 3 (1)(e), 207 TFEU, and has regulated its Anti-Dumping framework in Reg. (EU) 2016/1036. The investigating authority is the Commission, Art. 6 Reg. (EU) 2016/1036.

[185] Member States had to unify their industrial legislation and regulations on anti-dumping, Art. 8 (ii) GCC Agreement. This has happened in the GCC Antidumping Law. The Bureau of the Technical Secretariat is the investigating authority, Sec. I Art. 10 (2) GCC Antidumping Law.

[186] The Commission (Art. 26–34 WAEMU Treaty) is the investigation authority, Art. 31–36 Reg. N. 09/2003.

[187] Even though the Common External Tariff already applies: Trade Policy Review Body, 'Trade Policy Review, Report by the Secretariat, Trinidad and Tobago', WT/TPR/S/388, 27.3.2019, p. 29.

[188] Final Determination by the Minister of Trade and Industry Arising out of an Investigation into the Allegation of The Dumping of Imports of Aluminium Extrusions Originating in the People's Republic of China, Legal Supplement Part B—Vol. 55, No. 30, 3.3.2016.

[189] Trade Policy Review Body, 'Trade Policy Review, Report by the Secretariat, Guinea', WT/TPR/S/370, 24.4.2018, p. 19.

[190] Trade Policy Review Body, Trade Policy Review, Report by the Secretariat, The Member Countries of the West African Economic and Monetary Union (WAEMU), WT/TPR/S/362, 14.9.2017, p. 47.

relevant legislation for these customs unions is considered, there is no relevant practice to see how these systems will work.

The competence of the General Secretariat[191] in CAN is severely limited. In CAN, externally Decision 283 still applies to the extent that Decision 456 has not replaced it.[192] Decision 283 applies when practices originate in a third country and cause or threaten to cause injury to domestic production destined for export to another member country.[193] Distinguishing between which branch of the domestic industry is injured is not based on WTO law and it is practically difficult to make that distinction. The scope of the decision is best understood as applying to anti-dumping actions on behalf of a third country.[194] Above that, Decision 283 also applies in some cases in which the Common External Tariff—which is not yet operational[195]—applies.[196] Where Decision 283 does not apply, the member countries remain competent.[197]

Two interesting observations relating to other forms of integration derive from this.

First, the customs unions that have a common investigation authority also either prohibit or centralize the internal imposition of anti-dumping measures, with the exception of CARICOM. On the one hand this suggests that greater internal integration corresponds to external harmonization but on the other hand it reinforces that theoretically no internal integration is necessary for external harmonization to take place.

Second, those customs unions that have a central investigating authority usually also conduct the investigations on a union wide basis, with the exceptions of CAN and CARICOM.

Transferring investigatory competences to a centralized authority may lead to some practical difficulties as customs unions may depend on the cooperation with member state authorities to obtain or verify information. Moreover, transferring competences to a centralized authority can be politically controversial. Therefore, customs unions usually cushion these effects by granting various rights and obligations to their member states. There are three different rights and obligations that usually apply: (1) member states may have the right to request the initiation of an investigation, (2) member states may have to cooperate during the investigation, (3) member states may have certain information rights. Besides these specific rights,

---

[191] Art. 1 (e) Decision 425, Reglamento de Procedimientos Administrativos de la Secretaría General de la Comunidad Andina, 11.12.1997.

[192] Vallejo (2018) <https://www.ssrn.com/abstract=3209860> accessed 5 July 2021.

[193] Art. 2 (c) Decision 283.

[194] See below at: Sect. 3.5.3.

[195] Trade Policy Review Body, Trade Policy Review, Report by the Secretariat, Peru, WT/TPR/S/393, 27.8.2019, p. 37.

[196] Art. 2 (d) Decision 283.

[197] Art. 2 (3) Decision 283.

Table 3.3 Summary of additional rights and obligations if there is a centralized external investigating authority

RTA Name	Additional rights to initiate an investigation	Cooperation requirements in the investigation phase	Information requirements
Andean Community (CAN)	x	x	x
Caribbean Community and Common Market (CARICOM)			
Economic Community of West African States (ECOWAS)		x	x
Eurasian Economic Union (EAEU)			
European Union (EU)	x	x	x
Gulf Cooperation Council (GCC)	x		x
West African Economic and Monetary Union (WAEMU)		x	x

general information requirements and general cooperation requirements may exist.[198]

Table 3.3 summarizes which customs unions grant which additional rights.

Requesting the Initiation of an Investigation

According to the ADA, an anti-dumping investigation is initiated either upon request by or on behalf of the domestic industry,[199] which is usually the industry of the member state or by the investigating authority itself, if they have sufficient evidence of dumping, injury and a causal link.[200]

Customs unions may deviate from this by giving more groups of persons the right to request the initiation of an investigation. Member states may be competent to request the initiation of an investigation or the industry of a member state may request the initiation of an investigation.[201]

Only CAN and GCC grant additional rights to request the initiation of an investigation. CAN modifies the initiation in both ways and also includes that

---

[198] E.g. in the EU: Art. 6 (1) Reg. (EU) 2016/1036.

[199] Art. 5.1 ADA. The relevant quorum is defined in Art. 5.4 ADA.

[200] Art. 5.6 ADA.

[201] In the EU member states should communicate any evidence relating to dumping, injury and causation to the Commission, Art. 5 (1)(3) Reg. (EU) 2016/1036. This does not give member states any additional rights but rather constitutes a form of information exchange.

individual corporations can initiate an investigation to the extent permitted by national law.[202] In the GCC either a GCC industry or an industry of a member state may request the initiation of an investigation.[203]

Conducting the Investigation

In principle, the central authority conducts the investigation. However, some customs unions allow the central authority to delegate some tasks to the authorities of the member states. This means that the central authority can demand information by the members or can demand that the members gather information on its behalf.

Both of these modifications appear in the EU,[204] the CAN,[205] ECOWAS,[206] and WAEMU.[207]

Moreover, during the verification of the information, the central authority may require the same assistance. The central authorities of the EU,[208] CARICOM,[209] ECOWAS,[210] and WAEMU[211] can delegate the verification of the information to member states' authorities.

Information Rights

Customs unions may regulate that the customs union must share or that member states may demand certain information. The information exchange thereby differs between the initiation and investigation phase. During the initiation phase, the additional information requirements usually oblige the central authority to share each request for initiation and the member states to share evidence of dumping and injury. During the investigation stage, member states can request non-confidential information on the investigation.

All customs unions that have a central investigating authority except for CARICOM and the EAEU have some provisions concerning information exchange.

---

[202] Art. 10 Decision 283.

[203] Sec. II Art. 2.2 GCC Antidumping Law.

[204] Art. 6 (3), (4) Reg. (EU) 2016/1036.

[205] Art. 11 (1) Decision 283. Limitations exist if the information is confidential, Art. 13 Decision 283.

[206] Art. 33 (2), 34 (2) Reg. C/Reg.6/06/13.

[207] Art. 32, 33 (2) Reg. N. 09/2003.

[208] Art. 6 (3), (4) Reg. (EU) 2016/1036.

[209] Art. 132 (1) Revised Treaty of Chaguaramas.

[210] Art. 32 (2), 33 (4) Reg. C/Reg.6/06/13.

[211] Art. 33 (2) WAEMU Anti-Dumping Regulation.

During the initiation stage, the EU,[212] ECOWAS,[213] and WAEMU[214] have the strongest forms of information exchange. In addition to the two modifications mentioned—that each request for initiation must be notified to the members and that the members must forward any information on dumping and injury—the request for initiation can also be sent to the members which will then forward it to the central investigating authority. The GCC has relatively few additional information rights, but member governments shall be notified prior to the initiation of an investigation.[215]

During the investigation, members may request non-confidential information on the proceedings in the CAN,[216] EU,[217] ECOWAS,[218] and WAEMU.[219] No additional information rights exist during that stage exist in the GCC.

3.4.1.2 Member States Remain Competent

In the remaining nine of 16 (i.e. 56%) customs unions, the competence to conduct investigations remains with the member states. These are CEMAC, COMESA, EAC, MERCOSUR and SACU[220] where national regulations apply without modification by the customs unions on the one hand and CACM,[221] the customs unions between the EU and Andorra,[222] Turkey,[223] and San Marino[224] on the other hand.

---

[212] Member States must forward information on dumping and injury: Art. 5 (1) (3) Reg. (EU) 2016/1036; the Commission must forward any complaints or the intention to self-initiate an investigation: Art. 5 (1) (3) s. 2, 5 (6) s. 2 Reg. (EU) 2016/1036; the request for initiation can also be sent to the Member States: Art. 5 (1) (3) Reg. (EU) 2016/1036.

[213] Art. 23 (2) Reg. C/Reg.6/06/13.

[214] Art. 23 (2) Reg. N. 09/2003.

[215] Sec. II Art. 7 GCC Antidumping Law.

[216] Art. 11 (2) Decision 283. Limitations exist if the information is confidential, Art. 13 Decision 283.

[217] Art. 6 (3) Reg. (EU) 2016/1036. The requested information must be of general interest and non-confidential.

[218] Art. 33 (3) Reg. C/Reg.6/06/13.

[219] Art. 33 (3) Reg. N. 09/2003.

[220] Only South Africa has an investigating authority.

[221] Art. 1 (3) Resolucion 193/2007 defines the investigating authority the member states' authorities except in a regional procedure, where it is SIECA.

[222] Because Andorra must copy the EU's Anti-Dumping measures, only the EU has a competent investigating authority.

[223] Following Art. 12 of the Agreement, Turkey must mirror the Basic Anti-Dumping Regulation, which at the time was Council Regulation (EC) No 3283/94 of 22 December 1994 on protection against dumped imports from countries not members of the European Communities, OJ L 349/1, 31.12.1994. Nevertheless, the parties can implement Anti-Dumping measures independently, Chapter IV Section 3 Decision 1/95.

[224] Only the EU has a competent investigating authority.

Classification of the EU-Andorra and EU-San Marino customs unions and SACU into this category should be read with caution, as they follow a unique structure, which will be elaborated below.[225]

Relating to the other layers of integration and harmonization, three interesting observations can be made. First, all customs unions where the members have a competent investigating authority externally, also have the competence internally to conduct investigations. Second, apart from the three special cases of SACU and the EU-Andorra and EU-San Marino customs unions, none of the customs unions that leave the competence to conduct investigations with its members, have eliminated internal anti-dumping measures. Third, except for SACU, all investigations substantively only focus on the members and not the whole customs union.

To achieve some level of harmonization during the investigation, different cooperation requirements exist. The purpose of these cooperation requirements is, however, different than the cooperation requirements between a central investigating authority and the member states. Because investigations are usually limited to the territory of one member and the member states exercise authority over their territory, they can conduct the investigation without cooperation by other institutions. Cooperation requirements then follow the purpose to harmonize external actions, but they are not vital for their functioning. If a central investigating authority exists, only the member state authorities may be competent to verify information, which is why the central investigating authority must have the right to delegate this task to ensure that it effectively conducts the investigation. This also explains why empirically fewer cooperation requirements exist as compared to the situation in which a central authority acts.

Those customs union that do not have harmonized anti-dumping legislation on a customs union wide level, will not have cooperation requirements either. These are: CEMAC, COMESA, MERCOSUR, EAC, and SACU.

Of those customs unions that have harmonized anti-dumping regulation (CACM, EU-Andorra, EU-San Marino, EU-Turkey, MERCOSUR), only the EU-Turkey customs union contains some cooperation requirements during the investigation. The cooperation requirements in the EU-Turkey customs union are, however, limited to an exchange of information and consultations with the aim of coordinating their actions when conducting investigations against third countries.[226]

3.4.2   Imposition Decision

Following and during the investigation, several decisions must be taken. These decisions can either be taken by a central authority or by the member states. If

---

[225] See: sections "SACU" and "EU-Andorra, EU-San Marino".

[226] Art. 45 (2) Decision 1/95. This replaces the consultation and decision-making procedure referred to in Section II, Chapter V of the Decision.

decisions are taken centrally, this means that the organ either imposes the measure or that it allows the members to impose the measure.

3.4.2.1 Central Authority Is Competent

In seven of the 16 customs unions (i.e. 44%), the decision to impose definitive anti-dumping measures and certain other decisions are taken by a central authority. These are: the EU,[227] CARICOM,[228] EAEU,[229] GCC,[230] ECOWAS,[231] WAEMU,[232] and CAN.[233] This means all customs unions that have a central investigating authority also impose measures centrally and *vice versa*.

Even though these customs unions take the decision to impose anti-dumping measures centrally, member states participate in that process directly or indirectly by participating in central institutions.

Member states may participate directly, as in ECOWAS[234] and WAEMU,[235] where provisional anti-dumping measures can only be imposed upon request by a member state.

Member states' participation may also be ensured through the setup of the institutions that make the decisions. This is the case if the central authorities that take the relevant decisions are composed of member states' representatives. In ECOWAS[236] and WAEMU[237] member states participate in the Council of Ministers, responsible to take the relevant decisions. Similarly, in the GCC, the Ministerial

---

[227] Art. 7 (4) (Provisional Duties), 8 (1) (Undertakings), 9 (2) (Termination), 9 (4) (Definitive Anti-Dumping duty), 11 (6) (Reviews), 13 (3) (3) (Circumvention), 9 (8) (4) (Refund Requests) Reg. (EU) 2016/1036.

[228] Art. 133 (1) Revised Treaty of Chaguaramas. The same process applies as internally. See: section "CARICOM".

[229] Para. 78 (Provisional Duties), 90 (Undertakings), 100 (Definitive Anti-Dumping Measures), 109 (Reviews), 118 (Circumvention), Annex 8 EAEU Treaty.

[230] For definitive Anti-Dumping measures, the Ministerial Committee is competent Sec. I Art. 8.1 GCC Antidumping Law. For other measures, the Permanent Committee is competent, Sec. I Art. 9.2 (a) GCC Antidumping Law.

[231] The Commission imposes the following: Art. 40.3 (Provisional Measures), 42.1 (Undertakings) Reg. C/Reg.6/06/13. The Council of Ministers imposes the definitive Anti-Dumping measures, Art. 47 Reg. C/Reg.6/06/13.

[232] The Commission is responsible according to Art. 40.3 (Provisional Measures), 42.1 (Undertakings) Reg. 09/2003. The Council of Ministers imposes the definitive Anti-Dumping measures, Art. 47 Reg. 09/2003.

[233] Art. 20 Decision 283.

[234] Art. 40.3. Reg. C/Reg.6/06/13.

[235] Art. 40.3 Reg. 09/2003.

[236] Art. 10 ECOWAS Treaty.

[237] Art. 20 WAEMU Treaty.

Committee and Permanent Committee are composed of ministers[238] as well as undersecretaries of ministries[239] of member states.

The EU includes the member states in the decision making process through the comitology procedure.[240] In the EU, anti-dumping measures are adopted in the form of implementing regulations[241] by the Commission following an advisory procedure[242] or an examination procedure[243] in the Comitology—a committee mostly composed of representatives of the member states.[244] In advisory procedures, the committee's decision is not binding[245] whereas it is principally binding in examination procedures.[246] The Commission[247] and the committee[248] are organs of the EU.

In the EAEU, the Board of the Eurasian Economic Commission (EEC) takes the decisions to impose anti-dumping measures. The Board of the Commission is comprised of representatives of the member states, based on the principles of equal representation.[249] Nevertheless, the members of the board do not represent their countries but only serve the Commission.[250] Members may only influence the decisions indirectly.[251] Moreover, EAEU members can submit a proposal to amend

---

[238] Art. 3 GCC Antidumping Law.

[239] Art. 9 (1) GCC Antidumping Law.

[240] Art. 15 Reg. (EU) 2016/1036.

[241] Art. 291 (2) TFEU.

[242] Art. 4 Regulation (EU) No 182/2011 of the European Parliament and of the Council of 16 February 2011 laying down the rules and general principles concerning mechanisms for control by Member States of the Commission's exercise of implementing powers (Reg. (EU) 2011/182), OJ L 55/13, 28.2.2011. This procedure applies when imposing provisional Anti-Dumping measures (Art. 7 (4) Reg. (EU) 2016/1036), when accepting an Undertaking (Art. 8 (1) Reg. (EU) 2016/1036), when initiating a review (Art. 11 (6) Reg. (EU) 2016/1036), and when suspending a measure (Art. 14 (4) Reg. (EU) 2016/1036).

[243] Art. 5 Reg. (EU) 2011/182. This procedure applies when an investigation is terminated following the acceptance of an Undertaking (Art. 8 (5) Reg. (EU) 2016/1036), where an investigation is terminated without imposing definitive Anti-Dumping measures (Art. 9 (2) Reg. (EU) 2016/1036), where definitive Anti-Dumping measures are implemented (Art. 9 (4) Reg. (EU) 2016/1036), where measures are repealed, maintained or amended following a review (Art. 11 (6)(2) Reg. (EU) 2016/1036), where measures are amended following an absorption investigation (Art. 12 (3) Reg. (EU) 2016/1036), or where measures are extended following a circumvention investigation (Art. 13 (3) Reg. (EU) 2016/1036).

[244] For a critical analysis of the procedure see: Willems et al. (2019), p. 268.

[245] Art. 4 (2) Reg. (EU) 2011/182.

[246] Art. 5 (2), (3), (4) Reg. (EU) 2011/182. See the exception in Art. 7 Reg. (EU) 2011/182.

[247] Art. 17 TEU.

[248] Art. 3 (2) Reg. (EU) 2011/182.

[249] Art. 31, Annex 1 EAEU Treaty.

[250] Art. 9, 18 EAEU Treaty.

[251] The EEC has Advisory Bodies comprised of representatives by member states. For anti-dumping measures, in particular the Sub-Committee on Tariff, Non-Tariff Measures and Trade Remedies (Formed via: College of the Eurasian Economic Commission Decision, On the Advisory Committee on Trade, 7.3.2012 N. 6 (Decision No. 6), as amended on 24.1.2017). Even though the opinions of the Advisory Body are not binding, according to Ind. 3, para. 13 Decision No. 6 only if all members of the Advisory Body agree to a draft decision, would that decision be sent to the Board of the Commission for approval.

a decision taken by the Board of the EEC[252] or consumers can request a review of the measure.[253] In the past internal political problems have arisen where the only industry that was injured was Russian and the other EAEU members objected the imposition of the measure.[254]

3.4.2.2 Member States Remain Competent

In nine of the 16 customs unions, i.e. 56%, the member states are competent to take the relevant decisions relating to anti-dumping measures. These are CEMAC, COMESA, EAC, and MERCOSUR where national regulations apply without modification by the customs unions on the one hand and CACM,[255] the EU-Andorra, EU-San Marino[256] and EU-Turkey[257] customs unions, CARICOM[258] and SACU[259] on the other hand.

To harmonize external trade, cooperation requirements between the member states may be implemented. These cooperation requirements are, however, rare. Only CACM and the EU-Turkey customs union impose procedures for additional information exchange. In CACM, the imposition of an anti-dumping measure must be notified to SIECA.[260] In the EU-Turkey customs union, the Customs Union Joint Committee, a central authority, shall be informed of the imposition of a measure.[261]

Special provisions exist in the EU-Andorra, EU-San Marino customs unions and SACU. The composition of these three customs unions is similar in that they consist of one economically dominant member (the EU, South Africa) on the one hand and economically less significant parties (Andorra, San Marino, Botswana, Lesotho, Namibia, Eswatini) on the other hand.

---

[252] Art. 30, Annex 1 EAEU Treaty.

[253] The author would like to thank Maxim Shmelev for his invaluable help. All mistakes remain the author's.

[254] For an overview, how these situations were resolved, see: Makhinova (2020), p. 37.

[255] Art. 22 Resolucion 193/2007.

[256] See: section "EU-Andorra, EU-San Marino".

[257] See Chapter IV Section 3 Decision 1/95 which only adds some elements but does not substitute the members' Anti-Dumping legislation.

[258] Art. 133 (1) Revised Treaty of Chaguaramas. COTED is, however, competent to conduct a review if an applicant is not satisfied with the review conducted by the Member State, Art. 133 (3) (d) Revised Treaty of Chaguaramas, see above: section "CARICOM".

[259] See: section "SACU".

[260] Art. 22 Resolucion 193/2007.

[261] Art. 46 Decision 1/95.

SACU[262]

In 2019 South Africa had a GDP of 351.431 Mio. USD whereas the other customs unions members (BELN states) had a combined GDP of 37.527 Mio. USD equalling 10,6% of South Africa's GDP.[263]

Anti-dumping regulation in SACU still operates with a transitional mechanism. Even though the 2002 SACU Agreement provides for the creation of national investigating authorities[264] and a central authority, the Tariff Board,[265] competent to impose anti-dumping measures, most national investigating authorities are not yet operational[266] and the Tariff Board has not yet been set up. Once that is the case, anti-dumping investigations will be conducted on a union wide basis but each national investigating authority will conduct the investigation with respect to its territory.[267] The decision to impose the measure will be taken centrally by the Council of Ministers[268] following recommendation by the Tariff Board.[269]

Until this system is operational, the Council of Ministers has delegated tariff (including anti-dumping) decisions to the International Trade Administration Commission (ITAC),[270] a South African authority.[271] Legally, ITAC conducts investigations on a union wide basis and then recommends the imposition of definitive anti-dumping measures.[272] Approval takes place by the South African Minister of Trade and Industry,[273] even though tariff decisions have only been delegated to ITAC and not the ministry.[274] To conduct the investigation, ITAC may request information from other member states[275] and consider imports into the

---

[262] The author would like to thank Gustav Brink for his valuable help with this section. All mistakes remain the author's.

[263] Numbers according to: The World Bank, 'GDP (Current US$) | Data' <https://data.worldbank.org/indicator/NY.GDP.MKTP.CD> accessed 5 July 2021.

[264] Art. 14, Annex C SACU Agreement.

[265] Art. 11 SACU Agreement.

[266] Only South Africa's National Authority is operational. It is the International Trade Administration Commission (ITAC), International Trade Administration Act (ITAA), No. 71 of 2002. Botswana and Eswatini are in the process of setting up their own national investigating authorities.

[267] Art. 14.1 SACU Agreement.

[268] Art. 8.7 SACU Agreement.

[269] Art. 11.2 SACU Agreement.

[270] International Trade Administration Commission, sec. 7 ITAA, sec. 16 ITAA.

[271] Trade Policy Review Body, 'Trade Policy Review, Report by the Secretariat, South African Customs Union', WT/TPR/S/324, 30.9.2015, p. 29.

[272] S. 38.1 The International Trade Administration Commission, Anti-Dumping Regulations (Anti-Dumping Regulations) N. 3197 of 2003, 14.11.2003.

[273] S. 38.2 Anti-Dumping Regulations. For a critical analysis of South Africa's Institutional Set-up, see: Brink (2015), pp. 325, 327–328.

[274] Questioning legality of this practice: Brink (2013), pp. 419, 429–436.

[275] Art. 19 (c) ITAA.

entire customs union.[276] However, factually this rarely happens for the purpose of the injury determination, which usually only considers whether the South African industry is injured. In fact, there has only been a single application from an industry of Botswana, Eswatini, Lesotho or Namibia[277] and otherwise BELN industries have not contributed to injury determinations.[278]

EU-Andorra, EU-San Marino

In 2019 the EU had a combined GDP of 15.592.795 Mio. USD whereas Andorra had a GDP of 3.154 Mio. USD, equalling 0,02% of the EU's GDP and San Marino of 1.637 Mio. USD equalling 0,01% of the EU's GDP.[279]

The anti-dumping regime in the EU-Andorra and EU-San Marino is even more one-sided. In both customs unions, Andorra and San Marino are required to adopt "the laws, regulations and administrative provisions applicable to customs matters".[280] This includes the obligation to apply a common anti-dumping regime, i.e. to copy the EU's anti-dumping measures.[281] This means that the EU's anti-dumping measures apply to imports into the entire EU-Andorra and EU-San Marino customs union. However, when conducting investigations, the EU does not take Andorra's or San Marino's industry into account.[282]

3.4.3 Scope of Investigation and Measure

If a state conducts an anti-dumping investigation, the territorial scope[283] of that investigation considers all relevant imports into that state to determine dumping and

---

[276]E.g. ITAC, 'Investigation Into the Alleged Dumping of Clear Float Glass Originating in or Imported from Saudi Arabia and the United Arab Emirates: Final Determinations', Report No. 615, 18.10.2019.

[277]Definitive Anti-Dumping Measures on Soda Ash against the United States, GG37756, 19.6.14.

[278]For a thorough structural and legal analysis, see: Brink (2012) D12WP07/2012.

[279]The World Bank, 'GDP (Current US$) | Data' <https://data.worldbank.org/indicator/NY.GDP.MKTP.CD> accessed 5 July 2021.

[280]For EU—Andorra: Art. 7 (1) EU—Andorra Agreement. For EU—San Marino: Art. 7 (1) EU—San Marino Agreement.

[281]Committee on Regional Trade Agreements, 'Customs Union Between the European Community and the Principality of Andorra', WT/REG53/3, 12.11.1998, p. 4

[282]Art. 4 Regulation (EU) No 952/2013 of the European Parliament and of the Council of 9 October 2013 laying down the Union Customs Code (Reg. (EU) 952/2013 or Union Customs Code), OJ L 269/1, 10.10.2013.

[283]The territorial scope of an anti-dumping measure is also relevant with respect to which exporters and producers participate in the investigation. This dimension is not considered in this section. See below: Chap. 7.

considers the domestic production, which are certain producers within that state for the injury determination. The resulting measure then applies to the respective imports into that state. In exceptional circumstances, anti-dumping measures can also be regional, meaning that they apply only to imports into certain regions of a state.[284]

This may differ in customs unions as the territorial scope of the investigation and measure may also be union wide. This means that the export price must be the price paid or payable for the import of a like product into the territory of the customs union (instead of the member state) and the dumping must cause an injury to the entire union industry (instead of the member's industry). The resulting measure then applies to imports into the entire union (instead of one state).

3.4.3.1 Union Wide Investigation and Measure

In eight of the 16 customs unions, i.e. 50%, the territorial scope of the investigation or the measure are customs union wide. These are: the EU,[285] EAEU,[286] GCC,[287] ECOWAS,[288] WAEMU,[289] SACU.[290] In the EU-Andorra and EU-San Marino customs unions even though the investigation only relates to the territory of one member of the customs union (the EU), the measure applies to imports into the entire customs union.

One would expect that in all customs unions in which a central authority investigates and imposes anti-dumping measures, the investigations and the scope of the resulting measure would relate to the entire customs union. This is true with the exceptions of CAN and CARICOM, where the scope of the investigation and measure are only member state wide. However, no relevant practice exists to examine the effects of these arrangements.

---

[284] Art. 4.1(ii), 4.2 ADA.

[285] Art. 2 (8) Reg. (EU) 2016/1036; Art. 4 (1) Reg. (EU) 2016/1036. Exception to this: Art. 4 (1) (b) Reg. (EU) 2016/1036.

[286] Para. 7 Annex 8 EAEU Treaty.

[287] Sec. I Art. 3 GCC Antidumping Law.

[288] With regards to the export price: Art. 12.1 Reg. C/Reg.6/06/13. The injury determination relates to the Community market and the Community industry, Art. 17 Reg. C/Reg.6/06/13, both terms are defined in Art. 1 Reg. C/Reg.6/06/13.

[289] Export price: Art. 12.1 Reg. N. 09/2003; Injury determination: Art. 17–21 Reg. N. 09/2003; Scope of the measure: Art. 46–54 Reg. N. 09/2003.

[290] SACU industry is defined in Art. 7 Anti-Dumping Regulations. The export price is established in relation to the customs union, Art. 32 (2)(a) ITAA. The injury determination is made in relation to the SACU industry, Art. 13.1 Anti-Dumping Regulations.

3.4.3.2 Member Wide Investigation and Measure

The remaining eight of 16 customs unions, i.e. 50%, apply a member state wide scope to their investigation and the resulting measure applies on a member state wide basis. These are the customs unions where national regulations apply without modification by the customs union (CEMAC, COMESA, EAC, and MERCOSUR) as well as CAN,[291] CACM,[292] CARICOM, and the EU-Turkey customs union.[293]

Even though in COMESA WTO rules apply, they have included a rule on the scope of measures that is without legal framework not yet operational but may hint at future integration. In the Council Regulations Governing the COMESA Customs Union,[294] the term "regional industry" has been defined as all relevant producers in the customs union.[295] This has been done, even though a specific legislation for external anti-dumping measures does not exist yet.

Legislation in CARICOM is ambivalent on that matter. The legislation does not explicitly define which imports are taken into account for the export price[296] and the domestic industry is defined as "the [member states'] industry consistent with the provisions of Art. XXIV:8 (a) GATT".[297] The following chapter will argue that WTO law does not require but allows customs unions to change the scope to a union wide basis, which means that a member state wide definition of domestic injury is WTO compliant. The legislation is equally vague as to the territorial scope of the resulting measure.[298] Given that the domestic industry definition hints at the scope being member state wide and that this is the only interpretation that would allow internal anti-dumping measures, the legislation should be interpreted in that way.

3.4.4 Conclusions

The relevant distinction externally is between centralizing the investigation, imposition decision and extending the scope of the investigation and the measure one the one hand and leaving the competences with the member states as well as leaving

---

[291] Export price: Art. 5 (1) Decision 283. Injury determination: Art. 17 Decision 283 (interestingly the injury determination is not limited to the domestic production but concerns the entire Member State). Scope of the measure: Art. 20 Decision 283.

[292] Scope of the investigation: Art. 5 (2) Resolucion 193/2007. Scope of the measure: Art. 22 Resolucion 193/2007.

[293] This is not explicit in Chapter IV Section 3 of the Decision but is apparent as the decision only adds certain elements but does not replace the legislation of the parties.

[294] 9.6.2009, OJ. Vol. 15 No. 1.

[295] Art. 21 Council Regulations Governing the COMESA Customs Union.

[296] Art. 126.3 Revised Treaty of Chaguaramas.

[297] Domestic industry definition: Para. 4 Annex 1 Revised Treaty of Chaguaramas.

[298] Art. 133 Revised Treaty of Chaguaramas.

the scope of the investigation and measure on a member state wide basis on the other hand.

The customs unions that have harmonized fully are the EU, EAEU, and GCC as well as ECOWAS and WAEMU, even though no relevant practice exists as regards the latter two customs unions. Moreover, the envisioned anti-dumping regime in SACU is interesting, as it is nearly as harmonized as these customs unions, but national investigating authorities remain competent and will have to cooperate in investigations. Until then SACU remains fully harmonized with all relevant powers delegated to a national authority, ITAC. Similarly, the EU-Andorra and EU-San Marino customs unions are fully harmonized, with Andorra and San Marino simply copying the EU's anti-dumping measures.

No harmonization has taken place in CEMAC, COMESA, EAC, and MERCOSUR, as they have not established an external anti-dumping regime yet, so that national laws apply without modification. Similarly, CACM and the EU-Turkey customs union have only minimally modified anti-dumping regulation. CARICOM and CAN have harmonized to some degree by both having a central investigating authority and in CAN that authority also has the competence to impose anti-dumping measures. No practice relating to either of these regimes functioning exists, however. Table 3.4 summarizes the results. An asterisk next to an x means that additional conditions apply.

3.5 Associated Problems

So far, this chapter has compared the different anti-dumping regimes in customs unions with a view to how they differ from the WTO anti-dumping rules as typically applied by states. The different modifications may, however, also necessitate amendments in associated areas. The last part of this comparative analysis therefore focuses on what problems arise from membership in multiple RTAs (under Sect. 3.5.1), with regards to Rules of Origin (under Sect. 3.5.2) and how situations in which the country of export does not coincide with the country of injury can be resolved (under Sect. 3.5.3).

3.5.1 Membership in Several RTAs

Customs unions or their members may conclude further RTAs. A multitude of different possibilities how this may occur exist. First, a distinction between the type of the RTA can be made. For this study only customs unions and FTAs that regulate trade in goods are considered.[299] Second, these RTAs can be distinguished

---

[299] Other Agreements that do not regulate the trade in goods but only e.g. trade in services or investment protection are not considered.

Table 3.4 Summary

Customs Union	Investigation		Imposition decision		Scope of investigation & measure	
	Central	Member State	Central	Member State	Union wide	MS wide
Andean Community (CAN)	X	X	X	X		X
Caribbean Community and Common Market (CARICOM)	X		X			X
Central American Common Market (CACM)		X		X		X
Common Market for Eastern and Southern Africa (COMESA)		X		X		X
East African Community (EAC)		X		X		X
Economic and Monetary Community of Central Africa (CEMAC)		X		X		X
Economic Community of West African States (ECOWAS)	X		X		X	
EU—Andorra		X		X	X*	
EU—San Marino		X		X	X*	
EU—Turkey		X		X		X
Eurasian Economic Union (EAEU)	X		X		X	
European Union (EU)	X		X		X	
Gulf Cooperation Council (GCC)	X		X		X	
Southern African Customs Union (SACU)	X		X		X	
Southern Common Market (MERCOSUR)		X		X		X
West African Economic and Monetary Union (WAEMU)	X		X		X	

by their parties. It is possible that the entire customs unions conclude RTAs. This includes RTAs concluded by the customs union itself, concluded by all member states of the customs union jointly, or a combination of the two.[300] Above that, cases also exist where only some members of customs unions have concluded RTAs.

Table 3.5 shows which RTAs have been concluded either by member states or customs unions. Only RTAs that have been notified to the WTO are considered but no distinction is made based on whether they were notified following the Enabling Clause or Art. XXIV GATT.[301] The data is limited to FTAs and Customs unions that

---

[300] E.g. Agreement establishing an Association between the EU and its Member States, on the one hand, and Central America on the other, OJ L 2012 346, 15.12.2012. It was concluded by the EU and its member states on the one hand and the member states of another customs union, CACM, on the other.

[301] Source: WTO, Regional Trade Agreements Database, available at: https://rtais.wto.org/UI/PublicMaintainRTAHome.aspx (accessed 5 July 2021).

Table 3.5 RTAs concluded by CUs or their MS

Customs Union	Members	RTAs by only some Members of a CU		RTAs by the CU Alone, all its Members or Jointly	
		FTA	CU	FTA	CU
Andean Community (CAN)	Bolivia, Colombia, Ecuador, Peru, Venezuela	23			
Caribbean Community and Common Market (CARICOM)	Antigua and Barbuda, Bahamas, Barbados, Belize, Dominica, Grenada, Guyana, Haiti, Jamaica, Montserrat, Saint Kitts and Nevis, Saint Lucia, Saint Vincent and the Grenadines, Suriname, Trinidad and Tobago	1		1	
Central American Common Market (CACM)	Costa Rica, El Salvador, Guatemala, Honduras, Nicaragua, Panama	20		6	
Common Market for Eastern and Southern Africa (COMESA)	Angola, Burundi, Comoros, Egypt, Eritrea, Eswatini, Ethiopia, Kenya, Lesotho, Malawi, Mauritius, Rwanda, Sudan, Somalia, Tanzania, Tunisia, Uganda, Zambia, Zimbabwe	13	2		
East African Community (EAC)	Burundi, Kenya, Rwanda, Tanzania, Uganda	1			1
Economic and Monetary Community of Central Africa (CEMAC)	Cameroon, Central African Republic, Chad, Congo, Equatorial Guinea, Gabon	1			
Economic Community of West African States (ECOWAS)	Benin, Burkina Faso, Cabo Verde, Côte d'Ivoire, Ghana, Guinea, Guinea-Bissau, Liberia, Mali, Niger, Nigeria, Senegal, Sierra Leone, Gambia, Togo	2	1		
EU—Andorra	EU (and its Member States), Andorra	+ EU			
EU—San Marino	EU (and its Member States), San Marino	+ EU			
EU—Turkey	EU (and its Member States), Turkey	19 + EU			
Eurasian Economic Union (EAEU)	Armenia, Belarus, Kazakhstan, Kyrgyz Republic, Russian Federation	18		3	
European Union	Austria, Belgium, Bulgaria, Croatia, Cyprus, Czech Republic, Denmark, Estonia, Finland France, Germany, Greece, Hungary, Ireland, Italy, Latvia, Lithuania, Luxembourg, Malta, Netherlands, Poland, Portugal, Romania, Slovak Republic, Slovenia, Spain, Sweden, United Kingdom			37	3
Gulf Cooperation Council (GCC)	Bahrain, Kuwait, Oman, Qatar, Saudi Arabia, United Arab Emirates	3		2	

(continued)

Table 3.5 (continued)

Customs Union	Members	RTAs by only some Members of a CU		RTAs by the CU Alone, all its Members or Jointly	
		FTA	CU	FTA	CU
Southern African Customs Union (SACU)	Botswana, Eswatini, Lesotho, Namibia, South Africa	2	1	3	
Southern Common Market (MERCOSUR)	Argentina, Brazil, Paraguay, Uruguay	1		2	
West African Economic and Monetary Union (WAEMU)	Benin, Burkina Faso, Côte d'Ivoire, Mali, Niger, Senegal, Togo	1			1

have been reported to the WTO. If an agreement is between two customs unions or members thereof, that agreement appears multiple times on the table.[302]

Several interesting points emerge from this table. Even though it would be expected that RTAs are concluded either at the level of the member states by them individually or at the level of the customs union, in many customs unions, RTAs exist on both levels. One reason for this may be historical. The competence to conclude RTAs may have only been centralized after some member states had already concluded an RTA. This could explain the situation of the EAEU, where all RTAs concluded by its members have been concluded prior to 2015.

Moreover, where a customs union has established a central authority that is competent to impose measures, this hints at a strong level of integration with respect to the common external tariff. It would be expected that the member states individually cannot conclude RTAs. It is thus surprising that in the EAEU, ECOWAS and CAN many FTAs by individual countries exist.

The specific issues that arise in the context of anti-dumping from the membership in multiple RTAs differ between FTAs (under Sect. 3.5.1.1) and customs unions (under Sect. 3.5.1.2).

3.5.1.1 Anti-Dumping Legislation in FTAs of Customs Unions or Its Members

The customs union, all of its members or both jointly on the one hand or some member states of a customs union on the other hand may conclude FTAs with third parties.

---

[302]The author would like to thank Anna Berg for her valuable help in this part. All mistakes remain the author's.

This is not problematic where either states remain competent to investigate and impose anti-dumping measures and states conclude FTAs or where a central investigating authority investigates and imposes measures and all members conclude the FTA.

Problems only arise where a central investigating authority investigates and imposes anti-dumping measures but member states conclude FTAs. As FTAs only liberalize internal trade,[303] anti-dumping rules included in those FTAs only regulate the relationship between the parties of the FTA. This study does not analyse how these FTAs modify anti-dumping legislation, but they are the same as the modifications in any FTA.[304] This means that usually the parties of the FTA will usually not modify WTO rules on anti-dumping but may also decide to incentivize or disincentivize the imposition of anti-dumping measures. Whether such modifications are legal in general will be dealt with in the next chapter.[305]

Beyond that, an interesting hypothetical question arises: if within a customs union that has a centralized anti-dumping system, one member concludes an FTA that disincentivizes the imposition of anti-dumping measures between its members and the central investigating authority applied the rules of the FTA as well, how could the other members of the FTA justify the deviations from the WTO Agreements? They are responsible for the measures of the investigating authority and the measures violate the MFN clause, as different rules are used depending on whether one is a member of the FTA or not. However, they may not raise the Art. XXIV:5 GATT defence, as they are not members of the FTA. It seems that this violates WTO law, calling into question many FTAs concluded by members of customs unions. Due to the hypothetical nature the question will not be dealt with extensively.

Beyond that, interesting issues concerning rules of competences may arise as well. Especially where anti-dumping measures are imposed following a central investigation and they apply on a customs union wide basis but individual members of the customs union conclude FTAs that modify anti-dumping rules between the parties of the FTA, problems may arise relating to the rules of competences within a customs union. These issues are, however, beyond the scope of this study, which is primarily focussed on the interaction of customs union law with WTO law.

3.5.1.2   Membership in Several Customs Unions

Where either a customs union, all of its members or both of them jointly on the one hand or some members of a customs union are members of another customs union as well, conflicts between the anti-dumping regimes contained in the customs unions may arise. The root of these conflicts is that customs unions not only liberalize internal trade but also harmonize external trade. If two customs unions share the

---

[303] Art. XXIV:8(b) GATT.
[304] For a comprehensive study, see: Rey (2016); Prusa (2016); Prusa and Teh (2011).
[305] See: Sect. 4.2.

Table 3.6 Overview of membership in several customs union

Shared members	Customs Union
Members of EAC	EAC; COMESA
Eswatini, Lesotho	COMESA; SACU
EU and/or its Members	EU; EU-Turkey; EU-San Marino; EU-Andorra
Members of WAEMU	WAEMU; ECOWAS

same members, these members may have to comply with the common external tariff of two different customs unions. Insofar as they diverge, conflicts arise between them.

Table 3.6 summarizes which customs unions have shared members.

Shared membership in multiple customs unions occurs in two ways: First, an entire customs union or its members (inner customs union) may be part of another customs union (outer customs union). Second, some members of one customs union may also be members of another customs union and the other customs union has further members as well (partial overlap).

There are four regulatory possibilities to avoid conflicting external trade regimes in the field of anti-dumping.

First, if there is an inner and an outer customs union, anti-dumping measures may apply to imports into the entire outer customs union. This is the case in the EU-San Marino and EU- Andorra customs unions. This setup is only compliant with WTO rules if the investigation leading to the measures relates to the outer customs union, which is also where problems arise in the EU-Andorra and EU-San Marino customs unions. In them, the investigation only relates to the inner customs union whereas the measure relates to the outer customs union. Such a set-up would violate WTO law for those countries that are not in both customs unions. As San Marino and Andorra are not WTO members, currently not problems arise, however.[306]

Second, if the outer customs union does not harmonize external anti-dumping measures, the other customs union may harmonize its external anti-dumping measures. Similarly, in the case of partial overlap only one customs union may harmonize its external anti-dumping measures. This is the case in the EU-Turkey customs union and with respect to those members that are part of SACU and COMESA (i.e. Eswatini and Lesotho).

Third, if neither customs union has harmonized external anti-dumping measures, no problems arise either. This is the case for the members of the EAC and COMESA.

Fourth, if some members of the customs unions are not WTO members, they are not bound by WTO law and different regulatory possibilities emerge. As Andorra and San Marino are not WTO members and the EU does not violate its WTO obligations, it is possible to distinguish between the scope of the investigation and the scope of application of the measure.

---

[306] See below: Section "Discrepancies Between the Scope of the Investigation and the Scope of the Measure".

Beyond these possibilities, external anti-dumping measures will conflict. Currently, the only example where this is the case is with regards to WAEMU as its members are also members of ECOWAS. Both WAEMU and ECOWAS foresee that a central institution will conduct and impose anti-dumping measures. This creates a conflict of laws: the WAEMU Commission cannot investigate and impose anti-dumping measures without violating the ECOWAS Secretariat's competence to impose anti-dumping measures and *vice versa*. This conflict did not materialize yet, as neither ECOWAS nor WAEMU have imposed anti-dumping measures by that system so far.[307]

If a conflict between the ECOWAS and WAEMU anti-dumping regimes arises in the future, this conflict will have to be solved using general rules of conflict. The conflict that arises thereby has to be seen in light of the African Economic Community's plan to economically integrate.[308] Established in 1994 through the Treaty of Abuja, the AEC foresees that its members progressively establish a customs union by integrating the different regional economic communities that exist in Africa.[309] As the integration occurs in steps, conflicts may arise on the way to this unified customs union. Steps towards realizing this are the conclusion of the AfCFTA in 2019.[310] Deciding which anti-dumping regime will ultimately prevail depends on the rules of the customs unions and their relationship to one another, which goes beyond the scope of this study.

3.5.2 Non-preferential Rules of Origin

Non-preferential rules of origin may be relevant during an anti-dumping investigation especially for the normal value determination and following the imposition of the measure to verify whether imports fall within the scope of the measure.[311] They are non-tariff trade barriers and not having to distinguish origin within the customs union further liberalizes internal trade. Rules of origin are national measures, and the WTO has not achieved to harmonize them yet, despite some efforts to do so. The WTO has set up a Harmonization Work Programme[312] in the Committee on Rules of

---

[307] See above: Table 3.1.

[308] Frimpong Oppong (2010), p. 92.

[309] Art. 28, 29 Treaty of Abujan.

[310] For an overview of the Anti-Dumping regulation contained therein: Taweel and Brink (2018), p. 157.

[311] They apply to Anti-Dumping measures following Art. 1.2 Agreement on Rules of Origin (RoO Agreement). See also: Inama (2009), pp. 113–117; Inama et al. (2009), pp. 293–295; Willems and Brolin (2018), p. 229.

[312] Art. 6.3 RoO Agreement.

Origin,[313] but harmonization efforts have halted since 2007.[314] One reason for this is the issue of implication: Members have polarised views on whether the non-preferential rules of origin should apply to other Agreements such as the ADA.[315]

Overall, the legal landscape with regards to non-preferential rules of origin is rather uncertain: some countries have notified the WTO to not apply non-preferential rules of origin despite being frequent anti-dumping users themselves.[316] This is why from a WTO perspective only little definitive remarks can be made with regards to the interaction between anti-dumping and non-preferential rules of origin.

The internal and external anti-dumping regime may, however, influence the necessity for origin verification within a customs union. If internal anti-dumping measures are prohibited and the scope of the external measures are harmonized, origin certificates for the purpose of applying anti-dumping measures only need to be verified upon entering the customs union but not on internal border crossings, thereby liberalizing internal trade further. Moreover, if anti-dumping investigations have a union wide scope, origin of the domestic industry does not need to distinguish between the member states of the customs unions, but it is sufficient to certify that the producer is a union producer. If the scope of the anti-dumping measures is member state wide and/or internal anti-dumping measures are possible, origin certificates also need to be verified on internal border crossings in the customs union. Moreover, investigating authorities may have to distinguish origin of domestic producers. Otherwise, an exporter could export into a country of the customs union that does not impose anti-dumping measures and then ship it to the country in the customs union that applies anti-dumping duties to circumvent the measures.

3.5.3 Anti-Dumping Action on Behalf of a Third Country

As customs unions liberalize internal trade, internal border crossings of goods will occur more frequently. If products can move relatively freely within a customs union, the situation that the country of import and injury do not coincide will occur more often. An example of how this may happen is if products are imported

---

[313] Art. 4.1 RoO Agreement.

[314] Committee on Rules of Origin, 'Report (2018) of the Committee on Rules of Origin to the Council for Trade in Goods', G/L/1266, 18.10.2018; Committee on Rules of Origin, 'Report (2013) of the Committee on Rules of Origin to the Council for Trade in Goods', G/L/1047, 10.10.2013, para. 3.

[315] Committee on Rules of Origin, 'Report (2013) of the Committee on Rules of Origin to the Council for Trade in Goods', G/L/1047, 10.10.2013, para. 3. For an overview, see: Azzam (2019), p. 467; Inama (2009), pp. 1–16.

[316] Committee on Rules of Origin, 'Report (2013) of the Committee on Rules of Origin to the Council for Trade in Goods', G/L/1047, 10.10.2013, para. 6, Inama et al. (2009), p. 298; Saluste (2017), p. 54.

into one member state at dumped prices and consumers start buying these products instead of buying the imports from another member state of the customs union which they did before dumping occurred. In that scenario, dumped products of a third country cause injury to the domestic production of one state within the customs union, even though the dumped products are imported into another state of the customs union.

For such situations, Art. 14 ADA provides the possibility that an anti-dumping action be carried out on behalf of a third country. The member state of the injured party can request the importing country to initiate an investigation.[317] The importing country will consider whether injury has occurred to the industry as a whole in the third country and not just to the part that exports to the importing country.[318] The decision to carry out the investigation and apply anti-dumping measures rests with the importing country but the measure can only be imposed following approval by the Council on Trade in Goods—a WTO organ which decides by consensus and in which a representative of the exporting member sits.[319] Unsurprisingly, this provision has never been invoked.[320]

If external anti-dumping measures are harmonized, no specific problems arise as injury to the entire customs union production will be considered either way. However, problems arise if externally anti-dumping measures are not harmonized but the customs union has the effect of increasing intra-regional trade, such a situation becomes more likely.

This is why some customs unions regulate anti-dumping actions by third parties and deviate from WTO provisions. The EAC simply transposed Art. 14 ADA into their anti-dumping regulation but without the obligation to request approval by the WTO's Council on Trade in Goods.[321] Similarly, in COMESA Art. 54.2 COMESA Treaty applies if dumped imports into one COMESA member injure the community industry. In that case, the importing member should conduct an investigation and the measure is then applied again without approval by the Council on Trade in Goods.

CACM and CAN even offer regional investigations to deal with these situations.

In CACM a request for a regional procedure must be sent to SIECA[322] which forwards it to the investigating authority of the importing state that is compelled to initiate a proceeding.[323] If the investigating authority does not initiate the

---

[317] Art. 14.1 ADA.

[318] Art. 14.3 ADA.

[319] Art. 14.4 ADA. Approval takes the form of a Waiver, Art. VI:6(b) GATT.

[320] For background, see: WTO, GATT Analytical Index (pre-1995), Article VI Anti-Dumping and Countervailing Duties (https://www.wto.org/english/res_e/publications_e/ai17_e/gatt1994_art6_gatt47.pdf), last accessed: 5 July 2021, pp. 247–248.

[321] Art. 18 East African Community Customs (Anti-Dumping Measures) Regulations. Even though Art. 18 (4) East African Community Customs (Anti-Dumping Measures) Regulations requires approval by the Council through the Committee, Art. 3 of the Regulation clarifies that the EAC's organs are meant by that.

[322] Art. 28 Resolucion 193/2007.

[323] Art. 29 Resolucion 193/2007.

investigation, SIECA will act as the investigating authority.[324] In such a case the decision to impose provisional[325] or definitive[326] measures rests with the Executive Committee, a central authority. The member states are obliged to implement the decisions.[327] Interestingly, the costs for the regional investigation should be borne by the domestic industry that brought the action before the requesting state party.[328]

In CAN a different legal instrument applies depending on whether the dumping originates from a CAN member or from a third party.[329] Nevertheless, in both situations the General Secretariat becomes the investigating authority that also applies the measures.

Either way, in none of these cases is approval sought by the Council on Trade in Goods. Although these provisions violate Art. 14 ADA, violations can be justified according to Art. XXIV:5 GATT, as will be argued for in the next chapter.

3.6 Conclusions

This chapter has compared how anti-dumping regimes differ in customs unions from WTO obligations as typically applied by states. Differences between the internal and external dimension exist. Internally, customs unions aim to integrate trade. The strongest form in which this can be achieved is by prohibiting the imposition of internal anti-dumping measures. Below that, the imposition of anti-dumping measures may be disincentivized and anti-dumping procedures may be harmonized to reduce the possibility that anti-dumping measures are only imposed for protectionist purposes. Externally, customs unions aim to harmonize trade. This can be done by having a central investigating authority, centralizing the imposition decision and changing the scope of the investigation and measure to consider the entire customs union. Again, below that different degrees of lesser harmonization exist.

Having considered why customs unions modify anti-dumping legislation and how they do so, the next question that arises is whether WTO law allows modifications to anti-dumping legislation.

---

[324] Art. 31 Resolucion 193/2007.

[325] Art. 33 Resolucion 193/2007.

[326] Art. 32 Resolucion 193/2007.

[327] Art. 34 Resolucion 193/2007.

[328] Art. 35 Resolucion 193/2007.

[329] Art. 2 (b) Decision 456 applies for internal situations of dumping on behalf of a third country. Art. 2 (c) Decision 283 applies in external situations of dumping on behalf of a third country.

References

Academic Texts

Andenas M, Andersen CB, Ashcroft R (2012) Towards a theory of harmonisation. In: Andenas M, Andersen C (eds) Theory and practice of harmonisation. Edward Elgar Publishing

Azzam MW (2019) Harmonization of non-preferential rules of origin. Global Trade Cust J 14:467

Boodman M (1991) The myth of harmonization of laws. Am J Comp Law 39:699

Brink G (2012) Anti-Dumping in South Africa. Tralac - Trade Law Centre, D12WP07/2012

Brink G (2013) The Roles of the Southern African Customs Union Agreement, the International Trade Administration Commission and the Minister of Trade and Industry in the Regulation of South Africa's International Trade. J South Afr Law/Tydskrif vir die Suid-Afrikaanse Reg 419

Brink G (2015) One hundred years of anti-dumping in South Africa. J World Trade 49:325

Frimpong Oppong R (2010) The African Union, the African economic community and Africa's regional economic communities: untangling a complex web. Afr J Int Comp Law 18:92

Fuders F (2008) Die Wirtschaftsverfassung des MERCOSUR: eine rechtsvergleichende Darstellung unter besonderer Berücksichtigung des Rechts der Europäischen Union. Duncker & Humblot

Gantz DA (2011) Commentary on "Contingent Protection Rules in Regional Trade Agreements". In: Bagwell K, Mavroidis PC (eds) Preferential trade agreements: a law and economics analysis. Cambridge University Press

Hage J (2014) Comparative law as method and the method of comparative law. In: Adams M, Heirbaut D, van Hoecke M (eds) The method and culture of comparative law: essays in honour of Mark Van Hoecke. Hart

Herrmann C Weiß W, Ohler C (2007) Welthandelsrecht, 2th edn. CH Beck

Husa J (2014) Research Designs of Comparative Law - Methodology or Heuristics? In: Adams M, Heirbaut D, van Hoecke M (eds) The method and culture of comparative law: essays in honour of Mark Van Hoecke. Hart Publishing Ltd

Inama S, Vermulst E, Eeckhout P (2009) Nonpreferential origin rules in antidumping law and practice. In: Bagwell KW, Bermann GA, Mavroidis PC (eds) Law and economics of contingent protection in international trade. Cambridge University Press

Kafeero E (2009) Customs Law of the East African Community in Light of WTO Law and the Revised Kyoto Convention. Rechtswissenschaftliche Fakultät der Westfälischen Wilhelms-Universität zu Münster <https://d-nb.info/99448609x/34>

Kasteng J, Prawitz C (2013) Eliminating Anti-Dumping Measures in Regional Trade Agreements: The European Union Example. Kommerskollegium 2013:5 <http://www.kommersse/publikationer/Rapporter/2013/Eliminating-Anti-Dumping-Measures-in-Regional-Trade-Agreements/> Accessed 5 July 2021

Krueger AO (1997) Free Trade Agreements versus customs Unions. J Dev Econ 54:169

Makhinova A (2020) How to suspend Trade defence remedies applied in the Eurasian economic union: recent trends. Global Trade Cust J 15:37

Marceau G (1994) Anti-dumping and anti-trust issues in free-trade areas. Oxford University Press

Mavroidis PC (2015) The regulation of international trade: GATT, vol 1. The MIT Press

Mossner LE (2016) Westafrikanische Wirtschaftsintegration im Mehrebenensystem: Normkonflikte und Koordinierung, 1st edn. Nomos

Orford A (2005) Beyond harmonization: trade, human rights and the economy of sacrifice. Leiden J Int Law 18:179

Prusa T (2016) Antidumping provisions in preferential trade agreements. In: Bhagwati JN, Krishna P, Panagariya A (eds) The world trade system: trends and challenges, 1st edn. MIT Press Ltd

Prusa T, Teh R (2011) Contingent protection rules in regional trade agreements. In: Bagwell K, Mavroidis PC (eds) Preferential trade agreements: a law and economics analysis. Cambridge University Press

Rey J-D (2016) Do regional anti-dumping regimes make a difference? In: Acharya R (ed) Regional trade agreements and the multilateral trading system. Cambridge University Press

Sagara N (2002) Provisions for trade remedy measures (anti-dumping, countervailing and safeguard measures) in preferential trade agreements. Research Institute of Economy, Trade and Industry, 02-E-013

Saluste M (2017) Rules of origin and the anti-dumping agreement. Global Trade Cust J 12:54

Taweel KE, Brink G (2018) Trade defence instruments in Africa: possible scenarios for implementation under the TFTA. Afr J Int Comp Law 26:157

Vallejo S (2018) Anti-Dumping in the Andean Community: Rethinking Regionalism in the Americas in Unsettling Times. SSRN Electronic Journal <https://www.ssrn.com/abstract=3209860> Accessed 5 July 2021

Willems A, Jinaru A, Moroni A (2019) Accountability in antidumping: the silent death of lisbon. Global Trade Cust J 14:268

Willems AR, Brolin MJ (2018) The unhappy marriage of customs and anti-dumping legislation: tensions relating to product description and origin. Legal Iss Econ Integr 3:229

Yanning Y (2008) Circumvention and anti-circumvention measures: the impact of anti-dumping practice in international trade. Wolters Kluwer Law & Business

Chapter 4
WTO Framework

From an economic perspective, RTAs generally and customs unions specifically are not unequivocally good in the sense that they are always welfare enhancing. The negative effects of trade diversion may outweigh the positive effects of internal trade liberalization.[1] WTO law should encourage the conclusion of welfare enhancing and prohibit the conclusion of welfare reducing RTAs. This requires an effective mechanism that distinguishes which RTAs are welfare enhancing and which are welfare reducing and that mechanism must have clear legal rules as well as being enforced effectively.

Unfortunately, in the WTO neither exists: Art. XXIV GATT and the Enabling Clause, the main provisions dealing with RTAs in the WTO, are highly ambiguous with regards to their requirements and the DSB as well as the CRTA and CTD have proven ineffective in giving clear guidance and enforcing rights and obligations associated with RTAs.[2] There are several reasons why especially the DSB is structurally ineffective to give guidance on WTO law in that regard: Panels are risk averse on the subject due to the gravity of the judgement (303 RTAs will potentially be illegal) coupled with the little guidance WTO primary law offers on the matter.[3] Moreover, there is a collective action problem that stems from the adversarial procedure. As all WTO members have RTAs and will want to conclude more in the future any clarification by the Appellate Body will be a restriction of their future freedom, thereby disincentivizing any challenge.[4] This means that the DSB is unlikely to clarify the matter in the future.

---

[1] See above: Sect. 2.2.1.

[2] Explaining why these provisions do not sufficiently distinguish between welfare enhancing and reducing RTAs: Krishna (2018), pp. 21–22. Denying any regulatory function of these provisions: Hilpold (2003), p. 219, 242. For an extensive critique see also: Devuyst and Serdarevic (2007), p. 1, 5.

[3] Mavroidis (2006), pp. 209–210.

[4] Negotiating Group on Rules, 'Compendium of Issues Related to Regional Trade Agreements, Background Note by the Secretariat, Revision', TN/RL/W/8 Rev.1, 1.8.2002, para. 18, 20.

© The Author(s), under exclusive license to Springer Nature Switzerland AG 2021   89
F. Bickel, *Customs Unions in the WTO*, European Yearbook of International
Economic Law 20, https://doi.org/10.1007/978-3-030-86312-8_4

Bearing these structural deficiencies in mind, this chapter sketches the limits WTO law sets on its members with respect to anti-dumping legislation in RTAs. This question has generally received a lot of academic attention and the focus has usually been on whether certain internal modifications can be justified according to Art. XXIV:5 GATT. This study emphasises the preliminary question which modifications violate which WTO provisions, also considers the Enabling Clause to justify those violations, focuses on whether external modifications can be justified as well, and considers legality of customs unions where some of its members are not WTO members. Finally, it incorporates the Appellate Body's more recent decisions into the different strands of argumentation that have been developed.

The structure of WTO law in this regard is as follows: WTO law contains certain obligations such as the ones in Art. VI GATT or the ADA. These must be fulfilled for the imposition of anti-dumping measures to be legal. If they are violated, there is a breach of a WTO obligation. This first step is often overlooked in the discussion and this study argues that Art. VI GATT and the ADA contain sufficient flexibilities so that most modifications only violate the MFN principle (under Sect. 4.1). Breaches can then be justified. Breaches may be justified according to WTO provisions, which are Art. XXIV:5 GATT or Para. 2 (c) or (d) Enabling Clause (under Sect. 4.2). If that is not possible, a justification may stem from the customs union agreement, as it is an instrument of international law (under Sect. 4.3). Finally, as not all states or customs territories are members of the WTO as well, the rules applicable to customs unions with non-WTO-members will be considered (under Sect. 4.4).

4.1 Breach of WTO Provisions

The previous chapter has clarified how customs unions modify the rules to impose internal and external anti-dumping measures in various ways. This section now considers whether these modifications violate WTO law.

The main argument of this section is that Art. VI GATT and the ADA contain many flexibilities so that most modifications do not violate them. Moreover, even though the MFN principle applies to some modifications and is sometimes violated, it does not apply to all modifications either. Overall, violations of WTO obligations are rarer than typically advocated for.[5] Especially transferring the competences to investigate and impose anti-dumping measures to a central authority and conducting the investigation and applying the measure on a customs union wide basis does not violate WTO obligations.

Mavroidis also points to the costs of litigation, thereby referring to Bown and Hoekman (2005), p. 43; and discusses the political considerations when initiating a dispute: Mavroidis (2006), pp. 210–212; Mavroidis (2011), p. 375.

[5]For the general point that RTAs adopt WTO language and comply with WTO obligations more often than typically assumed: Allee et al. (2017), p. 333.

This is relevant for one practical and one legal reason. First and from a practical perspective the DSB has so far been hesitant to apply and clarify the justification contained in Art. XXIV:5 GATT. The finding that no WTO provision is violated so that Art. XXIV:5 GATT does not have to be invoked gives greater legal certainty to legislators. Second and from a legal standpoint, as the Enabling Clause only justifies violations of Art. I:1 GATT, the finding that most modifications only violate Art. I:1 GATT means that they may be justified by the Enabling Clause.

The WTO provisions that may be breached are on the one hand the respective provisions contained in Art. VI GATT and the ADA that customs unions modify (under Sect. 4.1.1) and on the other hand the MFN principle (under Sect. 4.1.1). They will be considered in turn.

4.1.1 Violation of Art. VI GATT, ADA

Customs unions modify WTO obligations in various ways. Internally, customs unions have prohibited anti-dumping measures, disincentivized them or integrated anti-dumping procedures.[6] Beyond that, they may also incentivize them. Externally, customs unions have harmonized anti-dumping measures by integrating procedures and varying the scope of the investigation or resulting measure.[7]

The analysed modifications can be grouped along the lines that they either add the WTO requirements or replace them.

In the EU-Turkey customs union interim measures can only be in place for three instead of 4 to 6 months, in MERCOSUR expiry reviews must be conducted after 3 years instead of five and member states must consult before the initiation of an investigation.[8] These changes are substantive and procedural, but they add to the WTO requirements by raising the respective thresholds and making it more difficult to impose anti-dumping measures or by requiring some additional procedural steps. Cases in which requirements are added to the WTO provisions do not violate the respective provision in Art. VI GATT, ADA that they modify (under Sect. 4.1.1.1).

This is different from lowering the respective thresholds, introducing new ways in which the normal value may be calculated taking environmental dumping into account or including societal costs in the injury determination. These modifications are hypothetical as they have not occurred yet, but they would violate the respective ADA provision they modify. This is because they allow the imposition of anti-dumping measures even though the requirements in the ADA have not been satisfied. Such a violation is not apparent for all deviations from the ADA, however. Cases in which a the violation is not straight-forward are: the decision to change the scope of the investigation and resulting measure to a union wide basis (under Sect.

---

[6] See: Sect. 3.3.

[7] See: Sect. 3.4.

[8] See more generally: Sects. 3.3, 3.4.

4.1.1.2), to grant competences to a centralized authority (under Sect. 4.1.1.3) or to allow anti-dumping action on behalf of third countries (under Sect. 4.1.1.4). As in these situations the requirements do not simply apply in addition to the WTO requirements, but they replace WTO requirements, their legality is not as straight-forward.

4.1.1.1 Adding to WTO Obligations

Where customs unions add to the WTO requirements, this does not violate the respective WTO provision.

Customs unions impose additional requirements in several ways. Substantively, this covers all legislation that disincentivizes anti-dumping measures and prohibits their imposition internally. Procedurally, this includes any additional procedural step or right granted to a member state. These provisions thereby deviate from the WTO rules on anti-dumping.

Not every deviation from Art. VI GATT and the ADA constitutes a breach of Art. VI GATT or the ADA, however. According to Art. VI:2 GATT, a WTO member "*may* levy [...] an anti-dumping duty" on any dumped product. The term "may" has thereby been interpreted as giving "[m]embers a choice between imposing an anti-dumping duty *or not,* as well as a choice between imposing an anti-dumping duty equal to the dumping margin *or imposing a lower duty.*"[9] More generally, Art. VI GATT and the ADA set out the minimum requirements to impose anti-dumping measures but members are free to deviate from them as long as it disincentivizes the imposition or reduces the impact of anti-dumping measures. This applies to additional substantive as well as procedural requirements. Only if a customs union falls short of the requirements set out in Art. VI GATT and the ADA, does that violate the respective provision. This means that adding additional requirements does not violate the requirements contained in Art. VI GATT and the ADA.

4.1.1.2 Changing the Scope of the Investigation and Measure

In customs unions external anti-dumping measures are either investigated on a union or on a member state wide basis. The first question is whether WTO law allows investigations to be union wide. Usually, the scope of the resulting measure also corresponds with the scope of the investigation. The second question is whether it violates WTO law if the scope of the investigation and the scope of the measure do not correspond.

---

[9] *United States - Anti-Dumping Act of 1916* [2000] WTO Appellate Body Report WT/DS136/AB/R; WT/DS162/AB/R [116].

Scope of the Investigation and Measure

The first question is whether investigations can be conducted on a union-wide basis and whether customs unions may impose anti-dumping measures to imports into the entire customs union.

Art. 4.3 ADA provides,

> where two or more countries have reached under the provisions of [Art. XXIV:8 GATT] such a level of integration that they have the characteristics of a single, unified market, the industry in the entire area of integration shall be taken to be the domestic industry referred to in [Art. 4.1 ADA].

This means that customs unions can be set up to consider injury to the domestic production of the entire customs union. As Art. 4.3 ADA not only refers to Art. XXIV:8 GATT but additionally requires that the integration has reached a level characterized as a *single, unified market,* this means that a distinction can be made between the different customs unions. Customs unions that do not fulfil these additional requirements can investigate injury based on the domestic industry of the member states. Interestingly, Art. 4.3 ADA does not give discretion to customs unions to choose whether they should investigate injury on union wide basis. Rather, if the additional requirements are fulfilled, they *shall* conduct the injury analysis on a union wide basis. As there are no customs unions that have the characteristics of a *single, unified market* but do not calculate injury on a union wide basis, this distinction has not become relevant yet.

No parallel provision exists for the calculation of the export price stating that customs unions may take exports into the entire customs union into account or concerning the scope of the resulting measure stating that the measure may apply to imports into the entire customs union. It is therefore questionable, whether beyond its wording, Art. 4.3 ADA generally allows that customs unions may conduct investigations on a union wide basis and that the resulting measures' scope is union wide.

For safeguard measures, Footnote 1 SG provides:

> A customs union may apply a safeguard measure as a single unit or on behalf of a member State. When a customs union applies a safeguard measure as a single unit, all the requirements for the determination of serious injury or threat thereof under this Agreement shall be based on the conditions existing in the customs union as a whole. When a safeguard measure is applied on behalf of a member State, all the requirements for the determination of serious injury or threat thereof shall be based on the conditions existing in that member State and the measure shall be limited to that member State. Nothing in this Agreement prejudges the interpretation of the relationship between Article XIX and paragraph 8 of Article XXIV of GATT 1994.

The Appellate Body in *Argentina – Footwear (EC)* added the third possibility that a member state may conduct investigations and impose Safeguard measures.[10]

---

[10] *Argentina - Safeguard Measures on Imports of Footwear* [1999] WTO Appellate Body Report WT/DS121/ABRR [106–108].

Footnote 1 SG is more extensive than Art. 4.3 ADA as it relates to all requirements and the scope of the measure. Even though a parallel provision does not exist in the ADA, Footnote 1 SG should guide the interpretation of Art. 4.3 ADA, meaning that Art. 4.3 ADA should apply beyond its wording to also allow the calculation of the export price being union wide and the measure to apply to all imports into the union. Otherwise, Art. 4.3 ADA would be void of meaning. As the next section will argue, the investigation and scope of the measure must coincide. The only possibility in which an investigation can consider imports into the entire customs union is if it is unionwide and if the resulting measures apply to imports into the entire customs union. Art. 4.3 ADA therefore applies by way of analogy for the calculation of the export price and the scope of the measure.

Discrepancies Between the Scope of the Investigation and the Scope
of the Measure

If it is possible to conduct anti-dumping investigations on a union wide basis and the scope of the resulting measures is union wide as well, the second question is whether the scope of the investigation must always align with the scope of the resulting measure. A divergence between the two may happen if legally the investigation is limited to one member of a customs union, but the measure applies to the entire customs union, as is the case in the EU-San Marino and EU-Andorra customs unions. This may also happen factually if an investigating authority only considers the industry of a certain geographical area in their investigation. This is the case in SACU where ITAC usually only considers the South African industry in their injury determination.[11]

   In the EU-Andorra and EU-San Marino customs unions, the EU limits its investigation to the territory of the EU and imposes the measures that then apply to all imports into the territory of the EU. Andorra and San Marino then apply the EU's anti-dumping measures as well.[12] The problems that may arise from this setup are mainly hypothetical as Andorra and San Marino are not WTO members and are therefore not bound by Art. VI GATT or the ADA.[13]

---

[11] For an explanation of the setup, see above: section "SACU".

[12] For an explanation of this setup, see above: section "EU-Andorra, EU-San Marino". A violation of the EU's WTO obligation might occur if San Marino or Andorra made up for large parts of the overall domestic industry so that the EU's industry requesting an investigation would no longer meet minimum requirements or if only the EU's industry was injured with the consequence that overall in the EU-San Marino or EU-Andorra customs union no injury exists and the EU has not limited the investigation and application of the measure only to the EU. This situation is not explored as it seems very hypothetical.

[13] See below at: Sect. 4.4. It may be problematic for the EU if the industry in Andorra or San Marino were so large that the EU industry would no longer meet minimum thresholds to initiate an investigation or if only EU industry was injured but the majority of the industry in San Marino or Andorra was nor injured.

As a starting point, Art. 1 ADA sets out that anti-dumping measures can only be introduced pursuant to "investigations initiated and conducted". If anti-dumping measures apply to imports into a territory that has not been part of the investigation, no investigation took place with regards to that territory and the measure is in violation of Art. 1 ADA. With regards to the EU-Andorra and EU-San Marino customs unions this is straight forward, as the customs union legislation limits the scope of the investigation to the territory of the EU.

Spotting whether a certain territory has not been within the scope of the investigation may, however, not always be as straightforward. Problems arise if an investigating authority should take data from the entire customs union into account but factually only considers the data of certain member states of the customs union. As the domestic industry does not include every producer, the question arises whether a factual bias by an investigating authority to only consider the domestic industry of parts of the territory to which the investigation refers, violates WTO provisions. An example of this are potentially the investigations by ITAC in SACU. ITAC is the investigating authority and is supposed to carry out investigations taking the entire customs union industry into account. However, it only rarely considers the domestic industry of other countries than South Africa.

As ITAC claims that the investigation considers all of SACU, this does not violate Art. 1 ADA. However, it may violate Art. 3.1, 4.1 ADA. The injury determination must be objective which requires that the "domestic industry, and the effects of dumped imports, be investigated in an unbiased manner, without favouring the interests of any interested party, or group of interested parties, in the investigation."[14] This requirement is violated if there is a "material risk of distortion in defining the domestic industry" an example of which is "excluding a whole category of producers of the like product."[15] If certain industries are continuously not considered because of their geographical location (i.e. because they are located in Botswana) this risks distorting the definition of domestic industry. Due to the extreme asymmetry of economic strength between the members of SACU, where the BELN members combined only make up 10,6% of South Africa's GDP, it will often be difficult to prove that sufficient portions of BELN were omitted. This means that usually the objectivity of the industry determination will not be questioned, but this may happen in individual cases. This means that if factually an investigation is limited to only certain geographical parts, this may violate Art. 3.1, 4.1 ADA. Proving such a bias may prove difficult in practice, however.

---

[14] *United States - Anti-Dumping Measures on Certain Hot-Rolled Steel Products from Japan* [2001] WTO Appellate Body Report WT/DS184/AB/R [193].

[15] *European Communities - Definitive Anti-Dumping Measures on Certain Iron or Steel Fasteners from China* [2011] WTO Appellate Body Report WT/DS397/AB/R [414].

4.1.1.3 Central Authorities

Concerning the procedural modifications, the same principles apply as internally: the procedural requirements contained in Art. VI GATT and the ADA only set minimum requirements. Additional requirements can be introduced but it is not possible to go below that standard.

Problems may arise if customs unions establish a centralized authority that is competent to investigate or impose the measures. Whereas the ADA mostly sets out obligations to "authorities",[16] sometimes it mentions "authorities of the importing Member".[17] The ADA does not define "authorities"[18] but it is questionable whether a centralized organ of a customs union is an authority of "the importing Member". Only the EU is a member of the WTO. The question thus arises whether a central authority can be an "authority of the importing Member" where that member is not a customs union.

This study argues that reference to "authorities of the importing Member" is an attribution requirement and must be interpreted widely.[19] If the acts by the central authority can be attributed to a member state that is also a WTO member, acts by the central authority may discharge that state's WTO obligations. This study argues that acts by central authorities of customs unions may be attributed to their member states,[20] which is why they are "authorities of the importing Member". Delegating competences to a central authority therefore does not violate WTO obligations.

4.1.1.4 Anti-Dumping Investigations on Behalf of a Third Country

Some customs unions include special provisions that deal with the situation in which the country of injury and import do not coincide. Art. 14 ADA regulates this situation but since the WTO's Council for Trade in Goods, i.e. *inter alia* the country targeted by the measures, must approve them, this provision has never been invoked.[21]

Customs unions have regulated this situation because due to the internal economic integration such a situation is more likely to arise. Insofar as customs unions have included provisions that deal with this situation, these provisions do not require approval by the WTO's Council for Trade in Goods. As Art. 14.4 ADA leaves no room for interpretation in that regard so that any deviations violate that provision.

---

[16]E.g. Art. 2.2.1; 2.3; 2.4; 3.2 ADA.

[17]E.g. Art. 8.2; 8.5; 8.6 ADA.

[18]Footnote 3 ADA merely explains that the term "authorities" refers to the authorities at an appropriate senior level without defining the term.

[19]See: Sect. 5.1.2.

[20]See: Sect. 5.3.

[21]See: Sect. 3.5.3.

4.1.2 Violation of the MFN Principle

If customs unions distinguish between internal and external anti-dumping rules and thereby distinguish based on the origin of a good or their anti-dumping legislation at least has that effect, this may violate the MFN principle contained in Art. I:1 GATT.

As a preliminary point, Art. I:1 GATT would have to apply in the anti-dumping context. Art. I:1 GATT does not expressly exclude anti-dumping measures from its application. There are, however, two reasons why Art. I:1 GATT might not apply to anti-dumping measures.

First, the ADA may contain a *lex specialis* to Art. I:1 GATT. According to Art. 9.2 ADA, when an anti-dumping duty is imposed in respect of any product, it shall be collected "on a non-discriminatory basis on imports of such products from all sources *found* to be dumped and causing injury" (emphasis added). Some have argued that this expresses a more general non-discrimination requirement. This study argues that the scope of Art. 9.2 ADA is limited and only constitutes a *lex specialis* in those cases where dumping causing injury has been found. Above that, Art. 4.3 ADA may also constitute a *lex specialis*. As it is not possible to conduct a union wide investigation internally but only externally, this presumes that in some cases it is possible to distinguish based on the origin of the goods (under Sect. 4.1.2.1).

Second, anti-dumping measures only apply against the exporters and producers of the country under investigation and not against all exporters or producers of the product globally. Anti-dumping measures are therefore an exception to the MFN principle. The requirements for that exception may have been exclusively listed in Art. VI GATT and the ADA, potentially leaving no room for the MFN principle in Art. I:1 GATT (under Sect. 4.1.2.2).

However, neither of these is convincing. This study argues that the MFN principle in Art. I:1 GATT generally applies to anti-dumping measures. The last section considers whether the different modifications violate Art. I:1 GATT (under Sect. 4.1.2.3).

4.1.2.1 Are Art. 9.2 ADA or Art. 4.3 ADA *lex specialis* MFN Requirements?

According to Art. 9.2 ADA:

> When an anti-dumping duty is imposed in respect of any product, such anti-dumping duty shall be collected in the appropriate amounts in each case, on a non-discriminatory basis on imports of such product from all sources found to be dumped and causing injury, except as to imports from those sources from which price undertakings under the terms of this Agreement have been accepted. The authorities shall name the supplier or suppliers of the product concerned. If, however, several suppliers from the same country are involved, and it is impracticable to name all these suppliers, the authorities may name the supplying country concerned. If several suppliers from more than one country are involved, the authorities may

name either all the suppliers involved, or, if this is impracticable, all the supplying countries involved.

Panels and the Appellate Body have interpreted this provision only scarcely. The term "all sources" has so far only been interpreted in that it refers to the individual exporters subject to the investigation and not the country as a whole.[22] This means that anti-dumping duties cannot be imposed in a discriminatory manner on only some exporters or producers subject to the investigation. The last sentence of this provision clarifies that the provision also applies if several countries are subject to the same investigation. This could be understood in a way that the investigating authority cannot discriminate between countries once it has found the requirements to be met with the different countries.

Nevertheless, the wording of the provision is limited to cases in which the investigating authority *found* there to be dumping which causes injury. It is not clear if above that Art. 9.2 ADA also applies to other forms of discrimination in which the investigating authority has not (yet) found there to be dumping causing injury.

Some have argued in favour that Art. 9.2 ADA constitutes a general non-discrimination requirement for anti-dumping measures. They support this by referring to the importance of non-discrimination in the WTO framework.[23]

Such an interpretation of the clause cannot be reconciled with the rules on interpretation and is not necessary in light of Art. I:1 GATT. The customary rules on international law relating to interpretation as codified in Art. 31, 32 VCLT[24] apply in the WTO.[25] A treaty must be interpreted "with the ordinary meaning given to the terms of the treaty in its context and in the light of its object and purpose", Art. 31.1 VCLT. The Appellate Body has clarified that the importance of an interpretative exercise depends on the clarity of the plain textual meaning of the treaty terms.[26] The more difficult and ambiguous a term is, the more importance will be given to the object and purpose of the treaty in its interpretation.[27] Art. 9.2 ADA does not leave any ambiguity and it is difficult to read the term "found" to mean "found or not found". This is also confirmed by the context of the provision. The rest of Art. 9 ADA only deals with special rules that apply during the imposition stage, i.e. after the end of the investigation. It is therefore unclear why Art. 9.2 ADA should be the only exception. Finally, it is not necessary to interpret Art. 9.2 ADA in such an

---

[22] *EC — Fasteners (China)* (n 15) para 338.

[23] Müller-Ibold (2018), pp. 206–208. See also: Jackson (1969), p. 421. In a later work he seemed to cast doubt on that opinion, however: Jackson (2007), p. 62.

[24] *United States - Standards for Reformulated and Conventional Gasoline* [1996] WTO Appellate Body Report WT/D2/AB/R 17; *Japan — Taxes on Alcoholic Beverages* [1996] WTO Appellate Body Report WT/DS8/AB/R; WT/DS10/AB/R; WT/DS11/AB/R 10.

[25] Art. 3.2 DSU.

[26] *Peru - Additional Duty on Imports of Certain Agricultural Products* [2015] WTO Appellate Body Report WT/DS457/AB/R; WT/DS457/AB/R/Add.1 [5.94].

[27] Ibid.

extensive manner, as Art. I:1 GATT could apply. The application of Art. I:1 GATT is even preferable, as there is more practice concerning its interpretation.[28]

It is, therefore, more convincing to understand Art. 9.2 ADA only within its literal meaning.[29] This means that where an investigating authority has found a certain product to be dumped and causing injury from several countries, it cannot treat one of the exporting countries more favourably than any of the others. Cases in which this happens are very rare, raising the question why that provision exists at all. One possible explanation is that the drafters wished to harmonize the provision with Art. 2.2 SG, which has a similar wording.

Understood in that light, Art. 9.2 ADA is only *lex specialis* to Art. I:1 GATT in rare cases where an investigation against exporters of several countries has been successful and the investigating authority wishes to discriminate between them.[30] Substantively, Art. 9.2 ADA imposes the same obligations as Art. I:1 GATT. Future references to Art. I:1 GATT will include reference to Art. 9.2 ADA insofar as it applies.

Above that, Art. 4.3 ADA may also constitute a *lex specialis* to Art. I:1 GATT. Art. 4.3 ADA allows—beyond the scope of its wording—that customs unions investigate and impose anti-dumping measures on a union wide basis.[31] If customs unions impose externally customs union wide anti-dumping measures, it is impossible to do so internally as well. This is because the target of the anti-dumping measure would coincide with the territory protected by it.[32] This means that where Art. 4.3 ADA applies, a distinction is made based on the origin of goods and that distinction possibly also amounts to an advantage for the goods within the customs union, thus violating Art. I:1 GATT. In that situation, Art. I:1 GATT and Art. 4.3 ADA address the same subjects, and both impose obligations concerning the imposition of anti-dumping measures. Finally, as Art. 4.3 ADA allows the imposition of anti-dumping measures on a union-wide basis and Art. I:1 GATT possibly prohibits this they are mutually exclusive. Therefore, Art. 4.3 ADA is insofar *lex specialis*. This means that if externally customs unions have harmonized their anti-dumping

---

[28] The same criticism can be raised against another interpretative idea. Müller-Ibold advocates that Art. 9.2 ADA should be limited to specific cases, excluding those cases where internal anti-dumping measures are not economically justified, see: Müller-Ibold (2018), pp. 206–208. It is not possible to reconcile this interpretation with the limits of interpretation.

[29] See also: Jackson (1969), p. 421.

[30] The requirements of the *lex specialis* principle are laid down in *Indonesia—Certain Measures Affecting the Automobile Industry* [1998] WTO Panel Report WT/DS54/R; WT/DS55/R; WT/DS59/R; WT/DS64/R 649. The two provisions oblige the same parties and cover the same subject matter.

[31] See: section "Scope of the Investigation and Measure".

[32] It is possible that internally member states are allowed to impose anti-dumping measures on a member state wide basis. In such a case a distinction between internal and external anti-dumping measures would still exist, also violating Art. I:1 GATT.

regime following Art. 4.3 ADA, the MFN principle does not apply to the difference between the external and internal relation of the customs union.[33]

4.1.2.2   Relationship Between Art. VI GATT, the ADA and Other WTO Provisions

Except where Art. 4.3, 9.2 ADA constitute a *lex specialis,* the MFN principle in Art. I:1 GATT could apply to all other situations if there are no other reasons why it should not apply. Anti-dumping measures are an exception to the MFN principle[34] as they disadvantage the country they are imposed against. It has been argued that Art. I:1 GATT cannot apply to its exceptions.[35]

This question arose in *EC – Fasteners (China).* China argued that the EU's normal value calculation violates Art. I:1 GATT as it distinguishes between NMEs and market economies.[36] Although the EU argued *inter alia* that Art. I:1 GATT does not apply in the context of anti-dumping measures,[37] the Panel accepted China's submission that Art. I:1 GATT applies without analysing the relationship between the ADA and Art. I:1 GATT.[38] The Appellate Body overturned the decision for lacking to answer the question whether the MFN principle applies to anti-dumping measures, without providing an answer to that question itself.[39]

The same issue arose again in *EU – Footwear.* Again, China challenged the EU's anti-dumping provision[40] on the basis of which the determination of the duty differs

---

[33] Above that, the MFN principle applies, e.g. if the customs union externally discriminates between two countries as in *European Union — Anti-Dumping Measures on Certain Footwear from China* [2011] WTO Panel Report WT/DS405/R.

[34] *EC — Fasteners (China)* (n 15) para 392.

[35] Müller-Ibold (2018), p. 204.

[36] *European Communities - Definitive Anti-Dumping Measures on Certain Iron or Steel Fasteners from China* [2010] WTO Panel Report WT/DS397/R [7.119]. The challenge related to Art. 9 (5) Council Regulation (EC) No 384/96 of 22 December 1995 on protection against dumped imports from countries not members of the European Communities (Reg. (EC) 384/96), OJ L 056/1, 6.3.1996, the predecessor of Reg. (EU) 2016/1036. See also: Espa and Levy (2018).

[37] *EC - Fasteners (China)* (n 36) para 7.120.

[38] Ibid 7.122–7.127.

[39] *EC — Fasteners (China)* (n 15) paras 392–398. The Appellate Body thereby referred to *Brazil - Measures Affecting Desiccated Coconut* [1997] WTO Appellate Body Report WT/DS22/AB/R 21. In that case, the Appellate Body upheld the Panel's decision (*Brazil - Measures Affecting Desiccated Coconut* [1996] WTO Panel Report WT/DS22/R [280–281]) that where Art. VI GATT does not apply because the investigation had been initiated before 1.1.1995, a claim cannot rest on Art. I:1 GATT either (Appellate Body Report, p. 21). It is not clear whether this finding really supports the proposition that Art. VI GATT and Art. I:1 GATT apply in conjunction. The finding could also be explained as any other finding would have undermined Art. 32.3 SCM (the provision defining the temporal application of the SCM).

[40] *EU — Footwear (China)* (n 33). In *EU – Footwear* the relevant provision was Art. 9 (5) Council Regulation (EC) No 1225/2009 of 30 November 2009 on protection against dumped imports from countries not members of the European Communities (Reg. (EC) 1225/2009), OJ L 343/51,

between NMEs and market economies.[41] The EU advanced the same reply arguing *inter alia* that Art. I:1 GATT does not apply due to the *lex specialis* principle.[42] The Panel held that Art. I:1 GATT is an additional requirement independent of Art. VI GATT and the ADA[43] and provided the missing analysis the Appellate Body requested in *EC – Fastener*.

The Panel analysed whether the *lex specialis* principle applies. Crucially, it requires a conflict[44] in the sense that the provisions must impose mutually exclusive obligations.[45] The Panel held that because it is possible to fulfil both the requirements of the MFN principle in Art. I:1 GATT and the requirements in Art. VI GATT and the ADA, these are not mutually exclusive obligations.[46] In the specific case, the EU could simply not have distinguished between NMEs and market economies. Thus, the *lex specialis* principle does not apply and the MFN principle applies to anti-dumping measures.[47]

The finding that there is no conflict between the two provisions can be supported by the general presumption against conflict and the presumption that general GATT rules apply to supplementary agreements, unless there is an explicit exemption.[48] Moreover, the fact that there is no conflict between Art. VI GATT and the ADA on the one hand and the MFN principle on the other hand, is also demonstrated by Art. 1.1 ADA. It stipulates that no anti-dumping measure can be applied except in accordance with the GATT (and not simply with Art. VI GATT).[49]

Consequently, Art. VI GATT and the ADA are not *lex specialis* to Art. I:1 GATT. This means that WTO members must not only fulfil the requirements imposed in Art. VI GATT and the ADA but must also comply with Art. I:1 GATT and other more general GATT provisions.

22.12.2009, the predecessor of Reg. (EU) 2016/1036, which is identical to Art. 9 (5) Reg. (EC) 384/96.

[41] Ibid 7.94.

[42] Ibid 7.95.

[43] Ibid 103.

[44] A conflict is also required for the General Interpretative Note to Annex 1 A of the WTO Agreement to apply, which is what the EU used for their argumentation.

[45] Laying down the three requirements that must be satisfied for the *lex specialis* rule to apply: *Indonesia - Auto* (n 30) n 168. The other two requirements are that the treaties concerned must have the same parties and the treaties must cover the same substantive subject matter. The other two requirements are fulfilled.

[46] *EU — Footwear (China)* (n 33) para 7.104.

[47] This has not ended problems associated with the treatment of China. See e.g.: Suse (2017); Espa and Levy (2018); Antonini (2018); Herrmann and Müller (2017), p. 500.

[48] Mahncke (2014), pp. 209–210.

[49] Ibid. 196–197. Different opinion, yet without a clear analysis of what the *lex specialis* principle entails: Jackson (1969), p. 421. Consider, however, that Jackson in a later work (previous to the discussed cases) doubted whether the MFN principle really does not apply: Jackson (2007), p. 63.

4.1.2.3 Application of the MFN Principle

As the MFN principle applies except if Art. 4.3, 9.2 ADA are *lex specialis*, the subsequent question is whether the different modifications that occur in customs unions *prima facie* violate the MFN principle. The anti-dumping regulation or the measures violate Art. I:1 GATT, if rules and formalities in connection with the importation grant an advantage, favour, privilege, or immunity of the type covered by Art. I GATT, which is not immediately and unconditionally accorded to all like products of all WTO members.[50]

The decisive question is if the various modifications of anti-dumping provisions constitute an advantage.[51] Anti-dumping measures and regulations are rules and formalities in connection with importation, no exception in Art. I GATT applies and if they are an advantage, they are not immediately and unconditionally accorded to all like products of all WTO members.

An advantage exists if there is first, a discrimination which second, has the effect that one exporter has a commercial advantage over another.[52] Art. I:1 GATT thereby covers *de jure* as well as *de facto* discrimination.[53] A *de facto* discrimination exists if a provision is on its face country neutral but in fact discriminates against a source of supply. This is the case if a measure modifies the conditions of competition to the detriment of imported goods and the change in competition cannot be justified other than by the origin of the good.[54] A *de jure* discrimination exists if a provision distinguishes between the origin of the good. The finding that this discrimination results in a commercial advantage for an exporter is not contingent on actual trade effects of a measure, as Art. I:1 GATT also protects the expectation of equal competitive opportunities.[55] Moreover, although the requirements must be assessed holistically,[56] the assessment does not allow balancing more favourable treatment under some procedure against less favourable treatment under another.[57]

---

[50] Art. I:1 GATT, *EU — Footwear (China)* (n 33) para 7.99; *Indonesia - Auto* (n 30) para 14.138.

[51] The rules and formalities applied in anti-dumping investigations, fall within the scope of the "rules and formalities in connection with importation" referred to in Art. 1:1, *EU — Footwear (China)* (n 33) para 7.100. Similarly, if the anti-dumping regulations are advantages, favours, privileges, or immunities, they are not immediately accorded to all like products of all WTO Members, as they specifically only apply in relation to other members of the customs union.

[52] *European Communities - Regime for the Importation, Sale and Distribution of Bananas* [1997] WTO Panel Report WT/DS27/R/USA [7.239].

[53] *Canada - Certain Measures Affecting the Automotive Industry* [2000] WTO Appellate Body Report WT/DS139/AB/R; WT/DS142/AB/R [78].

[54] As applied in *EC - Bananas III* (n 52) para 7.239. The general rule has been formulated in: Mavroidis (2012), p. 134.

[55] *European Communities - Measures Prohibiting the Importation and Marketing of Seal Products* [2014] WTO Appellate Body Report WT/DS400/AB/R; WT/DS401/AB/R [5.87].

[56] *United States - Measures Concerning the Importation, Marketing and Sale of Tuna and Tuna Products* [2015] WTO Art 215 DSU Appellate Body Report (Mexico) WT/DS381/AB/RW [7.280].

[57] *EC - Bananas III* (n 52) para 7.239.

It has been argued that none of the modifications are an advantage because the imposition of anti-dumping measures is discretionary.[58] Because a WTO member is free to choose not to impose anti-dumping measures at all, it is also free to adopt them only partially, the logic goes. This argument must be rejected on the basis that whether an advantage exists depends on the effects of a provision rather than on the formulation of the provision. If discretion is used in a discriminatory manner, this amounts to a commercial advantage and frustrates the expectation of equal competition opportunities. This is also why it violates the MFN principle if tariffs as applied differ even if they are below the bound level or if they are unbound.[59]

If customs unions distinguish between internal and external trade in their anti-dumping provisions and include additional requirements internally, this constitutes a *de jure* discrimination. Similarly, where customs unions include specific regulation to deal with anti-dumping action on behalf of another member state, this also constitutes a *de jure* discrimination. If the modifications incentivize or disincentivize anti-dumping measures, this also amounts to a commercial advantage: where anti-dumping measures are internally disincentivized or even eliminated, members of the customs union will gain a competitive advantage over third parties.

A commercial advantage is less apparent concerning the procedural modifications, as their intent may be to delineate competences between the customs union and its member states. Where additional procedural steps must be taken, this may reduce the likelihood of imposing anti-dumping measures and thereby amount to a commercial advantage to the producers and exporters of the customs union. Although some empirical evidence suggests that procedural integration disincentivizes anti-dumping measures,[60] this is controversial in the individual case. Chapter 19 of NAFTA[61] allowed binational reviews, i.e. included an additional procedural step similar to consultations, and has been studied extensively for its effects on internal anti-dumping filings. Although evidence suggests that NAFTA had an effect on anti-dumping filings,[62] it is difficult to attribute that solely to Chapter 19.[63] There is some evidence that at least subjectively US policy makers felt that Chapter 19 curtailed their possibility to protect themselves properly against dumping.[64] Such an effect would have to be proven, however.

Even if customs unions do not deviate from Art. VI GATT and the ADA, differences in the use of anti-dumping measures may amount to a *de facto* discrimination. Regional economic integration puts a strain on certain parts of the domestic

---

[58] Voon (2010), p. 625, 661.

[59] *Spain - Tariff Treatment of Unroasted Coffee* [1981] GATT 1947 Panel Report L/5135 [4.3].

[60] Prusa and Teh (2011), p. 63.

[61] North American Free Trade Agreement, 17.12.1992, entered into force: 1.1.1994, being the predecessor of Agreement between the United States of America, the United Mexican State, and Canada, 13.12.2019. This is an FTA but is also illustrative for customs unions.

[62] Prusa (2016), pp. 133–139.

[63] Blonigen (2005), pp. 407, 409–410.

[64] Gagné and Paulin (2013), pp. 413, 418–420.

industry that now face greater import competition. To counter these effects, countries within a customs union may be more likely to impose anti-dumping measures against third countries.[65] The selective nature of anti-dumping measures as well as the great degree of discretion in interpreting data afforded to investigating authorities make this "protection diversion" even more likely than other forms of trade diversion.[66] There is some evidence that the effect exists in practice[67] but the effect will have to be proven in the individual case. If this effect can be proven, it also amounts to a commercial advantage.

This means that generally any distinction between internal and external anti-dumping measures will *prima facie* violate Art. I:1 GATT, if it applies. If the modified measure is purely procedural, some additional evidence may be required that there is a commercial advantage. Similarly, if no modification has occurred, this may also violate Art. I:1 GATT but evidence of protection diversion will need to be provided as well.

4.1.3 Conclusions

Not every deviation from the WTO rules on anti-dumping also breaches WTO obligations. The relevant obligations are contained in Art. VI GATT, the ADA and Art. I:1 GATT.

Internal modifications either prohibit anti-dumping measures or disincentivize their imposition and integrate procedures. Prohibiting anti-dumping measures or disincentivizing them does not violate Art. VI GATT or the respective provision in the ADA. Insofar as procedurally additional cooperation requirements are established, this does not violate Art. VI GATT or the ADA either. Only if customs unions fall below the WTO requirements, do they violate WTO provisions. This has, however, not happened in the existing customs unions. If procedural integration happens by handing competences to centralized institutions, this does not violate Art. VI GATT or the ADA if the acts of those institutions are attributable to the customs union, they are, as will be developed below.[68]

External modifications either change the scope of the investigation and measure to a union wide basis or integrate procedures. Changing the scope of the investigation and measure does not violate Art. VI GATT or the ADA if the scope of the investigation and measure coincide. Procedural integration may happen by including additional cooperation requirements or by handing competences to central authorities. Neither violates Art. VI GATT or the ADA, if the acts of the central authority

---

[65] Prusa (2016), p. 140.

[66] Ibid.

[67] Ibid 139–143; Prusa and Teh (2010); James (2000); Bown et al. (2014); Tabakis and Zanardi (2018).

[68] See: Sect. 5.1.2.

Table 4.1 Overview Breaches of WTO Obligations

	Violates Art. VI GATT, ADA	Violates MFN Principle
No modification		(X)
AD action on behalf of third party	Art. 14 ADA	X
Internal modifications		
• Prohibition of internal ADMs		X
• Disincentivizing internal ADMs		X
• Central IA		(X)
• Cooperation requirements between MS		(X)
• Central imposition decision		(X)
External modifications		
• Central IA		N.a.
• Cooperation requirements between MS		(X)
• Central imposition decision		N.a.
• Union wide Inv. & measure	Pot. Art. 3.1, 4.1 ADA	N.a.
• MS Inv. & union wide measure	Art. 1 ADAs	
Further potential modifications		
• Incentivizing ADMs	X	X

remain attributable to its members, as will be developed below. Finally, any deviation from Art. 14 ADA violates it.

Any distinction between internal and external anti-dumping measures *prima facie* violates Art. I:1 GATT, however, the MFN principle does not apply especially if the investigation and measure are union wide, Art. 4.3 ADA.

Overall, Art. VI GATT and the ADA are sufficiently flexible so that most modifications do not violate them. Table 4.1 summarizes the results. (x) thereby means that a violation of the MFN principle is possible but additional information will have to be provided. N.a. means that a provision is not applicable. Note that if the MFN principle is not applicable due to an external modification, it is not applicable to the internal modifications that correspond either. Where customs unions harmonize anti-dumping measures externally, the internal modifications will not violate the MFN principle either.

4.2 Justifications According to WTO Provisions

The anti-dumping legislation contained in some customs unions violates different WTO provisions. These violations may, however, be justified according to WTO law. WTO law contains specific justifications in Art. XXIV:5 GATT and Para. 2 (c) and (d) Enabling Clause.[69]

As these grounds for justification are vague and WTO bodies have not clearly defined their limits yet, the applicable sources of law will be identified first (under Sect. 4.2.1). This section then considers how violations may be justified according to Art. XXIV:5 GATT (under Sect. 4.2.2) or the Enabling Clause (under Sect. 4.2.3).

4.2.1 Sources of Law

The primary source of law is the text of Art. XXIV GATT as well as the Enabling Clause, being an integral part of the GATT.[70] Because both provisions contain vague terms such as "substantially all the trade" or that duties and other restrictive regulations of commerce (ORRC) cannot "on the whole" be "higher or more restrictive", substantial interpretation of the relevant provisions is necessary. WTO members have agreed on some interpretations concerning Art. XXIV GATT and have adopted the Understanding on the Interpretation of Article XXIV of the General Agreement of Tariffs and Trade 1994 (RTA Understanding).[71]

Above that, the interpretation of the provisions follows the general rules. The interpretation of the provisions must be in accordance with customary rules of international law,[72] as codified in Art. 31, 32 VCLT.[73] A treaty must be interpreted "with the ordinary meaning given to the terms of the treaty in its context and in the light of its object and purpose", Art. 31.1 VCLT.

---

[69] No other justification in the WTO Agreement applies. The measures cannot be justified via Art. XX (d) GATT as in most customs union the union law is not directly applicable and Art. XX (d) GATT only applies to directly applicable law (*Mexico — Tax Measures on Soft Drinks and Other Beverages* [2006] WTO Appellate Body Report WT/DS308/AB/R [148]) and because modifications to Art. VI GATT or the ADA are not necessary to secure compliance with the WTO Agreement.

[70] The Enabling Clause has become an integral part of the GATT 1994 as it is another decision of the contracting parties to the GATT 1947 within the meaning of Art. 1 (b)(iv) GATT 1994, see: *European Communities - Conditions for the Granting of Tariff Preferences to Developing Countries* [2004] WTO Appellate Body Report WT/DS246/AB/R [90].

[71] Panels have not yet ruled on their legal nature. Mavroidis argues that it is an international agreement in the sense of the VCLT: Mavroidis (2006) n 21.

[72] Art. 3.2 DSU.

[73] *US - Gasoline* (n 24) 17; *Japan - Alcoholic Beverages II* (n 24) 10.

Interpretations of these provisions take place in the WTO either in the CRTA or CTD on the one hand or Panels and the Appellate Body in the context of the DSB on the other hand.

Because RTAs are not always economically beneficial and because they undermine a multilateral trade system, the agreements provide for a review process of RTAs. This process has now changed. Initially, Art. XXIV:7 (a) GATT obliged members that entered into an RTA to notify it to the WTO, or more specifically the Committee on Regional Trade Agreements (CRTA).[74] The CRTA would then review the notified RTA and according to Art. XXIV:7 GATT had the power "to make such reports and recommendations to contracting parties as they may deem appropriate". Similarly, Para. 4 (a) Enabling Clause required notification of RTAs in the sense of Para. 2 (c) and (d) Enabling Clause to the Committee on Trade and Development (CTD) and Para. 4 (b) Enabling Clause gave a wide mandate for consultations to reach "solutions satisfactory to all such contracting parties." It is not clear whether the choice under which clause notification happens has substantive implications[75] but notification is not constitutive.[76]

The CRTA as well as its predecessor, the Art. XXIV GATT Working Parties, have not made use of this discretion in an effective way and have never found that an RTA to be inconsistent with the GATT.[77] Overall, no useful insights on the interpretation of Art. XXIV:5 GATT emerged.[78] Similarly, the CTD has not made

---

[74] Committee on Regional Trade Agreements, 'Rules of Procedure for Meetings of the Committee on Regional Trade Agreements, Adopted by the Committee on Regional Trade Agreements on 2 July 1996', WT/REG/1, 14.8.1996.

[75] This issue mainly arose when the GCC changed the provision under which it notified its customs union: see, e.g. Committee on Trade and Development, 'Systematic and Specific Issues Arising out of the Dual Notification of the Gulf Cooperation Council Customs Union, Communication from China, Egypt and India', WT/COMTD/W/175, 30.9.2010. The General Council Decision on this topic did not add clarity: General Council, Decision of 14 December 2010, Transparency Mechanism for Preferential Trade Arrangements, WT/L/806, 16.12.2010.

[76] Art. XXIV:7 (a) GATT requires prompt notification but does not regulate that the absence of the notification impacts the validity of the RTA. The same is true for Para. 4 (a) Enabling Clause. See also *Brazil—Certain Measures Concerning Taxation and Charges* [2018] WTO Appellate Body Report WT/DS472/AB/R; WT/DS497/AB/R 5.416–5.427. Despite the AB's finding that the Para. 4 (a) Enabling Clause Requirements had not been fulfilled, the only impact this had was procedural. Substantively, only the question whether the measure at issue has a genuine link to the measures justified pursuant to Para. 2 (c) Enabling Clause was relevant. The same should apply in the context of Art. XXIV:5 GATT.

[77] Four RTAs were judged "broadly" consistent with the GATT and only the RTA between the Czech and Slovak Republic has been unambiguously accepted: Schott (1989); Mavroidis (2015b), pp. S107, S109.

[78] This may be because decision had to be reached by consensus (Committee on Regional Trade Agreements, 'Rules of Procedure for Meetings of the Committee on Regional Trade Agreements, Adopted by the Committee on Regional Trade Agreements on 2 July 1996', WT/REG/1, 14.8.1996, Rule 33), which has led members to adopt a decision whereby the disagreement was notified but no interpretation put forward: Mavroidis (2006), p. 198.

use of its wide discretion either. No meaningful conclusions on the interpretation of Para. 2 (c) and (d) Enabling Clause have emerged.

This system has been refined with the Transparency Mechanism in 2006.[79] Members are still obliged to notify the WTO of RTAs but the CRTA has stopped to make substantive assessments on WTO compliance altogether. The CRTA will circulate a factual abstract and a factual presentation focused on the content of the RTA rather than on its relationship to WTO law. Members will subsequently be able to ask questions. Argumentative value may be drawn from the opinions expressed during the questions, as they sometimes refer to substantive issues. Factually, the same has happened in the CTD and the only argumentative value on substantive questions can be derived from the discussions in the committee.[80]

Moreover, RTAs can be subject to proceedings in the DSB. Although Panel or Appellate Body Reports only bind the parties to the particular dispute but do not create binding precedent, the Appellate Body has stressed that it aims to honour the legitimate expectation of WTO members to see prior case-law applied in future cases, if appropriate.[81] Panel reports that have been overturned on appeal will not develop this *de facto* precedence but will have an argumentative value, nevertheless. Panels or the Appellate Body have only rarely ruled on the interpretation of Art. XXIV GATT and have never done so on Para. 2 (c) and (d) Enabling Clause.

This means that Panel reports that have not been overturned, and Appellate Body reports create a *de facto* precedence, whereas overturned Panel reports and opinions voiced in the CRTA or CTD merely have argumentative value.

4.2.2 Art. XXIV:5 GATT

Violations of WTO provisions may be justified according to Art. XXIV:5 GATT. The following customs unions have been notified according to Art. XXIV:7 (a) GATT and can only be justified according to this provision: CARICOM, CACM, ECOWAS, EU-Andorra, EU-San Marino, EU-Turkey, EAEU, GCC,

[79]General Council, 'Transparency Mechanism for Regional Trade Agreements', WT/L/671, 14.12.2006; General Council, 'Decision of 14 December 2006, Transparency for Preferential Trade Arrangements', WT/L/672, 14.12.2006.

[80]Mavroidis (2015a), pp. 300–303; Bossche and Zdouc (2017), pp. 692–693; Matsushita et al. (2017), pp. 514–518.

[81]*Japan - Alcoholic Beverages II* (n 24) n 30; *India - Patent Protection for Pharmaceutical and Agricultural Chemical Products* [1998] WTO Panel Report WT/DS79/R [7.30]; *United States - Import Prohibition of Certain Shrimp and Shrimp Products* [2001] WTO Art 215 DSU Appellate Body Report WT/DS58/AB/RW [109]; *United States - Definitive Safeguard Measures on Imports of Circular Welded Carbon Quality Line Pipe from Korea* [2002] WTO Appellate Body Report WT/DS202/AB/R [102]. A good example is the acceptance of *amicus curiae* briefs which has no legal basis in WTO law, but Panels and the Appellate Body frequently refer to prior decisions when justifying taking them into account: e.g. *European Communities - Trade Description of Sardines* [2002] WTO Appellate Body Report WT/DS231/AB/R [155–156].

SACU. The following customs unions are notified under para. 4(a) of the Enabling Clause and primarily justified through the Enabling Clause: CAN, COMESA, EAC, CEMAC, MERCOSUR and WAEMU. For them Art. XXIV:5 GATT is relevant for violations other than the MFN principle.[82]

According to Art. XXIV:5 GATT, "the provisions of *this Agreement* shall not prevent, as between the territories of contracting parties, *the formation of a customs union* or of a free-trade area [. . .]; *Provided* that:" (a) the duties and other regulations of commerce (ORCs—not to be confused with ORRCs) are "on the whole" not higher or more restrictive than the general incidence of the duties and ORC prior to the formation of the customs union (emphasis added).

This provision has been interpreted by the Appellate Body in *Turkey – Textiles* to require several things: (1) there must be a customs union in the sense of Art. XXIV:8 (a) GATT, (2) the customs union must fulfil the requirements of Art. XXIV:5 (a) GATT; (3) the measure is adopted upon the formation of an RTA, and (4) the formation of a RTA would be prevented if the measure were disallowed.[83] The scope of the justification is thereby limited to violations of "the Agreement".[84] Each requirement will be considered in turn following an examination of the scope of the justification.

The justification of a WTO inconsistent measure according to Art. XXIV:5 GATT follows two steps: first, certain requirements that pertain to the entire customs union must be met and second, certain requirements that pertain to the specific measure in violation of a WTO obligation must be met as well.

The justification is therefore relevant where certain anti-dumping provisions in customs unions violate WTO obligations but also where anti-dumping provisions do not violate any WTO provisions. The anti-dumping regulation must meet both sets of requirements where it violates WTO law. Moreover, since a customs union agreement necessarily affords preferential treatment to its members, other provisions of the agreement will violate the MFN principle. These measures could be justified by Art. XXIV:5 GATT. Even if the anti-dumping regulation does not violate WTO law itself, the regulation should not stand in the way of a successful justification of another measure. Consequently, anti-dumping regulation should not be of such nature as to make a justification of the requirements pertaining to the entire customs union impossible to meet.[85]

The elements must be interpreted according to the words used in the treaty, read in their context, and in light of the object and purpose of the treaty.[86] Art. XXIV:4 GATT sets out the purpose of the provision:

---

[82] See below at: Sect. 4.2.3.1.

[83] *Turkey - Restrictions on Imports of Textile and Clothing Products* [1999] WTO Appellate Body Report WT/DS34/AB/R [45, 46, 51].

[84] Ibid 13.

[85] Pauwelyn (2004), p. 109, 126.

[86] Art. 3.2 DSU; Art. 31, 32 VCLT.

The Members recognize the desirability of increasing freedom of trade by the development, through voluntary agreements, of closer integration between the economies of the countries parties to such agreements. They also recognize that the purpose of a customs union or of a free-trade area should be to facilitate trade between the constituent territories and not to raise barriers to the trade of other Members with such territories.

More context on the exception in Art. XXIV:5 GATT is provided in the RTA Understanding. Accordingly, WTO members recognize the contribution to the expansion of world trade through RTAs. The higher the elimination of internal trade restrictions, the greater that contribution. WTO members also reiterate that adverse effects on third countries should be avoided "to the greatest extent possible".[87]

4.2.2.1   Scope of the Justification

The scope of Art. XXIV:5 GATT is limited to "this Agreement", i.e. the GATT.[88] Any violation of Art. I:1 GATT falls within the scope of this exception. It is less clear if that also includes violations of the ADA.

The Appellate Body in *Turkey—Textiles* applied the justification to a violation of Art. 2.4 ATC, even though the justification failed for other reasons. It argued that this is within the scope of the justification because Art. 2.4 ATC expressly refers to the GATT.[89] The Panel in *US—Wheat Gluten* understood this to mean that Art. XXIV:5 GATT can be invoked as a defence if the GATT is "somehow incorporated" into the provision or agreement.[90] Art. 1 ADA clarifies that "the following provisions govern the application of Art. VI [GATT]". This means that the ADA is a concretization of Art. VI GATT which justifies a sufficient link to be considered part of "this Agreement".[91]

---

[87] RTA Understanding, Preamble.

[88] See also: Yangyang Huang, *Trade Remedy Measures in the WTO and Regional Trade Agreements* (The University of Edingburgh) 173–175. Compare generally: Kallmayer (2005).

[89] *Turkey - Textiles* (n 83) n 13.

[90] *United States - Definitive Safeguard Measures on Imports of Wheat Gluten from the European Communities* [2000] WTO Panel Report WT/DS166/R [8.180].

[91] Agreeing and proposing that it depends on the "wording and context" of a provision to fall within the scope of the justification: Lockhart and Mitchell (2005), p. 9. See also with regards to Safeguards measures: *United States - Definitive Safeguard Measures on Imports of Circular Welded Carbon Quality Line Pipe from Korea* [2001] WTO Panel Report WT/DS202/R [7.150]. The Panel requires a "close interrelation" between the relevant provision and the GATT. The AB held that the finding has no legal effect, however, *US - Line Pipe* (n 81) paras 198, 199. Agreeing that the entire ADA falls within the scope of the justification: Huang (n 88), p. 181. Agreeing in the similar situation concerning Safeguards: Pauwelyn (2004), pp. 128–129. Only Müller-Ibold suggests that Art. VI GATT and the ADA do not fall within the scope of the exception: Müller-Ibold (2018), pp. 205–206. The view rests on the false assumption that Art. VI GATT and the ADA are *lex specialis* to other provisions in the GATT, however. See: Sect. 4.1.2.2.

In principle, any violation of the ADA can therefore be justified by Art. XXIV:5 GATT, the only limitation being that Art. XXIV:5 GATT requires a certain nexus between the WTO member invoking the justification and the customs union agreement. Art. XXIV:5 GATT cannot be invoked to justify a measure which grants WTO-inconsistent advantages to customs territories not party to the customs union agreement or for a measure that cannot be characterized as a measure of the customs union.[92] In *Canada – Auto* Art. XXIV:5 GATT could not be invoked to justify an import duty exemption that did not solely depend on the origin of the goods for lacking that special nexus.[93] The only situation in which this limitation will be relevant for anti-dumping measures is if an anti-dumping measure derives from national legislation and the customs union has not yet harmonized anti-dumping matters. If that measure violates WTO obligations, this cannot be justified by Art. XXIV:5 GATT.

4.2.2.2 Existence of a Customs Union

There must be a customs union in the sense of Art. XXIV:8 (a) GATT.

Procedurally, it is not clear whether absent any arguments on this there is a presumption that this requirement has been met. In *Turkey – Textiles* the Panel did not address whether the customs union between Turkey and the (then) EC met the requirements of Art. XXIV:8 (a) GATT. Rather, it even held that "it is arguable" that Panels may not have jurisdiction to assess the overall compatibility of customs unions with the requirements of Art. XXIV GATT at all.[94] Absent any arguments by the parties and following the principle of judicial economy, it assumed that the requirement was met.[95] The issue was not appealed and therefore the Appellate Body could not rule on it.[96] As regards justiciability, the Appellate Body nevertheless referred to *India – Quantitative Restrictions*[97] where the Appellate Body affirmed justiciability of Balance-Of-Payments provisions. Some have interpreted this reference to imply that Panels have jurisdiction to review whether the conditions of Art. XXIV:8(a) GATT are met.[98] As regards whether there is a presumption that

---

[92] *Canada - Certain Measures Affecting the Automotive Industry* [2000] WTO Panel Report WT/DS139/R; WT/DS142/R [10.55].

[93] Ibid 10.56.

[94] *Turkey - Restrictions on Imports of Textile and Clothing Products* [1999] WTO Panel Report WT/DS34/R [9.53].

[95] Ibid 9.54–9.55.

[96] *Turkey - Textiles* (n 83) para 60.

[97] *India - Quantitative Restrictions on Imports of Agricultural, Textile and Industrial Products* [1999] WTO Appellate Body WT/DS90/AB/R [102–105] is concerned with the question whether Balance-Of-Payments issues are justiciable.

[98] The argument is that Balance-Of-Payments are structurally similar to RTAs. See: Roessler (2001), p. 316. See also Para. 12 RTA Understanding, which indicates the same result. The result is controversial and some argue that because the conclusion and terms of RTAs are inherently

the requirements have been met, the Appellate Body held that they "expect a panel, when examining such a measure, to require a party to establish that both of these conditions have been fulfilled",[99] implying that a Panel cannot assume that the requirements have been met.[100] This is also reflected in the Panel Report in *US – Line Pipe,* which has, however, been overturned by the Appellate Body in that regard.[101] The party relying on the defence must therefore prove that the customs union fulfils the requirements of Art. XXIV:8 (a) GATT and there is no presumption to this extent.

Internal Requirements: Art. XXIV:8 (a)(i) GATT

Art. XXIV:8(a)(i) GATT sets out the internal requirements of a customs union. A customs union requires that a single customs territory substitutes two or more customs territories so that

> duties and other restrictive regulations of commerce (except where necessary, those permitted under Art. XI, XII, XIII, XIV, XV, and XX) are eliminated with respect to substantially all the trade between the constituent territories or at least with respect to substantially all the trade in products originating in such territories.

Duties and ORRCs must therefore be eliminated between the constituent territories at least with regards to substantially all the trade and referring to at least those products that originate within those territories. The duties and ORRCs listed in the parenthesis are exempt from this requirement.

The provision is ambiguous in several regards: it is unclear (1) whether anti-dumping measures or regulation are duties or ORRCs, (2) what modifications to the anti-dumping provisions remain within the limit of "substantially all the trade", and (3) what the nature of the list of exceptions in the parenthesis is and if that list also includes Art. VI GATT.

Duties or ORRCs?

Although there has been some debate on the issue, no one suggests that anti-dumping *measures* are neither duties nor ORRCs. Because the purpose of anti-dumping measures is to restrict the cross-border movement of certain products by

---

political, justiciability may offset the institutional balance of the WTO, see ibid. and Bartels (2004a), pp. 861, 881–882.

[99] *Turkey - Textiles* (n 83) para 59.

[100] Interpreting the AB Report as presuming the requirements will be met: Bartels (2005), p. 691, 713.

[101] The findings with regards to Art. XXIV GATT has been overturned and the issues have been solved relying on the Parallelism requirement. For argumentative value see: *US - Line Pipe* (n 91) para 7.142–7.146.

levying tariffs or by accepting undertakings, they are at least restrictive regulations of commerce and Art. II:2(b) GATT suggests that they are duties.[102]

It is less clear if the regulatory framework to impose anti-dumping measures, i.e. the anti-dumping regulations of customs unions *as such* are duties or ORRC.[103] Although this question may seem overly meticulous, it is relevant as the measures that can be subsumed under duties and ORRCs should be eliminated. It makes a difference if only measures must be eliminated or if the internal anti-dumping framework must prohibit internal anti-dumping measures.

The mere possibility to impose an anti-dumping duty is not a duty because if no measure has been imposed no additional charge will have to be paid upon the border crossing of a good. Consequently, anti-dumping legislation would have to be an ORRC. This depends on what an ORRC is, which is not clear. Some suggest that ORRCs are only those measures that restrict the cross-border movement of goods as opposed to all marketplace regulations that are restrictive for commerce.[104] This debate need not be decided here, as anti-dumping measures restrict cross-border movement, meaning they can be ORRCs even following the narrower definition. However, to be an ORRC, the regulation must also be *restrictive*. The assessment of restrictiveness thereby focuses on the effects on commerce rather than the form of the regulation.[105] The mere possibility to impose anti-dumping measures will not have a restrictive effect. Only if the regulation has been used or its use has been announced (e.g. if an investigation has been initiated) will it have a chilling effect on trade. Regardless of the question whether any chilling effect is enough to qualify a border-measure as an ORRC, the chilling effect does not derive from the regulation but from its use or the announcement of its use. Consequently, anti-dumping regulations are not ORRCs but only anti-dumping measures.

Some have argued that anti-dumping regulations are duties or ORRCs as anti-dumping measures can only be said to have been *eliminated* as opposed to *not applied*, if the anti-dumping regulation does not allow internal anti-dumping measures.[106] Moreover, focusing on the measures instead of the regulation would result in the assessment of WTO compliance varying depending on whether the regulation

---

[102] Arguing that they are either duties or ORRCs: Gobbi Estrella and Horlick (2006), pp. 909, 916–920; Huang (2013), p. 183, 196; Mathis (2006), p. 87; Lockhart and Mitchell (2005), pp. 14–15; Mitchell and Lockhart (2009), pp. 240–242. For safeguard measures, see: *US - Line Pipe* (n 91) para 7.141. The AB Report overturned the findings in that regard: *US - Line Pipe* (n 81) paras 198, 199. It has been argued that they are not restrictive, as they are designed to offset unfair trading practices. The same could, however, be true with Art. XX GATT, which is listed and must thus be an ORRC. See: Voon (2010), p. 662.

[103] *Duties* is thereby different from the term *measure*.

[104] Lockhart and Mitchell (2005), p. 14. Lockhart and Mitchell also include marketplace regulations that discriminate against foreign products: Mitchell and Lockhart (2009), p. 241.

[105] Lockhart and Mitchell (2005), p. 14; Mitchell and Lockhart (2009), p. 241.

[106] Estrella and Horlick (2006), pp. 934–935.

is used.[107] This view should be rejected.[108] Ultimately, anti-dumping regulation would have to be subsumed under the term ORRC and it is difficult to see what trade restrictive effect anti-dumping regulation—irrespective of its use—has.

Further points support the finding that anti-dumping legislation is not an ORRC. This view corresponds with the fact that generally the effects of certain measures rather than the measures themselves are used to determine compliance with the requirements contained in Art. XXIV GATT. This is why for the exercise in Art. XXIV:5(a) GATT, the weighted average duties and not the bound duty rates are considered[109] and when Panels have applied Art. XXIV:5 GATT in the context of safeguard measures, they have always considered the individual measures and not the regulatory framework.[110] Finally, this also corresponds with the wording in the parenthesis ("except where necessary, *those permitted* under . . .") which suggests that the actual measures and not the transposed framework to implement those measures are duties and ORRCs. This means that whereas anti-dumping measures are duties or ORRCs, anti-dumping regulation is not.

Substantially All the Trade

Duties and ORRC must be eliminated with respect to substantially all the trade. In *Turkey – Textiles* the Appellate Body defined the term "substantially all the trade" as not being the same as all the trade but considerably more than some of the trade,[111] thereby not adding clarity to the term. Whereas the definition of duties and ORRC indicate the type of measures that must be liberalized, the substantially all the trade requirement refers to the degree of liberalization.[112]

Because only duties and ORRCs but no other measures must be eliminated with regards to substantially all the trade, this requires the elimination of anti-dumping

---

[107] Ibid. 937.

[108] The arguments can also be challenged directly: the difference between the terms *eliminated* and *not applied* is not compelling. If countries decide to drop all existing anti-dumping measures upon the formation of a customs union, it can be said that they have eliminated anti-dumping measures. The term eliminated is not as precise as advocated for and there is not necessarily a distinction to the term *not applied*. Furthermore, the fact that the assessment may vary merely highlights the inherent difficulties in assessing whether the requirements have been met. Since the test whether duties and ORRCs have been eliminated with respect to substantially all the trade also requires an examination of trade flows, it is also subject to constant change. On the second point, see Mitchell and Lockhart (2015), pp. 93–96; Voon (2010), p. 660.

[109] Para. 2 RTA Understanding.

[110] *Argentina - Safeguard Measures on Imports of Footwear* [1999] WTO Panel Report WT/DS121/R [8.97]. Note that the finding has been reversed the Appellate Body found that the parallelism requirement had been violated, *Argentina - Footwear (EC)* (n 10) para 109. See also:*US - Line Pipe* (n 91) para 7.141. The findings have been reversed by the AB in this respect: *US - Line Pipe* (n 81) paras 198, 199.

[111] *Turkey - Textiles* (n 83) para 48.

[112] Mitchell and Lockhart (2015), p. 97.

measures but not the elimination of anti-dumping regulation.[113] Put differently, only an insubstantial amount of internal trade can be subject to anti-dumping measures.

Different approaches exist to examine what "substantially all the trade" is. The alternatives are to follow either a quantitative or a qualitative approach. Following the quantitative view, a statistical threshold of trade liberalization must have been reached.[114] This may require that a certain amount of tariff lines have been liberalized or that a certain amount of trade flow has been liberalized.[115] The qualitative approach requires that trade has been liberalized with regards to every major sector of the economies of the customs union.[116] The rationale for this approach is that an exception to WTO rules is only justified if the parties to it have shown commitment to closer economic integration. That commitment is lacking if major sectors are excluded.[117]

In *Turkey – Textiles,* the Appellate Body held that the "substantially all the trade" test requires in principle that both a certain percentage of trade must have been liberalized and that no major sector can be excluded but the requirements should allow flexibility.[118] In *US – Line Pipe,* the Panel accepted the US' submission[119] that NAFTA liberalizes 97% of the Parties' tariff lines and 99% of trade volumes to establish *prima facie* that NAFTA met the FTA requirements, without explaining why the substantially all the trade test was satisfied.[120] Neither the US' submission nor the Panel's examination of it thereby referred to internal anti-dumping measures which remain possible in NAFTA.[121,122]

---

[113] Estrealla and Horlick argue that the imposition of internal anti-dumping measures must be prohibited. They argue that otherwise although substantial duties and ORRCs will have been eliminated, this is different than the required elimination of all duties and ORRC on substantially all the trade. They argue that the comparison to Art. XXIV:8 (a)(ii) GATT supports such a reading. Whereas paragraph 8 (a)(ii) requires that "substantially the same" duties and ORC are applied, paragraph 8 (a)(i) requires that duties and ORRCs are eliminated with respect to "substantially all the trade". This difference can only mean that paragraph 8 (a)(i) requires a complete elimination of all types of duties and ORRC, such as anti-dumping measures, but leaves the possibility open that in some sectors, the right to impose Anti-Dumping measures remains: Estrella and Horlick (2009), pp. 936–937. These arguments all rely on the false presumption that the possibility to impose anti-dumping measures, i.e. anti-dumping legislation, constitutes a duty or ORRC. Reaching the same result: Müller-Ibold (2018), pp. 204–205; Pauwelyn (2004), p. 127; Mitchell and Lockhart (2009), p. 242.

[114] Lockhart and Mitchell (2005), p. 11; Mitchell and Lockhart (2009), p. 238.

[115] Lockhart and Mitchell (2005), p. 12.

[116] Ibid.; Mitchell and Lockhart (2009), p. 238.

[117] Lockhart and Mitchell (2005), p. 12; Mitchell and Lockhart (2009), p. 237.

[118] *Turkey - Textiles* (n 83) para 48.

[119] *US - Line Pipe* (n 91) para 7.142. The findings were reversed by the AB in this regard.

[120] Ibid. 7.144. The findings were reversed by the AB in this regard.

[121] See especially Art. 1902 NAFTA.

[122] *US - Line Pipe* (n 91) para 7.142, 7.144. The findings have been reversed by the AB in this regard.

The flexibility in this approach should recognize the specifics of anti-dumping measures. Using trade flows to measure whether anti-dumping measures have been eliminated with respect to substantially all the trade is not appropriate, as the purpose of anti-dumping measures is to distort trade flows.[123] As tariff lines do not always correspond with the products subject to an anti-dumping measure, that approach may give a distorted impression as well.[124] Similarly, the qualitative approach may lead to misguiding results because market asymmetries may exist with respect to entire sectors, which may explain why several anti-dumping measures have been imposed on one specific sector.[125] That such general determinations may be difficult has been recognized in the context of Art. XXIV:5 (a) GATT where the general incidence of the duties and "other regulations of commerce" (ORC) applicable before and after the conclusion of a customs union must be assessed. Para. 2 RTA Understanding clarifies that the quantification and aggregation of some measures may be difficult and suggests that "the examination of individual measures, regulations, products covered, and trade flows affected may be required." The same cautious remarks should apply by analogy to the exercise under Art. XXIV:8 (a)(i) GATT.

As the assessment considers the entire customs union, nothing definitive can be said with regards to anti-dumping measures. It is possible that members of a customs union apply anti-dumping measures against each other and that substantially all the trade has nevertheless been liberalized. It is also possible that either because not sufficient other trade has been liberalized or because too many anti-dumping measures have been imposed that the customs union no longer meets the requirements. No duty to modify anti-dumping regulation in a certain way derives from this.

Nature of the List of Exceptions?

Art. XXIV:8 (a)(i) GATT includes a list of exceptions to the requirement that duties and ORRCs must be eliminated. Namely, "where necessary, those exceptions permitted under Art. XI, XII, XIII, XIV, XV and XX [GATT]", must not be eliminated between the parties of a customs union. The effect of that list is that if these exceptions are retained in a customs union, the retention of these exceptions cannot be used to argue that substantially all the trade has not been liberalized.

Historically, some have argued in favour of the list being illustrative and that Art. VI GATT should be contained in that list as well. They have advanced that there is no historical reason why other Articles than the mentioned ones have not been considered.[126] Moreover, Art. XXI GATT is not listed either. Art. XXI GATT is

---

[123]Mitchell and Lockhart (2015), p. 94.

[124]For problems resulting from differing product definitions in anti-dumping measures and other customs issues: Inama et al. (2009), pp. 282–288.

[125]E.g. a country may subsidize steel. All exporters of products with steel may therefore dump.

[126]Committee on Regional Trade Agreements, 'Systemic Issues Related to "Other Regulations of Commerce" – Background Note by the Secretariat (Revision)', WT/REG/W/17/Rev.1, 5. February 1998, para. 6. Challenging this claim: Estrella and Horlick (2006), p. 940.

an overarching exception and the requirements of forming a customs union would be too high if it were impossible to retain that exception.[127] Neither of these reasons are, however, convincing. Just as there is no historical reason why Art. VI GATT was not included in that list, it would have been easy to include it. Not including it is indicative that it should not be extended to Art. VI GATT.[128] As regards Art. XXI GATT, it is an exception with a special meaning in the GATT. The wording of it indicates that it works as an exception to the entire GATT and it can therefore apply in customs unions even without it being mentioned in the parenthesis.[129] This interpretation of the list is also supported by the general principle that exceptions must be applied restrictively.[130] Therefore, the list is exhaustive. As Art. VI GATT is not mentioned, anti-dumping measures are not an exception to the duty to liberalize substantially all the trade.

External Requirements: Art. XXIV:8 (a)(ii) GATT

Art. XXIV:8 (a)(ii) GATT sets out the external requirements of a customs union. Accordingly, a customs union requires the substitution of a single customs territory for two or more customs territories so that: "substantially the same duties and other regulations of commerce are applied by each of the members of the union to the trade of territories not included in the union."[131]

Whereas internally a customs union must liberalize trade, it must harmonize trade externally. This means that a common external trade regime[132] must apply. Similar ambiguities exist as with Art. XXIV:8(a)(i) GATT. Like the internal requirements, the common external trade regime must cover duties and other regulations of commerce (under section "Duties or ORC?") and only substantially but not all duties and ORC must be harmonized (under section "Substantially the Same").

Duties or ORC?

Duties and ORC must be harmonized to some extent. Like the internal dimension, the meaning of duties and ORC is not clear. Similar arguments as to the internal dimension can be made concerning the question whether anti-dumping measures and/or regulations are duties or ORC.

---

[127] Huang (2013), p. 198; Pauwelyn (2004), pp. 126–127.

[128] Marceau (1994), p. 188.

[129] Estrella and Horlick (2006), p. 939.

[130] Müller-Ibold (2018), p. 205; Lockhart and Mitchell (2005), p. 16; Huang (2013), p. 197; Mitchell and Lockhart (2009), p. 243. Also referring to *Turkey - Textiles* (n 12) para 48, stating that "certain restrictive regulations" are permitted, suggesting that the list is exhaustive.

[131] Subject to Art. XXIV:9 GATT with excludes the preferences in Art. I:2 GATT from this requirement.

[132] *Turkey - Textiles* (n 83) para 49.

Anti-dumping measures are duties or because they are border-measures[133] that have the effect and purpose of restricting trade, they are at least ORC.[134]

Whether anti-dumping regulations of a customs union are ORCs is again more problematic. The Panel in *Turkey – Textiles* defined ORCs as "any regulation having an impact on trade (such as *measures* in the fields of [. . .] anti-dumping)" (emphasis added).[135] This indicates that the Panel only considered measures but not anti-dumping regulation as such an ORC.[136] A reason for this could be that as long as the members apply the same anti-dumping measures, there is no reason to call the harmonization of the regimes defective. An example of this could be the envisaged SACU system. All members of SACU will have their own anti-dumping regulation and every SACU member will conduct investigations with respect to its territory. One SACU member will then combine the results and make the determination on a union wide basis. In that situation, not the same anti-dumping legislation applies (as national anti-dumping legislation continues to apply) but ultimately anti-dumping measures are union wide and the ADA and GATT should leave sufficient flexibilities to allow such results.[137] This means that anti-dumping measures are duties or at least ORC, but anti-dumping regulation as such is not.

Substantially the Same

Substantially the same duties and ORC must be imposed against third countries. The Appellate Body in *Turkey—Textiles* defined this as closely approximating "sameness", whereby members have a "certain degree of flexibility" to retain individual restrictions on external trade.[138] The circumstances under which this is the case remain unclear.

Different factors have been suggested to make that assessment: the number of harmonized ORCs compared to the number of unharmonized ORCs or the products and value of trade affected by these different harmonisations.[139]

When considering whether substantially the same anti-dumping measures apply, the specifics of trade defence measures must be respected. The same problems arise as when making the internal determination whether substantially all the trade has

---

[133] Mitchell and Lockhart (2015), p. 104.

[134] The same discussion applies as internally, see: Fn. 102.

[135] *Turkey - Textiles* (n 94) para 9.120. This has not been reversed by the AB. This has been criticized as too broad. The criticism is, however, directed against market measures and not border measures. See: Estrella and Horlick (2006), p. 918.

[136] This claim can be contested, as reference to *measures* could be interpreted as reference to measure as required in the DSB. This includes *as such* measures, i.e. anti-dumping legislation.

[137] See also: Mitchell and Lockhart (2015), p. 103.

[138] *Turkey - Textiles* (n 83) para 50.

[139] Mitchell and Lockhart (2015), p. 107.

been liberalized. When deciding upon the exact methodology Para. 2 RTA Understanding can be guiding.[140]

Due to the limited guidance little can be suggested with regards to anti-dumping measures. As Art. XXIV:8 (a)(i) GATT includes the possibility that rules of origin apply in customs unions, because only substantially the same duties and ORC must apply and because Art. 4.3 ADA indicates that only certain customs unions must conduct union wide investigations, it remains possible for customs unions not to completely harmonize their external anti-dumping regimes. Nevertheless, not harmonizing sufficient duties and ORCs may lead to a customs union not fulfilling these requirements despite a harmonious application of anti-dumping measures and *vice versa*.

4.2.2.3 Not More Restrictive Externally: Art. XXIV:5 (a) GATT

According to Art. XXIV:5 (a) GATT:

> the duties and other regulations of commerce imposed at the institution of any such [customs union] in respect of trade with contracting parties not parties to such union [...] shall not on the whole be higher or more restrictive than the general incidence of the duties and regulations of commerce applicable in the constituent territories prior to the formation of such union [...].[141]

This prohibits that "overall" third countries do not face higher duties and ORC after establishing a customs union. More specifically, this requires that the internal liberalization and external harmonization do not make third countries face higher duties or more ORCs. The assessment of this requires a two-step approach. The "general incidence" of duties and ORCs prior to the establishment of the union and the applicable harmonised and un-harmonised duties[142] and ORCs after establishing the union must be identified. These are then compared, and the requirement is not fulfilled if the ORCs post-establishment of the union are "on a whole" more restrictive.

Anti-Dumping Prior and After the Establishment of the Customs Union

First, the "general incidence" of duties and ORCs prior to and after the establishment of the customs union must be identified.

Consistent with the classification that only anti-dumping measures are ORCs in the context of Art. XXIV:8(a)(ii) GATT and with the purpose of the assessment to determine restrictive effects which cannot flow from the anti-dumping regulation but

---

[140] See above at section "Substantially all the Trade".

[141] The provision also applies to interim customs unions.

[142] Lockhart and Mitchell (2005), p. 22.

only from the measures, this assessment only considers the anti-dumping measures but not anti-dumping regulation.[143]

The assessment shall be in respect of an "overall assessment of weighted average tariff rates and customs duties collected" which takes place "on a tariff-line basis and in values and quantities".[144] The same problems arise as with regards to the assessment in Art. XXIV:8 (a)(i) GATT: the values and quantities of products as well as the customs duties collected will not be helpful as the purpose of anti-dumping measures is to deter their importation. An assessment on a tariff-line basis is difficult as it does not relate to the value and the importance of the imports. Para. 2 RTA Understanding recognizes that the quantification and aggregation of some measures may be difficult and suggests that "the examination of individual measures, regulations, products covered, and trade flows affected may be required."[145]

Comparison

The duties and ORCs before and after the establishment of the customs union must be compared and they cannot "on the whole" be more restrictive post-establishment of the customs union.

Whereas the MFN requirement does not allow that a more trade restrictive measure is weighed against a more liberalized measure,[146] as the object is to assess "overall"[147] if duties and ORCs have become more restrictive, such a balancing is possible under this provision.

The results of this exercise will not only depend on anti-dumping measures. It is possible that post formation more external anti-dumping measures apply due to "protection diversion",[148] but nothing definitive can be said about the results of this on the overall assessment of whether the customs union complies with Art. XXIV:5(a) GATT.

4.2.2.4 The Measure Is Adopted Upon the Formation of the RTA

All requirements that were considered so far related to the entire customs union and anti-dumping legislation or measures should comply with these requirements so as to not stand in the way of an Art. XXIV:5 GATT defence for a measure that violates provisions of "this Agreement". The second set of requirements focuses on the

---

[143] Similarly, Mitchell and Lockhart (2015), p. 103.

[144] Para. 2 RTA Understanding.

[145] See also above: section "Substantially all the Trade".

[146] *EC - Bananas III* (n 52) para 7.239.

[147] *Turkey - Textiles* (n 94) para 9.121.

[148] See for more detail: Prusa (2016), pp. 139–143; Prusa and Teh (2010); James (2000); Bown et al. (2014); Tabakis and Zanardi (2018).

measures and not on the customs union in general. This means that they must only be fulfilled if anti-dumping regulation violates a WTO obligation.

According to the chapeau of Art. XXIV:5 GATT, the GATT shall not prevent the "formation of a customs union". The Appellate Body in *Turkey – Textiles* has interpreted this to require that Art. XXIV:5 GATT can only justify those measures that have been "introduced upon the formation of a customs union".[149]

Applied literally this is a requirement that refers to the time at which a measure has been introduced. Only if the measure has existed at the time at which the customs union was formed, can it be justified following Art. XXIV:5 GATT. In the context of anti-dumping measures this greatly restricts the Art. XXIV:5 GATT defence seemingly without normative justification. Only where a country challenges anti-dumping regulation *as such* and that anti-dumping regulation has been introduced at the time at which the customs union has been formed, will the justification apply. Any later modifications of the anti-dumping regulation will no longer have been introduced *upon the formation* of the customs union. Moreover, if the regulation is challenged *as applied*, the challenged measure will be the specific anti-dumping measure. Except for transposed anti-dumping measures, all anti-dumping measures will have been introduced after the formation of the customs union and the defence will on the face of it not apply.

To cushion the great limitations the requirement understood in that way brings about, the Panel in *US – Line Pipe* has restricted that requirement in the context of safeguard measures and held that as long as the mechanism for imposing safeguard measures was established on the formation of the RTA, the requirement is fulfilled.[150]

Although the restriction of this requirement is sensible, it is not clear how far reaching this restriction is.[151] If primary law in customs unions merely gives the customs union the competence to adopt anti-dumping regulation, will secondary law introduced after the customs union has already been established have been established "upon the formation" of the customs union? If it does, can the legislators modify the anti-dumping regulation as it will be based on the same title of competences? If those are answered in the affirmative, are changes to the customs union agreement to centralize anti-dumping legislation "upon the formation" of the customs union?

The best view is to answer all of these questions in the affirmative. Art. XXIV:4 GATT recognizes the goal of economic integration which must also require that future improvements of customs unions are possible.[152] If a customs union that is

---

[149] *Turkey - Textiles* (n 83) para 48.

[150] *US - Line Pipe* (n 91) n 128. The finding has been reversed by the AB in this regard. Agreeing with the distinction: Lockhart and Mitchell (2005), p. 7.

[151] Bartels (2005), pp. 712–713.

[152] Pauwelyn (2004), p. 132. To illustrate he gives the example that two States that form an RTA but liberalize all trade except for Bananas. Later on, they decide to liberalize trade in Bananas as well. Because this violates the MFN principle and cannot be justified by Art. XXIV:5 GATT, as it does not happen upon the formation of the RTA, the requirement prohibits later liberalization efforts.

initially imperfect allows internal anti-dumping measures, future integration should be encouraged so that the MFN violation that goes along with the elimination of internal anti-dumping measures can be justified. If the requirement is interpreted in such a way that this is allowed, the purpose and the scope of this requirement become questionable. Ultimately, the temporal interpretation of the terms "for the formation of" adopted in *Turkey – Textiles* should be rejected altogether.[153]

4.2.2.5 The Formation of an RTA Would Be Prevented Were the Measure Disallowed

That the GATT "shall not prevent [. . .] the formation of a customs union" in Art. XXIV:5 GATT has been interpreted by the Appellate Body in *Turkey – Textiles* to include a second requirement as well. The Appellate Body held that Art. XXIV:5 GATT can only be used as a defence to the extent that "the formation of a customs union would be prevented if the introduction of the measure[s] were not allowed".[154]

This seems to require proof of hypothetical negative causality. The Appellate Body demonstrated of what is not sufficient to fulfil this requirement. In *Turkey – Textiles,* Turkey argued that it adopted the same quantitative restrictions as the EC because otherwise the EC would have excluded textile products from the customs union altogether and as these products account for 40% of exports from Turkey to the EC, the customs union would no longer have liberalized substantially all the trade.[155] The Appellate Body did not react to the importance of textiles (for Turkey) for overall internal trade liberalization but held that externally Turkey and the EC could have adopted rules of origins in that sector instead.[156]

Interestingly, neither the Panel Report,[157] nor the Appellate Body Report[158] deal with the question whether the lack of external quantitative restrictions in the area of textiles meant that the customs union did not sufficiently harmonize external trade and thus violate Art. XXIV:8 (a)(ii) GATT. That the alternative is WTO compatible was just assumed. Moreover, considering the political nature of customs union agreements, it is questionable how far the Panels' jurisdiction goes in assessing whether an alternative route could have been pursued.[159] More specifically, it is not clear how important the argument that otherwise an agreement could not have been

---

[153] On an alternative interpretation: Sect. 4.2.2.6).

[154] *Turkey - Textiles* (n 83) para 48.

[155] Ibid. 61.

[156] Ibid. Referring to *Turkey - Textiles* (n 25) para 9.152, which does not deal with Art. XXIV:8 (a) (ii) GATT either.

[157] *Turkey - Textiles* (n 94) para 9.152.

[158] *Turkey - Textiles* (n 83) para 61.

[159] In the case this was not problematic, as the EU and Turkey had agreed that rules of origins apply to the extent that Turkey was unable to replicate the EU's RTAs with third countries, Art. 12 Decision 1/95.

reached is. The reference to the fact that Turkey and the EC had agreed to use rules of origin with respect to other parts of the customs union has been used as evidence that Turkey could have acted differently.[160] Would that outcome have changed if the EC and Turkey had wanted to abolish all rules of origin?[161] The necessity test thus requires a complex balancing of alternative arrangements and their political likelihoods, which is problematic concerning the inherently political nature of RTAs and the fact that justiciability is not clear which can at least be used to argue that Panels should be cautious in how far reaching their hypotheticals are.[162]

These practical and normative difficulties have led the Panel in *US – Line Pipe* to suggest that the necessity test only applies concerning external but not internal requirements. Conveniently, that case concerned an FTA where external trade is not harmonized. The Panel argued that insofar as eliminating duties and ORRCs violate WTO rules, the elimination is always necessary, as it is "the very raison d'être of any [FTA]".[163] To support this finding, some have argued that as Art. XXIV:5 (a) GATT aims to prevent increases in the level of external trade restrictions, it makes sense to impose an additional requirement externally.[164] In contrast, internally the purpose of Art. XXIV GATT is to eliminate internal trade restrictions[165] and the necessity test undermines that purpose, as it will be impossible to liberalize more internal trade than the minimum necessary to eliminate duties and ORRCs on "substantially all the trade".[166]

Although the reasoning to disapply the necessity test is good, the distinction between the internal and external element should be disregarded. Rather, the same objections can be raised externally. In the same way that internal liberalization constitutes the "raison d'être" of an FTA, external harmonization constitutes part of the "raison d'être" of a customs union. Applying the necessity test will only allow external harmonization up to the point that just reaches the "substantially the same" test. Any further harmonization cannot be justified as the customs union would have passed the test in Art. XXIV:8 (a)(ii) GATT.[167] Moreover, it will be impossible to improve a customs union, as any further external harmonization or internal liberalization will not be necessary.[168]

---

[160] *Turkey - Textiles* (n 94) para 9.152.

[161] Similarly: Trachtman (2003), pp. 459, 475.

[162] The Panel Report in *US – Line Pipe* highlights the difficult nature of this in Footnote 137. It gives an example of an FTA that eliminates duties on peanuts but not on cars. It could be argued that eliminating duties on peanuts was not necessary as the duties on cars could have been eliminated instead. They thereby ask the question what role the political process in finding an agreement (here: to eliminate duties on peanuts but not on cars) plays. For an analysis of the legal uncertainties of the test: Bartels (2004b), pp. 269–271.

[163] *US - Line Pipe* (n 91) para 7.148. These findings have been reversed on appeal.

[164] Lockhart and Mitchell (2005), p. 8.

[165] See Preamble, RTA Understanding.

[166] Lockhart and Mitchell (2005), p. 8. For a similar argument, see: Huang (2013), p. 210.

[167] Herrmann et al. (2007) para 626.

[168] Pauwelyn (2004), p. 135.

It is therefore better to disregard this requirement as well. Such a restriction can be justified on the basis that the wording of Art. XXIV:5 GATT does not include a necessity test. The term "the provision in the Agreement shall not prevent . . ." in the chapeau of Art. XXIV:5 GATT can also be interpreted to mean that GATT provisions must be carved out so as to permit the formation of an RTA.[169] That this requirement cannot be read as an additional requirement becomes evident when comparing Art. XXIV:5 GATT to Art. XX (b) GATT.[170] Art. XX (b) GATT states that "nothing in this Agreement shall be construed to prevent the adoption or enforcement [. . .] of measures [. . .] *necessary* to protect human [. . .] health" (emphasis added). Art. XX (b) GATT contains a necessity requirement as the text clearly provides for it. As the text in Art. XXIV:5 GATT does not clearly provide for a necessity requirement, it cannot be assumed.[171]

4.2.2.6   Alternative Requirements

Overall, it is better to drop the additional requirements the Appellate Body developed in *Turkey – Turkey Textiles* and instead adopt a different approach. The recent case *Peru – Agricultural Products* gives the relevant precedent to do that.

In *Peru – Agricultural Products* the Appellate Body considered whether an internal measure that is more instead of less trade restrictive could be justified based on Art. XXIV:5 GATT. Even though much of the Appellate Body report covered more general questions on the interaction of WTO law with other instruments of international law—here: RTAs –, in its *obiter dictum* the Appellate Body subsumed the issues of the case under Art. XXIV GATT and rejected a possible justification following that article. It held that because Art. XXIV:4 GATT requires there to be closer integration between the RTA parties, Art. XXIV:5 GATT cannot be used "as a broad defence for measures in FTAs that 'roll back on Members' rights and obligations under the WTO Agreements."[172]

Commentary on that decision has almost entirely focussed on the parts of the decision that deal with the relationship between WTO law and other international law instruments.[173] The fact that the Appellate Body has to some extend departed from its *Turkey – Textiles* requirements has been overlooked.

---

[169] Ibid. 134.

[170] Ibid.

[171] Ibid.

[172] *Peru - Agricultural Products* (n 26) para 5.116. See also: Joost Pauwelyn, 'Interplay between the WTO Treaty and Other International Legal Instruments and Tribunals: Evolution after 20 Years of WTO Jurisprudence' [2016] SSRN Electronic Journal 23 <http://www.ssrn.com/abstract=2731144> accessed 5 July 2021.

[173] Mathis (2015), p. 97; Shaffer and Winters (2017), p. 303; Tagle and Claros (2016), p. 44; Vidigal (2019), p. 187; Zhang (2016), p. 122; Saggi and Wu (2016), p. 259; Izadnia (2015), p. 727; Shadikhodjaev (2017), p. 109; Zang (2019), p. 33; McRae (2019), p. 1; McRae (2000), p. 27.

To begin, the decision cannot be explained using the *Turkey – Textiles* requirements. The Appellate Body reached its conclusion without explicitly applying the additional requirements. It is also difficult to see how the result could be justified applying those requirements. On the face of it, the PRS system—the measure at issue—was adopted "upon the formation" of the FTA and the conclusion of the FTA would have been prevented had that measure not been included. In *Turkey – Textiles,* the Appellate Body also took political considerations of whether the customs union could also have been formed alternatively into account. In *Peru – Agricultural Products* a finding that the FTA could also have been concluded with different terms would have been difficult. Peru relied on the inclusion of the PRS and upon the challenge of that provision, Peru even refused to put the agreement into force. As the Appellate Body neither engaged with this nor referred to the necessity requirement and addressed a change of it, it is unlikely that the Appellate Body wanted to fit its ruling into the system it developed in *Turkey – Textiles.*

The Appellate Body's approach in that report is best understood in a way that it did not want to specify where its statement fits in systematically but just establish the general rule that Art. XXIV:5 GATT cannot be used to justify a measure that rolls back on the WTO rights of the members of an RTA. Structurally, this means that the Appellate Body established an additional negative requirement that the measure must meet. Whether this applies alongside or instead of the *Turkey – Textiles* requirements is not clear. However, the Appellate Body's complete lack of referral to them may suggest that these requirements will either no longer apply or be applied less restrictively in the future.

Some have concluded that at least where a party to the FTA challenges a measure in that FTA, only the requirements in Art. XXIV:8 GATT must be satisfied and not also the additional *Turkey – Textiles* requirements.[174] This idea has been rejected by some as expanding the scope of the Art. XXIV:5 GATT justification too much.[175] However, whether a party to an FTA or whether a third party requests a Panel should not influence materially what requirements must be fulfilled for a successful defence under Art. XXIV:5 GATT. Moreover, lowering the thresholds to invoke Art. XXIV:5 GATT may not necessarily be bad, as it would reflect the reality that Panels and the Appellate Body are reluctant to rule on the legality of RTAs as such.

Rather, beyond dismissing negatively that the *Turkey – Textiles* requirements should not apply, the Appellate Body has also introduced a negative requirement that must be fulfilled: Art. XXIV:5 GATT cannot be used as a *broad defence* for measures that roll back on members' rights. The Appellate Body did not add specificity answering whether a WTO-minus measure could ever be justified but the qualification that Art. XXIV:5 GATT cannot serve as a *broad defence* suggests that some WTO minus measures are possible.[176]

---

[174] Shaffer and Winters (2017), p. 322.

[175] Zang (2019), p. 54.

[176] Pauwelyn (2016), p. 23.

However, what that means precisely is far from clear. It is best understood in a way that a measure is weighed against the purpose of RTAs as expressed in Art. XXIV:4 GATT. If a measure furthers the aim to facilitate trade, it may be justified and if it does not, Art. XXIV:5 GATT would be used as a broad defence to roll back on members' rights. Customs unions deviations may violate the MFN clause, Art. 14 ADA and Art. 1, 3.1, 4.1 ADA. Beyond that, hypothetical violations for environmental or social reasons are possible.

Most modifications that occur only violate the MFN principle. In that case certain members gain preferential treatment, but no rights of other WTO members are 'rolled back'. Moreover, all RTAs violate the MFN clause in some aspect, so that the exception of Art. XXIV:5 GATT would be void of meaning if a justification fails due to an inherent condition of an RTA. This means in turn that MFN violations may be justified according to Art. XXIV:5 GATT.

The situation is more difficult as regards modifications to Art. 14.4 ADA, however. Usually, Art. 14 ADA does not pose problems as the situation that the country of import and injury do not coincide happens only rarely. If customs unions integrate internally, there is a higher likelihood that the country of import and injury do not coincide. This is because goods are in free circulation. If the customs union is sufficiently integrated, no problems arise, as Art. 4.3 ADA allows investigations to take place on a union wide basis. If investigations are union wide, the fact that the country of import and injury do not coincide will not matter, as the elements are assessed on a union wide basis. It would seem that below union wide investigations WTO law offers no possibilities deal with the increased importance of conducting anti-dumping action on behalf of another customs union member. This is difficult to reconcile with the general aim to incentivize RTAs, Art. XXIV:4 GATT. To not deter the formation of customs union below the level of Art. 4.3 ADA, justifying a violation of Art. 14.4 ADA with Art. XXIV:5 GATT is not a *broad defence* to roll back on members' rights.

A violation of Art. 1 ADA or Art. 3.1, 4.1 ADA cannot be justified accordingly. There is no inherent reason that directly stems from Art. XXIV:4 GATT why the EU and San Marino or Andorra and the SACU members could not have agreed to legally include the territory of San Marino and Andorra on the one hand and to factually consider BLN territories more often. This means that a violation of these provisions cannot be justified according to Art. XXIV:5 GATT.

Finally, the interesting question emerges whether further hypothetical modifications could be justified. Potential examples are provisions that allow the construction of the normal value if one country operates with 'significant market distortions' something that is also influenced by adherence to environmental standards.[177] Even though one could argue that such a modification does not serve the facilitation of trade in a strict sense[178] one could also argue that this creates a level-playing field that is a prerequisite for trade facilitation. Overall, such a measure could be justified.

---

[177] Compare to Art. 2 (6)(a) Reg. (EU) 2016/1036.
[178] Marceau and Wyatt (2010), p. 67, 92, 93.

Besides the requirements directly expressed in *Peru – Agricultural Products,* alternative requirements have been proposed as well.

It has been argued that because Art. XXIV:6 GATT requires compensation where tariff duties have been increased above their bindings following the formation of an RTA, new quantitative restrictions cannot be imposed without compensation following the formation of an RTA.[179] To avoid that, quantitative restrictions are treated differently from tariff duties, this is sensible and should also apply.

Similarly, it has been argued that allowing RTA partners to retain trade remedies internally contradicts the purpose of RTAs to liberalize trade, as expressed in Art. XXIV:4 GATT.[180] This is, however, not necessarily the case. There are good reasons why parties in an RTA may want to keep the possibility to impose anti-dumping measures against each other. Keeping the possibility to impose trade remedy measures may act as a pressure valve that enables the conclusion of the RTA and despite trade liberalization that fulfils the Art. XXIV:8 GATT requirements, there may still be an asymmetric market access that justifies the retention of anti-dumping measures.[181] Retaining trade defence measures does, therefore, not *per se* contradict the purpose of RTAs.

Although the rules that members cannot roll back on their WTO rights and that compensation must be given for increases in quantitative restrictions seem sensible, it is not clear where they fit in structurally. Because the rules derive from Art. XXIV:4 and 6 GATT, these provisions could constitute additional (negative) requirements. This would deviate from the Appellate Body's finding in *Turkey – Textiles* that Art. XXIV:4 GATT is limited to the interpretation of Art. XXIV:5 GATT.[182] Moreover, it is difficult to reconcile this with the operative language of the provision. Alternatively, the phrase "shall not prevent [...] the formation of a customs union or Free Trade Area" in Art. XXIV:5 GATT seems sufficiently vague to allow inclusion of several additional negative requirements.[183]

4.2.2.7 Conclusions

For a successful justification under Art. XXIV:5 GATT, general customs union requirements as well as measure specific requirements must be met. The general customs union requirements must also be met if there is no violation of a WTO provision. No specific requirements relating to anti-dumping regulation emerge from these general requirements. Above that, some measure specific requirements must be met. In the context of anti-dumping, the only relevant requirement is that Art. XXIV:5 GATT cannot be used as a broad defence for measures that roll-back on

---

[179] Pauwelyn (2004), p. 138.

[180] Voon (2010), p. 659.

[181] See above at: Sect. 2.3.

[182] *Turkey - Textiles* (n 83) paras 56, 57.

[183] See also: Pauwelyn (2004), pp. 136–139.

Table 4.2 Justifications following Art. XXIV:5 GATT

	WTO Violation of the measure	General RTA Requirements	Measure Specific Requirements
No modification	Pot. MFN	(+)	+
AD action on behalf of third party	Art. 14 ADA, MFN	(+)	+
Internal modifications			
• Prohibition of internal ADMs	MFN	(+)	+
• Disincentivizing internal ADMs	MFN	(+)	+
• Central IA	Pot. MFN	(+)	+
• Cooperation requirements between MS	Pot. MFN	(+)	+
• Central imposition decision	Pot. MFN	(+)	+
External modifications			
• Central IA	−		
• Cooperation requirements between MS	Pot. MFN	(+)	+
• Central imposition decision	−		
• Union wide Inv. & measure	Pot. Art. 3.1, 4.1 ADA	(+)	−
• MS Inv. & union wide measure	Art. 1 ADA	(+)	−
Further potential modifications			
• Incentivizing ADMs	ADA, MFN	(+)	(+)

member's rights. This is not the case where members deviate from Art. 14.4 ADA or in some cases where environmental or political aims are pursued with anti-dumping measures. Violations of the MFN principle can be justified to the extent that they relate to the distinction between customs union members and non-members.

Table 4.2 summarizes the results for the possible modifications.

4.2.3 Enabling Clause

Violations of WTO provisions can also be justified according to the Enabling Clause.

Para. 1 Enabling Clause provides a general exception to Art. I GATT as "contracting parties may accord differential and more favourable treatment to developing countries, without according such treatment to other contracting parties." Para. 2 (c) Enabling Clause specifies that this refers to "Regional or global arrangements entered into amongst less-developed contracting parties for the mutual reduction or elimination of tariffs and, in accordance with criteria and conditions which may be prescribed by the Contracting Parties, for the mutual reduction or elimination of non-tariff measures, on products imported from one another". According to para. 2 (d) Enabling Clause, this also refers to "[s]pecial treatment on the least developed among the developing countries in the context of any general or specific measures in favour of developing countries". Para. 3 Enabling Clause limits this freedom and specifically Para. 3 (a) Enabling Clause provides that any differential and more favourable treatment "shall be designed to facilitate and promote the trade of developing countries and not to raise barriers to or create undue difficulties for the trade of any other contracting parties".

Although para. 2 (c) and (d) Enabling Clause are justifications for certain violations, their scope is limited to violations of Art. I GATT (under Sect. 4.2.3.1). The justifications differ in their requirements.

Para. 2 (c) has several requirements, three of which relate to the entire RTA and one relates to the measure that must be justified. First, para. 2 (c) Enabling Clause is limited to arrangements between less-developed countries (under Sect. 4.2.3.2); second, the arrangement must meet the requirements concerning the reduction of tariffs and non-tariff measures (under Sect. 4.2.3.3); third, the specific requirement of para. 3 (a) Enabling Clause must be met (under Sect. 4.2.3.4). Above these codified requirements, the Appellate Body has introduced the requirement that there must be a genuine link between the measure and the arrangement, the only requirement that relates to the measure and not the entire RTA (under Sect. 4.2.3.5).

Para. 2 (d) applies to arrangements between the least developed countries (LDCs) (under Sect. 4.2.3.2). They must also meet the requirement of para. 3 (a) Enabling clause (under Sect. 4.2.3.4) and the Appellate Body's requirement that there must be a genuine link between the measure and the arrangement (under Sect. 4.2.3.5).

Procedurally, some specifics exist with regards to this justification. The Appellate Body in *EC – Tariff Preferences* noted that the justification according to Para. 2 (a) Enabling Clause is not a "typical 'exception', or 'defence' in the style of Article XX of the GATT 1994 or other exception provisions."[184] Usually defences are raised by the defending party. The Enabling Clause is an exception to this as the complaining party must already identify and notify the parties and third parties in its panel request of the relevant provisions in the Enabling Clause it sees violated, even before the defending party raises the defence.[185] This has, however, no impact on the burden of proof. The defending party must still prove consistency with the Enabling Clause.[186]

The Appellate Body in *Brazil – Taxation* further clarified this duty and recognised that it also applies in the context of Para. 2 (c) Enabling Clause. A complaining party is only required to raise the Enabling Clause and identify the relevant requirements it sees not met in its panel request if a measure according differential and more

---

[184] *EC - Tariff Preferences* (n 70) paras 106, 110.

[185] Ibid. 113.

[186] Ibid. 114.

favourable treatment is: (1) plainly taken pursuant to the Enabling Clause, or if it is clear from the face of the measure itself that it has been adopted pursuant to the Enabling Clause; and/or (2) notified pursuant to paragraph 4 (a) of the Enabling Clause.[187]

These requirements are usually met where the customs unions legislate in matters of anti-dumping: even if anti-dumping measures are adopted by national authorities based on national legislation it is clear that the national legislation implements the customs union agreement. Only where the customs union agreement is silent to the possibility of imposing anti-dumping measures, is this requirement not fulfilled.

This means that if a member challenges anti-dumping measures or legislation by a customs union which has been notified under Para. 4 (a) Enabling Clause, it must notify the other parties of the relevant provisions of the Enabling Clause it believes are not fulfilled. Currently the following customs unions are notified under Para. 4 (a) Enabling Clause: CAN, COMESA, EAC, CEMAC, MERCOSUR, and WAEMU.[188]

4.2.3.1   Scope of the Justification

According to Para. 1 Enabling Clause: "notwithstanding the provisions of Article I [GATT], contracting parties may accord differential and more favourable treatment to developing countries, without according such treatment to other contracting parties." Thus, on the face of it, the Enabling Clause only justifies violations of the MFN principle.[189] This raises the question whether other violations of the GATT or of other covered agreements can be justified by the clause as well. In the context of anti-dumping measures, it specifically raises the question whether violations of Art. VI GATT or the ADA can be justified.

The starting point of this interpretation is the text. Para. 1 Enabling Clause is relatively straight forward and seems to leave little ambiguity as to its scope being limited to violations of Art. I GATT.

Nevertheless, this issue arose in the CTD after the members of the GCC, which was initially notified under Art. XXIV:7 (a) GATT,[190] changed its notification to one under para. 4 (a) Enabling Clause.[191] Specifically, the US and EC remarked that the Enabling Clause could only justify violations of Art. I GATT. Because the tariff

---

[187] *Brazil — Taxation (Japan)* (n 76) para 5.365.

[188] WTO RTA Database (https://rtais.wto.org/; last accessed: 5 July 2021).

[189] *EC - Tariff Preferences* (n 70) para 90.

[190] Committee on Regional Trade Agreements, 'Gulf Cooperation Council Customs Union, Notification from Saudi Arabia', WT/REG222/N/1, 20.11.2006.

[191] Committee on Regional Trade Agreements, 'Gulf Cooperation Council Customs Union, Notification from Saudi Arabia, Corrigendum', WT/REG222/N/1/Corr. 1, 31.3.2008; Committee on Trade and Development, 'Notification of Regional Trade Agreement, Gulf Cooperation Council', WT/COMTD/N/25, 31.3.2008. Later the members of the GCC notified the customs union again under Art. XXIV:7 (a) GATT: Committee on Regional Trade Agreements, 'Notification of

bindings of some members of the GCC were below the external tariffs as applied by the GCC, this violated Art. II GATT and Para. 2 (c) Enabling Clause could not justify a violation thereof.[192] The procedure of Art. XXIV:6 GATT could be subverted if para. 2 (c) Enabling Clause constituted a justification for this violation.[193] The same argument applies to justifications according to para. 2 (d) Enabling Clause.

Although the premise of the argument—that a notification under Para. 4 (a) Enabling Clause bars the application of Art. XXIV:5 GATT outside the scope of it—is not necessarily correct,[194] the observation related to the scope of para. 1 Enabling Clause is good. Further arguments also speak in favour of limiting the scope of the justification to Art. I GATT. Whereas Art. XXIV:5 GATT includes additional requirements, namely that the measure is adopted upon the formation of an RTA, such requirements do not exist in the context of the Enabling Clause. The purpose of these additional requirements is to limit the freedom of the contracting parties, ultimately recognizing the ambivalent nature of RTAs and the necessity to distinguish between welfare enhancing and welfare reducing RTAs.

Therefore, the scope of a justification pursuant to the Enabling Clause is limited to violations of Art. I GATT. This means that modifications of Art. 14 ADA and violations of Art. 1 ADA cannot be justified via the Enabling Clause.

As the scope of the Enabling Clause is narrower than Art. XXIV:5 GATT, the logical follow-up question is what the relationship between the Enabling Clause and Art. XXIV:5 GATT is. Although the EU's and US' arguments why the GCC could not change the provision under which it was notified presumed that Art. XXIV:5 GATT could not supplement the Enabling Clause, no arguments related specifically to why that should not be possible were brought forward.

Applying general principles, the better view is that Art. XXIV:5 GATT applies insofar as the Enabling Clause does not apply. The Secretariat argued in its legal note on RTAs under the Enabling Clause that Para. 2 (c) and (d) Enabling Clause are *lex specialis* to the justification of Art. XXIV:5 GATT.[195] As the scope of the Enabling Clause is limited to violations of Art. I GATT for other violations than Art. I GATT,

---

Regional Trade Agreement, Gulf Cooperation Council, Revision', WT/REG276/N/1/Rev.1, 17.11.2009.

[192] Committee on Trade and Development, 'Gulf Cooperation Council Customs Union – Saudi Arabia's Notification (WT/COMTD/N/25), Communication from the United States, Addendum', WT/COMTD/66/Add.1, 24.11.2008, para. 4–5.

[193] Committee on Trade and Development, 'Gulf Cooperation Council Customs Union – Saudi Arabia's Notification (WT/COMTD/N/25), Communication from the European Communities, Addendum', WT/COMTD/66/Add.2, 25.11.2008, para. 6–7.

[194] Committee on Trade and Development, 'Gulf Cooperation Council Customs Union – Saudi Arabia's Notification (WT/COMTD/N/25), Communication from Bahrain, the United Arab Emirates, Saudi Arabia, Oman, Qatar and Kuwait, Addendum', WT/COMTD/66/Add.3, 5.12.2008, para. 10–11.

[195] Committee on Trade and Development, 'Legal Note on Regional Trade Arrangements under the Enabling Clause, Note by the Secretariat', WT/COMTD/W/114, 13.5.2003, para. 5.

the provisions do not cover the same subject matter. Moreover, the purpose of the Enabling Clause is to encourage regional trade amongst developing and least-developed countries and not make it more difficult to justify. Accordingly, the Enabling Clause is only *lex specialis* within its limited scope. Therefore, Art. XXIV:5 GATT applies to cases not within the scope of the Enabling Clause.[196] This also corresponds with the practice under the GATT 1947 as following the notification of MERCOSUR the terms of reference of the CTD stated that it should "examine [MERCOSUR] in the light of the relevant provisions of the Enabling Clause and the GATT 1994, including Article XXIV."[197] This means that any violation of Art. I GATT can be justified by the Enabling Clause and other violations can be justified according to Art. XXIV:5 GATT.

4.2.3.2 Developing Countries

Para. 2 (c) Enabling Clause only applies to regional or global arrangements entered into amongst *less-developed contracting parties*. These are categorized into least developed countries (LDCs) and developing countries.

LDCs are those countries that have been identified by the UN as such.[198] Developing countries are defined on a self-election principle. In the DSB upon adoption of the Appellate Body Report in *Korea – Various Measures on Beef*,[199] the EC noted that it disagreed with South Korea's self-characterization as a developing country in the context of the Agreement on Agriculture.[200] Although the EC's remark had no impact on the substance of the case, this highlights that self-characterization may lead to controversial results and it is not clear if the self-election may be challenged.

All members of the regional or global arrangement must be LDCs or developing countries.

Para. 2 (d) Enabling Clause applies to arrangements amongst LDCs. All members of the arrangement must be LDCs. Beyond that, no specific requirements exist apart from the general limitation contained in para. 3 (a) Enabling Clause. This means that

---

[196]For the *lex specialis* Principle to apply, the two provisions must cover the same subject matter: *Indonesia - Auto* (n 30) n 168. If Para. 2 (c) Enabling Clause is limited to providing an exception to violations of Art. I GATT and Art. XXIV:5 GATT provides a justification for all GATT violations, the provisions do not cover the same subject matter for violations other than Art. I GATT. See also: Jalal Alavi (2011), pp. 26–28 <http://www.ssrn.com/abstract=1737233> accessed 5 July 2021.

[197]Committee on Trade and Development, 'Third (Special) Session, Note of the Meeting of 14 September 1995', WT/COMTD/M/3, 23.10.1995, p. 1.

[198]https://www.un.org/development/desa/dpad/wp-content/uploads/sites/45/publication/ldc_list. pdf (last accessed: 24.08.2021).

[199]*Korea - Measures Affecting Imports of Fresh, Chilled and Frozen Beef* [2000] WTO Appellate Body Report WT/DS161/AB/R; WT/DS169/AB/R.

[200]Dispute Settlement Body, 'Minutes of the Meeting, Held in the Centre William Rappard on 10 January 2001', WT/DSB/M/96, 22.2.2001, para. 14.

any customs union amongst LDCs can be subsumed under para. 2 (d) Enabling Clause.

4.2.3.3 Regional or Global Arrangements

Substantively, para. 2 (c) Enabling Clause applies to

> regional or global arrangements [...] for the mutual reduction or elimination of tariffs and, in accordance with criteria or conditions which may be prescribed by the contracting parties, for the mutual reduction or elimination of non-tariff measures, on products imported from one another.

This sets out internal liberalization requirements whereby the degree of required liberalization differs between tariffs and non-tariff measures. Tariffs must be mutually reduced or eliminated whereas non-tariff measures must be reduced or eliminated in accordance with criteria and conditions prescribed by the contracting parties. There are no external requirements.

Anti-dumping measures as well as anti-dumping regulation are tariff measures.[201] They must be reduced or eliminated internally or if other tariff measures are reduced or eliminated internally, they may remain the same. Compared to Art. XXIV:8 GATT, there is no requirement concerning the degree to which tariff measures must be eliminated and consequently there are no limits on the extent to which anti-dumping legislation is modified.

Para. 2 (c) Enabling Clause is relatively imprecise as to which level of regional economic integration it envisages. This has led to two special problems which raise the question whether para. 2 (c) Enabling Clause contains a ceiling on the level of regional integration it allows: (1) Can non-tariff measures be eliminated even without the WTO members having set the necessary criteria or conditions and (2) may arrangements go beyond internal trade liberalization and also harmonize trade externally, i.e. does Para. 2 (c) Enabling Clause apply to customs unions?

Non-Tariff Measures

If the arrangement also reduces or eliminates non-tariff measures but no criteria or conditions have been set by the WTO members—which is currently the case—, this may stand in the way of a justification following the Enabling Clause. More specifically, the question is whether non-tariff measures can be liberalized even without WTO members having set the conditions for that. The legal note issued by

---

[201] Estrella and Horlick argue that anti-dumping measures are not duties within the meaning of Art. XXIV:8 GATT. Estrella and Horlick (2009), p. 917. "Tariff measure" does not appear in the GATT and must be interpreted in its context. It is best understood to at least encompass the measures in Art. II GATT, which specifically refers to anti-dumping measures in Art. II:2 (b) GATT. Moreover, as it refers to "measures", it applies to anti-dumping regulation *as such* and *as applied*.

the Secretariat concerning RTAs under the Enabling Clause already identified this issue but explicitly did not answer it.[202] This question became relevant when the members of the GCC changed the notification from Art. XXIV:7 (a) GATT to one under para. 4 (a) Enabling Clause. The EC argued that a change of the provision under which notification takes place is not possible as the Enabling Clause could not be invoked for any arrangement that not only eliminates tariff but also non-tariff measures. Non-tariff measures could only be eliminated insofar as the contracting parties provide conditions and criteria for their elimination. The EC argued that above that the situation is like for general systems of preferences (GSPs) under para. 2 (a) Enabling Clause, where Panels have accepted that they cannot eliminate non-tariff measures.[203] Following that view, arrangements would have to be justified following Art. XXIV:5 GATT. The GCC members rejected this argumentation as the cited case only dealt with GSPs which are dealt with under para. 2 (a) Enabling Clause. Moreover, the language in para. 2 (c) Enabling Clause does not require conditions to be set but merely provides for that possibility.[204]

Nevertheless, the question remains unresolved, and China, Egypt and India identified this question as one of the systemic concerns concerning the Enabling Clause which they wanted to discuss and resolve.[205] These concerns were discussed in nearly every CTD Meeting between 2008 and 2020,[206] and Art. 28 of the Nairobi Ministerial Declaration[207] requested the CRTA to discuss the "systemic implications of RTAs for the multilateral trading system and their relationship with WTO rules." This includes the discussion of the systemic questions concerning the Enabling Clause.[208]

---

[202] Committee on Trade and Development, 'Legal Note on Regional Trade Arrangements under the Enabling Clause, Note by the Secretariat', WT/COMTD/W/114, 13.5.2003, para. 53 (b).

[203] Committee on Trade and Development, 'Gulf Cooperation Council Customs Union – Saudi Arabia's Notification (WT/COMTD/N/25), Communication from the European Communities, Addendum', WT/COMTD/66/Add.2, 25.11.2008, para. 5. Referring to *United States - Denial of Most-Favoured Nation Treatment as to Non-Rubber Footwear from Brazil* [1992] GATT 1994 Panel Report DS18/R - 39S/128 [6.15]. The Panel stated "it was clear that the Enabling Clause expressly limits the preferential treatment accorded by contracting parties in favour of developing contracting parties under the GSP to tariff preferences only".

[204] Committee on Trade and Development, 'Gulf Cooperation Council Customs Union – Saudi Arabia's Notification (WT/COMTD/N/25), Communication from Bahrain, the United Arab Emirates, Saudi Arabia, Oman, Qatar and Kuwait, Addendum', WT/COMTD/66/Add.3, 5.12.2008.

[205] Committee on Trade and Development, 'Systematic and Specific Issues Arising out of the Dual Notification of the Gulf Cooperation Council Customs Union, Communication from China, Egypt and India', WT/COMTD/W/175, 30.9.2010, p. 2.

[206] See WTO Documents: WT/COMTD/M/67- WT/COMTD/M/109.

[207] Ministerial Conference, 'Tenth Session, Nairobi, 15–18 December 2015, Nairobi Ministerial Declaration, Adopted on 19. December 2015', WT/MIN(15)/DEC, 21.12.2015.

[208] For this view, see: e.g. Committee on Trade and Development, 'Note on the Meeting of 15 November 2017', WT/COMTD/M/104, 19.3.2018, para. 63.

In the CTD disagreement still exists as to whether these issues could be discussed in that forum.[209] In the meetings on the CRTA, although a systemic discussion was whished for by the members of the Committee, the number of topics that should be discussed were vast[210] and the members were not able to agree on a procedure.[211] The Chairman ultimately concluded that the members would not be able to agree on parameters to conduct such discussions.[212] After a failed attempt to first decide on the right format with the members informally,[213] the Chairman took the item off the agenda.[214] Although a Draft Ministerial Decision was proposed in the following Ministerial Conference in Buenos Aires,[215] it was not adopted.

Absent agreement by the WTO members, the general rules of interpretation apply. Para. 2 (c) Enabling Clause gives WTO members the discretion to prescribe criteria and conditions for the reduction or elimination of non-tariff measures but does not regulate the consequence of not making use of that discretion. The aim of these arrangements is to "facilitate and promote the trade of developing countries."[216] Of course like any other RTA, these arrangements are not unambiguously good because negative effects of trade diversion may outweigh the positive trade creating effects. As the WTO members have a mandate to avoid these negative effects by adopting criteria and conditions with the aim to delineate between welfare enhancing and welfare reducing reductions of non-tariff measures, the absence of that action should not negatively impact the freedom of developing countries that want to conclude RTAs. On the contrary, the aim to facilitate and promote trade of

---

[209] Committee on Trade and Development, 'Note on the Meeting of 5 April 2019', WT/COMTD/M/108, 21.6.2019, para. 71–75; Committee on Trade and Development, 'Note on the Meeting of 28 June 2019', WT/COMTD/M/109, 8.11.2019, para. 59–64.

[210] Members wanted to discuss, e.g. electronic commerce, rules of origin, TBT, SPS, fisheries subsidies. See: Committee on Regional Trade Agreements, 'Note on the Meeting of 27 June 2016', WT/REG/M/81, 12.7.2016, para. 1.48.

[211] Committee on Regional Trade Agreements, 'Note on the Meeting of 27 June 2016', WT/REG/M/81, 12.7.2016, para. 1.47; Committee on Regional Trade Agreements, 'Note on the Meeting of 27 September 2016', WT/REG/M/82, 4.11.2016, para. 1.29.

[212] Committee on Regional Trade Agreements, 'Note on the Meeting of 7–8 November 2016', WT/REG/M/83, 7.12.2016, para. 1.116.

[213] Committee on Regional Trade Agreements, 'Note on the Meeting of 9–10 November 2017', WT/REG/M/87, 5.12.2017, para. 1.40.

[214] Committee on Regional Trade Agreements, 'Note on the Meeting of 19–20 June 2018', WT/REG/M/89, 25.6.2018, para. 1.38.

[215] Ministerial Conference, 'Eleventh Session, Buenos Aires, 10–13 December 2017, Draft Ministerial Decision on Improvement of Transparency for Regional Trade Agreements, Communication from the Russian Federation', WT/MIN(17)/28, 8.12.2017.

[216] Para. 3 Enabling Clause. The Secretariat is of the opinion that this requirement is more stringent compared to Art. XXIV:4 GATT according to which RTAs should (instead of shall) facilitate trade between the constituent territories, Committee on Trade and Development, Legal Note on Regional Trade Arrangements under the Enabling Clause, Note by the Secretariat, WT/COMTD/W/114, 13.5.2003, para. 53.

developing countries is better achieved by deeper forms of integration which require the elimination of non-tariff measures as well.

Customs Unions

Para. 2 (c) Enabling Clause does not contain external requirements. This raises the question if external harmonization bars Para. 2 (c) Enabling Clause.

The absence of specific regulation on external requirements could be used to argue that Para. 2 (c) Enabling Clause does not justify MFN violations of customs unions, as advocated by the EU in CTD meetings.[217] However, Para. 18 Transparency Mechanism requires that the CTD should examine "RTAs" falling under Para. 2 (c) Enabling Clause. RTAs are "trade agreements of a mutually preferential nature",[218] which includes FTAs and customs unions.[219] Moreover, the practice of WTO members which have notified several customs unions under the Enabling Clause also confirms this.[220] More fundamentally, the same arguments can be made as regards the question whether non-tariff measures can be liberalized in these arrangements. WTO law encourages trade liberalization and there is no reason why too much liberalization should result in the justification under Para. 2 (c) Enabling Clause not applying any longer.

To conclude, Para. 2 (c) Enabling Clause applies to customs unions that liberalize tariff and non-tariff measures. It does not include requirements as to the level of liberalization or harmonization expected. Therefore, no limits as regard to possible modifications of anti-dumping measures emerge.

4.2.3.4   Para. 3 Enabling Clause

According to Para. 3 (a) Enabling Clause, any more favourable treatment provided under this clause "shall be designed to facilitate and promote the trade of developing countries and not to raise barriers to or create undue difficulties for the trade of any other contracting parties". This applies to arrangements under para. 2 (c) and 2 (d) Enabling Clause.

---

[217]E.g. Committee on Trade and Development, 'Note on the Meeting of 15 November 2017', WT/COMTD/M/104, 19.3.2018, para. 63; Committee on Trade and Development, 'Note on the Meeting of 28 June 2019', WT/COMTD/M/109, 8.11.2019, para. 61.

[218]Third preambular paragraph Transparency Mechanism.

[219]Committee on Trade and Development, 'Gulf Cooperation Council Customs Union – Saudi Arabia's Notification (WT/COMTD/N/25), Communication from Bahrain, the United Arab Emirates, Saudi Arabia, Oman, Qatar and Kuwait, Addendum', WT/COMTD/66/Add.3, 5.12.2008, para. 10.

[220]For a similar result, see: Lissel (2015), p. 122 <https://www.tralac.org/publications/article/8273-safeguard-measures-in-multilateral-and-regional-trade-agreements.html> accessed 5 July 2021.

This has been interpreted in the CTD by the US as constituting a threshold requirement for RTAs.[221] Such a view should be rejected, as even if trade is only liberalized to a small degree, it can be designed to facilitate and promote the trade of developing countries. Rather, Para. 3 Enabling Clause resembles Art. XXIV: 5 (a), (b) GATT, but does not include the same specificity of requirements. Regardless of the interpretation, no limitations with regards to anti-dumping regulations flow from this, however.

4.2.3.5 Genuine Link

The Appellate Body in *Brazil – Taxation* introduced the additional criterion that a measure can only be justified by the Enabling Clause if that measure "has a 'genuine' link or a rational connection with the regional or global arrangement adopted and notified to the WTO."[222]

This requirement also exists for justifications according to Art. XXIV:5 GATT.[223] Because customs union agreements or secondary legislation contain specific rules on the imposition of anti-dumping measures, laying out procedural as well as substantive requirements, there will always be a genuine link to the customs union agreements insofar as they have legislated on the issue.

4.2.3.6 Conclusion

The scope of the Enabling Clause is narrower than Art. XXIV:5 GATT and the requirements are less strict as well. The Enabling Clause only applies to customs unions of developing countries (para. 2 (c) Enabling Clause) and of least-developed countries (para. 2 (d) Enabling Clause) and only justifies violations of Art. I GATT. Within the scope of para. 2 (c) Enabling Clause, the three requirements of the justification constitute a low burden to fulfil, so that no modification to anti-dumping legislation will *per se* not be covered by this. The measure specific requirements are always fulfilled if customs unions have legislated on anti-dumping. The burden is even lower for customs unions between LDCs, which will virtually always be justified (para. 2 (d) Enabling Clause).

---

[221] E.g. Committee on Trade and Development, 'Dedicated Session on Regional Trade Agreements, Preferential Trade Agreement Between Chile and India (Goods), Questions and Replies', WT/COMTD/RTA/4/2, 4.5.2010; Committee on Trade and Development, 'Dedicated Session on Regional Trade Agreements, Preferential Trade Agreement Between Chile and India (Goods), Questions and Replies', WT/COMTD/RTA/4/3, 26.7.2010, where the US questioned whether this requirement was met as the FTA between Chile and India was of a severely limited scope.

[222] *Brazil — Taxation (Japan)* (n 76) para 5.434.

[223] See above: Sect. 4.2.2.1.

Table 4.3 Justification following the enabling clause

	Justification Following para. 2 (c), (d) Enabling Clause			
	WTO Violation of the measure	Within Scope of the Justification	General RTA Requirements	Measure Specific Requirement
No modification	Pot. MFN	+	(+)	+
AD action on behalf of third party	Art. 14 ADA, MFN	−		
Internal modifications				
• Prohibition of internal ADMs	MFN	+	(+)	+
• Disincentivizing internal ADMs	MFN	+	(+)	+
• Central IA	Pot. MFN	+	(+)	+
• Cooperation requirements between MS	Pot. MFN	+	(+)	+
• Central imposition decision	Pot. MFN	+	(+)	+
External modifications				
• Central IA	−			
• Cooperation requirements between MS	Pot. MFN	+	(+)	+
• Central imposition decision	−			
• Union wide Inv. & measure	Pot. Art. 3.1, 4.1 ADA	−		
• MS Inv. & union wide measure	Art. 1 ADA	−		
Further potential modifications				
• Incentivizing ADMs	ADA, MFN	−		

Table 4.3 summarizes the results. As no differences exist concerning anti-dumping measures, no distinction between para. 2 (c) and (d) Enabling Clause occurs.

4.3 Justification According to the RTA: Resolving the Conflict of Laws

Only if the violations of WTO provisions cannot be justified according to Art. XXIV:5 GATT or the Enabling Clause, is WTO law violated.[224] In that case, there is a conflict of laws between the WTO Agreement and the Agreement of the customs union. This is because parties subject to the customs union agreement are internationally bound to obey the customs union agreement as well as the WTO Agreements. In doing so, they necessarily violate one obligation.[225] Various interesting questions arise but for this study only the question how the WTO's DSB resolves that conflict of laws is relevant. Although the conflict of laws may also become relevant in the customs unions dispute settlement systems, because these systems vary so greatly, they will not be considered further.[226]

Resolving this conflict may depend on who brings the claim before the DSB. In most cases third parties will bring a claim and argue that a specific provision in the RTA violates a WTO obligation of a WTO member that concluded the RTA. The responding party cannot use the RTA as a defence. Otherwise, an agreement to which the claimant is not part could diminish its WTO rights (under Sect. 4.3.1). If a member of the RTA brings a claim against another member of the RTA in the WTO's DSB, the RTA may potentially be used as a defence, however (under Sect. 4.3.2).

4.3.1 Third Party Claims

If a third party brings a claim in the DSB against the customs union or a member thereof, that member of the customs union cannot defend itself by arguing that the customs union agreement justifies the action.

Otherwise, the DSB would not "serve to preserve the rights and obligations of members under the *covered agreements*"[227] and would "diminish the rights [. . .] provided in the *covered agreements*".[228] This is also reflected in international law by the general conflict rule in Art. 30 (4)(b) VCLT according to which the treaty to which both are a party to (i.e. the WTO Agreement and not the customs union agreement to which only the defendant is a party) defines their relationship.

---

[224] On the interpretation that Art. XXIV:5 GATT is not a conflict rule but provides an exception: Mitchell et al. (2015), p. 134.

[225] Nele Matz-Lück, 'Treaties, Conflicts Between', *Max Planck Encyclopedia of Public International Law [MPEPIL]* (2010) para 5 <https://opil.ouplaw.com/view/10.1093/law:epil/9780199231690/law-9780199231690-e1485> accessed 5 July 2021.

[226] E.g. for the EU: Pickett and Lux (2016), p. 408.

[227] Art. 3.2 DSU.

[228] Art. 19.2 DSU.

Moreover, this is also reflected in the general principle that third parties' rights cannot be diminished without their consent in a treaty to which they are not a member.[229]

4.3.2   Claims by Members of the Customs Union

The situation is different if a member of the customs union challenges a measure. Even though this constellation has been at issue in *Peru—Agricultural Products* with respect to an FTA, cases concerning anti-dumping measures will be rare, making this only a hypothetical. A situation is imaginable in which a customs union makes the imposition of anti-dumping measures easier to combat asymmetric market access or to use anti-dumping measures as a tool against environmental or social dumping. This would violate the respective provisions of Art. VI GATT and the ADA. Only insofar as it cannot be justified according to Art. XXIV:5 GATT, a conflict of laws arises, raising the question whether the customs union agreement can serve as a justification.

Although claims can only be brought under the covered agreements, i.e. no claim can be brought directly under the customs union agreement,[230] the customs union agreement could potentially influence the WTO rights and obligations of the members to the agreement in different ways.[231] The customs union agreement may mean that bringing a claim against a provision agreed upon in that agreement before the DSB violates the good faith requirement in Art. 3.7 DSU[232] or that the WTO rights and obligations have been modified between the parties to the agreement.[233] Above that, other influences of the agreement on WTO rights and obligations are possible.[234]

---

[229] Art. 34 VCLT.

[230] Art. 3.2 DSU.

[231] The Appellate Body did not answer the preliminary question Guatemala raised, whether the Panel could consider other law than the covered Agreements, *Peru - Agricultural Products* (n 26) para 7.53, 7.511. This is, however, disputed. Arguing Against: Bartels (2014) 59/2014 16; Mavroidis (2008), p. 421; Bartels (2017). Arguing For: Pauwelyn (2003), pp. 460–466; Pauwelyn and Salles (2009), p. 77.

[232] *Peru - Agricultural Products* (n 26) para 5.28–5.28. Criticizing the requirements: Shaffer and Winters (2017), pp. 318–319. For comments see also: Mathis (2015), p. 99.

[233] Holding that Art. 41 VCLT does not apply due to the *lex specialis* provisions in Art. IX, X WTO Agreement: *Peru - Agricultural Products* (n 26) para 5.112. For criticism: Zang (2019), p. 53; Shaffer and Winters (2017), p. 320; Tagle and Claros (2016), pp. 26–27.

[234] The relationship to Art. 20, 45 ARSIWA is not clear. For an overview of how FTAs may impact WTO rights and obligations, see: Pauwelyn (2016), pp. 20–25; Pauwelyn (2014) <https://ielp.worldtradelaw.net/2014/12/waiving-wto-rights-in-an-fta-panel-report-on-peru-agricultural-products.html> accessed 5 July 2021. For a discussion of other ways in which rights to establish a Panel could have been relinquished or why the FTA could not influence the interpretation of WTO obligations, see generally: *Peru - Agricultural Products* (n 26).

The issues this raises are diverse but because of the limited practical relevance for the context of anti-dumping, the issues will not be discussed in this study.

4.4 Customs Unions with Non-WTO Members

The legal analysis so far has only considered customs unions where all of its members are WTO members as well. Although the WTO has 164 members that comprise 98% of international trade,[235] this leaves 31 countries that are not WTO members.

If a customs union only comprises non-WTO members, no WTO related problems arise, as neither is bound by the WTO Agreements. However, the situation is different if only some members of the customs union are WTO members as well. The core of the difficulties is that those customs unions members that are WTO members as well are bound by WTO law whereas non-WTO members are not. Only WTO law violations by WTO members are thus legally relevant. In practice the EU-San Marino and EU-Andorra customs unions as well as CARICOM, COMESA, CEMAC, ECOWAS, and EAEU are customs unions that include WTO members and non-WTO members.

As the members of the customs union that are WTO members as well are bound by WTO law, the same questions arise as with customs unions that only have WTO members: (1) does the customs union violate WTO provisions and (2) can they be justified? Specific issues arise in both dimensions.

Concerning the first question—whether a customs union arrangement violates WTO provisions—the following differences arise: The MFN obligation partially also applies against non-WTO members. Whereas it is possible to grant non-members less favourable treatment, it is not possible to treat them more favourably. Art. I:1 GATT holds that any "advantage favour, privilege or immunity granted by any contracting party to any product originating in or destined *for any other country*" shall be accorded to the like product originating in "the territories of all other *contracting parties*". The fact that Art. I:1 GATT distinguishes between *contracting party* and *any other country* can only be intentional. This means that the contracting parties cannot be treated less favourably than non-WTO members.[236] Art. I:1 GATT does not grant non-WTO members rights, as they could not invoke them anyway, since they cannot initiate disputes in the DSB.

The same principle applies concerning the requirements contained in the ADA. The relevant provisions that may be breached are Art. 14 ADA if customs unions allow anti-dumping action on behalf of third parties without the approval of the

---

[235] 'What Is the WTO?' (*WTO.org*) <https://www.wto.org/english/thewto_e/thewto_e.htm> accessed 5 July 2021.

[236] Choi (2005), pp. 825, 828–830.

WTO's Council for Trade in Goods[237] or Art. 9.2, 3.1, 4.1 ADA if the scope of investigation does not legally or factually correspond to the scope of the measure.[238] Art. 14.1 ADA applies to anti-dumping action on behalf of a "third country" and not a third members. Similarly, Art. 9.2 ADA requires that the anti-dumping duty be imposed against "all sources" and not just those sources of WTO members. Similar extensive language can be found in Art. 3.1, 4.1 ADA. Because the ADA limits some provisions to WTO members, such as Art. 15 ADA, according to which special regard must be given to developing country members, other provisions also apply against non-WTO members. This means that WTO members have a claim if they are treated less favourably than non-WTO members, but non-WTO members do not have a claim, as they cannot even participate in the DSB.

However, as non-WTO members are not bound by the WTO Agreements, a distinction must be made of who violates WTO provisions. On the face of it, the anti-dumping regime in the EU-Andorra and EU-San Marino customs unions violate Art. 1 ADA. Anti-dumping measures apply to imports into Andorra or San Marino, without the investigation considering them, potentially violating Art. 9.2 ADA. Nevertheless, this is not problematic. The EU does not violate its WTO obligations as it fulfils its duties under the ADA and Andorra and San Marino are not bound by the WTO Agreements, so that Art. 1 ADA does not apply against them. The EU-Andorra or EU-San Marino customs unions are not WTO members so that any potential violation of the WTO Agreements by it—presuming it has international legal personality—is not relevant either.

Like RTAs between WTO members, customs unions violate at least the MFN principle and therefore need to be justified. The two possible justifications are those contained in Art. XXIV GATT and the Enabling Clause.

Whether Art. XXIV:5 GATT applies also to RTAs between WTO members and non-members is contentious. Those that argue that they do not highlight that Art. XXIV:5 applies to RTAs "as between the territories of contracting parties" and not "as between states" and that RTAs between members and non-members are possible through a waiver in Art. XXIV:10 GATT.[239]

Others highlight that the practice among WTO members suggests that there is no membership requirement for Art. XXIV:5 GATT to apply. Art. XXIV:10 GATT has only been invoked twice—in the 50s, despite there being numerous RTAs between members and non-members. 57 RTAs notified to the WTO include non-WTO members and the EU alone has 11 RTAs with non-members.[240]

The situation is similar concerning the Enabling Clause. Some argue that para. 2 (c) Enabling Clause cannot be used to justify a violation of the MFN principle as para. 2(c) Enabling Clause applies to "less-developed *contracting parties*".[241]

[237] See above at: Sect. 4.1.1.4.

[238] See above at: Sect. 4.1.1.2.

[239] Choi (2005); Devuyst and Serdarevic (2007), p. 21 ff.; Islam and Alam (2009), p. 1, 29 ff.

[240] Mossner (2014), pp. 633, 635–641.

[241] Choi (2005), pp. 851–852.

However, RTAs amongst LDCs can be justified following para. 2(d) Enabling Clause, as it applies to "the least developed among developing countries" and not just contracting parties.[242] Others argue that the purpose of para. 2(c) Enabling Clause to allow differential treatment of developing countries is better served through a wide interpretation of the clause, including RTAs with non-WTO members.[243]

Regardless of which view one follows, no specific problems arise in the area of anti-dumping: if one believes that RTAs with non-members cannot be justified, the RTA will violate the WTO Agreement regardless of the rules on anti-dumping. If one follows the view that Art. XXIV:5 GATT and the Enabling Clause apply against non-WTO members as well, the same applies as with customs unions between WTO members.

4.5 Conclusions

Overall, WTO law is rather flexible towards the modifications of anti-dumping rules that can be explained using the justifications developed in Chapter B. Where customs unions prohibit, disincentivize or integrate procedures for internal anti-dumping measures or where customs unions integrate procedures for external anti-dumping measures, in general this will not violate the MFN requirement. This study argues that complete external harmonization neither violates Art. VI GATT nor the ADA and bars the application of Art. I:1 GATT so that no justification will have to be invoked. If anti-dumping measures are not fully harmonized externally, the MFN principle may be violated and if Art. 14 ADA is modified that provision is violated as well. Both violations can be justified according to Art. XXIV:5 GATT. A violation of the MFN principle can also be justified according to the Enabling Clause.

In general, modifications that cannot be rationalized following the lines of argumentation developed in Chapter B, are prohibited by WTO law, however. If customs unions incentivize anti-dumping measures or if the scope of investigation and application of the measure do not align, this cannot be justified according to Art. XXIV:5 GATT and because it violates specific provisions in Art. VI GATT and the ADA, it cannot be justified by the Enabling Clause either. If anti-dumping measures are encouraged to account for an asymmetric market access or to combat social or environmental dumping, it is not clear whether that can be justified. The approach advocated in this thesis is that Art. XXIV:5 GATT should be interpreted widely so as to generally allow these modifications. The same principles apply if only some members of the RTA are members of the WTO as well.

Table 4.4 summarizes these results.

---

[242] Ibid. 852–853.
[243] Mossner (2014), pp. 645–648.

Table 4.4 Overview of WTO legality of modifications

	WTO Violation of the measure	Justification via Art. XXIV:5 GATT	Justification via Enabling Clause
No modification	Pot. MFN	+	+
AD action on behalf of third party	Art. 14 ADA, MFN	+	−
Internal modifications			
• Prohibition of internal ADMs	MFN	+	+
• Disincentivizing internal ADMs	MFN	+	+
• Central IA	Pot. MFN	+	+
• Cooperation requirements between MS	Pot. MFN	+	+
• Central imposition decision	Pot. MFN	+	+
External modifications			
• Central IA	−		
• Cooperation requirements between MS	Pot. MFN	+	+
• Central imposition decision	−		
• Union wide Inv. & measure	Pot. Art. 3.1, 4.1 ADA	−	−
• MS Inv. & union wide measure	Art. 1 ADA	−	−
Further potential modifications			
• Incentivizing ADMs	ADA, MFN	−	−

References

Academic Texts

Alavi SJ (2011) Regional Trade Arrangements Among Developing Countries: Enabling Clause Re-Visited. SSRN Electronic Journal <http://www.ssrn.com/abstract=1737233> Accessed 5 July 2021

Allee T, Elsig M, Lugg A (2017) The Ties between the World Trade Organization and preferential trade agreements: a textual analysis. J Int Econ Law 20:333

Antonini R (2018) A "MES" to be adjusted: past and future treatment of Chinese imports in eu anti-dumping investigations. Global Trade Cust J 13:79

Bartels L (2004a) The separation of powers in the WTO: how to avoid judicial activism. Int Comp Law Q 53:861

Bartels L (2004b) WTO dispute settlement practice on Article XXIV of the GATT. In: Ortino F, Petersmann E-U (eds) The WTO dispute settlement system, 1995–2003. Kluwer Law International

Bartels L (2005) The legality of the EC mutual recognition clause under WTO law. J Int Econ Law 8:691

Bartels L (2014) Jurisdiction and applicable Law in the WTO. University of Cambridge 59/2014

Bartels L (2017) Jurisdictions and applicable law in the WTO. In: Bourgeois JHJ, Bronckers MCEJ, Quick R (eds) WTO dispute settlement, time to take stock. PIE Peter Lang

Blonigen BA (2005) The effects of NAFTA on antidumping and countervailing duty activity. World Bank Econ Rev 19:407

Bossche P, Zdouc W (2017) The law and policy of the World Trade Organization: text, cases and materials, 4th edn. Cambridge University Press

Bown CP, Hoekman BM (2005) WTO Dispute Settlement and the Missing Developing Country Cases: Engaging the Private Sector. 43

Bown CP, Karacaovali B, Tovar P (2014) What do we know about preferential trade agreements and temporary trade barriers? The World Bank, WPS6898

Choi W-M (2005) Legal problems of making regional trade agreements with non-WTO-Member States. J Int Econ Law 8:825

Devuyst Y, Serdarevic A (2007) The World Trade Organization and Regional Trade Agreements: bridging the constitutional credibility gap. Duke J Comp Int Law 18:1

Espa I, Levy PI (2018) The analogue method comes unfastened - the awkward space between market and non-market economies in EC-Fasteners (Article 21.5). World Trade Rev 17:313

Estrella ATG, Horlick G (2006) Mandatory abolition of anti-dumping, countervailing duties and safeguards in customs Unions and free-trade areas constituted between world trade organization members: revisiting a long-standing discussion in light of the appellate body's turkey-textiles ruling. J World Trade 40:909

Gagné G, Paulin M (2013) The Softwood Lumber dispute and US allegations of improper NAFTA Panel review. Am Rev Can Stud 43:413

Herrmann C, Müller S (2017) 'Die Gewährung Des "Marktwirtschaftsstatus" Gegenüber China Im Antidumpingrecht. Europäische Zeitschrift für Wirtschaftsrecht 500

Herrmann C Weiß W, Ohler C (2007) Welthandelsrecht, 2th edn. CH Beck

Hilpold P (2003) Regional integration according to Article XXIV GATT - between law and politics. Max Planck Yearb United Nations Law Online 7:219

Huang Y (2013) Trade remedy measures in the WTO and Regional Trade Agreements. The University of Edinburgh

Inama S, Vermulst E, Eeckhout P (2009) Nonpreferential origin rules in antidumping law and practice. In: Bagwell KW, Bermann GA, Mavroidis PC (eds) Law and economics of contingent protection in international trade. Cambridge University Press

Islam MR, Alam S (2009) Preferential Trade Agreements and the Scope of Gatt Article XXIV, Gats Article V and the enabling clause: an appraisal of Gatt/WTO Jurisprudence. Neth Int Law Rev 56:1

Izadnia R (2015) Peru - agricultural products, DS457 case summaries. World Trade Rev 14:727

Jackson JH (1969) World Trade and the law of GATT (a legal analysis of the general agreement on tariffs and trade). The Bobbs-Merrill Company Inc

Jackson JH (2007) The jurisprudence of GATT & the WTO: insights on treaty law and economic relations. Cambridge University Press

James WE (2000) The rise of anti-dumping: does regionalism promote administered protection? Asian-Pac Econ Liter 14:14

Kallmayer A (2005) Verbot und Rechtfertigung von Präferenzabkommen im GATT. 1. Aufl, Nomos-VerlGes

Krishna P (2018) The economics of PTAs. In: Lester S, Mercurio B, Bartels L (eds) Bilateral and regional trade agreements - commentary and analysis. Cambridge University Press

Lissel E (2015) Safeguard measures in multilateral and regional trade agreements. Trade Law Center (tralac) <https://www.tralac.org/publications/article/8273-safeguard-measures-in-multilateral-and-regional-trade-agreements.html> Accessed 5 July 2021

Lockhart N, Mitchell A (2005) Regional Trade Agreements under GATT 1994: an exception and its limits. In: Mitchell A (ed) Challenges and prospects for the WTO. Cameron May International Law & Policy

Mahncke H (2014) The relationship between WTO anti-dumping law and GATT non-discrimination principles. Schulthess

Marceau G (1994) Anti-dumping and anti-trust issues in free-trade areas. Oxford University Press

Marceau G, Wyatt J (2010) Dispute settlement regimes intermingled: regional trade agreements and the WTO. J Int Disp Settlement 1:67

Mathis JH (2006) Regional Trade Agreements and domestic regulation: what reach for "other restrictive regulations of commerce"? In: Bartels L, Ortino F (eds) Regional Trade Agreements and the WTO legal system. Oxford University Press

Mathis JH (2015) WTO Appellate Body, Peru - additional duty on imports of certain agriculture products, WT/DS457/AB/R, 20 July 2015. Legal Iss Econ Integr 43:97

Matsushita M et al (2017) The World Trade Organization: law, practice, and policy, 3rd edn. Oxford International Law Library

Mavroidis P (2008) 'No outsourcing of law? WTO law as practiced by WTO Courts. Am J Int Law 102:421

Mavroidis P (2012) Trade in goods: the GATT and other WTO agreements regulating trade in goods, 1st edn. Oxford University Press

Mavroidis PC (2006) If I Don't Do It, Somebody Else Will (Or Won't): testing the compliance of preferential trade agreements with the multilateral rules. J World Trade 40:187

Mavroidis PC (2011) Always look at the bright side of non-delivery: WTO and preferential trade agreements, yesterday and today. World Trade Rev 10:375

Mavroidis PC (2015a) The regulation of international trade: GATT, vol 1. The MIT Press

Mavroidis PC (2015b) Dealing with PTAs in the WTO: falling through the Cracks between "Judicialization" and "Legalization". World Trade Rev 14:S107

McRae D (2000) The WTO in international law: tradition continued or new frontier? J Int Econ Law 3:27

McRae D (2019) The relationship between international economic law and public international law: the role of self-contained regimes. Indian J Int Econ Law 11:1

Mitchell AD, Lockhart NJS (2009) Ensuring compliance between a Bilateral PTA and the WTO. In: Jayasuria S, MacLaren D, Magee G (eds) Negotiating a preferential trading agreement. Edward Elgar Publishing

Mitchell AD, Lockhart NJS (2015) Legal requirements for PTAs under the WTO. In: Lester S, Mercurio B, Bartels L (eds) Bilateral and regional trade agreements - commentary and analysis, 2nd edn. Cambridge University Press

Mitchell AD, Voon T, Sheargold E (2015) PTAs and public international law. In: Lester S, Mercurio B, Bartels L (eds) Bilateral and regional trade agreements - commentary and analysis, 2nd edn. Cambridge University Press

Mossner LE (2014) The WTO and regional trade: a family business - the WTO compatibility of regional trade agreements with Non-WTO-Members. World Trade Rev 13:633

Müller-Ibold T (2018) EU trade defence instruments and free trade agreements: is past experience an indication for the future? Implications for Brexit? In: Bungenberg M, others (eds) The future of trade defence instruments: global policy trends and legal challenges, vol 1

Pauwelyn J (2003) Conflict of norms in public international law: how WTO law relates to other rules of international law. Cambridge University Press

Pauwelyn J (2004) The Puzzle of WTO safeguards and regional trade agreements. J Int Econ Law 7:109

Pauwelyn J (2014) Waiving WTO rights in an FTA? Panel Report on Peru - agricultural products. International Economic Law and Policy Blog, 3 December 2014) <https://ielp.worldtradelaw.net/2014/12/waiving-wto-rights-in-an-fta-panel-report-on-peru-agricultural-products.html> Accessed 5 July 2021

Pauwelyn J (2016) Interplay between the WTO treaty and other international legal instruments and tribunals: evolution after 20 Years of WTO Jurisprudence. SSRN Electronic Journal <http://www.ssrn.com/abstract=2731144> Accessed 5 July 2021

Pauwelyn J, Salles LE (2009) Forum shopping before international tribunals: (real) concerns, (im)possible solutions. Cornell Int Law J 42:77

Pickett E, Lux M (2016) The status and effect of WTO law before EU courts. Glob Trade Cust J 11:408

Prusa T (2016) Antidumping provisions in preferential trade agreements. In: Bhagwati JN, Krishna P, Panagariya A (eds) The world trade system: trends and challenges, 1st edn. MIT Press Ltd

Prusa T, Teh R (2011) Contingent protection rules in regional trade agreements. In: Bagwell K, Mavroidis PC (eds) Preferential trade agreements: a law and economics analysis. Cambridge University Press

Prusa TJ, Teh R (2010) Protection reduction and diversion: PTAs and the incidence of antidumping disputes. National Bureau of Economic Research, Working Paper 16276

Roessler F (2001) Are the judicial organs of the World Trade Organization overburdened? In: Porter RB, and others (eds) Efficiency, equity, and legitimacy: the multilateral trading system at the millennium. Brookings Institution Press

Saggi K, Wu M (2016) Understanding agricultural price range systems as trade restraints: Peru -agricultural products. World Trade Rev 15:259

Schott JJ (1989) More free trade areas? In: Schott JJ (ed) Free trade areas and U.S. trade policy. Institute for International Economics

Shadikhodjaev S (2017) The "Regionalism vs Multilateralism" issue in international trade law: revisiting the Peru–agricultural products case. Chic J Int Law 16:109

Shaffer G, Winters LA (2017) FTA Law in WTO dispute settlement: Peru–additional duty and the fragmentation of trade law. World Trade Rev 16:303

Suse A (2017) Old Wine in a new bottle: the EU's response to the Expiry of Section 15(a)(Ii) of China's WTO protocol of accession. J Int Econ Law 20:951

Tabakis C, Zanardi M (2018) Preferential trade agreements and antidumping protection. Lancaster University Management School, 2018/002

Tagle Y, Claros R (2016) The Law of Regional Trade Agreements in the WTO Dispute Settlement System: Lessons from the Peru-Agricultural Products Case. SSRN Electron J 44

Trachtman JP (2003) Toward open recognition?: standardization and regional integration under Article XXIV of GATT. J Int Econ Law 6:459

Vidigal G (2019) The return of voluntary export restraints? How WTO law regulates (and doesn't regulate) bilateral trade-restrictive agreements. J World Trade 53:187

Voon T (2010) Eliminating trade remedies from the WTO: lessons from regional trade agreements. Int Comp Law Q 625

Zang MQ (2019) When the multilateral meets the regionals: regional trade agreements at WTO dispute settlement. World Trade Rev 18:33

Zhang W (2016) Tracing GATT-Minus provisions on export restrictions in regional trade agreements. Global Trade Cust J 11:122

Chapter 5
Responsibility for and Attribution of Anti-Dumping Measures

The previous chapters have answered why customs unions deviate from the WTO's provisions on anti-dumping, how they do so and what flexibility WTO law offers them in doing so. The remainder of this study deals with the consequences that these modifications have. This chapter focuses on the consequences that the various modifications have on the responsibility for and the attribution of anti-dumping measures.

Even though responsibility and attribution are highly controversial in international law, usually no problems arise in the context of anti-dumping measures. Typically, state authorities conduct investigations and impose anti-dumping measures. Naturally, these measures can then also be attributed to the state and the state is responsible for any violations of WTO law that occurred in the process. Complexities arise in the context of customs unions, as anti-dumping measures can potentially be attributed to the member states of the customs union and/or the customs union itself. The purpose of this chapter is to delineate attribution and responsibility between the customs union on the one hand and their member states on the other.

So far, questions of responsibility have arisen in the WTO DSB only in a severely fragmented manner. In the context of the EU, sometimes the question arose whether the EU is responsible for certain acts committed by its or the member states' authorities. In other customs unions questions of responsibility sometimes arose to answer whether member states of customs unions were responsible for certain acts by central organs of the customs union. The reverse, namely whether EU member states are responsible or whether other customs unions are responsible, has not been the focus of any dispute yet. This is, of course, due to the fact that the EU is the only customs union that is also a WTO member, meaning that other customs union cannot be defendants in a dispute and because the EU always assumed responsibility a proper demarcation between the EU's and its member states responsibility never became necessary.

F. Bickel, *Customs Unions in the WTO*, European Yearbook of International Economic Law 20, https://doi.org/10.1007/978-3-030-86312-8_5

However, questions of responsibility should be answered independently of whether a customs union is a member of an international organization.[1] This chapter sets out a framework to do so.

The main argument of this chapter is that responsibility should depend on the institutional setup within a customs union. In general, actions by an authority of a member state are usually only attributable to the state and actions by centralized authorities are attributable to the customs unions and to the member states. This argument results from an application of ARIO[2] and ARSIWA[3] interpreted in accordance with relevant case law. More specifically, this study argues that most of the academic debate relating to responsibility in international organizations generally and the EU specifically can be subsumed under the definition of the term organ or agent. This study advocates an extensive definition of the term organ or agent that only considers whether an entity fulfils functions of the customs union or member state. In doing so, this study offers an interpretation of ARIO and ARSIWA that produces workable results when delineating responsibility between customs unions and their member states that is in conformity with WTO DSB reports and can apply beyond the EU also to other customs unions.

This argument is developed after clarification of some preliminary points. Responsibility and attribution are defined and their practical and theoretical relevance highlighted (under Sect. 5.1), the applicable law for answering questions on responsibility and attribution is categorized (under Sect. 5.2) and the different stages of centralization in relation to anti-dumping are recollected so that they can serve as a demarcation for the purpose of attribution (under Sect. 5.3).

After a clarification of these preliminary points, this chapter defines the circumstances under which an anti-dumping measure can be attributed to a customs union (under Sect. 5.4) or a state (under Sect. 5.5). Finally, the relationship between the different forms of responsibility that arise will be analysed (under Sect. 5.6).

Questions on attribution and responsibility bear significant practical and conceptual relevance. Practically, responsibility is relevant as it defines who must answer for a violation of the WTO Agreements in the DSB. The finding that member states are not responsible for acts of their customs unions would therefore mean that they can evade responsibility by outsourcing tasks to the customs union level. Moreover,

---

[1] The ECtHR's decisions are often criticized as being politically motivated because the EU is not a member of the ECHR yet, see e.g.: Hoffmeister (2010), pp. 723, 735. Interestingly, the same criticism is usually not voiced against the WTO DSB whose decisions could be equally politically motivated but for the opposite reason, namely because the EU is a WTO member.

[2] Responsibility to an international organization is similar and regulated in the Articles on the Responsibility of International Organizations (ARIO), ILC Report on the Work of its Sixty-third Session, UNGAOR 66th Sess, Supp. No. 10, UN Doc. A/66/10 (2011); Commentary to the Articles on the Responsibility of International Organizations, ILC Report on the Work of its Sixty-third Session, UNGAOR 66th Sess., Supp. No. 10, UN Doc. A/66/10 (2011) (ARIO Commentary).

[3] Articles on Responsibility of States for Internationally Wrongful Acts, ILC *Yearbook* 2001/II(2); Commentary to the Articles on Responsibility of States for Internationally Wrongful Acts, ILC *Yearbook* 2001/II(2) (ARSIWA Commentary).

this study argues that attribution is an implicit requirement of anti-dumping mea-sures. Conceptually, this is relevant as explaining WTO cases using the ILC's articles on responsibility, highlights the WTO's place in the international legal order.

5.1   What Is Responsibility and What Is Attribution?

This section will define responsibility and attribution in the abstract (under Sect. 5.1.1) before considering what the definitions mean in the context of anti-dumping (under Sect. 5.1.2) and laying down the practical relevance of the concepts (under Sect. 5.1.3).

5.1.1   Definitions in International Law

The ILC has codified international customary law on responsibility and attribution in the ARIO and ARSIWA. What responsibility is, is best understood through the requirements following which it arises and the consequences that stem from it. Accordingly, responsibility for an act arises if there is an internationally wrongful act of a state or an international organization.[4] There is an internationally wrongful act of a state or an international organization if an act that constitutes a breach of an international obligation is attributable to the state or the international organization.[5] If responsibility arises, the state or the international organization is under a duty to (a) cease the act, (b) to offer appropriate assurance of non-repetition, if circum-stances so require[6] and to potentially make full reparation of injury caused.[7]

This also broadly corresponds with traditional definitions of responsibility.[8] Thus, responsibility is concerned with the identification of the proper respondent which is different from the question whether that respondent can effectively remedy the alleged breach. A state or an international organization can be responsible even if that actor cannot provide an effective remedy.[9]

For responsibility to arise, two requirements must be met: (1) an act must violate an international obligation and (2) that act must be attributable to a state or an international organization.

---

[4] Art. 3 ARIO, Art. 1 ARSIWA.

[5] Art. 4 ARIO, Art. 2 ARSIWA.

[6] Art. 30 ARIO, Art. 30 ARSIWA.

[7] Art. 31 ARIO, Art. 31 ARSIWA.

[8] For a historical overview of different approaches to responsibility and their differences to the approach in the ARIO and ARSIWA, namely that there is no longer a requirement of damages, see: Pellet (2010), pp. 5–11.

[9] See also: Herrmann and Streinz (2014) para 90.

Responsibility requires a breach of an international obligation. The question whether a state or an international organization is bound by an international obligation is therefore a condition for responsibility to arise and not synonymous with responsibility.[10] An international obligation arises through conventions or treaties, international customary law and general principles of law.[11]

Attribution concerns the relationship of a certain action or omission with a state or an international organization such as if it exists, that act or omission can be attached to the state or international organization.[12] It is thereby distinct from the question whether the actor acted within its competences.[13] Whereas rules of competences regulate internally who is allowed to act, attribution considers factually whether an act can be attached to an entity.[14] Attribution is one of the conditions of responsibility, but attribution can also serve as an international obligation independently of responsibility.[15]

5.1.2 Responsibility, Attribution, International Obligations and Anti-Dumping Measures

After having considered what responsibility and attribution are in principle, the following will now tie these abstract definitions to anti-dumping.

For anti-dumping measures, Art. VI GATT and the ADA contain international obligations in the form of preconditions that must be fulfilled before measures that would otherwise violate Art. I, II GATT can be imposed. Because the WTO Agreement is a "single undertaking", all WTO members are fully bound by these obligations, whether they are states or customs unions.[16] Thus, obligations are not

---

[10] Bartels (2016); Bartels (2017), p. 83. It seems, however, that attribution is a precondition for certain international obligations to arise. If consent is not given by a state because it is not attributable to that state, that state cannot be bound by a treaty (Art. 34 VCLT). If a custom cannot be attributed to a state, that state cannot be bound by international customary law.

[11] Art. 38 Statute of the International Court of Justice (ICJ Statute), 18.4.1946.

[12] Art. 2 Rec. (12) ARSIWA Commentary. The relationship is thereby normative and not merely factual as parties may agree to different rules of attribution, Ch. II, Rec. 4 ARSIWA Commentary.

[13] Herrmann and Streinz (2014) para 95.

[14] For a discussion on the differences between the two concepts, see Sect. 5.2.2.2.

[15] Crawford and Murphy (2010), p. 283. For examples how attribution serves as requirements in International Investment Law: Kovács (2018), pp. 35–43.

[16] Because there is no Declaration of Competence, this flows from the principle *pacta sund servanda*, Art. 26 Vienna Convention on the Law of Treaties between States and International Organizations or between International Organizations (VCLTIO), 21.3.1986, as internal rules cannot be invoked to justify the violation of an international obligation, Art. 27 (1), (2) VCLTIO. See also: Durán (2017a), pp. 697, 703.

apportioned.[17] Only WTO members are bound by these obligations. Except for the EU, customs unions are not WTO members so that usually only the member states of customs unions but not the customs unions are bound by WTO obligations. In the case of the EU both the EU as well as its member states are WTO members and thus bound.

Art. VI GATT and the ADA condition anti-dumping measures on a successful investigation[18] and a decision to impose an anti-dumping duty.[19] Although neither Art. VI GATT nor the ADA explicitly require that the investigation and the decision to impose measures must be attributable to the respective WTO member, this is implicitly required.

The ADA refers to "the authorities" 120 times. This means that the ADA requires *authorities* instead of any natural or legal person to take the required actions and because it sometimes refers to "the authorities of the importing Member"[20] this indicates generally that it is not enough that any authority fulfils the required conduct. It is thus not possible for one WTO member to copy the normal value determination made by another WTO member in the course of another anti-dumping investigation or outsource the dumping, injury, and causation determinations to private actors such as the domestic industry or law offices and accountants. The fact that there is no practice by WTO members in that regard also indicates a shared understanding of this implicit requirement. Moreover, as Art. 5.7 SPS Agreement allows reliance on information by international organizations or other WTO members to adopt SPS Measures in specific circumstances[21] this means conversely that usually this is not possible in anti-dumping proceedings. Rather, the limitation that certain *authorities* must act constitutes a requirement that concerns the link of a measure to a WTO member, i.e. is concerned with attribution.

This raises the question who *the authorities of the importing member* are or what kinds of attribution the ADA requires. Because the ARSIWA Commentary explicitly refers to authorities as being specific organs of a state,[22] one could understand the term as a subset of organ as defined in ARIO and ARSIWA. This could limit the possible grounds of attribution to Art. 6 ARIO and Art. 4 ARSIWA. As the ADA precedes ARSIWA and ARIO the wording should, however, not be overanalysed. Reference to "the authorities" should rather be understood in an extensive manner,

---

[17] It seems settled that as a general principle international obligations are not apportioned, except if declarations of competences exist: Bartels et al. (2006), pp. 457–459; Hoffmeister (2010), pp. 743–744. Nevertheless, the EC has argued this in its comments to the ILC ARIO Drafts, ILC, 'Comments and observations received from international organizations', 2004, A/CN.4/545, p. 26 para 1–5 and the EC's view has found prominent supporters, e.g.: Kuijper and Paasivirta (2013); Paasivirta and Kuijper (2005), p. 169; Eeckhout (2011), pp. 457–460.

[18] Art. 5, 6, ADA. This includes a review of existing measures, Art. 11 ADA.

[19] Art. 9.1 ADA.

[20] E.g. Art. 9.1 ADA.

[21] On the extent of this, see: *EC - Measures Concerning Meat and Meat Products (Hormones)* [1998] WTO Appellate Body WT/DS26/AB/R; WT/DS48/AB/R [190].

[22] Art. 4, Rec. 3, 9 ARSIWA Commentary.

following its purpose and aim. The purpose of the term is to clarify that WTO members are responsible for acts during the investigation of anti-dumping measures. The purpose is fulfilled irrespective of the ground of attribution. *Authorities of the importing member* are, therefore, all entities that are attributable to the WTO member relying on the anti-dumping measure.

This interpretation can also be supported by a historical analysis of Art. 9.1 ADA. Its predecessor, Art. 8.1 1967 Anti-Dumping Code, provided that "[the decision to impose anti-dumping measures is a decision] made by the authorities of the importing country or customs territory." The term "country or customs territory" has now been replaced by the term "the authorities of the importing Member". The reason for the change in the terminology are not obvious. During the Uruguay negotiations, Hong Kong, the Republic of Korea, Japan, the EEC, the Nordic Countries and Canada all submitted proposals to modify Art. 8.1 1967 Anti-Dumping Code. None of the modifications concerned the phrase "importing country or customs territory".[23] Following informal meetings[24] the proposal changed in such a way that removed mentioning customs territories and substituted it by requiring that an authority of the importing member takes the relevant decision. This change is best understood as an emphasis that the WTO Agreements can only bind its members and that its obligations must be fulfilled by its members and not by any entity. The change thus emphasises that a special relationship between the entity imposing a measure and a WTO member is required. That relationship is provided by attribution requirements.

In case that any of the requirements in Art. VI GATT and the ADA are not fulfilled, the imposition of an anti-dumping measure constitutes a violation of an international obligation. If the measure is then attributable to a WTO member, that WTO member is responsible for the violation of WTO law.

This means that in the context of anti-dumping measures, attribution is required twice: first, to discharge the requirements contained in Art. VI GATT and the ADA and second, to tie a measure to a WTO member to establish responsibility.

In case that there is no violation of an international obligation, i.e. the imposition of the anti-dumping measure complies with all requirements, Art. VI GATT and the ADA allow the imposition of anti-dumping measures. This has two benefits. First, WTO members may levy duties in violation of Art. I:1, II GATT and second, the WTO member cannot be obliged to repeal the measure but must only conduct

---

[23] Negotiating Group on MTN Agreements and Arrangements, 'Report of the acting Chairman of the Informal Group on Anti-Dumping', MTN/GNG/NG8/W/83/Add5, 23.7.1990, pp. 96–97.

[24] Negotiating Group on MTN Agreements and Arrangements, 'Meeting of 18 October 1990', MTN.GNG/NG8/21, 29.10.1990, p. 3; Negotiating Group on MTN Agreements and Arrangements, 'Report of the Negotiating Group on MTN Agreements and Arrangements to the Group of Negotiations on Goods', MTN.GNG/NG8/W/85, 30.10.1990.

newcomer,[25] interim,[26] or expiry[27] reviews[28] or grant refund requests[29] if the requirements to do so have been met.

5.1.3 Practical Relevance of Responsibility and Attribution

Responsibility and attribution are abstract concepts that have been the focus of a lot of academic debate. Before diving into the details of that debate, the practical and theoretical relevance of these abstract concepts should be highlighted. Responsibility and attribution are relevant for three reasons.

First, responsibility is relevant in the dispute settlement system to define who must answer for a violation of an international obligation. In the WTO's DSB only WTO members are liable for WTO law violations. This is practically relevant, as—other than the EU—no customs union is a WTO member as well. This means the finding that only customs unions but not their members are responsible for anti-dumping measures undermines effective enforcement of WTO law, as violations could not be addressed in the WTO's DSB. To avoid that, rules of responsibility should be interpreted to not undermine effective enforcement of WTO rules.[30] Conversely, if member states are responsible for the behaviour of centralized institutions, this may enable targeting member states of customs unions more strategically. Members may choose to only initiate proceedings against Russia or Germany for anti-dumping measures imposed on the EAEU or EU level because they may wish to potentially only suspend concessions against one country of the customs union for political reasons.[31]

Second, attribution is also an implicit requirement of anti-dumping measures. In most cases this requirement will not pose difficulties. However, it becomes relevant in the context of customs unions. Attribution provides the justification why it is legal for WTO members to establish centralized authorities in customs unions. The criterion then becomes visible in cases of economic integration and disintegration. This study argues that the UK can apply the EU's anti-dumping measures following its withdrawal from the EU if the investigations are attributable to it, which this study affirms.[32] More generally, attribution provides the legal framework in which circumstances the territorial scope of anti-dumping measures can change.

---

[25] Art. 9.5 ADA.

[26] Art. 11.2 ADA.

[27] Art. 11.3 ADA.

[28] See: Sect. 6.3.4.

[29] Art. 9.3.3 ADA.

[30] Klabbers (2015), pp. 9, 82.

[31] Following the principles in Art. 22.3 DSU.

[32] See: Sect. 6.3.3.

Third, responsibility has received a lot of attention due to the ILC's attempts to codify the international customary law on responsibility. Tying WTO law as applied by its members into that practice also highlights the WTO's place within the context of international law.

5.2 Applicable Law

The ILC has attempted to codify the international customary law on the responsibility of states in ARSIWA and the responsibility of international organizations in the ARIO. As the ILC does not have the competence to change international law, it can only clarify existing international customary law. Conversely, insofar as the codifications by the ILC do not codify existing international customary law but change it, it does not apply. Some have argued categorically that ARIO and ARSIWA do not codify customary international law in the context of the WTO[33] or the EU[34] as they do not take their peculiarities into account. Whether that criticism is true is, however, equally impossible to establish as the question whether ARSIWA and ARIO successfully codify international law on responsibility. Rather, the provisions should be applied cautiously and whether the provision constitute a general practice accepted as law[35] should be considered.

General international customary law may, however, not apply if the WTO (under Sect. 5.2.1) or the law of the customs unions[36] (under Sect. 5.2.2) contain more specific rules, i.e. are *lex specialis*.[37]

---

[33] Herrmann and Streinz (2014) para 92.

[34] Kuijper and Paasivirta (2013), p. 69.

[35] Art. 38 (1)(b) ICJ Statute.

[36] That internal rules of customs unions can contain more specific rules, has been codified in Art. 64.2 ARIO.

[37] *Korea - Measures Affecting Government Procurement* [2000] WTO Panel Report WT/DS163/R [7.96, 7.101]. The same relationship of subsidiarity between the ARSIWA and ARIO and WTO law is expressed in Art. 55 ARSIWA; Art. 64 ARIO. On the conditions for the *lex specialis* principle to apply: *Indonesia - Auto* (Chap. 4, n 30) n 649.

5.2.1 Special Rules of Responsibility in WTO Law

ARIO and ARSIWA contain provisions on attribution,[38] the breach of an international obligation,[39] secondary forms of responsibility,[40] justifications,[41] secondary obligations,[42] and the invocation of responsibility.[43]

The WTO Agreement contains rules on the breach of obligations, justifications, secondary obligations, and the invocation of responsibility.[44] These provisions in the WTO are *lex specialis* to ARIO and ARISWA. However, general customary international law as codified in ARIO and ARSIWA may still be relevant in the WTO when interpreting WTO provisions. ARIO and ARISWA may provide evidence as to the "subsequent practice" in the application of the WTO Agreement and "relevant rules of international law" both of which "shall be taken into account, together with the context" in the interpretation of the WTO Agreements.[45] Nevertheless, as the issues that arise in this regard are not specific to anti-dumping measures, the remainder of this chapter will not focus on these requirements.

No provision of WTO law explicitly deals with attribution and secondary forms of responsibility,[46] which is why WTO law is not *lex specialis* concerning these provisions in the ARIO and ARSIWA.[47] This is why WTO Panels have referred to general principles of international law[48] and more specifically ARIO[49] and

---

[38] Art. 6–9 ARIO, Art. 4–11 ARSIWA.

[39] Art. 10–13 ARIO, Art. 12–15 ARSIWA.

[40] Art. 14–19, 58–63 ARIO, Art. 16–19 ARSIWA.

[41] Art. 20–27 ARIO, Art. 20–27 ARSIWA.

[42] Art. 28–42 ARIO, Art. 28–41 ARSIWA.

[43] Art. 43–57 ARIO, Art. 42–54 ARSIWA.

[44] Flett (2017), pp. 853–872; Ruka (2017) ch 2.V.1.

[45] Art. 31 (3) VCLT.

[46] Herrmann and Streinz (2014) para 92; Steinberger (2006), pp. 837, 840; Flett (2017), pp. 859–862. Art. 4.3 DSU has been used to argue that WTO Law follows a principle of attribution based on territoriality. It has been rightly pointed out against this view that (1) Art. 4.3 DSU only deals with responsibility and not with attribution and (2) the claim of territoriality does not help in the EU context, as the acts take place within the EU's and the Member States' territories: Delgado Casteleiro (2016), pp. 175–178.

[47] The relationship is like the relationship between the rules VCLT rules on interpretation and WTO law. In that case there even is a WTO provision, but it does not displace Art. 31.3 (a) VCLT: Pauwelyn, 'Interplay between the WTO Treaty and Other International Legal Instruments and Tribunals' (Chap. 4, n 172), p. 21; Pauwelyn (2001), pp. 535, 538–540.

[48] E.g. *Australia - Measures Affecting Importation of Salmon - Recourse to Article 215 by Canada* [2000] WTO Panel Report WT/DS18/RW [7.12–7.13]; *Turkey - Textiles* (Chap. 4, n 94) para 9.41–9.43. For more detail on the relationship, see: Ruka (2017) chs 73–79; Flett (2017), p. 853.

[49] *European Communities - Selected Customs Matters* [2006] WTO Panel Report WT/DS315/R 932.

ARSIWA[50] when confronted with questions of attribution. As WTO law is not *lex specialis* to questions of attribution, ARIO and ARSIWA apply. The remainder of this chapter explores how the rules of attribution contained in ARIO and ARSIWA apply in the WTO.

5.2.2 Special Rules of Responsibility in the Internal Laws of the Customs Unions

Art. 64 ARIO clarifies that special rules that supplement or replace the codified international customary law "may be contained in the rules of the organization applicable to the relations between an international organization and its members." What kind of rules are meant by that is, however, not clear.[51]

The ARIO Commentary offers an example that aims to clarify the scope of the measure (under Sect. 5.2.2.1) and some have argued that the rules refer to the distribution of competences between the customs union and its members (under Sect. 5.2.2.2).

5.2.2.1 ARIO Commentary

The ARIO Commentary does not define which special rules between an organization and its members constitute *lex specialis* to ARIO within the meaning of Art. 64 ARIO. According to the Commentary, it is "impossible to [. . .] identify each of the special rules and their scope of application."[52] Interestingly, the Commentary does not refer to rules of competences and does not explain their relevance in this context.

Instead, the Commentary refers to the situation in which the EU member states implement a binding EU act as one example of such a special rule.[53] The example will be dealt with in detail below,[54] but the Commentary highlights the seeming disparity between the ECHR's approach according to which the member states are responsible on the one hand[55] and the approach in the WTO Panel's approach in

---

[50] *Thailand - Customs and Fiscal Measures on Cigarettes from the Philippines* [2010] WTO Panel Report WT/DS371/R 533; *Brazil - Measures Affecting Imports of Retreaded Tyres* [2007] WTO Panel Report WT/DS332/R 1480.

[51] Although Art. 2 (b) ARIO defines "rules of the organization", this definition does not help to understand which rules of the organization can be *lex specialis*.

[52] Art. 64 (2) ARIO Commentary.

[53] Art. 64 (2) ARIO Commentary.

[54] See: Sect. 5.4.2.1.

[55] Art. 64 (3), (5), (6) ARIO Commentary.

EC – Geographical Indications[56] according to which the EC is responsible on the other hand.[57] Although the Commentary does not resolve that conflict, it explains that following the view expressed in *EC – Geographical Indications,* the predecessor of Art. 291 (1) TFEU is an example of a rule that supplements the ARIO, as it defines organ within Art. 6 ARIO further.[58] Interestingly, the Commentary does not necessarily suggest that these rules replace ARIO and ARSIWA but rather that they supplement it.

Nevertheless, this still misses the important question under which circumstances internal laws are relevant externally. Although this supports that the institutional setup of an international organization has some impact on the responsibility of the international organization and its members, it does not help to answer what that impact is exactly.

5.2.2.2 Rules on Competences

Some have argued that rules of competences constitute *lex specialis* to the general rules of international responsibility.[59] Accordingly, the actor that is competent to act should be responsible for the action: if a customs union is exclusively competent in the fields of anti-dumping, it should be responsible for anti-dumping measures.[60]

The application of rules of competences has been justified on several grounds. The idea is that the rules that allow a state or an international organization to act should correspond with the consequences that flow from that action.[61] Moreover, the common use of declarations of competences when concluding international agreements also demonstrates an acceptance of such a view, making the principle that competences coincide with responsibility part of the international customary law.[62]

---

[56] *European Communities - Protection of Trademarks and Geographical Indications for Agricultural Products and Foodstuffs* [2005] WTO Panel Report DT/DS174/R [7.725].

[57] Art. 64 (4) ARIO Commentary.

[58] Art. 64 (4) ARIO Commentary.

[59] Kuijper and Paasivirta (2013), pp. 67–69; Paasivirta and Kuijper (2005), pp. 212–216; Hoffmeister (2010), p. 745; Hernández (2012), p. 643; Kuijper (2010). Although the argument is more refined, Dúran's Competence/Remedy model is at least to some extent based on this assumption: Dúran (2017a, b).

[60] Note, however, that this view is different from the EC's comments to the ILC proposals. The EC argued that international obligations should be apportioned and after an international obligation had been apportioned to the EC or its Member States, responsibility would lie with the bearer of the obligation. See. e.g. ILC, Comments and observations received from international organizations, 2004, A/CN.4/545, p. 26 para 1–5. For an explanation of the EC's position, see: Eeckhout (2011), pp. 457–463. Leinarte mischaracterizes the EC's position by not distinguishing between attribution and apportionment: Leinarte (2018), pp. 171–174.

[61] Kuijper and Paasivirta (2013), p. 54.

[62] ibid 57, 68. For examples on the use of declarations of competences: Leinarte (2018), p. 183.

Practically, this is also sensible as only the competent entity can provide restitution for the violation.[63]

Ultimately, these reasons are not convincing. Declarations of competences are more concerned with apportionment than attribution and where there is no such declaration—as in the WTO—it cannot be inferred that their intended effect should arise nevertheless. Beyond that, the question whether a responsible party can provide restitution is independent of the question whether a party is responsible and it is not clear why responsibility should arise for the party that was *allowed to act* instead as for the party that *acted*.

Above that, there are several reasons why rules on competences should not be *lex specialis* to the ARIO and ARSIWA. First, on a practical level it is difficult to ascertain who is competent in the individual case. With regards to the EU, it is often unclear beforehand, whether a specific action falls within the competence of the EU or its member states.[64] Especially in areas of shared competences, questions of whether the EU has exercised its competences are not always easy to answer.[65] These practical difficulties coincide with political problems that WTO Panels should not decide internal questions of competences of customs unions.[66] Second, where an entity acts *ultra vires* that entity should still be responsible. Because competences answer who *should have* acted instead of who *acted,* it is difficult to reach a satisfactory conclusion if an actor *acted* even though that actor *should not have acted*.[67] Third, the competences model has difficulties applying in situations of executive federalism.[68] Where a customs union is exclusively competent to legislate in a certain area, but its members are competent to execute the legislation, difficulties arise if the application of a measure is challenged. Although supporters of the competence model argue that since the customs union legislates it has "normative control"[69] and that this should be decisive, this is systematically still difficult to reconcile with the fact that the members and not the customs union are competent to execute legislation and that as a consequence they should be responsible. Fourth, WTO members should not be able to escape responsibility by transferring rights to an international organization that is not necessarily a WTO member itself.

Above that and more fundamentally, the *lex specialis* requirements are not fulfilled. ARIO and ARSIWA enable the attribution of conduct for acts where an entity is not competent. Attribution occurs with regards to acts of an organ of an autonomous unit within a state even where the autonomous unit is exclusively competent (Art. 4 ARSIWA). Attribution also takes place where an organ acts in excess of its authority i.e. not within its competences (Art. 7 ARSIWA). Finally,

---

[63] Hoffmeister (2010), p. 745; Kuijper and Paasivirta (2013), p. 55.

[64] On the complexities with implied powers: Delgado Casteleiro (2016), pp. 20–24.

[65] Art. 2 (2), 3 (2) TFEU.

[66] Bartels et al. (2006), p. 459.

[67] Eeckhout (2011), p. 459.

[68] This concept will be considered below, see: section 'Control'.

[69] Kuijper and Paasivirta (2013), p. 55.

involuntary attribution under Chapter IV includes the attribution of conduct of entities not organs of the state that act within the competences of a different state. Because the system in ARSIWA and ARIO itself decouples responsibility from internal competences, it highlights the different nature of the concepts. The rules on competences and rules on responsibility therefore do not regulate the same subject matter. Ultimately, rules of competences regulate who is allowed to act internally but do not regulate externally who must respond to an act. As they cover a different subject matter, they are not *lex specialis.*[70]

5.2.3   Conclusions

Neither WTO law nor internal laws of customs unions provide *per se* a *lex specialis* to ARIO and ARSIWA. Insofar as ARIO and ARSIWA codify international customary law, they apply to questions of attribution and responsibility in the WTO.

5.3   Degrees of Centralization

This Chapter argues that the institutional setup of customs unions determines attribution of anti-dumping measures. Chapter 2 has analysed the different procedural modifications that have occurred in customs unions with respect to anti-dumping measures. Procedurally, the investigation or the decision taking mechanism may be harmonized. This harmonization can be characterised into three different steps. The difference between these three stages of harmonization is one of degree. The degree to which institutions are centralized impacts attribution of acts to the customs union or its member states.

First, institutions may have been fully centralized. This means that central authorities have been established. For the investigation this means that there is a central investigating authority competent to investigate all cases of anti-dumping. Decisions are then taken centrally. Even though member states may still influence the decision, this happens through institutions that have been set up by the customs union and that operate on a customs union level. Such authorities exist in the EU, EAEU, GCC, WAEMU, and ECOWAS.

Second, there may be partial centralization. This means that in some cases member state authorities investigate and take decisions and, in some cases, central

---

[70]The ECJ seems to support this under the auspices of what it calls the principle of (external) autonomy. See generally: *Opinion 2/13* [2014] Judgment of the CJEU ECLI:EU:C:2014:2454. See also: Jed Odermatt, 'When a Fence Becomes a Cage: The Principle of Autonomy in EU External Relations Law' (European University Institute - Robert Schuman Centre for Advanced Studies) EUI Working Paper MWP 2016/07; Barents (2003); Parish (2012), p. 141; White and Collins (2011).

authorities investigate and take decisions. The relationship between the member state authorities and the central authorities can be vertical so that central authorities act as supervisory bodies. This has happened for the investigation and imposition of certain internal anti-dumping measures in CARICOM and CACM. It has also happened as regards certain imposition decisions in the EAC and the EU-Turkey customs union. The relationship between the member state authorities and the central authorities can also be horizontal, meaning that each is competent in set cases. This has happened in CAN. A combination of the two may also exist.

Third, the authorities of the member states may still be competent to conduct investigations and take decisions. One reason for this is that the customs union may have delegated its competence back to one member of the customs unions, such as has happened for the interim system in SACU. Another reason may be that other members of the customs union are obliged to copy the anti-dumping measures of one member, as is the case in the EU-Andorra and EU-San Marino customs unions. Finally, it is possible that member states simply have retained the right to investigate and impose anti-dumping measures. This is the case in MERCOSUR, COMESA, CEMAC. In the EAC and the EU-Turkey customs union member states have retained the competence to investigate anti-dumping measures. Customs unions may have imposed cooperation requirements such as that consultations must take place or that additional information rights must be fulfilled.[71]

## 5.4	Attribution of Anti-Dumping Measures to Customs Unions

Having defined responsibility and attribution, the applicable law and the different stages of centralization, the ground is now set to answer the first substantive question relating to attribution: Which acts in relation to anti-dumping measures can be attributed to customs unions?

The relevant acts that take place surrounding an anti-dumping measure are the initiation of an investigation, the investigation itself, the imposition of the measure and the review of a measure. The question is therefore which of these acts can be attributed to which customs unions according to customary international law as practiced in the WTO and as codified in ARIO.

Even though ARIO applies to all acts, including the enactment of legislative measures,[72] it only codifies international customary law with respect to international organizations. Which customs unions are international organizations will be

---

[71] See above at: Chap. 3, section 'Cooperation Requirements'.

[72] ARSIWA and ARIO also apply to legislative measures, as on the one hand they clarify that the enactment of a legislative measure can violate an international obligation Art. 12 (12) ARSIWA Commentary, but on the other hand not specific rules of attribution are included for legislative measures.

considered first. ARIO includes several grounds to establish attribution. The four most relevant in the context of anti-dumping measures will be considered in turn.

5.4.1 International Organizations

ARIO only applies to International Organizations.[73] ARIO defines an international organization as "an organization established by a treaty or other instrument governed by international law and possessing its own international legal personality. International organizations may include as members, in addition to states, other entities."[74]

All customs unions notified to the WTO have been established through a treaty. The problematic requirement is whether they possess international legal personality.

The ARIO Commentary remains vague as to when an organization has international legal personality. It characterises the ICJ's approach to international legal personality in its advisory opinion *Reparation for Injuries* as taking a liberal view of the acquisition of legal personality under international law. Accordingly, the acquisition of international legal personality depends upon objective criteria, i.e. the recognition by other subjects of international law as an entity with international legal personality is not constitutive.[75]

The WTO does not regulate according to which criteria customs unions gain international legal personality. The issue arose in *Turkey – Textiles* with regards to the EC-Turkey customs union. The relevant considerations that led the Panel to conclude that the customs union does not have international legal personality were that the customs union does not have a legislative body that implements laws applicable in the territory of the customs union. This is because the actions of the Association Council require "independent implementation by the parties" without any enforcement process which means that the Association Council cannot force the parties to act.[76] An example to assess whether a customs union has international legal personality concerns the conclusion of international treaties. Where each party to the customs union signs the international treaty separately, the customs union probably does not have international legal personality. The Panel argued that the reason for this to be the decisive factor is that it is a "recognition that each party to the customs union may adopt measures, to some extent different" which confirms "the

---

[73] Art. 1.1 ARIO.

[74] Art. 2 (a) ARIO.

[75] Art. 2 (8)-(10) ARIO Commentary. The Commentary neither endorses an objective nor a subjective approach to international legal personality. On the objective theory: Seyersted (1963); Seyersted (2008), pp. 43–64; Crawford (2012), p. 679 ff; Gazzini (2011), p. 35; Amerasinghe (2005), pp. 79–80. On the subjective theory: Sands et al. (2001), p. 470 ff.; Schermers and Blokker (2018) para 1565; Kelsen (1951). See also: Klabbers (2013), pp. 47–51; Ipsen and Epping (2018). For a historical overview of the term, see: Potter (1945), p. 803.

[76] *Turkey - Textiles* (Chap. 4, n 94) para 9.40.

ability of the parties to act independently."[77] Put differently, "unless a customs union is provided with distinct rights and obligations (such as the European Communities) each party to the customs union remains accountable for measures it adopts for application on its specific territory."[78]

Besides rejecting international legal personality of the EU-Turkey customs union, WTO Panels have accepted international legal personality of the EU and EAEU.[79] Where customs unions have a centralized system to impose anti-dumping measures, this could indicate the will of its members that the customs union is able to act independently. Beyond the EU and EAEU, there are strong indications that the GCC and SACU are international organizations as well, as they have reached a similar degree of economic integration and their institutional setup is at least comparable.

Answering which customs unions have international legal personality is difficult and depends on the general setup of the customs unions. Because it is ultimately not relevant for the purposes of explaining attribution of anti-dumping measures, no definitive answer will be provided. Several points speak in favour of this. First, international legal personality does not depend on the anti-dumping regime. This means that other changes in the setup of the customs union that do not relate to anti-dumping may lead to a customs union gaining or losing international legal personality. Second, principles expressed in ARIO apply even if the customs union is not an international organization.[80]

5.4.2 Art. 6 ARIO: Organs or Agent of the International Organization

According to Art. 6 ARIO, the conduct of any "agent or organ of an international organization in the performance of functions of that organ or agent" shall be attributed to the international organization. The distinction between organ and agents made in the ARIO is purely terminological.[81]

The WTO Appellate Body has recognized that the "acts or omissions of the organs of the state" are attributable to the WTO member generally[82] and acts of organs of an international organization are attributable to that international

---

[77] ibid.

[78] ibid 272.

[79] The EU is a WTO member. For the EAU: *Russia - Tariff Treatment of Certain Agricultural and Manufacturing Products: Report of the Panel* [2016] WTO Panel Report WT/DS485/R [7.42].

[80] Art. 2 (2) ARIO Commentary.

[81] Art. 6 (5) ARIO Commentary.

[82] E.g. *United States - Sunset Review of Anti-Dumping Duties on Corrosion-Resistant Carbon Steel Flat Products from Japan* [2003] WTO Appellate Body Report WT/DS244/AB/R 79.

organization[83] more specifically. This indicates that within the WTO this ground of attribution has already been recognized as customary international law.

The main argument of this part is that most of the debate that takes place concerning attribution to the EU can be subsumed under this ground of attribution. Relevant practice can be understood as defining what an organ or agent is and conceptually this is sensible in the framework of ARIO (and ARSIWA), as this is the only ground of attribution concerned with the institutional setup of international organizations.

The main complexity of this ground of attribution is that it is not clear what an organ or an agent is (under Sect. 5.4.2.1). After exploring different interpretations of the term, an observation follows whether the different authorities that act in connection with anti-dumping measures are organs of the relevant customs union (under Sect. 5.4.2.2). Finally, whether the organs have acted in the performance of their functions will be discussed (under Sect. 5.4.2.3).

5.4.2.1 Definition of Organ and Agent

Art. 2 (c) ARIO defines an organ of an international organization as "any person or entity which has that status in accordance with the rules of the organization". Similarly, Art. 2 (d) ARIO defines an agent of an international organization as "an official or other person or entity, other than an organ, who is charged by the organization with carrying out, or helping to carry out, one of its functions, and thus through whom the organization acts".[84]

The definitions apply in a straight-forward manner to centralized authorities of international organizations: they usually have the status of an organ according to the rules of the organization and they carry out the functions of the international organization. It is less clear if authorities of member states are under some circumstances organs or agents of international organizations as well. WTO practice has evolved around the question whether the authorities of the EU member states are organs or agents of the EU insofar as they implement EU law.[85] Whether this is the case ultimately depends on the definition of organ or agent.

The general academic debate on whether acts by the EU member states can be attributed to the EU if they implement EU law has typically been conducted irrespective of Art. 6 ARIO. The arguments presented in that regard may, however, be used to form two possible approaches to define whether an entity has the required "status in accordance with the rules of the organization" or carries out the "functions" of the international organization and is thus an organ or an agent. One focuses

---

[83] *European Communities and its Member States - Tariff Treatment of Certain Information Technology Products: Report of the Panel* [2010] WTO Panel Report WT/DS375/R; WT/DS376/R; WT/DS377/R [7.1172].

[84] For an overview of the foundation of these articles, see: McArdle (2013), pp. 126–134.

[85] For an overview of WTO case law, see: Flett (2017); Cook (2015), pp. 31–48.

on whether an entity is structurally integrated into the international organization and the other one focuses on whether the entity carries out the functions of the international organization. After presenting the two approaches, WTO practice on the matter will be evaluated.

Structural Approach

It has been argued that only those entities that are structurally integrated into the apparatus of the international organization are organs of that organization.[86]

This view focuses on the definition of organ in accordance with Art. 2 (c) ARIO which limits organs to those entities who have been awarded that status by the rules of the organization. With regards to the EU, supporters of this definition conclude that the main institutions named in Art. 13 TFEU or other bodies, offices, and agencies as established by secondary legislation within the meaning of Art. 51 TFEU are organs of the EU.[87] Conversely, when executing EU law, the EU member states' authorities do not act as organs of the EU, as they are not integrated into the structure of the EU.

It seems as though the Commentary to Art. 6 ARIO follows this approach because "an organ or agent of an international organization may be an organ or agent who has been seconded by a State or another international organization. The extent to which the conduct of the seconded organ or agent has to be attributed to the receiving organization is discussed in the commentary on Art. 7 [ARIO]."[88] Some have concluded from this that this leaves no room for any wider definition of organ or agent.[89]

This view should be rejected for several reasons. First, it disregards that acts of agents can also be attributed to international organizations and that agents do not have to be named as such within the rules of the organization, according to Art. 2 (c) ARIO. Rather, it suffices that an entity carries out the functions of the international organization. The question is therefore rather, what the functions of an international organization are. The definition of agent is also not in conflict with the cited provision in the commentary to Art. 6 ARIO, as Art. 7 ARIO only applies subsidiarily to Art. 6 ARIO. Besides, Art. 7 ARIO was tailored for military operations[90] and its application in the WTO context is thus questionable to begin with.[91]

---

[86] E.g. Kuijper and Paasivirta (2013), pp. 49–53; Cortés Martín (2013), p. 195; Delgado Casteleiro (2016), pp. 69–71.

[87] Kuijper and Paasivirta (2013), pp. 50–51.

[88] Art. 6 (6) ARIO Commentary.

[89] Klein (2010), p. 299; Delgado Casteleiro (2016), p. 71.

[90] International Law Commission, 'Responsibility of International Organizations, Second report on responsibility of international organizations, by Mr. Giorgio Gaja, Special Rapporteur', DOC A/CN.4/541, 2.4.2004, 14.

[91] See below at Sect. 5.4.4.

Second, in ARSIWA the ILC adopted a wide definition of organ.[92] The reason for this is that states should not be able to avoid responsibility by internal subdivision. The same considerations should apply here. In the same way as acts by an autonomous subunit can be attributed to a state should acts by states that fulfil the functions of the international organization be attributed to international organizations as organs. This would also recognize on an institutional level that international organizations have generally a limited budget which is why execution of its decisions usually takes place at a member state level.[93] Third, this structural definition ignores the fact that normative decisions are taken at the level of the international organization.[94] Fourth, the term organ should be interpreted extensively to minimise the risk of third parties to name the wrong respondent and to minimise the necessity by Panels to interfere and interpret the rules of the organization. Lastly and most importantly, WTO practice does not support this view.[95]

Functional Approaches

The ARIO Commentary clarifies the definition of organ and agent by referring to the ICJ advisory opinion in *Reparation for Injuries*. The ICJ understood agent "in the most liberal sense, that is to say, any person who, whether paid official or not, and whether permanently employed or not, has been charged by an organ of the organization with carrying out, or helping to carry out, one of its functions – in short, any person through whom [the international organization] acts."[96] The ICJ confirmed in other cases that "the essence of the matter lies not in [the] administrative position [of the persons] but in the nature of their mission."[97] The ARIO Commentary argues that such an extensive approach also applies to the definition of an organ.[98]

The definition of an organ or an agent of an international organization therefore depends on the functions of the international organization and whether the entity in question carries out or helps to carry out the functions of the international organization. The ARIO Commentary does not clarify any further how this can be determined. To answer under which circumstances an entity carries out the functions of an international organization, two distinct arguments that are regularly made in the

---

[92] Art. 4 (1) ARSIWA Commentary; Ch. II(7) ARSIWA Commentary. The same considerations should apply to ARIO as well.

[93] Klabbers (2013), p. 279.

[94] Kuijper and Paasivirta (2013), p. 54.

[95] See below at section 'Practice'.

[96] *Reparation for Injuries Suffered in the Service of the United Nations* (1949) 1949 ICJ Rep 174 (ICJ Advisory Opinion) 177. See also: Art. 6 (2) ARIO Commentary.

[97] *Applicability of Article VI, Section 22, of the Convention on the Privileges and Immunities of the United Nations* (1989) 1989 ICJ Rep 177 (ICJ Advisory Opinion) 177. See also: Art. 6 (2) ARIO Commentary.

[98] Art. 6 (4) ARIO Commentary.

debate on responsibility of the EU for acts of the authorities of the EU member states may be used: one focuses on functional integration and one focuses on who controls a certain action.

Functional Integration

The first strand of argumentation has evolved around the question whether the EU's member states act as organs or agents of the EU when executing EU legislation in a field of exclusive EU competence. In matters concerning the common commercial policy, which includes anti-dumping action, the EU is exclusively competent.[99] Yet, the customs authorities of the member states execute the directly applicable EU legislative acts.[100] This separation between legislative competences and executive powers has been described as "executive federalism".[101] This view argues that because the EU member states still carry out "functions" of the EU, they act as organs of the EU.

When preparing the ARIO, the ILC invited international organizations to comment on applicable rules of attribution. The EC took the view that where member states carry out EC legislation, the acts of these authorities should be attributed to the EC[102] as they act as implementing authorities of EC law.[103] This seems to support that insofar as EC member states carry out EC law, they are organs of the EC.[104] The ILC's Special Rapporteur acknowledged this statement and tried to rebut it unsuccessfully in his Second report on responsibility of international organizations. He claimed that in such a case conduct can be attributed to member states but not the international organization, yet the EC could still be responsible even without attribution of conduct.[105] This claim is, of course, impossible to reconcile with Art. 4 (a) ARIO which requires attribution for responsibility to arise.[106] More importantly, however, the statement that conduct cannot be attributed to an international

---

[99] Art. 3 (e), 207 (1) TFEU.

[100] Art. 291 (1) TFEU.

[101] Schütze (2010), p. 1385.

[102] International Law Commission, 'Comments and observations received from international organizations', 2004, Doc A/CN.4/545, p. 29, para. 5.

[103] Information note of 7.3.2003, attached to a letter from the Director-General of the Legal Service of the EC, Mr. Michel Petite, addressed to the United Nations Legal Counsel, Mr. Hans Corell, quoted in International Law Commission, 'Reponsibility of International Organizations, Second report on responsibility of international organizations, by Mr. Giorgio Gaja, Special Rapporteur', 2004, Doc. A/CN.5.541, pp. 5, 6, para. 11. See also: Talmon (2005), p. 412.

[104] The EC does not specify that attribution should take place because the member states are organs of the EC but this is one way to interpret its arguments.

[105] International Law Commission, 'Reponsibility of International Organizations, Second report on responsibility of international organizations, by Mr. Giorgio Gaja, Special Rapporteur', DOC A/CN.4/541, 2.4.2004, para. 11.

[106] Talmon (2005), p. 409; Kuijper and Paasivirta (2004), pp. 111, 127. For a further discussion of Gajas reply in his third report and criticism thereof, see: Eeckhout (2011), p. 462.

organization because it is attributed to a state is made frequently but wrong as ARIO does not prescribe exclusive attribution but rather also allows dual attribution.[107] The EC's comments must thus be understood to mean that it supports that its members authorities act as its agents or organs[108] and the ILC's reply why this should not be the case is weak and must be disregarded.

Some authors have picked up the EC's statements and argued that where authorities of the member states merely carry out EU legislation, they are functionally integrated into the EU's administration.[109] Similarly, some have focused on the fact that EU law assigns the EU member states the function to carry out EU legislation[110] which makes them organs of the EU.[111]

The core of these arguments is that as opposed to states, international organizations are given certain functions. When carrying out these functions, the acting authority is an organ of the international organization. It is more difficult, however, to describe the functions of an international organization, especially as, unlike competences, it is not a well-defined and clear concept. The relevance of the functions of an international organization is highlighted in ARIO and ARSIWA as they distinguish between functions and competences, the former being more extensive.[112] The functions of an international organization refers to the general set-up of the international organization. It considers why the international organization has been created and which tasks it carries out in what ways. Those authorities that act to effectively carry out the tasks that have been assigned to the international organization are thereby organs of that international organization.

Control

A second set of arguments that has developed generally in the context of the EU's responsibility for acts of its member states focuses on control. These arguments can also apply to the definition of organ or agent. The definition of agent or organ thereby focuses on whether the international organization can exercise control over the entity in question. Control can thereby either refer to effective control or normative control.

It has been argued that if the role of the EU member states is confined to implementing and applying EU law, the authorities of EU member states' should

---

[107] See below at: Sect. 5.6.

[108] Talmon (2005), p. 413. Paasivirta and Kuijper acknowledge the merits of this argument but claim that the ILC has not adopted that approach: Paasivirta and Kuijper (2005), p. 215.

[109] Delgado Casteleiro (2016), p. 183; Kuijper and Paasivirta (2004), p. 127; Bartels et al. (2006), pp. 460–461.

[110] Art. 291 (1) TFEU.

[111] Flett (2017), p. 888; Messineo (2014), p. 76.

[112] Art. 8 ARIO covers the situation where an authority acts outside its competences but within the overall functions of the authority.

be considered as EU organs.[113] The EU effectively controls implementation by the EU member states, as the Commission has the ability to bring a claim against the member states if they fail to comply with EU law.[114]

It is, however, difficult to see how a potential violation claim by the Commission effectively controls member states. Member states are generally free to implement EU law in a way that they wish and the authorities remain under the state's control.[115] The EU can only correct an action by a member state or force a member state in the abstract to act, but cannot direct the member states' authorities.

A more nuanced approach is therefore to require normative control.[116] Member states act as agents of the EU, as they put into practice the will of the EU legislature, the compliance of which with primary law is ensured at Union level.[117] With regards to directives, the normative control stems from the fact that ultimately the legality of a measure still depends on Union law.[118]

In the abstract this means that an international organization exercises normative control if the international organization expresses its will in a legally binding manner. If the member states subsequently follow that will, they act under the normative control of the international organization, i.e. as their organs.

Because this approach focuses on a specific normative decision of the international organization, it has some difficulties applying to cases where there is no normative decision or where the member state's authorities acts in violation of the normative decision. If the international organization gives member states' authorities discretion any violation of an international obligation within the exercise of the discretion can hardly be attributed to the international organization. More generally, where a claim against a measure is not *as such* but only *as applied* as the member state authority incorrectly applied the international organization's legislation, it is difficult to see how the member state's authority acted under normative control of the international organization.

This also clarifies the difference to the arguments focussing on functional integration. Applying the functional integration line of reasoning would conclude in both cases that the acts of the member states' authorities can be attributed to the international organization. This is because regardless of who acted, ensuring a functioning customs policy is a function of the customs union. Any action that is

---

[113] Bartels et al. (2006), pp. 460–461.

[114] Art. 258 TFEU.

[115] International Law Commission, 'Responsibility of International Organizations, Third report on responsibility of international organizations, by Mr. Giorgio Gaja, Special Rapporteur', Doc. A/CN.4/553, 13.5.2005, para. 12.

[116] Hoffmeister (2010), p. 739. Hoffmeister argues that this is a situation of Art. 64 ARIO. It is, however, better to understand it as an application of Art. 6 ARIO. The nexus between internal laws and responsibility is only provided through the concept of normative control. Casteleiro would probably also support this, as he examines how to integrate considerations of normative control in Art. 6 ARIO but, wrongfully does not apply them: Delgado Casteleiro (2016), pp. 68–71.

[117] Hoffmeister (2010), p. 741; Kuijper and Paasivirta (2013), p. 55.

[118] Hoffmeister (2010), p. 742.

done to fulfil that function is done by an agent or organ of the customs union even if the member states make use of discretion or even violates legislation.

Practice

What the organs of international organizations are has been considered with regards to the EU in the WTO DSB, the ECHR, and the ECJ.

In the context of the WTO, the question whether acts by the member states' authorities of the EU can ever be attributed to the EU arose on several occasions.

EC – Computer Equipment concerned the customs classification of computer equipment. The measures at issue were a Commission Regulation, as well as binding tariff informations or similar measures, issued by the Ireland Revenue Commission,[119] the UK HM Customs and Excise,[120] and UK VAT and Duties Tribunal.[121] The US requested the establishment of Panels with the EC, United Kingdom, and Ireland. In its report, the Panel first focused on attribution to the EC and then found it unnecessary to rule with respect to the United Kingdom and Ireland.[122] Without explaining why it is possible, the Panel considered acts by EC member states' authorities as capable of raising legitimate expectations of the US against the EC, i.e. as attributing them to the EC.[123] The Panel did not dive into detailed explanations of why the actions could be attributed to the EC. Flett has argued that this decision can best be understood on the basis of Art. 6 ARIO as well as on the basis of Art. 9 ARIO.[124]

In *EC – Trademarks and Geographical Indications,* the Panel accepted the EC's submission[125] that EC laws are executed by EC member states acting as *de facto* organs of the EC. However, the Panel missed the opportunity to explain why the EC's member states act as *de facto* organs of the EC in that situation and it did not clarify the requirements for an authority to be considered a *de facto* organ of an international organization.

EC – Selected Customs Matter sheds some light on the questions that were left open in *EC – Trademarks and Geographical Indications.* The Panel held that during appeals in custom matters, the EC member states' customs authorities and judicial bodies or equivalent specialized bodies act as the organs of the EC and this setup does not violate Art. X:3(b) GATT.[126] In its reasoning, the Panel explicitly referred

---

[119] *European Communities - Customs Classification of Certain Computer Equipment* [1998] WTO Panel Report WT/DS62/R; WT/DS67/R; WT/DS68/R [2.18].

[120] ibid 2.19–2.21.

[121] ibid 2.22–2.24.

[122] ibid 8.15–8.16.

[123] ibid 8.32–8.59.

[124] Flett (2017), p. 888.

[125] *EC - Trademarks and Geographical Indications* (n 56) para 7.98.

[126] *EC - Selected Customs Matters* (n 49) para 7.553.

to Art. 4.1 ARSIWA in this context (the Report predates ARIO and Art. 4 ARSIWA is nearly identical to Art. 6 ARIO but applies to states[127]).[128] The Panel accepted the EC's argument that the reason customs authorities that review customs decisions act as organs of the EC is that of the preliminary reference procedure to the ECJ and the basic principles of primacy of EC law and direct effect.[129] The EC legal system has thereby been characterized as one of "executive federalism", whereby EC member states carry out the decisions taken by the EC organs.[130] Although the reference to the preliminary reference procedure could be used as evidence that the Panel endorsed a definition requiring control, the Panel also held that Art. X:3(b) GATT does not contain any requirements regarding the institutional structure of the review mechanisms as long as the reviews are undertaken by judicial, arbitral or administrative tribunals.[131] As this requirement could still be fulfilled without the preliminary reference procedure, the decisive arguments in this decision seem to have been that in the institutional setup of the EC, tasks have been divided in such a manner as can be described as "executive federalism". This report seems to clearly endorse the arguments surrounding an understanding of functional integration of the term organ.

All three Panel reports contradict the structural approach, as they all concerned attribution by entities that are not structurally listed as organs of the EU.

However, the WTO DSB practice seems to conflict with ECJ and ECtHR practice.

In *Kadi,* the question arose whether an act by the EC Commission could be attributed to the UN. To comply with the UN Resolution 1333/2000 and 1390/2002, the Commission implemented Regulation (EC) No. 467/2000 and No. 881/2002 which regulated that funds of *inter alia* Mr. Kadi should be frozen.[132] The ECJ ruled that the Commission did not act as a subsidiary organ of the UN.[133]

The ECJ relied on ECtHR jurisdiction which concerned the question whether acts by member states authorities can be attributed to the member states when implementing EU law to come to this conclusion. The ECJ distinguished between acts by the organs of the UN that have been listed as such and acts by other entities that seek to comply with UN Resolutions.[134] The ECJ then relied on *Bosphorus* to argue that the acts were attributable to the EC[135] and not the UN.[136]

---

[127] See below, Sect. 5.5.1.

[128] *EC - Selected Customs Matters* (n 49) n 932.

[129] ibid 7.550.

[130] ibid 2.13.

[131] ibid 7.552.

[132] *Kadi and Al Barakaat International Foundation v Council and Commission* [2008] Judgment of the CJEU ECLI:EU:C:2008:461 [11–45].

[133] ibid 314.

[134] ibid 311–312.

[135] ibid 313.

[136] ibid 314.

This decision clearly endorses a structural approach to the definition of organs. The ECJ reasoned that because the EU is not listed as an organ of the UN in its Charta, it is not an organ of the UN. However, both functional approaches would conclude that the EU acted as an organ of the UN by legislating. The UN Resolutions are binding upon its members and therefore constitute an instrument that expresses normative control. Hence, the EU is an organ following the normative control approach. Similarly, the UN is set up in a way that it enacts Resolutions that must then be transposed and implemented by its members. Hence, the structure of the UN resembles the one which can be described as executive federalism but to a much lesser degree than the EU.

It therefore seems as though *Kadi* is difficult to reconcile with the WTO practice as described above. The ILC's Special Rapporteur acknowledged the tension between these decisions in his Seventh Report on responsibility of international organizations but did not comment on the WTO practice. He simply asserted that *Kadi* does not "lend support to the proposal of considering that conduct implementing an act of an international organization should be attributed to that organization."[137] Above that he argued that the WTO's approach violates Art. 4 ARSIWA establishing that acts of member states authorities can be attributed to the states as they are their organs.[138]

This study argues that although *Kadi* has been decided correctly, it does not rule on whether the Commission acted as an UN organ, thereby releasing the tension with the WTO case law. The ECJ's explanation in *Kadi* falsely premises that dual attribution is not possible and the ECJ's arguments do not support the finding that attribution to the UN is not possible. The ECJ's finding whether or not an act by an authority of the EC could be attributed to the UN is irrelevant for the question that needed to be decided in the case. What should have been considered is whether the EC's Regulations could be attributed to the EC, which they quite clearly can, based on Art. 6 ARIO. Whether they could be attributed to the UN is a question that did not need to be answered in this case and that does not directly impact the EC's responsibility. This flaw is also highlighted by the ECJ's referral to *Bosphorus*. In *Bosphorus,* the ECtHR considered whether certain acts could be attributed to the member states of the EU and cannot be used as a ruling that consequently these acts cannot be attributed to the EU as well. *Bosphorus* therefore does not lend support either for the conclusion that the considered acts in that case cannot be attributed to the EU as well or that attribution to the member states is exclusive, as neither was at question in that case. The Special Rapporteur follows this by arguing that otherwise

---

[137] International Law Commission, 'Responsibility of International Organizations, Seventh report on responsibility of international organizations, by Mr. Giorgio Gaja, Special Rapporteur', Doc A/CN.4/610, 29.3.2009, para. 33. He also mentioned *Bosphorus Hava Yolları Turizm ve Ticaret Anonim Şirketi v Ireland* [2005] ECtHR Application no. 45036/98.

[138] International Law Commission, 'Responsibility of International Organizations, Seventh report on responsibility of international organizations, by Mr. Giorgio Gaja, Special Rapporteur', Doc A/CN.4/610, 29.3.2009, para. 33.

attribution could not occur to the member states of the international organization. Because ARIO explicitly allows dual attribution, this reasoning cannot hold.[139]

Hoffmeister has explained and defended why the cases were decided differently by pointing to the fact that whereas EU law is directly applicable, UN law is not.[140] More generally, direct effect as well as supremacy of EU law is often used as an argument why the EU should be treated differently to other customs unions on matters of responsibility.[141] Why these two concepts should be used to delineate attribution is usually not explained, however. Whether an authority is an organ of a customs union depends on the institutional setup of the customs union, i.e. the relationship between the customs union and its member states. Direct effect deals with the relationship between the customs union and natural persons. It is not clear why that relationship should have an impact on evaluating whether the member states may act as organs of the customs unions. However, it is understandable why supremacy of EU law is referred to and this implicitly supports a control-based approach to what an organ is. Yet, this should be one indication for control but not the only one, as effective control can be established even without supremacy of customs union law. Importantly, however, this discussion may be subsumed under the question what an organ is and using this approach it is possible to state that the EU is not an organ of the UN and *vice versa,* but the EU member state authorities are an organ of the EU.

All of the practice above concerned the situation in which EU member states enacted binding EU law in a field where the EU is exclusively competent. The responsibility of the EU has also become relevant in the WTO DSB outside the context of member states implementing EU law. Insights can be gained where EU member states do not simply execute EU law but make use of their competences.

Especially *EC – Biotech* may help to illustrate how attribution works not within an exclusive EU competence. That case concerned safeguard measures imposed by the member states but permitted under the relevant EU directive.[142] The measures were attributed to the EU and the Panel held that this was because the EC "never contested that, for the purposes of this dispute, the challenged member states measures are attributable to it and can be considered EC measures."[143] Besides the fact that the EU acknowledged the member states' behaviour, the fact that it permitted the imposition of safeguard measures can also be used to argue that it exercised some normative control and that overall the imposition of Safeguard

---

[139] For an argumentation on whether dual attribution is possible, see Sect. 5.6.

[140] Hoffmeister (2010), pp. 736–737. He also argues that there is no possibility in the UN by a person to challenge being on the list of sanctions. Although persons or entities can approach the UN Sanctions Committee to re-examine whether they should be on a sanctions list, that procedure is "in essence diplomatic and intergovernmental", where he refers to *Kadi v. Commission* (n 132) para 323.

[141] E.g. *EC - Selected Customs Matters* (n 49) para 7.550.

[142] *European Communities - Measures Affecting the Approval and Marketing of Biotech Products* [2006] WTO Panel Report WT/DS291/R; WT/DS292/R; WT/DS293/R [8.13–8.62].

[143] ibid 7.101.

measures falls within its functions so that arguments relying on executive federalism could apply.[144]

Overall, WTO practice supports the functional approaches to the definition of organs. Arguments can be made that it supports the definition using functional integration as well as a normative control-based approach. WTO practice is thereby consistent or at least does not stand in the way of ECJ and ECtHR practice.

5.4.2.2 Organs in Anti-Dumping Practice

The different acts associated with anti-dumping are either carried out by a fully centralized authority (under section 'Fully Centralized Authorities'), partially centralized authority (under section 'Partially Centralized Authorities') or by member state authorities (under section 'Member States' Authorities').

Fully Centralized Authorities

Where customs unions have completely centralized their anti-dumping regimes, the centralized authorities are organs of the customs union. These central authorities include e.g. the European Commission or the Eurasian Economic Commission. This also includes supporting organs whose purpose it is to accommodate for member states' opinions, such as the comitology in the EU.[145] Because internal laws of the customs union name them and give them the status of organs, they are organs of the customs union even following the structural approach.

The authorities of the member states may participate in this constellation exceptionally upon request by the central authority to e.g. verify information. The temporary and exceptional nature of the cooperation make it difficult to argue that from the perspective of the setup of the customs union the authority fulfils functions of the international organization. Such a case could possibly be resolved with Art. 7 ARIO.[146]

Partially Centralized Authorities

The more problematic cases are where authorities have only been centralized partially. This means that competences are divided between a central authority and the member states' authorities.

---

[144]Flett (2017), p. 894.

[145]Art. 4, 5 Reg. (EU) 2011/182.

[146]Arguing against: Kuijper and Paasivirta (2013), p. 47. They refer to Art. 64 ARIO Commentary, which supposedly leaves no room to the argument that Member States could be considered agents of the EU. The ARIO Commentary explicitly refers to the WTO cases stating the opposite, however.

If competences are divided horizontally, where member states are competent, the same principles apply as where no centralization has occurred. This means that their acts cannot be attributed to customs unions. Where the central authority is competent, the same principles apply as in instances of full centralization, meaning that acts can be attributed to the customs union.

If competences are divided vertically, the different definitions or organ reach different conclusions. Insofar as the central authority acts, it is structurally integrated into the customs union and thus an organ of it. Where member states act, they are not structurally integrated into the customs union. There may be normative control if the customs union legislated or if it can escalate cases to the central authority. Moreover, a functioning anti-dumping regime is within the functions of the customs union, which is why the member state authorities are functionally integrated into the customs union. This constellation resembles *EC – Biotech* which may be used in support of a functional definition of organ.

Member States' Authorities

Lastly, the member states' authorities may be competent for anti-dumping. There are three reasons why member state authorities conduct the investigation and impose the anti-dumping measure.

The first is that although the customs union has the competence for anti-dumping, it has delegated the competence to one of its members, such as is the case in SACU. Only the structural definition and functional integration definition conclude that ITAC is an organ of SACU. Following a structural definition of an organ, ITAC is an organ of SACU, as it has been given a mandate to conduct the investigations and impose the measures on behalf of the customs union. In SACU, the task of establishing a functioning anti-dumping system has been handed to the customs union. Because it is still setting up the anti-dumping system, it has temporarily mandated that task to South Africa, yet South Africa's authorities carry out functions of the customs union and are therefore organs of it. As SACU does not exercise control over how ITAC conducts its investigations, control-based definitions of organ would reject ITAC being a central organ.

The second is where one country is obliged to copy the anti-dumping measures of another country, such as is the case in the EU-Andorra and EU-San Marino customs unions. The Commission is not an organ of these customs unions under either definition. No centralized institutions have been created, which is why the Commission is not structurally integrated into these customs unions. Similarly, an anti-dumping regime is not a function of the customs union, as Andorra and San Marino simply copy the EU's regime. Finally, the customs union does not exert normative or factual control in the conduct of investigations or when decisions are taken. The Commission is thus not an organ of the customs union following all definitions.

The third is where member states have remained competent to impose anti-dumping measures. This includes the possibility that the customs union has harmonized procedures or includes some cooperation requirements that do not take the form of formal institutions. In that situation, the member state authorities are not organs or agents of the customs union under either definition. The member states' authorities are not mentioned in the customs union agreement as organs of the customs union and are thus not structurally integrated. Similarly, the effective functioning of an anti-dumping regime is not a function of the customs union, which is why the functional integration definition does not apply either. Finally, the customs union does not exert normative or factual control over the member states, as the investigation and imposition of the concrete measures solely depends upon the member states authorities. The views focusing on control therefore also reject that the authorities are organs of the customs union.

5.4.2.3 Has the Organ or Agent Acted Within Its Functions?

Even if an authority is an organ of a customs union, attribution following Art. 6 ARIO also requires that the organ acted "in the performance of [its] functions".

According to the ARIO Commentary, the functions of an agent or an organ are defined by "the rules of the organization".[147] As the rules of the organization "apply"[148] but are not the only source to define the functions of its organs or agents, it is possible that "in exceptional circumstances" an entity fulfils the functions of an international organization "even if this could not be said to be based on the rules of the organization".[149]

Generally, these rules of the organization refer to the rules on competences. If an authority acts *ultra vires,* Art. 8 ARIO applies. Because the rules of competences tend to be rather clear with regards to anti-dumping measures, typically no problems arise concerning this requirement.

5.4.3 Art. 7 ARIO: State Organs at the Disposal of an International Organization

According to Art. 7 ARIO the conduct of an organ of a state[150] that is placed at the disposal of another international organization is attributed to the international organization if the organization exercises effective control over that conduct.

Art. 6 and 7 ARIO are mutually exclusive grounds of attribution. Art. 7 ARIO only applies if the authority put at the disposal of the international organization is not an organ of the international organization.[151] This means that following a functional

---

[147] Art. 6.1 ARIO.

[148] Art. 6.2 ARIO.

[149] Art. 6 (9) ARIO Commentary.

[150] Or the conduct of an organ or agent of another international organization.

[151] Art. 7 (1) ARIO Commentary.

approach to the term organ or agent, it is not necessary in the area of anti-dumping to resort to Art. 7 ARIO.

Art. 7 ARIO applies if the seconded organ or agent acts on the one hand to a certain extent as organ of the seconding state[152] and on the other hand the international organization exercises effective control over that organ or agent. According to the ARIO Commentary, effective control refers to the "factual control that is exercised over the specific conduct taken by the organ or agent placed at the receiving organization's disposal."[153] The control is effective when it is exclusive and derives from a direct command.[154] The examples in the ARIO Commentary where this was the case all relate to military operations[155] and the ILC's Special Rapporteur acknowledged that the provision was tailored for military operations.[156] Because the test for effective control does not refer to normative elements of control, it is generally less adequate to apply in commercial contexts.[157]

Nevertheless, some have suggested to limit the definition of an organ to the structural approach and argued that the where EU member states execute binding EU law, this provision applies.[158] Yet, it is questionable whether the control exercised by the CJEU or the Commission upon the customs authorities can be qualified as deriving from a "direct command". The fact that member states are free in the way how they implement EU law has led most authors conclude that the degree of effective control exercised is not sufficient.[159]

The only situation where Art. 7 ARIO could apply is where a central authority is competent to investigate but may request assistance by a member state authority. The central authority will be able to decide if and how the member state authority participates in the investigation. This could constitute effective control but it is doubtful whether it passes the threshold of not simply acting "on instructions from the sending State" but can be described as "under its exclusive direction and control."[160]

---

[152] Art. 7 (1) ARIO Commentary.

[153] Art. 7 (4) ARIO Commentary. See also: *Al-Jedda v The United Kingdom* [2011] Judgment of the ECtHR Application no. 27021/08 [84–86]; Kuijper and Paasivirta (2004), p. 53; Hoffmeister (2010), p. 726.

[154] International Law Commission, 'Report of the International Law Commission on the work of its sixty-first session, Responsibility of International Organizations', Doc A/64/10, 2009, 114.

[155] Art. 7 (5)-(15) ARIO Commentary.

[156] International Law Commission, 'Reponsibility of International Organizations, Second report on responsibility of international organizations, by Mr. Giorgio Gaja, Special Rapporteur', Doc A/CN.4/541, 2.4.2004, 14.

[157] Hoffmeister (2010), p. 727.

[158] Steinberger (2006), p. 851.

[159] Kuijper and Paasivirta (2004), p. 127; Delgado Casteleiro (2016), p. 74.

[160] Art. 7 (4) ARIO Commentary, referring to Art. 6 (2) ARSIWA Commentary.

5.4.4 Art. 9 ARIO: Conduct Acknowledged and Adopted by an International Organization

According to Art. 9 ARIO, conduct can be attributed to an international organization if and to the extent that the organization acknowledges and adopts the conduct in question as its own.

The ARIO Commentary, by referring to Art. 11 ARSIWA Commentary, elaborates that the cases in which conduct was acknowledged and adopted as the organization's own must be distinguished from those in which an international organization merely supports or endorses conduct.[161]

The referral to Art. 11 ARSIWA is only of limited use, as Art. 11 ARSIWA primarily focuses on the delineation of conduct by private individuals to conduct of a state.[162] The situation in the context of ARIO is different as the question with regards to anti-dumping measures is whether conduct can be attributed to a state or an international organization and not if the conduct is public at all. However, the reference in the ARIO Commentary to *EC – Computer Equipment*[163] clarifies that Art. 9 ARIO should also apply to the question of attribution between a member state and the customs union.

The EU has internationally always acknowledged the conduct of its member states[164] which makes it difficult to identify for what particular reason the WTO DSB Panels and the Appellate Body have accepted that the conduct can be attributed to the EU.[165] Some authors even suggest that because the EU in the past always acknowledged the conduct of its member states, other WTO members can rely on this[166] and the EU would be estopped from denying attribution. Although some authors remain critical of this ground of attribution[167] the fact that the EU in the context of WTO Panels always explicitly acknowledged the conduct of its members could mean that Panels at least implicitly recognized this ground of attribution.

Nevertheless, the exact requirements of this ground of attribution are not clear. The WTO cases which deal with attribution through adoption by the EU always also involved other objective factors that could justify attribution.[168] It is, therefore, unclear whether acknowledging conduct alone is sufficient. Above that, not too

---

[161] Art. 11 (6) ARSIWA Commentary.

[162] See especially Art. 11 (2) ARSIWA Commentary.

[163] Art. 9 (3) ARIO Commentary.

[164] The ARIO Commentary distinguishes between acknowledging attribution or responsibility, without clarifying the meaning of it, Art. 9 (3) ARIO Commentary.

[165] E.g. In *EC – Computer Equipment* it is not entirely clear why the Panel attributed the conduct to the EC, *EC - Computer Equipment* (n 119) para 8.32–8.59.

[166] Herrmann and Streinz (2014) para 93.

[167] Delgado Casteleiro (2016), pp. 75–77.

[168] E.g. *EC – Computer Equipment* could also be interpreted to endorse attribution following Art. 6 ARIO, *EC - Computer Equipment* (n 119) para 7.15. See also: Delgado Casteleiro (2016), pp. 76–77.

much emphasis should be put on the will of the customs union to ensure legal certainty. Art. 9 ARIO should be an exceptional ground of attribution and should not be the norm, which is why it should be limited to the delineation between international organizations and private conduct.

5.4.5   Chapter IV: Subsidiary Responsibility

If an act can be attributed to the international organization following the previously mentioned grounds of attribution, it is not necessary to refer to Chapter IV of Part One of the ARIO, which deals with subsidiary forms of responsibility of an international organization.[169] Whereas the previous grounds of attribution followed the principle of independent responsibility[170] and identified whether an international organization has committed an own act, subsidiary attribution focuses on the collaboration of several states with international organizations.[171] Art. 19 ARIO thereby highlights that responsibility under this chapter is without prejudice to the responsibility of any other state or international organization.

Art. 17 ARIO is the central norm of attribution in Chapter IV Part One. It deals with the circumvention of international obligations. If an international organization circumvents responsibility, the act will be attributed to the international organization. Although circumvention sounds like a catch-all clause, Art. 17 ARIO defines two specific cases in which circumvention occurs. First, according to Art. 17.1 ARIO an international organization circumvents its responsibility if it adopts a binding decision on its members or another international organization to commit an act that would be internationally wrongful if committed by the international organization. Second, according to Art. 17.2 ARIO, an international organization circumvents its responsibility where it authorizes member states of an international organization to commit an act that would be internationally wrongful if committed by the former organization and the act in question is committed because of that authorization. The ARIO Commentary clarifies that Art. 17.2 ARIO also applies to acts of an international organization which may "be defined by different terms but present a similar character to an authorization".[172]

The ARIO Commentary limits the scope of this provision further by introducing another unwritten requirement. Accordingly, the term "circumvention" implies "an intention on the part of the international organization to take advantage of the separate legal personality of its members in order to avoid compliance with an international obligation."[173]

---

[169] Art. 57 (5) ARSIWA Commentary.

[170] Ch. IV (1) ARSIWA Commentary.

[171] Ch. IV (2) ARSIWA Commentary.

[172] Art. 17 (9) ARIO Commentary.

[173] Art. 17 (4) ARIO Commentary.

Responsibility arises under Art. 17.1 ARIO already before the member state commits the act because compliance by members of the international organization is to be expected.[174] Where under Art. 17.1 ARIO the member state is given some limited discretion and it would have been possible to carry out the act without committing an internationally wrongful act, responsibility only arises, as in Art. 17.2 ARIO,[175] if the act actually occurs.[176]

The only practice the ARIO Commentary refers to in order to justify this provision is the *Bosphorus* decision of the ECtHR.[177] Since that decision gives answers to the question whether states and not the international organization are responsible, it is difficult to see, how the case applies in this regard.

The difficulty of this provision is its delineation from Art. 6 ARIO. If one adopts a broad approach to the term organ, as this study advocates, why is the situation of Art. 17.1 or 17.2 ARIO not simply a case where an organ of the international organization acts?

First, it is doubtful that Art. 17 ARIO codifies international customary law in the commercial context. The ARIO Commentary does not refer to any cases that deal with circumvention in the commercial context and all cases that could fall under that provision have, especially in the WTO context, been dealt with using arguments that lead to an extensive reading of the terms organ or agent.[178] Especially the additional requirement that the international organization must intend to take advantage of the separate legal personality of its members seriously limits the scope of this provision[179] and that requirement has never been mentioned in the WTO context. Second, Art. 17 ARIO focuses more on individual acts for which international organizations are exceptionally responsible. The problems of responsibility in the context of customs unions for anti-dumping measures arise at an institutional level, however. A provision that focuses more on institutional structures is thus better suited to deal with these situations. Consequently, Art. 17 ARIO should not be applied to solve questions of responsibility in the context of anti-dumping measures.

Art. 14, 15 ARIO describe other situations in which the international organization is responsible. Because of their overlap with Art. 17 ARIO, their relevance in the WTO context is limited.[180]

According to Art. 14 ARIO, an international organization is responsible for aiding or assisting a state or another international organization in the commission of an internationally wrongful act, if the international organization does so with knowledge of the circumstances of the internationally wrongful act and the act

---

[174] Art. 17 (5) ARIO Commentary.

[175] Art. 17 (10) ARIO Commentary.

[176] Art. 17 (7) ARIO Commentary.

[177] Art. 17 (6) ARIO Commentary.

[178] See above: Sect. 5.4.2.

[179] Nedeski and Nollkaemper (2012), pp. 33, 48.

[180] Arguing that there is no overlap but rather a relationship of exclusivity between the provisions in Chapter IV: Delgado Casteleiro (2016), pp. 86–87.

would be internationally wrongful if committed by the international organization. Primary responsibility still lies with the state or international organization that aid has been given to.[181]

The ARIO Commentary gives the example of the United Nations Mission in the Democratic Republic of Congo (MONUC) giving support to the Forces Armées de la République Démocratique du Congo (FARDC). According to a United Nations Legal Council Document if MONUC has reasons to believe that FARDC violate international law, they must stop assisting them or else they would be responsible for their assistance.[182]

It has been argued that such a form of responsibility applies where a customs union authorises its member states to act, such as is the case in EU state aid cases.[183] By way of analogy this could also apply to cases where a central authority allows states to impose anti-dumping measures.

Using this provision has a similar weakness as Art. 17 ARIO. Art. 14 ARIO contains additional subjective requirements that have not been applied in the commercial context yet, which makes its validity as customary international law in that context questionable. Moreover, a provision that focuses more on institutional structures is better suited to deal with questions of responsibility for anti-dumping measures in customs unions. Ultimately, the application of Art. 14 ARIO for anti-dumping measures should thus be rejected as well.

According to Art. 15 ARIO responsibility also arises if an international organization directs or controls a state or another international organization in the commission of an internationally wrongful act, if the international organization does so with knowledge of the circumstances of the internationally wrongful act, and the act would be internationally wrongful if committed by that organization. This provision has considerable overlap with Art. 17 ARIO, which the Commentary acknowledges but does not find harmful.[184]

Like in Art. 7 ARIO, the question arises whether control refers only to effective control or whether it also includes normative control. The Commentary explains that if an international organization adopts a binding decision this could constitute direction or control.[185] The addressee should thereby not have discretion when carrying out the conduct.[186] Beyond that the Special Rapporteur hinted at the possibility that direction or control could include normative control by stating that where the obligation to carry out an act is accompanied "by elements that ensure

---

[181] Art. 14 (1) ARIO Commentary, Art. 16 (1) ARSIWA Commentary. See generally: Reinisch (2010), p. 63.

[182] Art. 14 (6) ARIO Commentary, referring to documents published in the New York Times on 9.12.2009.

[183] Flett (2017), p. 896.

[184] Art. 15 (5) ARIO Commentary.

[185] Criticizing the conception of direction and control: Reinisch (2010).

[186] Art. 15 (4) ARIO Commentary.

enforcement of those decisions".[187] In such a case "normative control would correspond in substance to factual control."[188]

Others argue, however, that Art. 15 ARIO only applies to instances of effective control. The wording of Art. 15 ARIO is nearly identical to Art. 17 ARSIWA and Art. 17 ARSIWA requires effective control.[189] Moreover, there is significant overlap in the terminology between Art. 17 ARIO and Art. 7 ARIO which could mean that a similar conception of control applies.[190]

Again, it could be argued that this provision should apply in the case where the international organization enacts anti-dumping measures and Art. 6 ARIO should be restricted to a structural approach of organ or agents. The same criticism applies with regards to the other provisions in Chapter IV Part One ARIO, which is why that argument should be rejected.

5.4.6 Conclusions

Whether ARIO applies in the WTO context is already highly contentious. The concrete application of ARIO is an even bigger minefield. This study proposes one reading of the different requirements with a focus on the institutional setup of customs unions subsumed under Art. 6 ARIO. This section also advocates that whether conduct should be attributed to a customs union depends on whether the authority is functionally integrated into the customs union.

The results that follow for anti-dumping measures are less controversial. Where a centralized authority acts, the actions can be attributed to the customs union. Where an authority of a member state acts, actions can be attributed to the customs union only if the customs union acts as a supervisory body or where the member state is mandated to conduct anti-dumping investigations by the customs union. Otherwise, i.e. where the customs union only harmonizes anti-dumping procedures or where the customs union is only competent in a specific set of cases, the acts by the member state authorities cannot be attributed to the customs union.

---

[187] International Law Commission, 'Responsibility of International Organizations, Third report on responsibility of international organizations, by Mr. Giorgio Gaja, Special Rapporteur', Doc. A/CN.4/553, 13.5.2005, para. 15.

[188] ibid.

[189] Art. 17 (7) ARSIWA Commentary.

[190] Reinisch (2010), p. 77. For a similar argumentation, see: Delgado Casteleiro (2016), pp. 85–86.

5.5   Attribution of Anti-Dumping Measures to the Member States of Customs Unions

The customary law on state responsibility has been codified in ARSIWA. Like ARIO, according to Art. 1 ARSIWA, every internationally wrongful act of a state entails the international responsibility of that state. An internationally wrongful act exists, according to Art. 2 ARSIWA, when conduct consisting of an action or omission is attributable to the state under international law and constitutes a breach of an international obligation of that state. This section focuses on the requirement that an act must be attributed to a state.

ARSIWA was adopted in 2001, 10 years before ARIO and most situations cover the distinction between a private act and a public act. This differs from the problem covered in this section. Regarding anti-dumping measures and the conduct surrounding the investigation and imposition of anti-dumping measures there is usually no dispute that the act is public. The relevant question is whether it should be attributed to the member states, the customs union or both.

It could be that ARSIWA does not apply in these situations. According to Art. 57 ARSIWA, ARSIWA does not apply to the responsibility of a state "for the conduct of an international organization". The ARSIWA Commentary clarifies that this limitation only applies to subsidiary responsibility. Accordingly, in cases of subsidiary responsibility, Part V ARIO applies.[191] Besides that, the grounds for attribution in Part One Chapter II ARSIWA apply as well.[192]

The ARSIWA Commentary muddies this distinction by stating that Part One Chapter II ARSIWA only applies for conduct that is not conduct performed by an organ of an international organization.[193] This qualification could mean that where an authority is an organ of an international organization, it cannot be an organ of a state as well. This statement could thus be used as an argument to endorse a structural approach to the definition of an organ or agent within Art. 6 ARIO.[194] Otherwise, it is difficult to see why authorities that are organs of an international organization as well as of a state should be treated differently to authorities that are only organs of a state. The better view is to disregard this statement altogether. First, according to Art. 57 ARSIWA, the ARSIWA does not answer questions on responsibility of an international organization. If the commentary is understood in a way to endorse a structural interpretation of the term organ or agent in Art. 6 ARIO and to prohibit dual attribution, ARSIWA answers questions on responsibility of international organizations. Second, this statement cannot be reconciled with the fact that the ARIO and ARSIWA endorse dual attribution.[195] Third, there is no international

---

[191] Art. 57 (4) ARSIWA Commentary.

[192] Art. 57 (5) ARSIWA Commentary. Casteleiro simply does not apply this part without justification why it should be barred: Delgado Casteleiro (2016), pp. 90–110.

[193] Art. 57 (5) ARSIWA Commentary.

[194] On that dispute, see above section 'Structural Approach'.

[195] See below at Sect. 5.6.

custom cited to support that statement but there is international custom to support a functional approach to the definition of organs.[196]

This means that Part One Chapter II ARSIWA applies to answer whether acts can be attributed to states even if that state is a member of a customs union. ARSIWA and ARIO provide for several grounds of attribution. The three most relevant grounds of attribution in the context of anti-dumping will be considered.

5.5.1   Art. 4 ARSWIA: Organs or Agents of a State

According to Art. 4 ARSIWA, the conduct of any "State organ" shall be attributed to that state. State organ thereby refers to "all the individual or collective entities which make up the organization of the State and act on behalf of it."[197] This includes all entities within the organization of the central government as well as that of a territorial unit regardless if they carry out legislative, executive, judicial or any other function.[198] Moreover, although internal law can give indications on the status of whether an entity is an organ,[199] it can also be determined by practice.[200]

This ground of attribution has also been recognized in several Appellate Body and Panel Reports. In *US – Corrosion-Resistant Steel Sunset Review,* the Appellate Body stated that "[t]he acts or omissions that are so attributable are, in the usual case, the acts or omissions of the organs of the state, including those of the executive branch."[201]

Because of the similarities of that provision with Art. 6 ARIO and since the Commentary of Art. 6 ARIO refers to Art. 4 ARSIWA,[202] the same definition of organ can be used. The three approaches to defining an organ are a structural approach, a functional integration approach and a definition based on control.[203]

Applied in the context of anti-dumping measures, it is questionable whether fully centralized or partially centralized authorities or authorities of member states are organs or agents of a state.

---

[196] See above at Sect. 5.4.2.

[197] Art. 4 (1) ARSIWA Commentary.

[198] Art. 4.1 ARSIWA.

[199] Art. 4.2 ARSIWA.

[200] Art. 4 (11) ARSIWA Commentary.

[201] *US - Corrosion-Resistant Steel Sunset Review* (n 82) para 81; *Thailand - Cigarettes (Philippines)* (n 50) para 7.120.

[202] Art. 6 (1) ARIO Commentary.

[203] See above at Sect. 5.4.2.

5.5.1.1 Fully Centralized Authorities

Whether acts of fully centralized authorities can be attributed to member states is contentious in theory and in practice. Both will be considered accordingly.

Theory

Applying the three possible definitions of an organ, only the functional integration approach concludes that fully centralized authorities are organs of the member states.

According to a structural definition of an organ, customs unions are distinct legal personalities and their authorities are not integrated into the structure of the state. Therefore, they are not organs of the state.[204] Moreover, states do not exercise effective control over central customs union authorities. Similarly, because the central authority takes the decision to investigate and implement anti-dumping measures, it is that authority's will that is reflected in the measures and not that of its member states. In the abstract, the international organization has been given certain competences and in complying with these competences it executes its own will and not the will of its member states. The definitions that centre around control therefore also conclude that the authorities of customs unions are not the authorities of the member states.[205]

Nevertheless, a definition that focuses on functional integration can be used to justify that central authorities are authorities of the member states as well.[206] Two strands of argumentation may support this view.

First, the arguments developed why EU member states that execute binding EU law are organs of the EU can be used in reverse. The "executive federalism" justification could apply the other way as well: In the same way that the EU makes use of the EU member states' executive organs for its decisions to be carried out, the EU member states make use of the EU's centralized organs to provide a legislative framework in fulfilling tasks they held before being in a customs union.[207] That handing over functions to the EU is an arrangement but cannot release the states from the fact that ultimately they are state functions is also clarified as the *Kompetenz-Kompetenz* remains with the EU member states, as the German Constitutional Court pointed out[208] and that the EU member states can unilaterally leave

---

[204] This is at least implicit in: Kuijper and Paasivirta (2013), pp. 49–53; Cortés Martín (2013), p. 195; Delgado Casteleiro (2016), pp. 69–71; Durán (2017a, b); Delgado Casteleiro and Larik (2013).

[205] Compare to: Bartels et al. (2006), p. 460; Hoffmeister (2010), p. 739; Kuijper and Paasivirta (2004, 2013); Delgado Casteleiro (2016), pp. 68–71.

[206] Reaching the same result: Talmon (2005), p. 413; Flett (2017), p. 888.

[207] Entities carrying out legislative functions are organs as well, Art. 4.1 ARSIWA.

[208] [1998] BVerfG, Order of the Second Senate 2 BvR 1877/97 and 2 BvR 50/98.

the EU.[209] This highlights that member states chose to outsource certain functions, but ultimately the functions remain state functions as well.

Second, a comparison to federal states can be made.[210] The division of power in an international organization is akin to the division of power within a federal state. In a federal state, the state is still responsible for the actions of autonomous sub-units, even if it does not have the power to compel the autonomous unit to abide by the state's international obligations.[211] Exceptions may exist, if the treaty has a federal clause,[212] which there has not been in the WTO Agreement.[213] This applies irrespective of the fact that the autonomous unit is a partial subject of international law.[214] The reason why actions should be attributed to states is because a state should not be able to escape liability through internal subdivision.[215]

The difference between a federal state and an international organization is of course that the autonomous unit is one within a federal state and the international organization is an international entity.[216] If a state should be responsible for an internal subunit it has no effective or normative control over even though that subunit is a partial subject of international law because a state should not be able to escape liability, the same should apply with regards to international organizations.[217]

Deciding between the three definitions, the same considerations apply as above.[218] Above that, there is a principled debate in international law whether member states should be responsible for the acts of international organizations. Two schools of thought exist on that issue.[219]

The first school of thought, often referred to as the constitutionalist view argues that the separate legal personality of an international organization blocks responsibility of its member states, except if the agreement of the international organization provides for instances that the members should be responsible.[220] Arguments of this school of thought could be used to defend a structural approach of organ or one based on control.

---

[209] Art. 50 TEU.

[210] On the extent to which this analogy is possible, see: Bordin (2019), pp. 49–86.

[211] Art. 4 (9) ARSIWA Commentary.

[212] Art. 4 (10) ARSIWA Commentary.

[213] Steinberger (2006), pp. 839–840.

[214] For German Federal States: Nettesheim (2018) para 34.

[215] Ch. II (7) ARSIWA Commentary.

[216] Generally: Bordin (2019).

[217] Leinarte applies a similar argumentation but does not focus solely on attribution or the definition of an organ: Leinarte (2018), p. 174.

[218] See above: Sect. 5.4.2.1.

[219] Brölmann (2012), p. 286; Klabbers (2012); Schermers and Blokker (2018) para 1585; Hartwig (1993), pp. 290–293.

[220] Proponents of this view include: Amerasinghe (1991), p. 259.

Opposing the constitutionalist view is the functionalist view, the second school of thought. It sees international organizations as a manifestation of the member states' will to cooperate to achieve certain objectives and the member states should thus be responsible for any acts by the international organization.[221] Arguments of this school of thought could be used to defend a functional definition of organ.

As the purpose of this chapter is to identify international customary law, the arguments of the two camps will not be presented and decided but relevant practice will be considered. Ultimately, relevant practice in the WTO and the ECtHR clearly favours the functional definition of organ.

WTO Practice

The issue of attributing the acts of central authorities by an international organization to its member states arose in the WTO with regards to three customs unions: the EU, the EU-Turkey customs union, and the EAEU.

EU

The issue of attribution between the EU and its member states arose several times. The focus of these proceedings has, however, almost entirely been attribution of acts to the EU. In the case that panels find acts attributable to the EU, the finding does not mean that acts cannot also be attributed to the EU member states, as acts can be attributed to more than one actor.[222] Rather, the decision by third-parties to only request a Panel against the EU and not the EU member states can be understood as judicial economy, as once EU liability is established, there is no necessity to establish the member states' liability.[223] Moreover and similarly, the omission by panels to not discuss attribution to the EU member states in the case that attribution to the EU has been established is more of an expression of judicial economy than of a finding and cannot be used in support of the case that no attribution to the member states is possible.[224] Rather, it could also demonstrate that there is a subsidiary form of attribution, whereby if an act can be attributed to the EU and a member state, the responsibility of the member state is moot.[225]

The Panel in *EC – Selected Customs Matters* supports this. It explicitly remarked that since the US had only argued that the EC violated a GATT provision and not its members, it would confine its attention to whether the EC is in violation of the

---

[221] Proponents of this view include: Brownlie (2005), p. 359; Yee (2005).

[222] Potentially differing opinion: Hoffmeister (2010), p. 734. Hoffmeister only refers to exclusive responsibility, which is an independent concept of attribution, however.

[223] Flett (2017), p. 902.

[224] Doing so, without explanation: Hoffmeister (2010).

[225] Flett (2017); Johansen (2019), p. 178.

relevant GATT provision, without explicitly ruling that the member states are not in violation.[226]

Whether EC acts can be attributed to the member states has only been explicitly raised in *EC and Member States – IT Products*. The US, Japan, and Chinese Taipei independently requested consultations[227] and the establishment of a panel[228] with the EC and its member states regarding the tariff treatment of the EC concerning certain IT products. The claims were directed against the EC as well as its members and were *as such* claims.

The Panel did not decide at the outset whether to rule on the claims directed against EC member states.[229] It noted, however, that it will consider the extent the EC and the EC member states have failed to comply with commitments in the goods schedules.[230] The panel then considered that "to the extent that the [EC member states] apply WTO inconsistent measures enacted by the [EC]" they consider it a reasonable basis to conclude that they have "acted inconsistently".[231] By using the words "acted inconsistently" the Panel came just short of declaring that the EC member states are responsible for EC measures. After establishing that the EC violated its WTO obligations, the Panel did not decide whether the EC measures could also be attributed to the EC member states. Rather it held that it was not necessary to examine whether the application of the measures by EC member states authorities would conflict their WTO obligations, as the claims made by the claimants were only claims of *as such* violations.[232]

The Panel has therefore not taken the opportunity to define attribution of actions taken by the EU to its member states. It is unclear, whether this means that the Panel did not see any ground to attribute actions by the Commission to EU member states or whether it simply means that the parties failed to make that argument.[233]

EU-Turkey Customs Union

Attribution to one of the members of the EU-Turkey customs union was at dispute in *Turkey – Textiles*. In that case, India challenged import restrictions on several categories of textile and clothing and argued that they violated Art. XI, XIII GATT, Art. 2.4 ATC.[234] Turkey argued that it could not be individually liable for the quantitative restrictions as they resulted from the implementation of the EC-Turkey customs union (now EU-Turkey customs union). According to its

---

[226] *EC - Selected Customs Matters* (n 49) para 7.548.

[227] *EC - IT Products* (n 83) para 1.1.

[228] ibid 1.5.

[229] ibid 7.89.

[230] ibid.

[231] ibid.

[232] ibid 8.2.

[233] Flett (2017), p. 892.

[234] *Turkey - Textiles* (Chap. 4, n 94) para 9.32.

view, Turkey is not responsible for acts that were collectively taken by the members of the EC-Turkey customs union through the institutions created by the agreement.[235]

Answering that claim, the Panel considered attribution to the different actors of the EC-Turkey customs union. The measures were attributed to Turkey because the measures were implemented through formal action by Turkey and published in its official Gazette, they were enforced by Turkish authorities and applied in the territory of Turkey only.[236] The Panel thus concluded that the measures were taken by Turkey.

The Panel then considered whether the measures could be attributed to the EC-Turkey customs union. This depended on whether the customs union has a distinct legal personality, which the Panel denied. Thus, the measures were not attributable to the customs union either.[237] The Panel did not consider if the principles of attribution could apply despite the EU-Turkey customs union not having international legal personality.

When considering attribution to Turkey, the Panel focused on actions taken by Turkish authorities and ignored the fact that Turkey was internationally obliged to act in that way. Moreover, since the Panel did not attribute the measures to the customs union, it is not surprising that the Panel did not attribute the measures to the EC. Overall, this case does not analyse to what extent acts by a central authority can be attributed to its members states in general.

EAEU

Whether acts by bodies of customs unions can be attributed to the member states of the customs union has been at issue in two cases against Russia.[238]

---

[235] ibid 9.33. More specifically, Art. 12 Decision 1/95 regulate that Turkey must adopt certain EC regulations concerning imports of textile and clothing and in particular Council Reg. 3030/93, which provided for the bilateral agreements with supplier countries to be implemented by a set of EC quantitative limits on certain imports. Based on this, Turkey adopted Quantitative Limits on certain products from India, see ibid 2.31–2.40.

[236] *Turkey - Textiles* (Chap. 4, n 94) para 9.36.

[237] ibid 9.40. See also above at Sect. 5.4.1 discussing legal personality.

[238] 5 Panel Reports against Russia exist. Attribution not been relevant in the following cases: *Russia – Railway Equipment* concerned Russia's suspension of certain conformity assessment certificates, denial to issue new certificates and denial to recognize certificates issued in other Members of the EAEU towards Ukrainian exporters of certain railway products. As the competence to issue conformity assessment certificates rested with Russia, the relationship with the EAEU was not discussed: *Russia - Measures Affecting the Importiation of Railway Equipment and Parts thereof* [2018] WTO Panel Report WT/DS499/R, WT/DS485/R/Corr.1, WT/DS485/R/Corr.2 [2.2]. *Russia – Traffic in Transit* concerned transit restrictions on transits from Ukraine to Kazakhstan and later the Kyrgyz Republic. These measures were adopted without the participation of the EAEU so that attribution did not become an issue: *Russia - Measures Concerning Traffic in Transit* [2019] WTO Panel Report WT/DS512/R [7.5–7.16].

Russia – Tariff Treatment

Russia – Tariff Treatment concerned duty rates in the Common Customs Tariff (CCT) of the EAEU. The EU argued that the measures are in excess of Russia's bound duty rates and Russia thereby violated Art. II:1(a) GATT 1994 *as such*.[239] Russia would apply the duty rates without any prior transposition.[240]

Interestingly, the EU argued that *Turkey – Textiles* serves as precedent "for the proposition that the members of a customs union may be held responsible [. . .] for *acts of that customs union,* at least in certain circumstances" (emphasis added).[241]

The Panel first recognized that the duty rates were adopted by the EAEU and not by Russia.[242] It then clarified that if Russian customs authorities apply the common customs tariff (CCT) duty rate, the act by the Russian authorities is attributable to Russia.[243] Since the challenge was *as such* there had not been any relevant act by the Russian customs authorities yet. The Panel nevertheless argued that because Russia is internationally and domestically bound to apply the CCT and Russia demonstrated conduct that it would apply the duty rates (it had issued customs declarations concerning the tariff lines at issues) future application could be presumed.[244] The Panel inferred from this that "the relevant CCT requirements are attributable to Russia, insofar as [. . .] it can be presumed that the CCT requirements will lead to the relevant duty rates being applied by Russia."[245]

The Panel therefore considered whether there was any act or whether there will be any act by a Russian authority and upon finding that there will be an act by a Russian authority the Panel concluded that the entire measure was attributable to Russia. Of course, there is a distinction between applying a measure and enacting one. The Panel gave no analysis why attribution of the legislative act—which was the *measure* at issue—could be inferred from the fact that the application of the measure is attributable to Russia. The report is best understood in the context of a functional approach of the term organ. As Russia somehow participates—by applying the customs procedures—customs remain a function of the member states. Whether Russia would implement the EAEU measures is relevant to determine if a system of executive federalism exists in the EAEU and the Panel's approach should be read as doing that.

The reasoning of the Panel gets less clear as the Panel went on to remark that since Russia asked the Panel to consider subsequent EAEU amendments to make findings that these are compliant with Russia's WTO obligations, Russia would agree

---

[239] *Russia - Tariff Treatment* (n 79) para 7.34.

[240] ibid 7.46.

[241] ibid 7.43.

[242] ibid 7.42.

[243] ibid 7.46.

[244] ibid.

[245] ibid.

attributing the relevant measures.[246] Although the Panel used this to demonstrate that Russia shared its views on attribution, this could also be understood as attributing the CCT because Russia acknowledged it.[247]

Russia – Commercial Vehicles

Russia – Commercial Vehicles, concerned an anti-dumping measure imposed by the EEC and applied by Russian customs authorities.[248] The Panel did not address the question of attribution of conduct, but throughout the Panel Report, the actions of the DIMD have been called Russia's actions[249] and the imposed anti-dumping measures have been called Russia's anti-dumping measures.[250]

The Appellate Body Report did not address attribution either; it noted in a footnote that although Russia is the respondent, it was the DIMD that completed the anti-dumping investigation. It also pointed to the fact that when the consultations were requested, Russia was the only customs union member that was also a WTO member.[251]

As Russia had already applied the anti-dumping duty, the Panel did not test whether Russia was likely to apply it. Like in the *Russia – Tariff Treatment* case, the Panel did not distinguish between the measure and the application of the measure. Attribution could be explained because Russia acknowledged the measure or because the EAEU's authorities are Russia's authorities as well. The interchangeable use of the DIDM and Russia as well as the fact that no requirements of attribution have been tested hints towards an understanding that the ground for attribution lies in the structure of the customs union i.e. that the EAEU's authorities are Russia's authorities as well.

Conclusion

Overall, WTO law offers only little support to explain whether and how attribution of acts by fully centralized authorities may be attributed to the member states. This question specifically has received a lot of attention and there is no clear answer to it. Following the approach adopted in Art. 4 ARSIWA and using a functional definition of organ, the conclusion is that acts of fully centralized authorities are

---

[246] ibid.

[247] According to Art. 11 ARSIWA, see below Sect. 5.5.2.

[248] *Russia - Anti-Dumping Duties on Light Commercial Vehicles from Germany and Italy* [2017] WTO Panel Report WT/DS479/R [2.1].

[249] E.g. ibid 7.279–7.280. Whereas the EU claims that the actions of the DIMD were inconsistent with Art. 1, 18.4 ADA and Art. VI GATT 1994, the Panel concluded that the Russian Federation acted inconsistently with those provisions.

[250] E.g. ibid 8.5.

[251] *Russia - Anti-Dumping Duties on Light Commercial Vehicles from Germany and Italy* [2018] WTO Appellate Body Report WT/DS479/AB/R 7.

attributable to the member states as well. *Russia – Tariff Treatment* may be used to endorse this result and the result is also favourable from a practical perspective, as it avoids circumvention of WTO obligations by outsourcing them to a centralized institution.

5.5.1.2   Partially Centralized Authorities

Authorities may have been partially centralized as well. Partial centralization may happen horizontally or vertically.[252] Where centralization has occurred horizontally, cases in which the central authority is competent may be answered in the same way as with fully centralized authorities. This means that they are organs of their member states as well. Where the member states are competent, the same arguments apply as if member states have remained competent and the organs are organs of the member states as well.

A similar argumentation may apply with respect to vertical relationships between the member states' authorities and central authorities. If the conduct of even fully centralized authorities may be attributed to the member states of customs unions, this should also apply to central authorities that have not been fully centralized. The same argumentation as if member states had remained competent applies if the member states' authorities act.

5.5.1.3   Member States' Authorities

Member states may be competent to conduct investigations and impose measures for three reasons: because the competence has been delegated, because the system obliges some members to copy anti-dumping measures or because member states have remained competent.

Where competences have been delegated to one member of the customs union, a different argumentation applies between the member that is competent and those members that are not competent. In SACU, ITAC is structurally integrated into South Africa and the South African state also exercises effective and normative control over its authorities. ITAC is, however, not structurally integrated into the BELN countries and they do not exercise effective or normative control. Functionally, ITAC is integrated into all SACU members, however. The same arguments apply as with respect to any centralized institution. This is because it should not make a difference for questions of attribution if a customs union decides to create a new authority or tasks an existing authority with the same task. The result of this may seem unintuitive. A proceeding may be initiated against Namibia for WTO violations in the area of anti-dumping committed by ITAC. Ultimately, this result is sensible, as Namibia also benefits from the measure that applies to imports into

---

[252] See above at: Sect. 5.3.

Namibia as well. Responsibility for a measure should coincide with being able to derive benefits from a measure.[253]

This situation is different from one in which one member state investigates and imposes measures and the other member states are obliged to copy these anti-dumping measures, as is the case in the EU-Andorra and EU-San Marino customs unions. In that case, the EU's Commission is structurally integrated into the EU, fulfils its functions and acts under its effective and normative control, i.e. is an organ of the EU. As anti-dumping is not a function of the EU-Andorra or EU-San Marino customs union, the argumentation employed as with SACU cannot apply. The Commission is not an organ of Andorra or San Marino.

Where member state authorities investigate and impose anti-dumping measures, the authorities are structurally integrated into the state. Following all definitions of an organ they are thus organs of the state. This is the case even if legislation on anti-dumping measures has been harmonized.

Russia – Pigs (EU) confirms this finding. It concerned the compliance of import bans on pork related products from the EU and specific countries[254] with the SPS agreement. Although the import bans were administrative decisions taken by the Russian Federal Service for Veterinary and Phytosanitary Supervision (FSVPS), the legislative framework upon which the Russian authorities acted was by the customs union.[255] The EU challenged the measures *as such* and *as applied.*[256] During the Panel proceedings, the Panel considered whether the measures were attributable to Russia.[257] The Panel thereby started off by affirming that acts of the organs of a state are attributable to it.[258] It then identified that FSVPS is an organ of Russia and its acts are attributable to it.[259] The Panel then described the requirements under the Customs Union Decision No. 317 and concluded that the measures also require "compliance with a number of requirements under the control of Russia's authorities."[260] The measure was thus attributed to Russia.[261] The latter connection was appealed by Russia to which the Appellate Body held that "we do not see on what ground the act of a member may not be attributed to that member due to the fact that

---

[253] Korhonen and Selkälä (2016), p. 845.

[254] *Russian Federation - Measures on the Importation of Live Pigs, Pork and other Pig Products from the European Union* [2016] WTO Panel Report WT/DS475/R [2.9].

[255] Decision by the Customs Union Commission on the Use of Veterinary-Sanitary Measures in the Customs Union, No. 317, 18.6.2010 (Customs Union Decision No. 317). For the relationship between the legislation and the executive decisions, see: ibid 7.75–7.83.

[256] ibid 2.9.

[257] The reason it considered this was because Art. 3.3 DSU has been interpreted in *US - Corrosion-Resistant Steel Sunset Review* (n 82) para 81 to mean that "any act or omission attributable to a WTO Member can be a measure of that Member for purposes of dispute settlement proceedings." See: *Russia - Pigs (EU)* (n 254) para 7.56.

[258] *Russia - Pigs (EU)* (n 254) para 7.75.

[259] ibid 7.79.

[260] ibid 7.82.

[261] ibid 7.83.

the basis for doing so is not contained in that member's municipal law."[262] The Appellate Body then distinguished between the measure and the legislative background of the measure. Although the legal foundation of a measure may be relevant to justify WTO compliance of the measure, only attribution of the measure is required.[263]

5.5.2   Art. 11 ARSIWA: Conduct Acknowledged and Adopted by a State

Conduct can also be attributed to a state, following Art. 11 ARSIWA, if and to the extent that the state acknowledges and adopts the conduct as its own. This is possible if at the time of commission, the conduct was not attributable to the state, but it was subsequently acknowledged and adopted by the state as its own.[264] The cases in which conduct was acknowledged and adopted as the state's own must be distinguished from those in which a state merely supports or endorses conduct.[265] Even though most cases falling under Art. 11 ARSIWA deal with the adoption and acknowledgement of private acts by a state,[266] the existence of the identical Art. 9 ARIO[267] and the application of Art. 9 ARIO to question of attribution between an international organization and a state[268] indicate that this provision also provides for the possibility to acknowledge and adopt acts attributable to an international organization as its own.

The Panel Report in *Russia – Tariff Treatment* could also be understood based on adoption by Russia. Because Russia used EAEU measures in their defence,[269] this could mean that it acknowledges all measures as its own. More generally, EAEU cases may all be subsumed under this provision. When Russia joined the WTO, it committed that to ensure that "the WTO obligations of the Russian Federation would be fully implemented, including in those areas where the CU Bodies had competency".[270] This could either be understood as a cheque blanche to acknowledge all

---

[262] *Russian Federation - Measures on the Importation of Live Pigs, Pork and other Pig Products from the European Union* [2017] WTO Appellate Body WT/DS475/AB/R [5.20].

[263] ibid.

[264] Art. 11 (1) ARSIWA Commentary.

[265] Art. 11 (6) ARSIWA Commentary.

[266] Art. 11 (2) ARSIWA Commentary.

[267] According to Art. 9 (2) ARIO Commentary the provision is identical to Art. 11 ARSIWA.

[268] Art. 9 (3) ARIO Commentary refers to *EC – Computer Equipment,* dealing with the question whether a clearly public act could be attributed to the EC, see above at Sect. 5.4.4.

[269] *Russia - Tariff Treatment* (n 79) para 7.46.

[270] Working Party on the Accession of the Russian Federation, 'Report of the Working Party on the Accession of the Russian Federation to the World Trade Organization' (Russia Accession Protocol), WT/ACC/RUS/70, WT/MIN(11)/2, 17.11.2011, para. 178.

acts by centralized authorities or as an expression of a functional interpretation of what an organ is.

Like Art. 9 ARIO it is, however, not clear whether this ground of attribution applies even without objective basis. For this reason and for the same reason as with regards to Art. 9 ARIO, it is best to limit Art. 11 ARSIWA so that it cannot apply in the context of anti-dumping.

5.5.3   Part Five ARIO: Subsidiary Responsibility

Part Five ARIO deals with subsidiary forms of attribution.[271] Whereas the previous grounds of attribution followed the principle of independent responsibility[272] and identified whether a state has committed an act of its own, subsidiary attribution focuses on the collaboration of several states and/or international organizations.[273]

According to Art. 61 ARIO, if a state takes advantage of the fact that an international organization has competence in relation to the subject matter of one of the state's international obligations, it circumvents that obligation by causing the organization to commit an act that, if committed by the state, would have constituted a breach of the obligation and is therefore responsible.[274]

For responsibility to occur, three conditions must be met: (1) the international organization must have competences in relation to the subject matter, (2) there must be a link between the conduct of the state and the international organization in that the act of the international organization must have been caused by the member state, and (3) the international organization must commit an act that if committed by the state would constitute a breach of an international obligation.[275] Above that, as an unwritten requirement, the state will only incur international responsibility if the result was intended by the state.[276]

Explaining the application of that provision, the ARIO Commentary refers to the ECtHR practice.[277] The cited case law is, however, better subsumed under Art. 4 ARSIWA. The same criticisms apply as against the application of Art. 17 ARIO. First, the subjective requirement in Art. 61 ARIO seriously limits the scope of the provision and this requirement is probably not part of international customary law.

---

[271] Art. 57 (5) ARSIWA Commentary.

[272] Ch. IV (1) ARSIWA Commentary.

[273] Ch. IV (2) ARSIWA Commentary.

[274] Art. 61 ARIO.

[275] Art. 61 (6)-(8) ARIO Commentary.

[276] Art. 61 (2) ARIO Commentary.

[277] Art. 61 (3)-(5) ARIO Commentary. For an overview of ECtHR practice, see: Janik (2010), p. 127; Leinarte (2018), pp. 176–179.

Second, Art. 61 ARIO is better suited to deal with individual acts rather than institutional set-ups. It is thus better to apply Art. 4 ARSIWA.[278]

The other provisions of Part Five ARIO do not apply either. Especially Art. 58 ARIO which establishes responsibility based on aid or assistance by a state in the commission of an internationally wrongful act by an international organization does not apply, as Art. 58.2 ARIO excludes acts of members of an international organization performed in accordance with internal rules from its scope. Art. 59.2 ARIO includes the same exclusion where a state directs or controls the commission of an internationally wrongful act by an international organization.

5.5.4 Conclusions

Especially the question whether acts by fully centralized authorities can be attributed to member states is extremely controversial and has attracted a lot of academic attention. This study provides one possible reading of the different cases and how they fit in with the ARSIWA and thereby produces a workable result: Where a centralized authority acts, WTO practice combined with a functional approach to the definition of organ guides the route towards member state attribution following Art. 4 ARSIWA.

If one accepts this, all other constellations can be attributed to member states as well. The main advantage of this result is that it avoids situations in which WTO members may circumvent WTO obligations by transferring competences to a customs union and it complies with the ARSIWA and WTO practice.

5.6 Relationship of the Responsibilities

As ARIO and ARSIWA include several grounds of attribution, it is possible that an act fulfils the requirements of more than one ground of attribution. There are numerous possible combinations. E.g. if an act is committed by an organ of an international organization (Art. 6 ARIO) and acknowledged by a state (Art. 11 ARSIWA). Similarly, an organ of an international organization (Art. 6 ARIO) may be an organ of a state (Art. 4 ARSIWA) as well. ARIO and ARSIWA do not specifically regulate if the attribution is exclusive and if it is exclusive, how the situation is dealt with if several grounds of attribution apply.[279]

---

[278] See above at Sect. 5.4.5.
[279] Flett (2017), p. 851.

The starting point is thus that acts can be attributed to multiple parties.[280] The ARIO Commentary seems to support this, most notably when it claims that "the existence for the organization of a distinct legal personality does not exclude the possibility of a certain conduct being attributed both to the organization and to one or more of its members or to all its members."[281]

The idea of dual attribution to states and international organizations has been rejected by some on the basis that it undermines the independent legal personality of the international organization.[282] There are several reasons why this is not the case. First, even if dual attribution leads to dual responsibility, this does not mean that the international organization is less of a legal personality. Legal personality derives from the ability to be responsible and not from the ability to be exclusively responsible. Interestingly, this claim is only made in international law. Under German company law, several persons can create a partnership.[283] Partnerships are characterized by the fact that the partnership itself as well as the shareholders are responsible for certain acts.[284] Despite that, their legal personality is undisputed. Similar provisions exist in other countries. Although this is not a strictly legal argument, it simply demonstrates the distinction between an entity being an international legal person and it being responsible and the latter not impacting the former. Second, even if there were a relationship between responsibility and international personality, attribution is distinct from responsibility. The objections could therefore also be understood to merely support subsidiary forms of liability.

The principle that one act can be attributed to multiple persons is also reflected in the Guiding Principles of Shared Responsibility in International Law, with Principle 3 (a) addressing such a situation.[285]

---

[280] ibid 852; Messineo (2014); Herrmann and Streinz (2014) para 94. For differing opinion on previous draft, see: Hoffmeister (2010), p. 727; Delgado Casteleiro and Larik (2013).

[281] Art. 2 (10) ARIO Commentary. See also: Part II, ch. 2, (4) ARIO Commentary; Art. 48 (3) ARIO Commentary. Art. 6 ARSIWA could also be interpreted to support this. Because it mentions that it covers a situation of exclusive attribution, the opposite must be the general rule. This is irrespective of which provision the attribution is based on.

[282] E.g. with regards to the EU: Wessel (2018), pp. 101, 116; Hoffmeister (2010), p. 731. Other arguments against dual attribution include that it would make the member states responsible for acts of the international organization (ibid 731). This argument will not be dealt with as it is rather a consequence and this study argues that it is a good thing, as it avoids that international obligations can be circumvented by forming a customs union. Many have also implicitly rejected dual attribution: Kuijper and Paasivirta (2013), pp. 67–69; Paasivirta and Kuijper (2005), pp. 212–216; Hoffmeister (2010), p. 745; Hernández (2012); Kuijper (2010); Durán (2017b); Durán (2017a); Kuijper and Paasivirta (2013); Paasivirta and Kuijper (2005); Delgado Casteleiro and Larik (2013); Delgado Casteleiro (2016).

[283] "Personengesellschaft" as opposed to "Kapitalgesellschaft". E.g. § 705 German Civil Code – Bürgerliches Gesetzbuch (BGB) (Civil Code in the version promulgated on 2.1.2002 (Federal Law Gazette [Bundesgesetzblatt] I page 42, 2909; 2003 I page 738), § 105 para. 1, 3 German Commercial Code – Handelsgesetzbuch (HGB) (Commercial Code in the version promulgated on 22.12.2015 (Federal Law Gazette [Bundesgesetzblatt] I page 2567, 2015).

[284] E.g. § 128, 105 para. (1) OHG.

[285] Nollkaemper et al. (2020), pp. 15–17; Gasbarri (2020), p. 1223.

If acts can be attributed to multiple parties, this leads to the follow-up question how the responsibilities that derive from that attribution relate to each other. The only example where this could become relevant in the WTO is the EU and its member states. As there is no WTO practice on this, nothing definitive can be said about it, however.

5.7 Conclusions

The discourse on responsibility and attribution is so vast that this chapter cannot summarize and contextualize it completely. Instead, what this chapter has done is to develop an argument that produces practical results and thereby complies with WTO practice and the ILC's codification of responsibility and attribution in ARIO and ARSIWA.

It does so in several steps. First, ARIO and ARSIWA apply in the context of the WTO for questions of attribution. This is because WTO law does not contain *lex specialis* attribution provisions. Second, the core provision in ARIO and ARSIWA that should be applied to resolve problems of attribution are Art. 4 ARSIWA and Art. 6 ARIO respectively. Acts by organs of states or international organizations are attributable. Discussions that have taken place generally in the context of attribution in the WTO may be subsumed under these grounds of attribution so that three definitions of organ have been developed: a structural, a functional integration approach and one focussing on control. The favoured approach is the functional integration definition. An organ depends on the functions of the entity. The functions of an entity relate to the question of why an entity has been created.

This framework applied to anti-dumping means that acts of central authorities may be attributed to customs unions but acts of member states' authorities may generally not. Acts of central authorities may be attributed to member states as well as acts of the member states' authorities. Table 5.1 summarizes these results as applied to the customs unions.

Finally, attribution is relevant with respect to anti-dumping, as anti-dumping measures are only legal if the acts that constitute the investigation and imposition of the measure are attributable to the WTO member. This explains why it is legal for WTO members to form customs unions that conduct anti-dumping investigations centrally, but why it is not possible to borrow the normal value determination of a third country. This also provides the framework to argue what consequences economic integration and disintegration has.

Table 5.1 Attribution of anti-dumping measures

	Customs unions		Attribution to	
	Investigation	Decisions	Customs union	Member states
Fully harmonized	EU, EAEU, GCC, WAEMU, ECOWAS	EU, EAEU, GCC, WAEMU, ECOWAS	Art. 6 ARIO	Art. 4 ARSIWA
Partially harmonized				
Horizontal	CAN	CAN	Art. 6 ARIO	Art. 4 ARSIWA
Vertical	CARICOM, CACM	CARICOM, CACM, EU – Turkey, EAC	Art. 6 ARIO	Art. 4 ARSIWA
Not centralized				
Redelegation	SACU	SACU	Art. 6 ARIO	Art. 4 ARSIWA for all
Duty to copy	EU – Andorra, EU – San Marino	EU – Andorra, EU – San Marino	(–)	Art. 4 ARSIWA for EU; (–) for Andorra, San Marino
MS remain competent	MERCOSUR, CEMAC, EAC, COMESA, EU - Turkey	MERCOSUR, COMESA, CEMAC	(–)	Art. 4 ARSIWA

References

Amerasinghe CF (1991) Liability to third parties of member states of international organizations: practice, principle and judicial precedent. Am J Int Law 85:259

Amerasinghe CF (2005) Principles of the institutional law of international organizations, 2nd edn. Cambridge University Press, pp 79–80

Barents R (2003) The autonomy of community law. Wolters Kluwer Law & Business

Bartels L (2016) The UK's status in the WTO after Brexit. SSRN Electron J 3–7. <https://www.ssrn.com/abstract=2841747>. Accessed 5 July 2021

Bartels L (2017) The UK's WTO schedules. Global Trade Customs J 12:83

Bartels L, Ortino F, Eeckhout P (eds) (2006) The EU and its member states in the WTO - issues of responsibility. In: Regional trade agreements and the WTO legal system, 1st edn. Oxford University Press, pp 457–459

Bordin FL (2019) The analogy between states and international organizations. Cambridge University Press, pp 49–86

Brölmann C (2012) International organizations and treaties. In: Klabbers J, Wallendahl Å (eds) Research handbook on the law of international organizations. Edward Elgar, p 286

Brownlie I (2005) The responsibility of states for the acts of international organizations. In: Schachter O, Ragazzi M (eds) International responsibility today: essays in memory of Oscar Schachter. Brill, p 359

Cook G (2015) A digest of WTO jurisprudence on public international law concepts and principles. Cambridge University Press, pp 31–48

Crawford J (2012) Brownlie's principles of public international law, 8th edn. Oxford University Press, p 679 ff

Crawford J, Murphy L (2010) International responsibility. In: Besson S, Tasioulas J (eds) The philosophy of international law. Oxford University Press, p 283

Delgado Casteleiro A (2016) The international responsibility of the European Union: from competence to normative control. Cambridge University Press, pp 175–178

Delgado Casteleiro A, Larik J (2013) The "odd couple": the responsibility of the EU at the WTO. In: Evans M, Koutrakos P (eds) The international responsibility of the European Union: European and international perspectives, 1st edn. Hart Publishing

Durán GM (2017a) Untangling the international responsibility of the European Union and its member states in the world trade organization post-Lisbon: a competence/remedy model. Eur J Int Law 28:697, 703

Durán GM (2017b) The EU and its member states in WTO dispute settlement: a "competence model", or a case apart, for managing international responsibility? In: Cremona M, Thies A, Wessel RA (eds) The European Union and international dispute settlement. Hart Publishing

Eeckhout P (2011) EU external relations law, 2nd edn. Oxford University Press, pp 457–460

Flett J (2017) The world trade organization and the European Union and its member states in the WTO. In: Nollkaemper A et al (eds) The practice of shared responsibility in international law. Cambridge University Press, pp 853–872

Gasbarri L (2020) On the benefit of reinventing the wheel: the notion of a single internationally wrongful act. Eur J Int Law 31:1223

Gazzini T (2011) Personality of international organizations. In: Klabbers J, Wallendahl Å (eds) Research handbook on the law of international organizations. Edward Elgar, p 35

Hartwig M (1993) Die Haftung der Mitgliedsstaaten für Internationale Organisationen, 1st edn. Springer, Berlin Heidelberg, pp 290–293

Hernández GI (2012) Beyond the control paradigm? International responsibility and the European Union. Camb Yearb Eur Leg Stud 15:643

Herrmann C, Streinz T (2014) Die EU als Mitglied der WTO. In: von Arnauld A, Hatje A, Müller-Graff P-C (eds) Europäische Außenbeziehungen. 1. Aufl, Nomos-Verl-Ges [u.a]

Hoffmeister F (2010) Litigating against the European Union and its member states - who responds under the ILC's draft articles on international responsibility of international organizations? Eur J Int Law 21:723, 735

Ipsen K, Epping V (2018) § 8. Internationale Organisationen. In: von Heinegg WH, Epping V (eds) Völkerrecht: ein Studienbuch, 7., völlig neu bearbeitete Auflage. CH Beck

Janik C (2010) Die EMRK Und Internationale Organisationen– Ausdehnung Und Restriktion Der Equivalent Protection-Formel in Der Neuen Rechtsprechung Des EGMR –. Zeitschrift für ausländisches öffentliches Recht und Völkerrecht 127

Johansen SØ (2019) Dual attribution of conduct to both an international organisation and a member state. Oslo Law Rev 6:178

Kelsen H (1951) The law of the United Nations: a critical analysis of its fundamental problems: with supplement. FA Praeger

Klabbers J (2012) Contending approaches to international organizations: between functionalism and constitutionalism. In: Klabbers J, Wallendahl Å (eds) Research handbook on the law of international organizations. Edward Elgar

Klabbers J (2013) An introduction to international institutional law, 2nd edn, 7. printing. Cambridge University Press, pp 47–51

Klabbers J (2015) The EJIL foreword: the transformation of international organizations law. Eur J Int Law 26:9, 82

Klein P (2010) The attribution of acts to international organizations. In: Crawford J et al (eds) The law of international responsibility. Oxford University Press, p 299

Korhonen O, Selkälä T (2016) Theorizing responsibility. In: Orford A, Hoffmann F, Clark M (eds) The Oxford handbook of the theory of international law, 1st edn. Oxford University Press, p 845

Kovács C (2018) Attribution in international investment law. Kluwer Law International B V, pp 35–43

Kuijper PJ (2010) International responsibility for mixed agreements. In: Hillion C, Koutrakos P (eds) Mixed agreements revisited: the EU and its member states in the world. Hart

Kuijper PJ, Paasivirta E (2004) Further exploring international responsibility: the European Community and the ILC's project on responsibility of international organizations. Int Organ Law Rev 1:111, 127

Kuijper PJ, Paasivirta E (2013) EU international responsibility and its attribution: from the inside looking out. In: Evans MD, Koutrakos P (eds) The international responsibility of the European Union: European and international perspectives. Hart Publishing

Leinarte E (2018) The principle of independent responsibility of the European Union and its member states in the international economic context. J Int Econ Law 21:171–174

Martín JMC (2013) European exceptionalism in international law? The European Union and the system of international responsibility. In: Brownlie I, Ragazzi M (eds) Responsibility of international organizations: essays in memory of Sir Ian Brownlie. Martinus Nijhoff Publishers, p 195

McArdle S (2013) The international responsibility of the European Union: a critique of the international law commission's articles on the responsibility of international organisations. pp 126–134. <https://ethos.bl.uk/OrderDetails.do?uin=uk.bl.ethos.632584>. Accessed 5 July 2021

Messineo F (2014) Attribution of conduct. In: Nollkaemper A, Plakokefalos I (eds) Principles of shared responsibility in international law: an appraisal of the state of the art. Cambridge University Press, p 76

Nedeski N, Nollkaemper A (2012) Responsibility of international organizations "in connection with acts of states". Int Organ Law Rev 9:33, 48

Nettesheim (2018) GG Art. 32. In: Maunz, Dürig (eds) Grundgesetz-Kommentar, 84th edn

Nollkaemper A et al (2020) Guiding principles on shared responsibility in international law. Eur J Int Law 31:15–17

Paasivirta E, Kuijper PJ (2005) Does one size fit all?: The European Community and the responsibility of international organizations. Neth Yearb Int Law 36:169

Parish M (2012) International courts and the European legal order. Eur J Int Law 23:141

Pauwelyn J (2001) The role of public international law in the WTO: how far can we go? Am J Int Law 95:535, 538–540

Pellet A (2010) The definition of responsibility in international law. In: Crawford J et al (eds) The law of international responsibility. Oxford University Press, pp 5–11

Potter PB (1945) Origin of the term international organization. Am J Int Law 39:803

Reinisch A (2010) Aid or assistance and direction and control between states and international organizations in the commission of internationally wrongful acts. Int Organ Law Rev 7:63

Ruka P (2017) The international legal responsibility of the European Union in the context of the world trade organization in areas of non-conferred competences. Springer

Sands P, Klein P, Bowett DW (2001) Bowett's law of international institutions, 5th edn. Sweet & Maxwell, p 470 ff

Schermers HG, Blokker N (2018) International institutional law: unity within diversity, Sixth revised edition. Brill Nijhoff

Schütze R (2010) From Rome to Lisbon: "Executive Federalism" in the (New) European Union. Common Market Law Rev 47:1385

Seyersted F (1963) Objective international personality of intergovernmental organizations: do their capacities really depend upon the conventions establishing them?

Seyersted F (2008) Common law of international organizations. Brill Nijhoff, pp 43–64

Steinberger E (2006) The WTO treaty as a mixed agreement: problems with the EC's and the EC Member States' membership of the WTO. Eur J Int Law 17:837, 840

Talmon S (2005) Responsibility of international organizations: does the European Community require special treatment? In: Schachter O, Ragazzi M (eds) International responsibility today: essays in memory of Oscar Schachter. Brill, p 412

Wessel R (2018) Consequences of BREXIT for international agreements concluded by the EU and its member states. Common Market Law Rev 55:101, 116

White ND, Collins RMD (2011) International organizations and the idea of autonomy: institutional independence in the international legal order. Taylor & Francis Ltd

Yee S (2005) The responsibility of states members of an international organization for its conduct as a result of membership of their normal conduct associated with membership. In: Schachter O, Ragazzi M (eds) International responsibility today: essays in memory of Oscar Schachter. Brill

Chapter 6
Economic Integration and Economic Disintegration

The previous chapter has considered how the different anti-dumping regimes influence questions of responsibility and more specifically attribution. The chapter argued that attribution is not only relevant to determine responsibility but is also a requirement in connection with anti-dumping measures. If the investigation and imposition of the measure are attributable to the respective WTO member, the measure is in compliance with WTO law. This requirement enables to resolve problems that arise in cases of economic integration and disintegration, which this chapter will discuss.

Customs unions are not static. New customs unions are created, customs unions integrate further by centralizing institutions, or they dissolve by transferring competences of its institutions back to its members. The composition of customs unions can also change as parties may join or leave customs unions.

Changes in the structure or composition of customs unions create problems with respect to anti-dumping measures. Especially the effects on those measures that apply at the time this change occurs is not clear. The core of the problem is that the existing anti-dumping measures were imposed following an investigation that took the situation before the instance of economic integration or disintegration into account. The question is then how later changes impact these findings or measures. This chapter will only focus on these measures.

Customs union law defines the consequences of economic integration and disintegration on existing anti-dumping measures. These effects must then comply with WTO obligations. WTO compatibility will be considered in this chapter. This will be done by first analysing the practice of WTO members in cases of economic integration (under Sect. 6.1) and economic disintegration (under Sect. 6.2) and second subsuming that practice under WTO obligations (under Sect. 6.3).

This is practically relevant as many anti-dumping measures remain in force for extended periods of time and because the question of compatibility with WTO law concerns all anti-dumping measures in force. It is conceptually relevant as centralized institutions are a defining feature of customs unions and the consequences of establishing or dissolving them are a crucial steps in defining the relationship

F. Bickel, *Customs Unions in the WTO*, European Yearbook of International Economic Law 20, https://doi.org/10.1007/978-3-030-86312-8_6

between the member states and the customs union. By answering these questions, this study constitutes the first comprehensive study that evaluates recent practice of cases of economic integration and disintegration and offers a first legal analysis from a WTO perspective. The main argument of this section is that the territorial scope of anti-dumping measures may change if the investigation remains attributable to the measure. Changes in the scope of the measure may warrant an interim review, but in fewer cases than typically advocated for.

6.1 Case Studies: Economic Integration

In this study economic integration refers to three situations: where a customs union is formed, where a customs union changes its internal structure so that it gains the competence to impose anti-dumping measures, which the member states previously held, or where a customs union is enlarged.[1]

Generally, economic integration will only have an impact on existing anti-dumping measures if it leads to a change in competences, i.e. if following the instance of economic integration, a central authority of the customs union becomes competent or if its competence covers a larger territory. If a state remains competent to investigate and impose anti-dumping measures after joining a customs union, joining the customs union will not have an effect on existing anti-dumping measures.

This is so, even if the customs union requires harmonization of national anti-dumping legislation. The possible changes to national legislation will not have other effects than any other change of legislation. Usually, legislative changes include a clause stipulating that the changes only apply to existing anti-dumping measures upon an expiry review.[2] Absent specific provisions, they constitute changed circumstances and may necessitate an interim review.

If competences change due to economic integration, several questions relating to the existing anti-dumping measures arise:

- In all cases of economic integration, it is questionable what happens to the existing measures of the states that lost their competence to investigate and/or impose anti-dumping measures. Under which circumstances do those measures no longer apply?
- In cases where a customs union is enlarged and that customs union is competent to legislate and/or impose anti-dumping measures, what happens to the measures that have been imposed by the customs union against the joining state?

---

[1]The previous Chapter developed that attribution depends on the functions of a customs union and rejected competences as a way to solve attribution. The reason that competences are considered here is because they are easier to ascertain and there is a clearer definition of them. Their interaction with the concept of the functions of customs unions is considered in the legal analysis below.

[2]E.g. Art. 11 (3)(4) Reg. (EU) 2016/1036.

- In cases where a customs union enlarges and that customs union is competent to legislate and/or impose anti-dumping measures, does the scope of the customs union's anti-dumping measures change? If that is the case, is there a duty to review those measures or must other measures be adopted to alleviate the economic pressure that results from the sudden extension in scope of the measures?

Beyond these immediate consequences, economic integration may change the economic structure of a customs union in a subtle way that may have long lasting impacts on anti-dumping measures. E.g. in the EU, the Commission initiated an *ex officio* interim review of an anti-dumping measure in 2012 (i.e. eight and five years after enlargements took place) partly because the 2004 and 2007 enlargements had led many union producers to move their production facilities to the new member states which may have decreased the cost of union production.[3] These effects could influence the result of interim reviews but as the effects stem from indirect changes in the market structure and not primarily from enlargements, such cases will not be considered further in this section.

Since 2000 several instances of economic integration in customs unions have occurred. The analysis has been limited to cases that occurred in the last twenty years, even though important insights could also be gained in prior cases, especially from the formation of the European Economic Community. Art. 26 Reg. (EEC) 459/68 contained a transition regime for anti-dumping measures which allowed member states to continue to impose member state- wide measures alongside introducing union-wide measures. The GATT 1949 including its dispute settlement system and reporting mechanisms were of course vastly different then, so that this is only of limited use today, which is why it will not be explored further.

Most instances of economic integration since 2000 have not had any effects on competences and will therefore not be considered further. No relevant practice can be deduced from the following cases of economic integration:

- The customs union between the EC and San Marino came into force on 1. April 2002. The EC remained competent to investigate and impose anti-dumping measures. San Marino lost its competence to impose anti-dumping measures but because it had no anti-dumping legislation in place let alone imposed anti-dumping measures, no practice relevant practice exists.
- The GCC was formed on 1. January 2003. As the joining members[4] had no anti-dumping measures imposed or reported at the time of formation,[5] no relevant practice exists.

---

[3]Council Reg. (EU) 502/2013 of 29 May 2013 amending Implementing Regulation (EU) No 990/2011 imposing a definitive anti-dumping duty on imports of bicycles originating in the People's Republic of China following an interim review pursuant to Article 11(3) of Regulation (EC) No 1225/2009, OJ L 153/17, 5.6.2013, Rec. 9.

[4]Saudi Arabia was not a WTO at that time but only joined the WTO on 11.12.2005.

[5]Committee on Anti-Dumping Practices, 'Report (2003) of the Committee on Anti-Dumping Practices', G/L/653, 28.10.2003, pp. 12–16.

- The 2002 SACU Agreement came into force on 15. July 2004. Under the predecessor, the 1969 Agreement, South Africa's customs duties, including anti-dumping measures, applied to all members.[6] Although the 2002 SACU Agreement foresees changes in the anti-dumping regime, the same anti-dumping regime applies on an interim basis as before that treaty was changed.[7]
- The EAC was formed in 2000 and Burundi and Rwanda acceded to the EAC in 2007. Neither the acceding members, the members of the EAC, nor the EAC itself have ever imposed anti-dumping measures.
- Venezuela joined MERCOSUR on 31. July 2012. As the member states are competent to impose anti-dumping measures, no changes in competence occurred and enlargement had no effect on existing anti-dumping measures.
- Panama acceded to CACM in 2013. As the member states are competent to impose anti-dumping measures, enlargement had no effect on existing anti-dumping measures.[8]
- The EAEU came into force on 1. January 2015. It succeeded the customs union between Russia, Belarus and Kazakhstan. The competences to impose anti-dumping measures did not change. Before and after the formation of the EAEU, a central customs union authority was charged with conducting anti-dumping investigations.
- Tunisia and Somalia acceded COMESA on 18, 19. July 2018.[9] As member states are competent to impose anti-dumping measures, enlargement had no effect on existing anti-dumping measures.

For the purpose of this study only the formation of the Russia, Belarus and Kazakhstan customs union and the EC/EU and EAEU enlargements contain relevant practice. Table 6.1 summarizes their effects.

The only practice that relates to the formation of a customs union is the formation of the customs union between Belarus, Kazakhstan and Russia. In cases in which a customs union is formed, the only question that arises is what happens to the anti-dumping measures by the member states that lost the competence to impose them. The members' measures could be terminated. On the one hand this seems sensible

---

[6] Art. 4 (1) Customs Union Agreement between the Governments of the Republic of South Africa, the Republic of Botswana, the Kingdom of Lesotho and the Kingdom of Swaziland (1969 SACU Agreement), 11.12.1969, entered into force: 1.3.1970.

[7] See above at: Chap. 3, section 'SACU'.

[8] The only anti-dumping measure in force was one measure by Costa Rica (Anti-Dumping Measure on Water-based latex paint from the United States, Final Resolution of 18.1.2007, published in Official Journal La Gaceta No. 21 of 30.1.2007, extended by Resolution of 21.11.2011, published in Official Journal La Gaceta, No. 3 of 5.1.2012), reported in Committee on Anti-Dumping Practices, 'Semi-Annual Report under Article 16.4 of the Agreement, Costa Rica', G/ADP/N/237/CRI, 18.2.2013. Costa Rica did not report any changes to its anti-dumping measure due to Panama's accession, Committee on Anti-Dumping Practices, 'Semi-Annual Report under Article 16.4 of the Agreement, Costa Rica', G/ADP/N/244/CRI, 24.9.2013.

[9] 'Tunisia, Somalia Join COMESA' The Southern Times (30 July 2018) <https://southerntimesafrica.com/site/news/tunisia-somalia-join-comesa> accessed 5 July 2021.

Table 6.1 Effects of economic integration on anti-dumping measures

Customs union	Form of integration	Date	MS measures drop	CU measures against MS drop	CU measures' scope extended	Interim reviews	Temporary measures
EC	25 Enlargement[a]	01.05.2004	+[b]	+[c]	+[d]	+[e]	+[f]
EC	27 Enlargement[g]	01.01.2007	h	+[i]	+[j]		
EU[k]	28 Enlargement[l]	01.07.2013	m	n	+[o]		
Customs Union of Belarus, Kazakhstan and Russia	Formation/ Centralising Competences	01.07.2010	−[p]	n.a.	n.a.	n.a.	n.a.
EAEU	Armenia Enlargement	02.01.2015	q	r	+[s]		
EAEU	Kyrgyz Enlargement	12.08.2015		t	+[u]		

+ = positive evidence; − = negative evidence; n.a. = not applicable; *empty* = No data available

[a] Documents concerning the accession of the Czech Republic, the Republic of Estonia, the Republic of Cyprus, the Republic of Latvia, the Republic of Lithuania, the Republic of Hungary, the Republic of Malta, the Republic of Poland, the Republic of Slovenia and the Slovak Republic to the European Union, OJ L 236, 23.9.2003

[b] Poland, Lithuania, and Latvia had definitive Anti-Dumping measures in place, which lapsed upon their accession: Committee on Anti-Dumping Practices, 'Semi-Annual Report under Article 16.4 of the Agreement, European Communities, Addendum', G/ADP/N/119/EEC/Add. 1, 14.9.2004

[c] The EC had definitive Anti-Dumping measures in place against Poland, the Czech Republic, the Slovak Republic, Hungary, and Lithuania. They lapsed upon their accession: G/ADP/N/119/EEC, pp. 43, 44

[d] European Commission, 'Notice regarding the application of anti-dumping and anti-subsidy measures in force in the Community following enlargement to include the Czech Republic, the Republic of Estonia, the Republic of Cyprus, the Republic of Latvia, the Republic of Lithuania, the Republic of Hungary, the Republic of Malta, the Republic of Poland, the Republic of Slovenia and the Slovak Republic and the possibility of review' (2004 Enlargement Notice), OJ C 91/2, 15.4.2004

[e] See below at: Sect. 6.1.2.2

[f] See below: Sect. 6.1.2.2

[g] Documents concerning the accession of the Republic of Bulgaria and Romania to the European Union, OJ L 157, 21.6.2005

[h] Romania and Bulgaria had no Anti-Dumping measures in force: Committee on Anti-Dumping Practices, 'Report (2007) of the Committee on Anti-Dumping Practices' G/L/830, 26.10.2007, pp. 11–15

[i] Committee on Anti-Dumping Practices, 'Semi-Annual Report under Article 16.4 of the Agreement, European Communities', G/ADP/N/158/EEC, 29.8.2007, p. 33

(continued)

Table 6.1 (continued)

[j] European Commission, 'Notice regarding the application of anti-dumping, anti-subsidy and safeguard measures in force in the Community following enlargement to include the Republic of Bulgaria and Romania and the possibility of review' (2007 Enlargement Notice), OJ C 297/12, 7.12.2006

[k] The findings concerning EU enlargements are consistent with: Müller et al. (2009) para I.64–I.66; European Commission (2013)

[l] Documents concerning the accession of the Republic of Croatia to the European Union, OJ L 112, 24.4.2012

[m] Croatia had no Anti-Dumping measures in force: Committee on Anti-Dumping Practices, 'Report (2013) of the Committee on Anti-Dumping Practices', G/L/1053, 29.10.2013, p. 10

[n] The EU had not Anti-Dumping measures against Croatia in force: Committee on Anti-Dumping Practices, 'Semi-Annual Report under Article 16.4 of the Agreement, European Union', G/ADP/N/244/EU, 20.9.2013, pp. 14–17

[o] European Commission, 'Notice regarding the application of anti-dumping and anti-subsidy measures in force in the Union following enlargement to include the Republic of Croatia and the possibility of review' (2013 Enlargement Notice), OJ C 137/9, 16.5.2013

[p] During a transition period until 9.2011 national measures were transposed into customs union law and applied to the entire union, see below: Sect. 6.1.1

[q] Armenia did not report anti-dumping measures: Committee on Anti-Dumping Practices, 'Report (2015) of the Committee on Anti-Dumping Practices', G/L/1134, G/ADP/22, 30.10.2015, p. 9

[r] Committee on Anti-Dumping Practices, 'Semi-Annual Report under Article 16.4 of the Agreement, Russian Federation', G/ADP/N/265/RUS, 20.3.2015, p. 6. Belarus and Kazakhstan were not WTO Members at the time and therefore did not report any measures

[s] Committee on Anti-Dumping Practices, 'Semi-Annual Report under Article 16.4 of the Agreement, Armenia', G/ADP/N/272/ARM, 3.10.2016, pp. 5, 6

[t] Committee on Anti-Dumping Practices, 'Semi-Annual Report under Article 16.4 of the Agreement, Russian Federation', G/ADP/N/280/RUS, 16.3.2016, pp. 5, 6

[u] Committee on Anti-Dumping Practices, 'Semi-Annual Report under Article 16.4 of the Agreement, Russian Federation', G/ADP/N/280/KGZ, 3.10.2016, pp. 6, 7

as, after all, the customs union and not the member states have the competence to impose anti-dumping measures. On the other hand, this may lead to a situation where territories that were previously protected by anti-dumping measures are no longer protected—at least until the customs union has imposed relevant measures. When the customs union of Belarus, Kazakhstan and Russia was formed, an interim system was put in place that allowed certain national measures to be transposed into union law. This system will be analysed further below (under Sect. 6.1.1).

All other relevant practice concerns enlargements. Enlargements have different effects. First, the measures of the joining member state may be terminated. This happened in the 2004 EC enlargement and will be considered further below (under Sect. 6.1.1). Second, the customs union's measures against the joining member may be terminated. This happened in the 2004 and 2007 EC enlargements. Finally, the scope of the customs union's measures may be extended to include the joining member as well. This has occurred in all considered cases. Because the scope of the anti-dumping measures changes, it begs the question whether it necessitates an interim review or whether other measures to alleviate the economic hardship caused by the sudden extension in scope of the measures should be implemented. The question of member practice concerning interim reviews generally and the EU's practice of interim reviews during its enlargements will be considered further as well (under Sect. 6.1.2).

This study is concerned with the effects of economic integration on definitive anti-dumping measures. However, the same arguments may also apply to other measures and during the stages of an investigation. Where the joining members' definitive anti-dumping measures drop, this also applies to undertakings or interim measures and investigations must be terminated. If the scope of the customs union's anti-dumping measures changes, pending investigations by the competent central authority continue and data from the enlarged customs union must only be considered if the period of investigation does not end before the accession. If accession takes place during the period of investigation, its scope changes during the investigation.[10] Nevertheless, in the EU, the Commission has on several occasions crosschecked whether the findings would be radically different had they been based on data relating to the enlarged union.[11] The anti-dumping measure resulting from such investigations will apply to the enlarged customs union.[12] Conversely, if anti-

---

[10] E.g. 2006/22/EC: Commission Decision of 20 January 2006 granting certain parties an exemption from the extension to certain bicycle parts of the anti-dumping duty on bicycles originating in the People's Republic of China imposed by Council Regulation (EEC) No 2474/93, last maintained and amended by Regulation (EC) No 1095/2005, and lifting the suspension of the payment of the anti-dumping duty extended to certain bicycle parts originating in the People's Republic of China granted to certain parties pursuant to Regulation (EC) No 88/97, OJ L 17/16, 21.1.2006.

[11] Müller et al. (2009) para I.66.

[12] ibid I.65–I.66.

dumping measures have widened in their scope, any review will consider the enlarged union.[13]

6.1.1   Measures of the State That Loses Its Competences

Before economic integration, the states that lose the competence to impose anti-dumping measure may have imposed anti-dumping measures. What happens to these measures?

Practice differs as to the fate of anti-dumping measures imposed by a state that loses its competence in matters of anti-dumping. As anti-dumping is a competence of the customs union following the instance of economic integration, it makes sense that the member states' measures can no longer apply. This has been the case in recent EU enlargements, where joining members were under an obligation to repeal measures or the measures lapsed following accession.[14] As the EU had an anti-dumping system already in place this outcome did not lead to a situation where a customs union had no measures in force.

This did not occur following the formation of the customs union of Belarus, Kazakhstan and Russia. In that customs union, some member states' anti-dumping measures were extended to apply on a union wide basis.

Although various commitments to set up a customs union between Belarus, Kazakhstan and Russia existed since 1993,[15] the Customs Union Agreement was signed on 6. October 2007[16] and the customs union between Belarus, Kazakhstan and Russia only became operational on 1. January 2010.[17] The Agreement on the

---

[13]Limited exceptions exist concerning circumvention proceedings: Council Regulation (EC) No 866/2005 of 6 June 2005 extending the definitive anti-dumping measures imposed by Regulation (EC) No 1470/2001 on imports of integrated electronic compact fluorescent lamps (CFL-i) originating in the People's Republic of China to imports of the same product consigned from the Socialist Republic of Vietnam, the Islamic Republic of Pakistan and the Republic of the Philippines, OJ L 145/1, 9.6.2005, Rec. 14.

[14]Compare the 2004 enlargement (where the measures lapsed) to the notice to the 2013 enlargement (where joining members were under a duty to repeal): European Commission (2013).

[15]E.g. the Treaty on Setting up the Economic Union of 24.9.1993, between Belarus, Kazakhstan and Russia; the Agreement on the Customs Union of 20.1.1995 between Belarus, Kazakhstan and Russia; Agreement on Customs Union and Common Economic Zone, 26.2.1999. For an overview (until 2008) see: Kembayev (2009).

[16]Treaty on the Establishment of the Common Customs Territory and the Formation of the Customs Union, 6.10.2007; Protocol on Rules on Entry into Force of International Treaties aimed at the Formation of the Legal Basis of the Customs Union, Withdrawal from them, and Accession to them, 6.10.2007. The Protocol gave the EurAsEC Interstate Council the power to list the international Agreements (as it did in Council Decision No. 14 of 27.11.2009) which together with the Treaty on the formation would then become the legal basis of the customs union.

[17]Russia Accession Protocol, para. 154. See also: 'Eurasian Economic Integration: Facts and Figures' (Eurasian Economic Commission) 1 H 2016 3–4.

common anti-dumping regime came into force on 1. July 2010.[18] It became operational following a transition period,[19] which ended in September 2011.[20]

During the transition period, three different kinds of measures were distinguished: (1) those that were already in force before the transition period began, (2) those that were in the investigation or imposition stage but not yet in force when the transition period began and (3) those where the investigation was initiated during the transition period.

Those anti-dumping measures that were in force when the transition period began remained in force[21] but were reviewed by national authorities to determine the share of the production of the like product in the member state compared to the rest of the customs union.[22] Where the domestic production of the like product constituted a major proportion of at least 25% of the union production, upon decision by the Commission of the customs union (the EEC), the measure would apply to the entire customs union.[23] In such a case, the national measure should be terminated.[24] Interestingly, after the transition period, the EEC[25] reviewed and extended the

---

[18] Agreement on the Application of Special Protective, Anti-dumping and Countervailing Measures against Third Parties of 25.1.2008 (2008 Agreement); Decision of the Commission of the Customs Union No. 191 of 26.2.2010 on the Application of Safeguard, Antidumping and Countervailing Measures in the Territory of the Customs Union of Belarus, Kazakhstan and the Russian Federation. All available at: Committee on Anti-Dumping Practices, 'Notification of Laws and Regulations under Articles 18.5, 32.6 and 12.6 of the Agreements, Russian Federation', G/ADP/N/1/RUS/1, 3.10.2012.

[19] Agreement on the Application of Special Protective, Anti-dumping and Countervailing Measures during the Transitional Period of November 19, 2010; Decision of the Customs Union Commission No. 339 of August 17, 2010. For an overview, see: Kozyrin and Yalbulganov (2015), pp. 185–186.

[20] On Some Issues of Special Protective, Anti-dumping and Countervailing Measures within the Common Customs Territory of the Customs Unions, Decision 802 of the Customs Union Commission of 23.9.2011.

[21] E.g. Anti-Dumping measures against Ukraine on Certain steel pipes and tubes: Resolution of the Government of the Russian Federation No. 297, 31.1.2006, published in Российская газета on 31.12.2005.

[22] Art. 6 (1), 1 Agreement on the Application of Special Protective, Anti-dumping and Countervailing Measures during the Transitional Period of November 19, 2010.

[23] Art. 2 Agreement on the Application of Special Protective, Anti-dumping and Countervailing Measures during the Transitional Period of November 19, 2010. E.g.: Anti-Dumping Measures against China on Rolling-element bearings (excluding needle roller bearings). The initial Russian measure: Resolution of the Government of the Russian Federation No. 868, 13.12.2007, published in Российская газета on 21.12.2007. Customs Union measure: Decision of the Commission of the Customs Union No. 705, 22.6.2011.

[24] Art. 4 Agreement on the Application of Special Protective, Anti-dumping and Countervailing Measures during the Transitional Period of November 19, 2010.

[25] The Department for Internal Market Defence of the Eurasian Economic Commission is the competent authority in Anti-Dumping measures since Decision of the Eurasian Economic Commission, No. 1, 7.3.2012 on some issues of safeguard, antidumping and countervailing measures in the common customs territory of the customs union.

measures following a sunset review.[26] Where the national production did not constitute a major proportion of union production, the national measure continued to apply for the member state but could not be extended to a union wide basis.[27]

Where an investigation had been initiated but the definitive measure was not yet in force, the national authority remained competent to conduct the investigation if the share of national production of like products was at least 25% of the total production volume of the customs union.[28] The national authority thereby applied national law which had to comply with the 2008 Agreement.[29] Accordingly, the investigations were then conducted on a union wide basis.[30] The EEC then imposed the measures.[31]

Investigations could be initiated during the transition period by the national authorities according to their laws but in compliance with the 2008 Agreement.[32] They were conducted on a union wide basis.[33] The EEC then imposed the measures.[34]

During the transition period none of the members of the customs union were WTO members. The transition period is nevertheless relevant practice because during Russia's accession negotiations WTO compliance of it was debated.[35] Beyond that, Russia acceded to the WTO on 22 August 2012 and committed to comply with WTO anti-dumping requirements without implementation period.[36] In Russia's first semi-annual report on anti-dumping measures, 18 out of its 22 anti-

---

[26] E.g. Definitive Anti-Dumping duties on Rolling-element bearings (excl. needle roller bearings) against China. Initial measure of 21.1.2008, Resolution of the Government of the Russian Federation published in No. 287, published in Российская газета on 21.12.2007. Extended on 19.10.2013, Decision of the EEC No. 197, 17.9.2013.

[27] Art. 5 Agreement on the Application of Special Protective, Anti-dumping and Countervailing Measures during the Transitional Period of November 19, 2010.

[28] Art. 6 (2), (3) Agreement on the Application of Special Protective, Anti-dumping and Countervailing Measures during the Transitional Period of November 19, 2010.

[29] Art. 6 (2) Agreement on the Application of Special Protective, Anti-dumping and Countervailing Measures during the Transitional Period of November 19, 2010.

[30] Art. 3 (2) 2008 Agreement. Art. 10 Agreement on the Application of Special Protective, Anti-dumping and Countervailing Measures during the Transitional Period of November 19, 2010 includes cooperation requirements between the different states.

[31] Art. 9 (4) Agreement on the Application of Special Protective, Anti-dumping and Countervailing Measures during the Transitional Period of November 19, 2010.

[32] Art. 9 (1) Agreement on the Application of Special Protective, Anti-dumping and Countervailing Measures during the Transitional Period of November 19, 2010.

[33] Art. 3 (2) 2008 Agreement. Art. 10 Agreement on the Application of Special Protective, Anti-dumping and Countervailing Measures during the Transitional Period of November 19, 2010 includes cooperation requirements between the different states.

[34] Art. 9 (4) Agreement on the Application of Special Protective, Anti-dumping and Countervailing Measures during the Transitional Period of November 19, 2010.

[35] Russia Accession Protocol, para. 577–620.

[36] Ministerial Conference, Accession of the Russian Federation, Decision of 16 December 2011, WT/MIN(11)/24, WT/L/839, 17.12.2011; Russia Accession Protocol, paras. 1450, 591.

dumping had undergone the review in the transition period and were originally Russia's national anti-dumping measures.[37] As Russia applied these measures, they had to be WTO compliant then. Similarly, when Armenia, a WTO member since 5 February 2003, joined the EAEU, Russia reported that in the EAEU three anti-dumping measures initially imposed by Russia but that had gone through the transition period regime were still in force.[38] One of them had not even undergone a sunset review by the EEC yet.[39] The same was the case when the Kygryz Republic—a WTO member since 20 December 1998—joined the EAEU and when Kazakhstan joined the WTO on 30 November 2015. Because the measures that resulted from the transition period were applied when the countries were bound by WTO law, they had to be in conformity with it. The transition period can thus be used as relevant practice in the WTO.

6.1.2 Interim Reviews: EU Case Law & the Commission's Opinion

In all cases of EU enlargement, the anti-dumping measures apply to the enlarged customs union following enlargement. A change in the scope of anti-dumping measures raises the question whether the measure must be reviewed as the changed scope may constitute changed circumstances.

The EU approach to this differed a little in the last three accessions: whereas in the 2004[40] accession it proposed a two-tier approach to first impose temporary measures to alleviate economic hardship (under Sect. 6.1.2.1) and second conduct interim reviews (under Sect. 6.1.2.2), in the 2007[41] and 2013[42] enlargements, it only informed about its willingness to conduct interim reviews.

6.1.2.1 Alleviating Economic Hardship Through Temporary Measures

Prior to the 2004 enlargement, the Commission recognized that automatically extending the scope of the EC's anti-dumping measures may cause "economic hardship for some operators" in the new member states.[43] Governments of third

---

[37] Committee on Anti-Dumping Practices, 'Semi-annual report under article 16.4 of the Agreement, Russia Federation', G/ADP/N/237/RUS, 5.3.2013, pp. 6–7.

[38] Committee on Anti-Dumping Practices, 'Semi-annual report under article 16.4 of the Agreement, Russia Federation', G/ADP/N/272/RUS, 17.9.2015, pp. 5–6.

[39] E.g. Anti-Dumping measures against Ukraine on Certain steel pipes and tubes, see: n. 21. Extended by, Decision of the Commission of the Customs Union No. 702, 22.06.2011.

[40] 2004 Enlargement Notice.

[41] 2007 Enlargement Notice.

[42] 2013 Enlargement Notice.

[43] 2004 Enlargement Notice.

parties and exporters were urged to identify such cases of economic hardship, following which the Commission would initiate interim reviews with the aim to provide transitional solutions.[44]

Interim reviews with the purpose to alleviate economic hardship were initiated on six[45] definitive anti-dumping measures (i.e. 3.8% of all definitive anti-dumping measures in force and 0% of all undertakings in force[46]).[47]

The reviews focused on the question whether the extension of the measures to the new member states was in the union's interest,[48] i.e. whether importers, users,

---

[44] 2004 Enlargement Notice.

[45] Council Regulation (EC) No 969/2000 of 8 May 2000 imposing a definitive anti-dumping duty on imports of potassium chloride originating in Belarus, Russia and Ukraine, OJ L 112/4, 11.5.2000; Council Regulation (EC) No 1100/2000 of 22 May 2000 imposing definitive anti-dumping duties on imports of silicon carbide originating in the People's Republic of China, the Russian Federation and the Ukraine and prolonging the undertaking accepted by Commission Decision 94/202/EC, OJ L 125/3, 26.5.2000; Council Regulation (EC) No 658/2002 of 15 April 2002 imposing a definitive anti-dumping duty on imports of ammonium nitrate originating in Russia, OJ L 102/1, 18.4.2002; Council Regulation (EC) No 132/2001 of 22 January 2001 imposing a definitive anti-dumping duty and collecting definitively the provisional duty imposed on imports of ammonium nitrate originating in Poland and Ukraine, and terminating the anti-dumping proceeding in respect of imports originating in Lithuania, OJ L 23/1, 25.1.2001; Council Regulation (EC) No 132/2001 of 22 January 2001 imposing a definitive anti-dumping duty and collecting definitively the provisional duty imposed on imports of ammonium nitrate originating in Poland and Ukraine, and terminating the anti-dumping proceeding in respect of imports originating in Lithuania, OJ L 23/1, 25.1.2001; Council Regulation (EC) No 151/2003 of 27 January 2003 imposing a definitive anti-dumping duty on imports of certain grain oriented electrical sheets originating in Russia, OJ L 25/7, 30.1.2003; Council Regulation (EC) No 398/2004 of 2 March 2004 imposing a definitive anti-dumping duty on imports of silicon originating in the People's Republic of China, OJ L 66/15, 4.3.2004.

[46] As of 31.12.2003, the EC had 157 Definitive Anti-Dumping Measures and 44 Undertakings in force: Committee on Anti-Dumping Practices, 'Semi-Annual Report under 16.4 of the Agreements, European Communities, G/ADP/N/112/EEC, 8.3.2004.

[47] European Commission, 'Notice of initiation of a partial interim review of the antidumping measures applicable to imports of certain products originating in the People's Republic of China, Russian Federation, Ukraine and the Republic of Belarus', OJ C 70/15, 20.3.2004.

[48] Art. 21 Reg. (EC) No. 384/96. E.g. Council Regulation (EC) No 992/2004 of 17 May 2004 amending Regulation (EEC) No 3068/92 imposing a definitive anti-dumping duty on imports of potassium chloride originating in Belarus, Russia or Ukraine, OJ L 182/23, 19.5.2004, Rec. 22.

distributors,[49] and consumers[50] in the new member states would suffer economic hardship if the measures were extended to them. Factors that were considered were whether import volumes were significant, a price difference existed between the joining EC10 and the existing EC15 or whether other exporters could fulfil the demand in the joining EC10.[51] Economic hardship was found in five out of the six cases.[52]

---

[49] Reg. (EC) 992/2004, Rec. 22; Council Regulation (EC) No 993/2004 of 17 May 2004 amending Regulation (EC) No 658/2002 imposing a definitive anti-dumping duty on imports of ammonium nitrate originating in Russia and Regulation (EC) No 132/2001 imposing a definitive anti-dumping duty and collecting definitively the provisional duty imposed on imports of ammonium nitrate originating in Poland and Ukraine, and terminating the anti-dumping proceeding in respect of imports originating in Lithuania, OJ L 182/28, 19.5.2004, Rec. 20; Council Regulation (EC) No 989/2004 of 17 May 2004 amending Regulation (EC) No 151/2003 imposing a definitive anti-dumping duty on imports of certain grain oriented electrical sheets originating in Russia, OJ L 182/1, 19.5.2004, Rec. 16; Council Regulation (EC) No 991/2004 of 17 May 2004 amending Regulation (EC) No 1100/2000 imposing definitive anti-dumping duties on imports of silicon carbide originating in the People's Republic of China, the Russian Federation and the Ukraine and prolonging the undertaking accepted by Commission Decision 94/202/EC, OJ L 182/18, 19.5.2004.

[50] Council Regulation (EC) No 785/2005 of 23 May 2005 terminating the partial interim review of the anti-dumping measures applicable to imports of silicon originating in the People's Republic of China, OJ L 132/1, 26.5.2004, Rec. 30.

[51] Reg. (EC) 992/2004, Rec. (19)-(21); Reg. (EC) 991/2004, Rec. (21)-(22); Reg. (EC) 993/2004, Rec. (18)-(19); Reg. (EC) 989/2004, Rec. (14)-(15); Reg. (EC) 875/2005, Rec. (8)-(26).

[52] It was found in the reviews of Reg. (EC) 969/2000 (see: Reg. (EC) 992/2004); Reg. (EC) 1100/2000 (see: 2004/498/EC: Commission Decision of 18 May 2004 accepting undertakings offered in connection with the anti-dumping proceeding concerning imports of silicon carbide originating, inter alia, in Ukraine, OJ L 267M/3, 12.10.2005; Reg. (EC) 991/2004); Reg. (EC) 658/2002 (see: Reg. (EC) 993/2004; Commission Regulation (EC) No 1001/2004 of 18 May 2004 accepting undertakings offered in connection with the anti-dumping proceeding concerning imports of ammonium nitrate originating in the Russian Federation and Ukraine and making imports of ammonium nitrate originating in the Russian Federation or Ukraine subject to registration, OJ L 183/13, 20.5.2004); Reg. (EC) 132/2001 (see: Reg. (EC) 993/2004; Reg. (EC) 1001/2004); Reg. (EC) 151/2003 (see: Reg. (EC) 989/2004; Council Regulation (EC) No 990/2004 of 17 May 2004 amending Regulation (EC) No 151/2003 imposing a definitive anti-dumping duty on imports of certain grain oriented electrical sheets originating in Russia, OJ L 182, 19.5.2004; Commission Regulation (EC) No 1000/2004 of 18 May 2004 accepting undertakings offered in connection with the anti-dumping proceeding concerning imports of certain grain oriented electrical sheets and strips of silicon-electrical steel with a width of more than 500 mm originating in the Russian Federation and making imports of certain grain oriented electrical sheets originating in the Russian Federation subject to registration, OJ L 183/10, 20.5.2004). It was not found in the review of Reg. (EC) 398/2004 (see: Reg. (EC) 785/2005).

To alleviate the economic hardship, the Commission accepted undertakings[53] which it characterised as special measures pursuant to Art. 22 (c) Reg. (EC) 384/96 (Now: Art. 22 (c) Reg. (EU) 2016/1036).[54] The undertakings restricted the export volumes to the acceding members[55] and/or imposed minimum import prices at prices below those that would usually be accepted.[56] The undertakings that were accepted were limited in their duration to six[57] or twelve[58] months and after that, some were prolonged.[59]

6.1.2.2   Interim Reviews

In all three enlargements since 2000, the Commission gave notice that it would conduct interim reviews of anti-dumping measures if interested parties submitted evidence that such a review was warranted. More specifically, it requested information that the measures would have been significantly different had the measure been based on information including the new member states.[60] In all three enlargements it highlighted that enlargement *per se* was not considered as a sufficient basis for a review to be initiated.[61]

---

[53] Commission Regulation (EC) No 1002/2004 of 18 May 2004 accepting undertakings offered in connection with the anti-dumping proceeding concerning imports of potassium chloride originating in the Republic of Belarus, the Russian Federation or Ukraine and making imports of potassium chloride originating in the Republic of Belarus and the Russian Federation subject to registration, OJ L 183/16, 20.5.2004; Commission Regulation (EC) No 498/2004 of 17 March 2004 adapting several regulations concerning the market of products processed from fruit and vegetables by reason of the accession of the Czech Republic, Estonia, Cyprus, Latvia, Lithuania, Hungary, Malta, Poland, Slovenia and Slovakia to the European Union, OJ L 80/20, 18.3.2004; Dec. (EC) No. 1001/2004; Reg. (EC) 1000/2004; 2004/782/EC: Commission Decision of 19 November 2004 accepting an undertaking offered in connection with the anti-dumping proceeding concerning imports of silicon carbide originating, inter alia, in Ukraine, OJ L 344/37, 20.11.2004.

[54] E.g. Dec. (EC) 1001/2004, Rec. 9; Reg. (EC) 1000/2004, Rec. 7; Commission Regulation (EC) No 858/2005 of 6 June 2005 accepting undertakings offered in connection with the anti-dumping proceeding concerning imports of potassium chloride originating in the Republic of Belarus or the Russian Federation and making imports of potassium chloride originating in the Republic of Belarus and the Russian Federation subject to registration, OJ L 143/11, 7.6.2005, Rec. 4.

[55] E.g. Reg. (EC) 993/2004, Rec. 24, only taking those export volumes into account that would not have been subject to trade defence measures by the acceding members prior to their accession; Reg. (EC) 989/2004, Rec. 20; Reg. (EC) 992/2004, Rec. 26.

[56] E.g. Reg. (EC) 993/2004, Rec. 24; Reg. (EC) 992/2004, Rec. 26.

[57] Reg. (EC) 1001/2004, Rec. 15; Reg. (EC) 1000/2004, Rec. 13; Dec. (EC) 498/2004, Rec. 14.

[58] Reg. (EC) 1002/2004, Rec. 14.

[59] Reg. (EC) 858/2005.

[60] 2004 Enlargement Notice, 2007 Enlargement Notice, 2013 Enlargement Notice.

[61] 2004 Enlargement Notice, 2007 Enlargement Notice, 2013 Enlargement Notice.

Following the 2004 enlargement, the Commission initiated interim reviews on three[62] undertakings (i.e. 0% of all definitive anti-dumping measures in force and 6.8% of all undertakings in force[63]). The Commission based the initiations on Art. 8, 11 (3), 22 (c) Reg. (EC) 384/96.[64] The undertakings were reviewed because they were subject to a quantitative element[65] which was adapted to the enlarged union market.[66] Where the price undertaking considered specific volumes that could be imported and those volumes depended on union consumption and there was significant consumption in the acceding members, the quantitative restrictions were adjusted to the new union consumption.[67]

Above that, enlargement became relevant in two further cases, but arguments surrounding enlargement failed. In one case, the Commission refused to initiate a review of a measure where the investigation was announced on 29 April 2004, two days before the 2004 enlargement and where the investigation periods related to the union prior to enlargement.[68] The reasons given were that imports from Vietnam, one of the countries under investigation, into the joining EC10 were negligible during the period of investigation. Furthermore, although imports from China, the other country under investigation, to the EC10 were significant, the export prices to the EC10 were below those of the EC15. Moreover, as there was significant production in the EC10, the dumping and injury margin would only have increased, had the investigation been extended and also covered the EC10.[69] In another case during the 2004 enlargement, the Commission refused to extend a partial interim

---

[62] Notice of initiation of a partial interim review of the antidumping measures applicable to imports of certain products originating in the People's Republic of China, Russian Federation, Ukraine and the Republic of Belarus, OJ C 70/15, 20.3.2004.

[63] As of 31.12.2003, the EC had 157 Definitive Anti-Dumping Measures and 44 Undertakings in force: Committee on Anti-Dumping Practices, 'Semi-Annual Report under 16.4 of the Agreement, European Communities', G/ADP/N/112/EEC, 8.3.2004.

[64] Now Art. 8, 11 (3), 22 (c) Reg. (EU) 2016/1036.

[65] The Notice also mentions that the Undertakings should be reviewed concerning the adaptation of a price element, this has, however, not occurred.

[66] European Commission, Notice of initiation of a partial interim review of the antidumping measures applicable to imports of certain products originating in the People's Republic of China, Russian Federation, Ukraine and the Republic of Belarus, OJ C 70/15, 20.3.2004.

[67] Council Regulation (EC) No 999/2004 of 17 May 2004 on the application of Regulation (EC) No 1531/2002 imposing a definitive anti-dumping duty on imports of colour television receivers originating in the People's Republic of China, the Republic of Korea, Malaysia and Thailand and terminating the proceeding regarding imports of colour television receivers originating in Singapore, OJ L 183/7, 20.5.2004; Reg. (EC) 991/2004; Council Regulation (EC) No 998/2004 of 17 May 2004 amending Regulation (EC) No 950/2001 imposing a definitive anti-dumping duty on imports of certain aluminium foil originating in the People's Republic of China and Russia, OJ L 183/4, 20.5.2004.

[68] Council Regulation (EC) No 1095/2005 of 12 July 2005 imposing a definitive anti-dumping duty on imports of bicycles originating in Vietnam, and amending Regulation (EC) No 1524/2000 imposing a definitive anti-dumping duty on imports of bicycles originating in the People's Republic of China, OJ L 183/1, 14.7.2005.

[69] Council Reg. (EC) No. 1095/2005, Rec. 18.

review focused on the product definition to a full interim review because insufficient evidence was submitted detailing the consequences of the enlargement upon the dumping and injury calculations.[70]

In the 2007 enlargement, no reviews were initiated because of the enlargement. Enlargement only became relevant in two reviews, that had been initiated for other reasons and the arguments raised by the exporters relating to enlargement ultimately failed. Arguments concerning enlargement were raised in an expiry review, but the Commission held that the accessions of Bulgaria and Romania did not change the union market significantly and the effects of enlargement were thus negligible.[71] In a partial interim review proceeding one party argued that the Commission should have initiated a full interim review *ex officio*. The Commission rejected this and held that it offered the possibility to review measures upon receiving sufficient facts on changed circumstances.[72] Since it had not received specific information, the Commission was of the view that it did not have to initiate an interim review *ex officio*.

In the 2013 enlargement no anti-dumping measures were reviewed because of the enlargement and arguments surrounding enlargement were not raised. The Commission published non-binding information on what kind of evidence it expected to initiate an interim review, however.

In that information, the Commission clarified that the reason it did not conduct automatic reviews of all measures was because Croatia—the joining country—only contributed to a small proportion of the entire union output and the imports of the products protected by the anti-dumping measures were small compared to the imports into the rest of the union. Moreover, findings are usually based on representative groups of producers or exporters and not every producer, importer, user, or exporter is considered anyway.[73]

---

[70] Council Regulation (EC) No 945/2005 of 21 June 2005 amending Regulation (EC) No 658/2002 imposing a definitive anti-dumping duty on imports of ammonium nitrate originating in Russia and Regulation (EC) No 132/2001 imposing a definitive anti-dumping duty on imports of ammonium nitrate originating in, inter alia, Ukraine, following a partial interim review pursuant to Article 11 (3) of Regulation (EC) No 384/96, OJ L 160/1, 23.6.2005, Rec. 10.

[71] Council Implementing Regulation (EU) No 1294/2009 of 22 December 2009 imposing a definitive anti-dumping duty on imports of certain footwear with uppers of leather originating in Vietnam and originating in the People's Republic of China, as extended to imports of certain footwear with uppers of leather consigned from the Macao SAR, whether declared as originating in the Macao SAR or not, following an expiry review pursuant to Article 11(2) of Council Regulation (EC) No 384/96, OJ L 352/1, 30.12.2009, Rec. 201.

[72] Council Regulation (EC) No 661/2008 of 8 July 2008 imposing a definitive anti-dumping duty on imports of ammonium nitrate originating in Russia following an expiry review pursuant to Article 11(2) and a partial interim review pursuant to Article 11(3) of Regulation (EC) No 384/96, OJ L 185/1, 12.7.2008, Rec. 8.

[73] European Commission, 'Enlargement: Impact on Trade Defence - Questions and Answers on the Possibilities for Enlargement-Related Interim Reviews of AD and AS Measures' 1 <http://trade.ec.europa.eu/doclib/html/150783.htm> accessed 5 July 2021.

The Commission also reiterated its invitation to interested parties to request an interim review[74] or if exporters did not export to the union during the investigation period but only to Croatia, they could apply for a newcomer review.[75]

According to the information, the request had to contain evidence on how the structural change of the union had an impact on the level or form of the measure.[76] In relation to the dumping margin, this could typically be the case if significant exports to Croatia existed and the pricing structure of these exports was different to those used for the investigation.[77] In relation to the product scope, it could be relevant if the products exported to Croatia differed in some ways from those exported to the rest of the union.[78] With regards to the union industry this could be relevant, where the union industry no longer has standing or the injury margin is higher or lower than the margin determined in the initial investigation.[79] With regards to the union interest this could be relevant if the measures at their current level could lead to an excessively negative effect on the union.[80] Overall, the evidence needs to demonstrate that the measures would have been significantly different, had they been based on information including Croatia.[81]

6.1.3   Conclusions

The relevant cases of economic integration are those in which either competences to impose anti-dumping measures have changed or where an authority is competent towards a larger territory following the economic integration.

Cases in which that has happened include the formation of the customs union between Belarus, Kazakhstan and Russia, where the anti-dumping regime has been centralized in 2010 as well as EU and EAEU enlargements.

Concerning the formation of a customs union, the question arises whether the anti-dumping measures that were imposed by the member states before formation of a customs union remain in force thereafter. In the customs union between Belarus, Kazakhstan and Russia they remained in force or were extended to cover imports into the entire customs union.

---

[74]European Commission, 'Enlargement: Impact on Trade Defence - Impact on Importers, Users, Suppliers and Consumers' 1 <http://trade.ec.europa.eu/doclib/html/150780.htm> accessed 5 July 2021; European Commission, 'Enlargement: Impact on Trade Defence - Impact on Exporters' 1 <http://trade.ec.europa.eu/doclib/html/150781.htm> accessed 5 July 2021.

[75]European Commission, 'Enlargement: Impact on Trade - Exporters' (n 74), p. 1.

[76]European Commission, 'Enlargement: Impact on Trade - FAQ' (n 73), p. 5.

[77]ibid.

[78]ibid.

[79]ibid 5–6.

[80]ibid 6.

[81]ibid 7.

In cases of enlargement several questions arise. The 2004 EU enlargement lends practice that anti-dumping measures by the joining member are terminated following enlargement and in the 2004 and 2007 enlargement anti-dumping measures against the joining member state by the customs union are terminated as well. In all cases of enlargement, the customs union's measures applied to the enlarged territory following enlargement. Finally, limited practice exists in the 2004 EC enlargement that some measures were reviewed and that they were disapplied to imports into the joining member states to alleviate economic hardship.

6.2   Case Study: Economic Disintegration (Brexit)

Economic disintegration refers to the opposite of economic integration. It describes a situation in which a customs union is less economically integrated after a change. This can occur by retransferring competences to the member states, by members withdrawing from the customs union or by dissolving the customs union completely.[82]

In general, no specific problems arise if the competences concerning anti-dumping do not change. Where anti-dumping measures are imposed at a member state level and a member leaves the customs union or the customs union dissolves, no problems with regards to anti-dumping measures arise: the relevant measure,s by that member as well as the measures by the other members of the customs union remain in force and but for the indirect economic changes that leaving the customs union or the dissolution bring about[83] no other relevant circumstances change.

This study therefore focuses on cases of economic disintegration that lead to changes in competences on anti-dumping. This is the case if following the disintegration either the customs union is no longer competent to investigate and impose anti-dumping measures or if its competence has been limited to a smaller territory. The effects of such changes on existing anti-dumping measures are not clear and this section examines the relevant precedence in that regard. Although there are instances of countries leaving a customs union, the only instance that provides practice is the UK's withdrawal from the EU (Brexit).

Venezuela withdrew from CAN in 2011, Namibia withdrew from COMESA in 2004 and Angola in 2007, and Venezuela was suspended from MERCOSUR in 2016. As in the CAN,[84] COMESA, and MERCOSUR member states are competent

---

[82] Compare this to typical characterizations of state succession: O'Connell (1967a), pp. 88, 91–112, 164; Bühler (2001), pp. 14–18; Zimmermann (2000), pp. 11–15. Although there is some structural overlap, the characterization here focuses more on the transferral of competences.

[83] See below at: section 'Data Relating to the Country Under Investigation'.

[84] When Venezuela withdrew from CAN, no measures that were based on the community procedure were in force (Committee on Anti-Dumping Practices, 'Report (2011) of the Committee on Anti-Dumping Practices', G/L/966, 26.10.2011, p. 18).

to impose anti-dumping measures, no competences changed, and no specific problems arose.

The effects of the UK's withdrawal from the EU on anti-dumping measures varied according to the stage of withdrawal. The UK withdrew from the EU on 31 January 2020. The process of leaving the EU can thereby be summarized into three stages: before leaving the EU (under Sect. 6.2.1), during the period in which the Withdrawal Agreement applied (transition period) and thereafter (under Sect. 6.2.2).

6.2.1 Before Leaving the EU

Following a referendum on 23 June 2016, the UK notified the European Council of its decision to withdraw from the EU on 29 March 2017[85] and thereby triggered the withdrawal procedure, according to Art. 50 (2) TEU.[86]

The UK should have left the EU two years after the notification, on 29 March 2019 (Art. 50 (3) TEU). This period was extended by agreement between the European Council and the UK according to Art. 50 (3) TEU on 21 March 2019[87] until 12 April 2019.[88] On 10 April 2019 the European Council and the UK agreed a further extension until 31 October 2019.[89] Finally, Prime Minister Johnson requested a third extension in accordance with the European Union (Withdrawal) (No. 2) Act 2019[90] which the European Council agreed to on 28 October 2019[91] to

---

[85] Theresa May, 'Prime Minister's Letter to Donald Tusk Triggering Article 50' <https://www.gov.uk/government/publications/prime-ministers-letter-to-donald-tusk-triggering-article-50/prime-min isters-letter-to-donald-tusk-triggering-article-50> accessed 5 July 2021.

[86] Treaty on European Union (TEU), Consolidated Version, OJ C 326/13, 26.10.2012.

[87] The UK requested an extension: Theresa May, 'Prime Minister's Letter to President Tusk: 20 March 2019' <https://www.gov.uk/government/publications/prime-ministers-letter-to-presi dent-tusk-20-march-2019> accessed 5 July 2021. The EU agreed: European Council decision taken in agreement with the United Kingdom, extending the period under Article 50 (3) TEU 2019 (EUCO XT 20006/19).

[88] The Withdrawal Agreement has been rejected for the third time on 29.3.2019: <https://hansard.parliament.uk/Commons/2019-03-29/division/B6052BBD-43BE-4A30-8365-E3A8B108009E/UnitedKingdom%E2%80%99SWithdrawalFromTheEuropeanUnion?outputType=Party>.

[89] The UK requested an extension: Theresa May, 'Prime Minister's Letter to President Tusk: 5 April 2019' <https://www.gov.uk/government/publications/prime-ministers-letter-to-president-tusk-5-april-2019> accessed 5 July 2021. The EU agreed: European Council Decision taken in agreement with the United Kingdom extending the period under Article 50(3) TEU 2019 (EUCO XT 20013/19).

[90] 9.9.2020.

[91] The UK requested an extension: Boris Johnson, 'Prime Minister's Letter to President Donald Tusk: 19 October 2019' <https://www.gov.uk/government/publications/prime-ministers-letter-to-president-donald-tusk-19-october-2019> accessed 5 July 2021. The EU agreed: European Council Decision taken in agreement with the United Kingdom extending the period under Article 50 (3) TEU 2019 (EUCO XT 20024/19 Rev 2).

extend the process until 31 January 2020. The UK left the EU on 31 January 2020. Until then, nothing changed in its position as an EU member from a union law and a WTO law perspective.[92]

During that time, Brexit only indirectly impacted anti-dumping investigations in that it affected the economic situation of the EU. In one investigation, this indirect effect of Brexit was used as an argument against causation. Exporters argued that the uncertain outlook of Brexit led to a contraction in demand on the specific market. The Commission rejected that argument not on fundamental grounds but on the basis that this could not explain why the exports from the country under investigation increased, i.e. that the claim was not substantiated enough.[93] Indirect effects could have impacted investigations but were difficult to prove.[94]

6.2.2   During the Transition Period

The EU treaties have ceased to apply to the UK on 31 January 2020 with the entry into force of the Withdrawal Agreement.[95,96] The transition period began when the Withdrawal Agreement came into force on 1 February 2020 and ended on 31 December 2020. It provided for the possibility to extend the duration by one or two years, but the parties did not agree to such an extension.

The Withdrawal Agreement consists of the main Agreement and three protocols which are integral parts of the Agreement.[97] In the main Agreement, the provisions on the transition period (Part Four) and the Protocol on Ireland/Northern Ireland contain provisions on anti-dumping. The other Protocols will not be considered further due to their limited practical relevance.[98]

Different parts of the Withdrawal Agreement apply during different time periods. The Withdrawal Agreement has entered into force following Art.

---

[92] Exporters argued in one proceeding that UK producers should be disregarded, which the Commission of course rejected: Commission Implementing Regulation (EU) 2018/1722 of 14 November 2018 amending Implementing Regulation (EU) No 999/2014 imposing a definitive anti-dumping duty on imports of ammonium nitrate originating in Russia following an interim review pursuant to Article 11(3) of Regulation (EU) 2016/1036 of the European Parliament and of the Council, OJ L 287/3, 15.11.2018, para. 59.

[93] Commission Implementing Regulation (EU) 2017/1480 of 16 August 2017 imposing a provisional anti-dumping duty on imports of certain cast iron articles originating in the People's Republic of China, OJ L 211/14, 17.8.2017, para. 189–191.

[94] More on indirect effects below at: section 'Data Relating to the Country Under Investigation'.

[95] Agreement of the Withdrawal of the United Kingdom of Great Britain and Northern Ireland from the European Union and the European Atomic Energy Community (Withdrawal Agreement), 19.10.2019.

[96] Art. 50 (3) TEU.

[97] The three protocols form an integral part of the Withdrawal Agreement, Art. 182.

[98] E.g. on the Gibraltar Protocol: Meinen (2018), p. 397.

185 (a) Withdrawal Agreement on 31 January 2020. Part Four regulating a transition period only applies until 31 December 2020. The Protocol on Ireland/Northern Ireland mainly applies after the transition period, but its effects are geographically limited to Ireland/Northern Ireland.[99] Beyond that, the Withdrawal Agreement does not regulate the future relationship between the UK and the EU.

During the transition period, the UK's position in the WTO did not change. It remained bound by the EU's Schedules, the plurilateral agreements the EU is a member of and the modifications of the WTO Agreements. Beyond the WTO, the UK's position in EU RTAs did not change either. The UK and the EU claimed that from an international perspective the UK should be treated like an EU member state.[100]

Union law applied to the UK during the transition period[101] and the applicable law had the same effect as if the UK were still a member of the EU meaning it applied directly and was supreme.[102] This included the application of Reg. (EU) 2016/1036 as well as all anti-dumping measures.

During the transition period, the UK no longer took part in the EU's institutions.[103] This included the comitology procedure.[104] There was, however, the possibility to exceptionally invite experts to meetings but they then had no voting rights.[105] Moreover, where draft union acts "identify or refer directly to specific member state authorities, procedures, or documents" the UK was consulted on drafts, with a view to ensuring the proper implementation and application of those acts by and in the UK.[106] This means that even though the UK no longer influenced the legislative process of anti-dumping measures, it remained bound by them.

6.2.3 After the Transition Period

The Withdrawal Agreement does not regulate the relationship between the EU and UK following the transition period with certain exceptions such as the measures in

---

[99] Art. 185 (5), (6) Withdrawal Agreement.

[100] General Council, The United Kingdom's Withdrawal From the European Union, Communication from the United Kingdom, WT/GC/2016, 1.2.2020. Director General, Communication from the European Union, WLI/100, 29.2.2020.

[101] Art. 127 (1) Withdrawal Agreement.

[102] Art. 127 (3) Withdrawal Agreement. See generally: Kenneth Armstrong and others, 'Implementing Transition: How Would It Work?' [2017] CELS/CLP Working Paper <https://www.ssrn.com/abstract=3052328> accessed 5 July 2021.

[103] Art. 7 (1) Withdrawal Agreement.

[104] Art. 7 (1)(c) Withdrawal Agreement.

[105] Art. 128 (5) Withdrawal Agreement.

[106] Art. 128 (7) Withdrawal Agreement.

the Protocol on Ireland/Northern Ireland. That relationship is governed by the
EU-UK Trade Cooperation Agreement (TCA).[107]

The UK's position in the WTO changed.[108] The UK remained a WTO Member,
as it was an original member of the GATT 1947 and as it ratified the 1995 Marrakesh
Agreement. As the WTO Agreements are a single undertaking, the UK remained
bound by modifications that are part of the single undertaking.[109] This is different to
plurilateral Agreements, such as the GPA,[110] which did not automatically continue
to apply. The UK applied and was granted independent membership in the GPA.[111]
Moreover, the EU and its member states do not have separate goods and services
schedules but only the EU's schedules.[112] Therefore, the UK has submitted new
goods[113] and services[114] schedules,[115] which are based on the EU's schedules.[116]

---

[107] Trade and Cooperation Agreement between the United Kingdom of Great Britain and Northern
Ireland, of the one part, and the European Union and the European Atomic Energy Community, of
the other part, 30. December 2020.

[108] For an overview, see: General Council, The United Kingdom's Withdrawal From the European
Union, Communication from the United Kingdom, WT/GC/2016, 1.2.2020; Fox (2016). Changes
from a practical perspective: Bacchus (2017).

[109] General Council, The United Kingdom's Withdrawal From the European Union, Communication from the United Kingdom, WT/GC/2016, 1.2.2020, Baetens (2018), pp. 133, 139; Herrmann
(2017a), p. 169.

[110] See generally: Ping Wang, 'Brexit and the WTO Agreement on Government Procurement
("GPA")' 1 34, 36; Sue Arrowsmith, 'Consequences of Brexit in the Area of Public Procurement'
(Directorate General for internal Policies 2017) IP/A/IMCO/2016-23 29; Bartels, 'The UK's Status
in the WTO after Brexit' (Chap. 5, n 10), p. 18; Wang (2018), p. 143.

[111] Committee on Government Procurement, Minutes of the Formal Meeting of 27 February 2019,
GPA/M/75, 28.5.2019, pp. 4–10. Referring to Committee on Government Procurement, Accession
of the United Kingdom to the Agreement on Government Procurement in its own right, GPA/ACC/
GBR/20/Rev.1, 6.2.2019; Committee on Government Procurement, Accession of the United
Kingdom to the Agreement on Government Procurement in its own right, GPA/CD/2/Add.1,
26.6.2019.

[112] The current EU Good Schedule is: Committee on Market Access, Rectification and modification
of Schedules, Schedule CLXXV – European Union, G/MA/TAR/RS/506, 17.10.2017. The EU's
Services Schedule is: Council for Trade in Services, European Communities and their Member
States, Schedule of Specific Commitments, GATS/SC/31, 15.04.1994. The EU25 Services Schedule has been certified but not yet ratified.

[113] Committee on Market Access, Rectification and modification of Schedules – Schedule XIX –
United Kingdom, G/MA/TAR/RS/570, 24.7.2018.

[114] Council for Trade in Services, Communication from the United Kingdom of Great Britain and
Northern Ireland, Certification of schedule of specific commitments, S/C/W/380, 3.12.2018; Coun-
cil for Trade in Services, Communication from the United Kingdom of Great Britain and Northern
Ireland, Certification of list of article II (MFN) exemptions, S/C/W/381, 3.12.2018.

[115] Department for International Trade, 'UK Goods and Services Schedules at the WTO' (GOV.UK)
<https://www.gov.uk/government/publications/uk-goods-and-services-schedules-at-the-wto>
accessed 5 July 2021.

[116] See generally: Gehring (2016); Lux and Pickett (2017), pp. 95–97; Baetens (2018), pp. 141–142;
Azevêdo (2016); Bartels, 'The UK's WTO Schedules' (Chap. 5, n 10); Herrmann (2017b), p. 963;
Ungphakorn (2016); Lorand Bartels, 'Understanding the UK's Position in the WTO after Brexit

Following reservations expressed by other WTO Members, neither has been certified yet.[117]

The UK was no longe bound by the EU's RTAs,[118] but "rolled-over" most[119] of them. This means that the deals were *copy and pasted* with the UK now being a party to them.[120]

6.2.3.1   Protocol on Ireland/Northern Ireland

The Protocol on Ireland/Northern Ireland applied from the end of the transition period onwards.[121]

The rules on anti-dumping differ from the general rules on customs. Generally, Northern Ireland is part of the customs territory of the UK.[122] However, a good can only be transported duty free from another part of the UK to Northern Ireland if that good is transported directly and that good is not at risk "of subsequently being moved into the Union, whether by itself or forming part of another good following processing."[123] Similarly, the UK's duties apply only if a good is moved by direct transport from a third country to Northern Ireland and that good is not at risk of "subsequently being moved into the Union, whether by itself or forming part of

---

(Part I – The UK's Status and Its Schedules)' (*International Centre for Trade and Sustainable Development*) <https://www.ictsd.org/opinion/understanding-the-uk> accessed 5 July 2021; Lorand Bartels, 'Understanding the UK's Position in the WTO after Brexit (Part II – The Consequences)' (*International Centre for Trade and Sustainable Development*) <https://www.ictsd.org/opinion/understanding-the-uk-0> accessed 5 July 2021; Boonekamp (2017). On agriculture: Downes (2017), p. 741; Matthews (2016); Swinbank (2017), p. 12.

[117] Kim (2019).

[118] Department for International Trade, 'Existing UK Trade Agreements with Non-EU Countries' (*GOV.UK*, 29 January 2020) <https://www.gov.uk/guidance/uk-trade-agreements-with-non-eu-countries> accessed 5 July 2021; Wessel (2018), pp. 115, 119–121; Volterra (2017); Odermatt (2017), pp. 1051, 1056; Kikarea (2019), p. 53; Denman (2016).

[119] On the UK-South Korea FTA, see e.g.: Ungphakorn (2019); Kim (2017). On the UK's relations to China and Russia, see: Henderson and Pils (2016), p. 473. On CETA, see e.g.: Hillman et al. (2017); Sosnow et al. (2017), p. 125.

[120] Department for International Trade, 'Existing UK Trade Agreements with Non-EU Countries' (n 118). Before the conclusion of the Withdrawal Agreement, it was controversial whether it would violate the sincere cooperation requirement if the UK negotiated FTAs with third parties prior to the Withdrawal Agreement: Wessel (2018), pp. 106–111; Wessel (2016), p. 197; Łazowksi and Wessels (2016), pp. 623, 523; Larik (2017), p. 102. The Withdrawal Agreement allows the UK to conclude RTAs during the transition period if they enter into force thereafter in Art. 129 (4) Withdrawal Agreement.

[121] Art. 185 (5) Withdrawal Agreement. Certain Articles apply from the entry into force of the Agreement already. None of those relate to anti-dumping measures, however. See generally: Connolly and Doyle (2019), p. 153.

[122] Art. 4 (1) Protocol on Ireland/NI, Withdrawal Agreement.

[123] Art. 5 (1)(1) Protocol on Ireland/NI, Withdrawal Agreement.

another good following processing."[124] Otherwise, the EU's customs legislation[125] applies with respect to Northern Ireland.[126]

Following an amendment to the Northern Ireland Protocol, the rules on anti-dumping now differ from these general rules.[127] Economic operators located in Northern Ireland are not considered part of the union market and are thus not considered in investigations. Similarly, economic operators in Northern Ireland may not request the initiation of investigations. However, the EU's anti-dumping measures apply to all goods brought to Northern Ireland (including ones coming from the rest of the UK) if they are at risk of being moved to the EU. Duties paid on goods with a customs clearance in Northern Ireland may be refunded.[128]

6.2.3.2   Trade and Cooperation Agreement[129]

Following some time of uncertainty and speculations of not reaching a deal,[130] the UK and EU have concluded the TCA. In the context of anti-dumping, two separate questions arise: (1) do the EU and UK impose the same trade defence measures against third countries (i.e. externally) and (2) can the EU and UK impose trade defence measures against each other (i.e. internally)?[131]

As the TCA is a Free Trade Agreement, it only liberalizes internal trade and external trade is not harmonized so that the EU and UK no longer impose the same trade defence measures externally. Internally, Art. Goods.17 TCA regulates that the EU and UK may impose trade defence measures against each other with minimal modifications to the WTO requirements. In addition to WTO requirements, interested parties should be granted an opportunity to defend their interests, provided that

---

[124] Art. 5 (1)(2) Protocol on Ireland/NI, Withdrawal Agreement. For a general explainer, see: Stojanovic (2020); Peers (2020); Terhechte (2020), pp. 20–21; Cabinet Office (2020).

[125] Art. 5 (2) Union Customs Code.

[126] Art. 5 (3) Protocol on Ireland/NI, Withdrawal Agreement.

[127] Art. 1 Nr. 9 Decision No3/2020 of the Joint Committee established by the Agreement on the withdrawal of the United Kingdom of Great Britain and Northern Ireland from the European Union and the European Atomic Energy Community of 17 of December 2020 amending the Protocol on Ireland and Northern Ireland to the Agreement on the withdrawal of the United Kingdom of Great Britain and Northern Ireland from the European Union and the European Atomic Energy Community.

[128] European Commission, Notice on the application of the trade defence legislation and measures of the European Union in Northern Ireland from 1 January 2021, OJ C 248/3, 25.6.2021.

[129] Bickel (2021), pp. 5, 9.

[130] See: Ungphakorn (2020a); Ungphakorn (2020b); Ungphakorn (2020c); Ungphakorn (2020d); Dolle and Leys (2017), p. 117; Vroom and de Wit (2018), p. 196; Hestermeyer and Ortino (2016), p. 452; Mandal (2017); Eeckhout (2018) PE 603.866; Piris (2015); André Sapir, 'Should the UK Pull out of the EU Customs Union?' (*Bruegel*) <http://bruegel.org/2016/08/should-the-uk-pull-out-of-the-eu-customs-union/> accessed 5 July 2021. If no agreement is reached, see: Aurich (2018), p. 443; Crowley et al. (2018).

[131] Bickel (2021), p. 9.

it does not delay the conduct of the investigation and members should also consider whether the imposition of anti-dumping and countervailing duties may not be in the public interest.[132] The effects for the EU and the UK will be considered in turn.

6.2.3.3 EU Obligations

Following the transition period, the EU's anti-dumping measures no longer applied to the UK except as to Northern Ireland in the circumstances laid down in the Protocol on Ireland/NI. The anti-dumping measures remained in force with regards to the rest of the union.

This meant that exporters that have only exported to the UK no longer had to pay the anti-dumping duties to the EU, but the measures remained applicable also against them with regards to the rest of the union.

In a similar way to instances of economic integration, the Commission announced that reviews could be requested if evidence was provided that the measure would have been different had they been based on information excluding the UK. It also highlighted that Brexit itself did not pose sufficient basis for a review.[133]

6.2.3.4 UK Obligations

Except as in the Protocol on Ireland/Northern Ireland, the UK is no longer bound by EU law following the transition period. This means that EU law, including all anti-dumping measures as well as Reg. (EU) 2016/1036 no longer apply in the UK.

The substantive rules on anti-dumping that apply in the UK are contained in Schedules[134] 4 and 5 Taxation (Cross-border Trade) Act 2018 which have been specified in the Dumping and Subsidisation Regulations,[135] as amended.[136] The investigating authority is the Trade Remedy Authority,[137] which has not yet been

---

[132] Article Goods.17.4, 6 TCA. Article Goods.17.5 TCA provides a lesser duty rule that merely replicates Article 9.1 ADA. Article Goods.17.7 TCA also provides that the same goods should not be subject to Safeguard measures and Agricultural Safeguard Provisions at the same time.

[133] European Commission, Notice regarding the application of anti-dumping and anti-subsidy measures in force in the Union following the withdrawal of the United Kingdom and the possibility of a review, OJ C 18/41, 18.1.2021.

[134] The Schedule are incorporated into the Act via Art. 13 (1) Taxation (Cross-border Trade) Act 2018, 13.9.2018.

[135] The Trade Remedies (Dumping and Subsidisation) (EU Exit) Regulations 2019 (Dumping Regulation), 4.3.2019.

[136] The Trade Remedies (Amendment) (EU Exit) Regulations 2019, 2.7.2019.

[137] Para. 8 (1) Schedule 4, Taxation (Cross-border Trade) Act 2018; Para. 6 (1) Schedule 5, Taxation (Cross-border Trade) Act 2018.

set-up.[138] Until then, the Secretary of State is the investigating authority.[139] The Secretary of State decides whether Trade Remedies should be imposed.[140]

The substantive rules establish a general anti-dumping regime that applies if the UK investigates and imposes measures[141] and a transitional regime whereby certain EU measures are transposed into UK law. The general rules will have to comply with WTO obligations, but no specific difficulties arise because of the economic disintegration from the EU.

In general, the UK Government was "committed to maintain" the EU anti-dumping measures that mattered to the UK.[142] These measures should, however, be reviewed to ensure that they are "tailored to the needs of the UK economy".[143] Part 12 Trade Remedies (Dumping and Subsidisation) (EU Exit) Regulations 2019[144] contain the legislative provisions that allow such transition.

With regards to anti-dumping measures, the Secretary of State decided to transition some EU measures.[145,146] Interestingly, prior to amendment in July 2019, the Secretary of State could only transition an EU anti-dumping measure had there been an application made by or on behalf of a UK industry of the respective goods.[147]

To identify which measures to transition, the Department for International Trade (DIT) ran a call for evidence from 28. November 2017 to 24. August 2018.[148] The measures are of interest to the UK, where there is an application by the domestic

---

[138] The Trade Bill 2017–2019 failed to complete its passage through Parliament before the end of the session in 2019.

[139] Part 13 Dumping Regulation.

[140] Para 20 Schedule 4 Taxation (Cross-border Trade) Act 2018; Para. 19 Taxation (Cross-border Trade) Act 2018. See generally on the setup of the UK: De Baere (2017); Peretz (2018); Townsend et al. (2018).

[141] The TRA can only initiate investigations once the EU's Trade Remedies no longer apply to the UK, reg. 95, 95A Dumping Regulation.

[142] 'UK Trade Remedies Authority: Government Response to the Committee's Third Report' (House of Commons International Trade Committee 2018) Third Special Report of Session 2017-19 HC1424 5; Liam Fox, 'Preparing for Our Future UK Trade Policy' (2017) White Paper Cm 9470 37 <https://www.gov.uk/government/publications/preparing-for-our-future-uk-trade-policy/preparing-for-our-future-uk-trade-policy> accessed 5 July 2021.

[143] Fox, 'Preparing for Our Future UK Trade Policy' (n 142), p. 37.

[144] This is based on s. 51 (1)(b) Taxation (Cross-border Trade) Act 2018.

[145] Measure only refers to definitive anti-dumping or anti-subsidy measures (Reg. 94 Dumping Regulation), i.e. not to provisional measures or Undertakings. Measures that undergo an expiry review at that time will also be maintained but only for 30 days, reg. 96B Dumping Regulation.

[146] Reg. 96 (1) Dumping Regulation.

[147] Para. 95 (1) Dumping Regulations.

[148] Department for International Trade, 'Call for Evidence to Identify UK Interest in Existing EU Trade Remedy Measures' (GOV.UK) <https://www.gov.uk/government/consultations/call-for-evidence-to-identify-uk-interest-in-existing-eu-trade-remedy-measures/call-for-evidence-to-iden tify-uk-interest-in-existing-eu-trade-remedy-measures> accessed 5 July 2021. To check whether maintaining Trade Remedy measures that were imposed after the call for evidence is in the UK's interest, the DIT actively approached UK producers to enquire whether maintaining these measures are in the UK's interest.

industry for the imposition of the trade remedy measure, the application is supported by the domestic industry[149] and the UK producers satisfy the minimal market share test.[150,151] The DIT has verified whether these conditions were met at the end of the transition period.[152] The DIT has identified 42 of 106 EU anti-dumping measures that it maintained.[153]

All anti-dumping measures that are maintained are under review.[154] The Trade Remedy Authority (TRA) can review the EU measures before they are transposed or can—after their transposition—review UK measures.[155] The review will consider whether (a) the continuing application of the measure is necessary or sufficient to offset dumping or the importation of the relevant subsidised goods into the UK and (b) there would be injury to the UK industry in those goods if the measure no longer applied.[156] The TRA may also consider other aspects in the review.[157]

---

[149] It is supported by the domestic industry if the quorum in Art. 5.4 ADA is met.

[150] The last requirement is only necessary because UK national law includes a market share requirement, reg. 51 Dumping Regulation. WTO law does not contain such a requirement.

[151] Department for International Trade, 'Final Findings of the Call for Evidence into UK Interest in Existing EU Trade Remedy Measures' (*GOV.UK*, 2 May 2019) para 7 <https://www.gov.uk/government/consultations/call-for-evidence-to-identify-uk-interest-in-existing-eu-trade-remedy-measures/outcome/final-findings-of-the-call-for-evidence-into-uk-interest-in-existing-eu-trade-remedy-measures> accessed 5 July 2021; Department for International Trade, 'Provisional Findings of the Call for Evidence into UK Interest in Existing EU Trade Remedy Measures' (*GOV.UK*, 24 July 2018) <https://www.gov.uk/government/consultations/call-for-evidence-to-identify-uk-interest-in-existing-eu-trade-remedy-measures/provisional-findings-of-the-call-for-evidence-into-UK-interest-in-existing-EU-trade-remedy-measures> accessed 5 July 2021; Department for International Trade, 'Trade Remedies If There's No Brexit Deal' (*GOV.UK*, 19 December 2018) <https://www.gov.uk/government/publications/trade-remedies-if-theres-no-brexit-deal/trade-remedies-if-theres-no-brexit-deal> accessed 5 July 2021.

[152] Department for International Trade, 'Final Findings of the Call for Evidence into UK Interest in Existing EU Trade Remedy Measures' (n 151) para 20; Department for International Trade, 'Trade Remedies Transition Policy' (*GOV.UK*, 6 February 2020) <https://www.gov.uk/guidance/trade-remedies-transition-policy> accessed 5 July 2021.

[153] Department for International Trade, 'Final Findings of the Call for Evidence into UK Interest in Existing EU Trade Remedy Measures' (n 152) para 29.

[154] Reg. 97 Dumping Regulation; Department for International Trade, 'Transition Reviews (Anti-Dumping and Countervailing Measures) - Trade Remedies Investigations Directorate (TRID) Dumping, Subsidisation and Safeguarding Investigations Guidance' (28 October 2019) <https://www.gov.uk/guidance/trade-remedies-investigations-directorate-trid-dumping-and-subsidisation-investigations-guidance/transition-reviews-anti-dumping-and-countervailing-measures> accessed 5 July 2021.

[155] Reg. 97 (2) Dumping Regulation. Transition of an EU measure into UK law during the review has no impact upon it, reg. 97A Dumping Regulation.

[156] Reg. 99A Dumping Regulation.

[157] Reg. 99A (2) Dumping Regulation.

6.2.4 Conclusions

The UK's withdrawal from the EU is the only relevant practice for the consequences of economic disintegration on existing anti-dumping measures. The main effects after the transition period are that the EU's measures will no longer apply to the territory of the UK except for Northern Ireland and the UK seek to transfer some EU measures into UK law to avoid a situation in which its producers are not protected.

6.3 WTO Law Limits

The laws of the member states or of the customs union define what consequences economic integration and disintegration have on existing anti-dumping measures. These consequences must, however, comply with WTO obligations. This part analyses which—if any—limits WTO law contains with regards to anti-dumping measures in the context of cases of economic integration and disintegration.

In general, WTO law does not directly regulate instances of economic integration, which is why members have great freedom when choosing the appropriate approach. The two questions that arise are which measures apply and if measures apply whether they must be reviewed. Which measures apply in cases of economic integration (under Sect. 6.3.1) must be answered separately from the question which measures apply in cases of economic disintegration (under Sect. 6.3.2). These sections will argue that the answer depends on the more fundamental question whether the territorial scope of anti-dumping measures can change. This more fundamental question will be dealt with separately (under Sect. 6.3.3). Finally, the situations that warrant a review will be examined (under Sect. 6.3.4).

6.3.1 Which Measures Apply Following Economic Integration?

Member states or customs unions regulate which anti-dumping measures apply following a case of economic integration and what the scope of these measures are. There are three categories of anti-dumping measures that must be distinguished: the measures previously imposed by the state that lost its competence to regulate (under Sect. 6.3.1.1), the measures of the customs union against the joining state (under Sect. 6.3.1.2) and the measures of the customs union against third states (under Sect. 6.3.1.3). The latter two only apply in cases of enlargement.

In all three categories no WTO problems occur if the measures continue to apply or are disapplied following the economic integration as long as their territorial scope of application does not change.

6.3.1.1   Measures of the State That Lost the Competence to Impose Anti-Dumping Measures Due to Economic Integration

The three alternatives that member states and customs unions have are either that the member state measures are terminated, that the measures continue to apply in the same way as prior to the economic integration or that the member state measures are transposed into customs union measures that then apply to imports into the entire customs union territory.

Because WTO members are not under an obligation to apply anti-dumping measures,[158] they can unilaterally repeal[159] all anti-dumping measures. No WTO problems arise in this constellation.

Similarly, even though this has not happened on a permanent basis in the past, maintaining member state measures will not violate WTO obligations even if in addition to these member state measures the customs union initiates and imposes customs union wide measures.[160] As customs unions may chose not to harmonize external anti-dumping measures, applying member state wide as well as customs union wide measures is possible within the limits of Art. XXIV:8 (a) GATT.[161]

Finally, as has happened to some extent during the formation of the customs union between Belarus, Kazakhstan and Russia, the member states could apply member state measures to the entire customs union. In such a case the territorial scope of a measure changes from previously only applying to Russia to now applying to the entire customs union. Whether that is legal will be discussed below.[162]

6.3.1.2   Enlargement: Customs Union Measures Against the Joining Member

The two options with regards to anti-dumping measures by the customs union against the joining member are either that they continue to apply or that they are repealed.

If the anti-dumping measures continue to apply, this is either because the customs union only follows a low degree of integration or because the customs union is internally divided into an initial customs union with a centralized anti-dumping regime and the joining members that have their own anti-dumping measures. Both

---

[158] Art. 9.1 ADA.

[159] Whether they are repealed or whether they lapse is of no difference for WTO compatibility.

[160] Compare to the EEC transition regime upon its foundation: Art. 26 Reg. (EEC) 459/68.

[161] On the limits of this exception, see: Sect. 4.2.2.

[162] See: Sect. 6.3.3.

options are legal, insofar the customs union still meets the requirements of Art. XXIV:8 (a) GATT.[163]

Similarly, repealing the anti-dumping measures will not violate WTO obligations. Repealing all anti-dumping measures against one country while keeping the anti-dumping measures against other countries in place could violate the MFN principle, however.[164] As this is done during the formation of an enlarged customs union, it can generally be justified according to Art. XXIV:5 GATT.[165]

Repealing the measures does not violate WTO law despite the potential negative effects this may have on third countries. Following the 2004 EC enlargement, anti-dumping measures against Slovakia on certain seamless pipes and tubes were terminated. Following the enlargement, an anti-dumping investigation was initiated on the same products but originating from Croatia, Romania (both were not EU members at the time), Russia and Ukraine. One exporter argued the fact that the anti-dumping measures against Slovakia were terminated should negate causation. The Commission rejected this claim on a factual basis as Slovakian exports to the rest of the EU had increased at a significantly lower rate than the exports of the countries under investigation.[166] However, even if it had not, because Slovakian producers were part of the union industry, this could only have lowered the injury margin[167] but would not have negated causation. The real problem in this case was, however, that Croatian, Romanian, Russian and Ukrainian exporters were relatively worse off, as Slovakian exporters no longer faced anti-dumping measures.[168] Because these negative effects of trade diversion are an inherent result of establishing customs unions[169] and because the formation of customs unions is allowed, third parties have no claim against these negative effects. This means that such an argument cannot be raised in a violation complaint, as the measures are legal. A non-violation

---

[163] Art. XXIV:5 GATT does not include a MFN requirement itself, as it is an exception of the MFN requirement. Because parties are free to conclude multiple differing RTAs, the MFN principle does not apply within RTAs either. In this scenario the parties could also have agreed to conclude two customs unions (as is the case in the EU-Turkey customs union). As it is a mere formality whether a customs union is defined as one customs union or two, this should not make a difference as to the legality of the setup.

[164] See above: Sect. 4.1.2.3.

[165] See above: Sect. 4.2.2. It could also be justified following the Enabling Clause: Sect. 4.2.3.

[166] Council Regulation (EC) No 954/2006 of 27 June 2006 imposing definitive anti-dumping duty on imports of certain seamless pipes and tubes, of iron or steel originating in Croatia, Romania, Russia and Ukraine, repealing Council Regulations (EC) No 2320/97 and (EC) No 348/2000, terminating the interim and expiry reviews of the anti-dumping duties on imports of certain seamless pipes and tubes of iron or non-alloy steel originating, inter alia , in Russia and Romania and terminating the interim reviews of the anti-dumping duties on imports of certain seamless pipes and tubes of iron or non-alloy steel originating, inter alia , in Russia and Romania and in Croatia and Ukraine, OJ L 175/4, 29.6.2006, Rec. 196–198.

[167] Even this is doubtful because of the small market shares of the Slovakian producers in the EU.

[168] This premise can be tackled, as in the EU due to the risk of arbitrage dumping should not be possible.

[169] See above at Sect. 2.2.1.

complaint[170] will also fail as it is questionable whether the fact that exporters or producers of another state no longer face anti-dumping duties upsets (i.e. nullifies or impairs) the competitive position of one state. Regardless of this, it can be reasonably anticipated that anti-dumping measures are lifted against states that join a customs union.[171]

6.3.1.3   Enlargement: Customs Union Measures Against Third Parties

Following enlargement, customs union measures against third parties can either apply to the enlarged customs union or to the customs union pre-enlargement only.

If the measures continue to apply to the customs union pre-enlargement only, no WTO problems arise. The customs union would be divided into two blocs: the union pre-enlargement and the joining members.[172] If they apply to the extended customs union, the territorial scope of the anti-dumping measure changes as it is extended. Again, this raises the question how WTO law deals with changes in the territorial scope of anti-dumping measures, which will be dealt below.[173]

6.3.2   Which Measures Apply Following Economic Disintegration

In cases of economic disintegration, the starting point is that there are only external measures that apply on a union-wide basis. Otherwise, competences would not change. Economic disintegration effects the former member states (under Sect. 6.3.2.1) and in cases of withdrawal from a customs union the remainder of the customs union as well (under Sect. 6.3.2.2).

---

[170] Following Art. 17.2 ADA.

[171] Requirements of non-violation complaints: *Japan - Measures Affecting Consumer Photographic Film and Paper* [1998] WTO Panel Report WT/DS44/R [9.5; 10.82]; *European Communities - Measures Affecting Asbestos and Asbestos-Containing Products* [2000] WTO Panel Report WT/DS135/R [8.288]; *European Communities — Measures Affecting Asbestos and Products Containing Asbestos* [2001] WTO Appellate Body Report WT/DS135/AB/R [185–186].

[172] Except if one argues that the MFN requirement applies to Art. XXIV:5 GATT as well. See Fn. 167.

[173] See below: Sect. 6.3.3.

6.3.2.1 Can the Former Member States Apply the Measures Implemented by the Customs Union?

Following a case of economic disintegration, the former member states can decide to either apply the measures that the customs union formerly implemented or can decide not to do so. This question arises in all cases of economic disintegration.

If the former member state does not transpose the (former) customs union's measures, this does not violate WTO law, as there is no obligation to impose anti-dumping measures.[174]

Former member states may have an incentive to transpose customs union measures, as this avoids a situation in which the producers of the member state are not protected by anti-dumping measures. In such a case an anti-dumping measure that was initially calculated to apply to an entire customs union now only applies to the reduced territory of one member state, meaning that its territorial scope diminishes. Again this is an instance of the territorial scope of a measure changing. Legality of this practice thus depends on whether it is legal for the scope of anti-dumping measures to change, which will be discussed below.[175]

6.3.2.2 Can the Customs Union Apply the Measures to the Reduced Customs Union?

A similar problem arises for the customs union. The question is whether the customs union can continue to apply the anti-dumping measures to the reduced territory of the customs union in the case where a member of the customs union has withdrawn from it.

Nothing obliges the customs union to keep the anti-dumping measures in force and it would not violate WTO provisions to repeal them.[176] If the customs union decides to keep applying the measures but to the reduced territory of the customs union, the situation is similar to when the member state transposes the anti-dumping measure. Again, the territorial scope of the anti-dumping measure is reduced and it is questionable how WTO law deals with these changes.

6.3.3 Can the Territorial Scope of Anti-Dumping Measures Change?

Overall, WTO law imposes few restrictions on its members in cases of economic integration and disintegration of customs unions. The only problematic question that

---

[174] Art. 9.1 ADA.
[175] See below at Sect. 6.3.3.
[176] Art. 9.1 ADA.

arises is whether the scope of an anti-dumping measure can change. This question arises in several constellations. In cases of economic integration, it is relevant to answer whether customs unions can apply the anti-dumping measures of certain member states to the entire union and to answer whether the customs unions' anti-dumping measures can be extended to also cover the joining member states. It is relevant in cases of economic disintegration concerning the question whether customs unions can continue to apply anti-dumping measures to the reduced territory of the customs union following the withdrawal of one member and whether member states can apply the customs union's measures with respect to their territory once they are no longer part of the customs union.

This general question has been discussed in connection with the debate on WTO legality of the UK's plan to transition the EU's anti-dumping measures. The consensus seems to be that the UK's proposed approach violates WTO law.[177] The UK Government has justified its approach on the basis that leaving the EU is an "exceptional and unprecedented" situation.[178] WTO law does not expressly address how to transition trade remedy measures when a member of a customs union leaves that union.[179] Therefore, they have adopted a "pragmatic" approach to minimise trade disruption.[180]

Strict critics argue that the transposition of the EU measures may conflict with the material requirements of Art. VI GATT and the ADA. This is because the determinations of dumping, injury, and causation have only considered the EU and not solely the UK market. Moreover, this may conflict with procedural requirements, as the investigation has been conducted by the EU Commission and not a UK authority.[181] Interestingly, supporters of this view do no suggest that the EU can no longer apply its anti-dumping measures to the reduced EU27 territory.

---

[177] Arguing for the legality: Oral evidence taken before the International Trade Committee on 29.11.2017, HC (2017-19) 603i, Q9-Q11, Q16 [Bernardine Adkins]; Oral evidence taken before the International Trade Committee on 14.3.2018, HC (2018-19) 743ii, Q50 [Bernard O'Connor]. Arguing against the legality: Oral evidence taken before the International Trade Committee on 29.11.2017, HC (2017-19) 603i, Q9-Q11, Q [Gareth Stace]; Van Bael & Bellis, 'The Impact of Brexit on EU Trade Relations' 4 <https://www.vbb.com/insights/trade-and-customs/brexit/the-impact-of-brexit-on-eu-trade-relations> accessed 5 July 2021; Lux and Pickett (2017), pp. 110–111; Herrmann (2017a), p. 177; Dunt (2019).

[178] Fox, 'Preparing for Our Future UK Trade Policy' (n 142), p. 37.

[179] ibid.

[180] ibid.

[181] E.g. Lux and Pickett (2017), pp. 92, 110; Herrmann (2017a), p. 177; Ni (2018), pp. 277–294; UK Steel, UK Implementation of Post-Brexit WTO-Compliant Trade Defence Remedies: a Steel Sector View (2017), at 21, Oral evidence taken before the International Trade Committee (29 November 2017), HC (2017-19) 603i, Q9-Q11, Q16 [Bernadine Adkins], http://data.parliament.uk/writtenevidence/committeeevidence.svc/evidencedocument/international-trade-com mittee/the-trade-bill/oral/75145.html (visited 6 September 2020); Oral evidence taken before the International Trade Committee (14 March 2018), HC (2018-19) 743ii, Q50 [Daniel Moulis]; 743ii, Q50 [Bernard O'Connor], http://data.parliament.uk/writtenevidence/committeeevidence.svc/evidencedocument/international-trade-committee/uk-trade-remedies-authority/oral/80553.html (visited 6 September 2020). For an overview of Expert Testimony during the legislative process: Khalfaoui and Gehring (2018), pp. 17–19.

Following this view the UK could not transition any EU measures. The UK could not even maintain the definitive anti-dumping duties on imports of high fatigue performance steel concrete reinforcement bars originating in China.[182] Some have argued that in that case the determinations would not be different as the dumped products are only exported to the UK market.[183] In that case, all the unrelated importers were UK importers[184] and probably all users were UK users too.[185] However, of the sampled union producers, only one was a UK producer.[186] Thus, the injury determination was not be limited to data from the UK. Yet, following this view, the anti-dumping measure could continue to apply against imports into the EU27 even though only imports into the UK were considered during the investigation. Moreover, following this view, the measure could presumably also continue to apply if EU producers that contributed data disappeared from the market due to insolvency or mergers or if new producers appeared.

A moderate view suggests that the UK's approach of mirroring the EU's anti-dumping measures is only permissible following a case-by-case analysis whether a hypothetical investigation limited to the UK would produce a different outcome. Only if the outcome would have been the same could the UK maintain the EU's measures.[187] This view is driven by practical considerations to ensure more workable results for the UK but it is not clear which WTO provision this can be based on.

Both views share the same premise that certain future changes in data have the effect that anti-dumping measures can no longer apply. This study argues that this premise is flawed. The UK can maintain the EU's anti-dumping measures[188] and

---

[182]Commission Implementing Regulation (EU) 2016/1246 of 28 July 2016 imposing a definitive anti-dumping duty on imports of high fatigue performance steel concrete reinforcement bars originating in the People's Republic of China, OJ L 204/70, 29.7.2016.

[183]'UK Implementation of Post-Brexit WTO-Compliant Trade Defence Remedies: A Steel Sector View' (n 181) n 35.

[184]Following the Notice of initiation (Notice of initiation of an anti-dumping proceeding concerning imports of high fatigue performance steel concrete reinforcement bars originating in the People's Republic of China, OJ C 143/12, 30.4.2015), four unrelated importers provided the requested information (Commission Regulation (EU) 2016/113 of 28 January 2016 imposing a provisional anti-dumping duty on imports of high fatigue performance steel concrete reinforcement bars originating in the People's Republic of China, OJ L 23/16, 29.1.2016, Rec. 11). Of these four a verification visit was conducted with one unrelated importer, Reg. (EU) 2016/113, Rec. 14 (a UK importer) and two unrelated importers subsequently withdrew. Nevertheless, three unrelated importers provided information concerning the retroactive application of the Anti-Dumping measures, Reg. (EU) 2016/1246, Rec. 10, those three were UK importers, see Reg. (EU) 2016/1246, Rec. 11.

[185]Initially there were five unrelated users and four related users. Three unrelated users subsequently withdrew their cooperation, Reg. (EU) 2016/113, Rec. 13. The four related users were all UK users, Reg. (EU) 2016/113, Rec. 14. The two unrelated users subject to verification visits were UK users, Reg. (EU) 2016/113, Rec. 14.

[186]Reg. (EU) 2016/113, Rec. 9, 14.

[187]Baetens (2018), p. 165.

[188]For a similar argument, see: Zhuang (2019).

changes in scope of anti-dumping measures are possible if the investigation remains attributable.

The argument is based on two steps: First, in principle future changes do not invalidate investigations and second, the two exceptions to this are that measures cannot be limited to only parts of a territory and that the investigation must remain attributable.

As a starting point, anti-dumping measures are always imposed on a future period of time based on the results of an investigation that concerned data from a past period of investigation.[189] This means that there is always a gap between the data upon which the calculations of the anti-dumping measures are based and the existing conditions under which the anti-dumping measures apply. To limit this gap, the ADA regulates that anti-dumping measures should only remain in force "as long as and to the extent necessary to counteract dumping which is causing injury."[190] If that is no longer the case, i.e. if the circumstances have changed between the investigation period and the period in which the measure applies or because too much time has passed between these points, the ADA foresees that the measures should be reviewed.[191]

The duty to conduct reviews is also a privilege. To not undermine the requirements that warrant a review, changed circumstances must only be taken into account insofar as the ADA has regulated that they trigger a review. This means that changed circumstances do not invalidate anti-dumping measures. Because changed circumstances reviews exist, it must be legal to apply anti-dumping measures even if the investigation is outdated. From a legal perspective this means that as the ADA lists the consequences of changing circumstances comprehensively, there is no room for interpretation to conclude that certain anti-dumping measures can no longer apply following changed circumstances.

The same principle applies where the territorial scope of a measure changes due to changes in the territory of the imposing state or customs union: first, the WTO Agreements contain no specific rules for territorial changes so that applying the general rules creates legal certainty. Second, the practical effects of changing the geographical scope of a measure are like other changes in the market structure. Factually, changes in the market structure such as a series of insolvencies[192] can be

---

[189] Although the ADA refers to a "period of investigation", it does not provide how that period should be defined. According to Committee on Anti-Dumping Practices, Recommendation Concerning the Period of Data Collection for Anti-Dumping Investigations, G/ADP/6, 16.5.2000, para. 1 (a) the period of investigation for the dumping investigation should normally be twelve months ending as close to the date of initiation as is practicable and according to para. 1 (c) the period of investigation for the injury determination should normally be at least three years and should include the entirety of the period of data collection for the dumping investigation.

[190] Art. 11.1 ADA.

[191] Art. 11.2, 11.3 ADA.

[192] That this does not invalidate antidumping measures: Commission Implementing Regulation (EU) 2018/1722 of 14 November 2018, OJ 2018 L 287, (47)–(61). This only relates to EU law, but is consistent with WTO law.

as permanent as territorial changes. Beyond that, the fact that territorial changes may originate from the decision of the imposing member should not impact the legal consequences as not all territorial changes depend on a decision by the imposing authority (e.g. the EU never consented to the UK's unilateral withdrawal). Additionally, consent does not play a role in other changes to market conditions, because changes may also originate from changes in market regulations. Third, there is WTO practice to support this. In all recent EU and Eurasian Economic Union (EAEU) enlargements, the scope of the measures was extended to include the joining states. The legality of this extension was only questioned with respect to the 2004 EC enlargement in two meetings of the Committee on Anti-Dumping Practices but no longer pursued after the EC answered questions on the modalities of the enlargement.[193] The issue did not arise again in later enlargements or in EAEU enlargements, which 'implies agreement on the interpretation of the relevant position'.[194] The fact that several enlargements by different WTO Members occurred without contention by other WTO Members also demonstrates a 'consistent, discernible pattern of acts' which is at least implicitly accepted by all WTO Members[195] and thus constitutes 'subsequent practice' in the sense of Art. 31(3)(b) VCLT.67 Although this subsequent practice only exists for enlargements, it demonstrates that territorial changes are possible in principle and nothing different should apply in the reverse situation.[196]

Exceptions may exist to this principle.

One exception may derive from Art. 4.1(ii) ADA. This provision allows limiting anti-dumping investigations to certain geographical territories within a state or customs union. Only exports into that limited territory will be considered and the injury only considers producers of that territory. The resulting measure then applies to the same limited geographic scope, according to Art. 4.2 ADA. Art. 4.1(ii) ADA only applies if

> (a) the producers within such market sell all or almost all of their production of the product in question in that market, and (b) the demand in that market is not to any substantial degree supplied by producers of the product in question located elsewhere in the territory.

These additional requirements could be circumvented were it allowed to change the scope of a measure without limitation. The situation is, however, different to the one considered in this chapter. This study deals with changes in the territory of

---

[193] Committee on Anti-Dumping Practices, Minutes of the Regular Meeting held on 1–2 May 2003, G/ADP/M/24, 17.10.2003, at 9–14; Committee on Anti-Dumping Practices, Minutes of the Regular Meeting held on 23–24 October 2003, G/ADP/M/25, 9.3.2004, at 11–21.

[194] *United States—Measures Affecting the Cross-Border Supply of Gambling and Betting Services* [2005], WT/DS285/AB/R, paras 192–93.

[195] *European Communities—Customs Classification of Frozen Boneless Chicken Cuts* [2005] WT/DS269/AB/R para 259. Practice only exists with respect to two customs unions, but they are the only two customs unions that had enlargements and have a harmonized trade defence system.

[196] This passage is based on Bickel (2021), pp. 14, 15.

customs unions as such and not to limiting measures to only certain parts of the customs union territory.

Another limitation may derive from the attribution requirement. This study argues that the ADA not only requires that an investigation concludes that the substantive requirements are met but that the acts to meet these requirements must be attributable to the WTO member imposing the measure.[197] It is not sufficient that these acts were only attributable at the time that they occurred but they must be attributable also at the time at which the measure is challenged, i.e. potentially permanently. Without attribution at the time of the challenge, the WTO member will not be able to rely on them.[198]

Accordingly, in cases of economic disintegration the former member state may apply the measures previously applied by the customs union limited to its territory and the customs union can apply its measures to the reduced territory. For Brexit this means that as the Commission acts are attributable to the member states as well, the UK may rely on the investigation that the EU initially conducted.[199] The UK may thus transpose the EU's measures.

Problems arise if following economic enlargement, a customs union applies anti-dumping measures imposed by member states to the entire territory of the customs union. Acts by the authorities of member states are not attributable to the customs union and especially since the customs union potentially did not even exist when the acts took place, investigations are not attributable. A violation of WTO rules could, however, be justified according to Art. XXIV:5 GATT. Yet, whether the justification applies is doubtful.[200]

Importantly, which anti-dumping measures apply following cases of economic integration and disintegration are not questions of state succession. Whether the principles of state succession apply in cases of withdrawals from a customs union at all is contentious.[201] There are three reasons, why irrespective of this, state succession does not apply to the question whether the territorial scope of anti-dumping measures can change.

---

[197] See above at: Sect. 5.1.2.

[198] The *moving frontiers* principle as expressed in Art. 29 VCLT is not required for this explanation. It applies to international treaties, whereas determining the scope of laws does not occur on the international plane but on the national plane but national law must comply with WTO obligations.

[199] See above at: Sect. 5.5.

[200] In the case where a state that has never implemented anti-dumping measures joins a customs union that implements Anti-Dumping measures, a justification according to Art. XXIV:5 GATT may not be available. The acceding member may apply more Anti-Dumping measures post-accession, which could be prohibited by Art. XXIV:4 GATT. See: Sagara (2002), p. 41. The author also points out that the *Turkey – Textiles* requirements would have to be met.

[201] For: Bartels, 'The UK's Status in the WTO after Brexit' (Chap. 5, n 10), p. 19; Kikarea (2019), pp. 72–75; Willemyns and Koekkoek (2017). Against e.g.: Khalfaoui and Gehring (2018), pp. 167–169; Häberli (2017), p. 87; Luca (2017), p. 479; Herrmann (2017a), p. 169; Sacerdoti (2017), pp. 905, 212; Mariani and Sacerdoti (2019), p. 187. See also generally: Bordin (2019).

First, the law of state succession applies where a state ceases to rule in a territory, while another takes its place.[202] Integral to this is that a new entity emerges and the law of state succession answers which rights and obligations that the former state had should be passed on to the new state.[203] This is different from the situation here. If acts are attributable to the withdrawing state, they are that state's acts. No transfer of rights or obligations must take place.[204] If there is attribution, no resort to state succession is necessary.

Second, it is difficult to see which rules on state successions apply to anti-dumping measures. The closest analogy of the provisions in the Vienna Conventions could be debts.[205] However, anti-dumping measures are charges payable by individuals and thus not state debts.[206] There are no codified rules of customary international law on state succession that answer issues of anti-dumping. Resorting to the principles of state succession therefore does not help in that regard.[207]

Third, there is precedence that the principles of state succession do not apply in the reverse situation. The ECJ had to decide whether EC anti-dumping measures initially applied against the Socialist Federal Republic of Yugoslavia (SFRY) could also apply against the Former Yugoslav Republic of Macedonia's (FYROM—now: North Macedonia) after its succession. Even though this is undoubtedly a case of state succession, the ECJ explicitly ruled that the law of state successions does not apply. Rather, the case was solved applying general principles.[208] Even though the ECJ and not a WTO Panel ruled on this, this case still has argumentative value.

In summary, the territorial scope of anti-dumping measures can change but two important limitations apply. A change in scope cannot undermine Art. 4.1(ii) ADA, i.e. it is not possible to limit anti-dumping measures to apply to only certain geographical parts of a customs territory and the investigation must remain attributable. The practical advantage of this solution is that it avoids a situation in which a customs territory experiences a protection vacuum following a case of economic integration or disintegration.

---

[202] See also: O'Connell (1967b), p. 3. See also generally: Zimmermann (2000); Bühler (2001).

[203] Compare to the situations covered in the Vienna Convention on Succession of States in respect of Treaties, 23.8.1978; Vienna Convention on Succession of States in respect of State Property, Archives and Debts, 8.4.1983 (jointly: Vienna Conventions).

[204] The only situation in which state succession could therefore apply is if an act is not attributable to the state or customs union but the territorial scope of the anti-dumping measures changes, nevertheless. This could explain the changing scope of Russian anti-dumping measures after the formation of the customs union of Belarus, Kazakhstan and Russia.

[205] Part IV Vienna Convention 1983.

[206] Art. 33 Vienna Convention 1983. See also: *Belgian State v Banque Indosuez and Other* [1997] Judgment of the CJEU ECLI:EU:C:1997:494 [25].

[207] Cheng develops a general approach to state succession that could apply in the present situation as well. However, it is doubtful whether this represents international customary law. See: Cheng (2006).

[208] *Belgian State v. Banque Indosuez and Other* (n 206). For a discussion of the case, see below at: Sect. 7.2.2.

If the territorial scope of a measure changes, certain data that has been used during the initial investigation will no longer be available or may have changed. The ADA deals with these changed circumstances by mandating changed circumstances reviews, according to Art. 11.2 ADA.

6.3.4 Must the Applicable Measures Be Reviewed?

If, following economic integration and disintegration, some anti-dumping investigations were repeated, the results of these investigations may be different. Especially in cases where the scope of the anti-dumping measures has changed, current data may not be in line with the initial investigations. WTO law deals with changed circumstances by requiring interim reviews.[209]

Above that, as there is no obligation to impose anti-dumping measures there is also no obligation to keep them in place at the given level. WTO members are free to conduct reviews or vary the measures to the benefit of exporters to accommodate for any economic hardship that arises following the sudden extension in scope of measures.

6.3.4.1 What Warrants a Review?

The purpose of an interim review is to ensure that the requirements of Art. 11.1 ADA are met, namely that an anti-dumping measure[210] only remains in force "as long as and to the extent necessary to counteract dumping which is causing injury."[211] In an interim review, the investigating authority considers whether the continued imposition of the measure is necessary to offset dumping and/or whether the injury is likely to continue or recur were the measure varied or removed.[212]

Interim reviews should be initiated by the investigating authority upon request or *ex officio* where warranted.[213] Where an investigating authority determines that "circumstances furnishing good and sufficient grounds for, or justifying, the self-initiation of a review" exist, it must self-initiate such review.[214] Above that, an

---

[209] Refund Requests, Art. 9.5 ADA, follow a similar principle limited to an examination of the dumping margin. The same threshold as applied in this study may be applied. If the dumping margin changes, exporters or producers may choose between requesting an interim review and/or refund requests. The difference between the two is that whereas interim reviews change the duty for the future, refund requests make it possible to get refunded for too much duty paid.

[210] Price Undertakings are reviewed following the same principles, see heading of Art. 11 ADA.

[211] *European Communities - Anti-Dumping Duties on Malleable Cast Iron Tube or Pipe Fittings from Brazil* [2003] WTO Panel Report WT/DS219/R [7.112].

[212] Art. 11.2 ADA.

[213] Art. 11.2 ADA.

[214] *United States - Anti-Dumping Measures on Certain Shrimp from Viet Nam* [2014] WTO Panel Report WT/DS429/R [7.375]. See also: *EC - Tube or Pipe Fittings* (n 211) para 7.112.

investigating authority must initiate an interim review upon request by an interested party[215] after a reasonable time,[216] if that request substantiates sufficiently the need for such review.[217] The interim review is thereby both forward and backwards looking: an investigating authority determines whether there is dumping or injury at the moment of the investigation but the investigating authority may also conduct a prospective analysis of whether there will be dumping[218] and injury[219] upon removal of the measure. This means that the absence of present dumping[220] or injury[221] does not in and of itself require revocation of the anti-dumping measure.

It could be the case that instances of economic integration and disintegration warrant a review.

In general, Panels and the Appellate Body have, so far, interpreted whether an interim review is warranted very restrictively. In the unadopted Panel Report *US – Swedish Steel Plate* the Panel decided that a review of a 20-year-old measure is not warranted even though Sweden had reduced Steel production, Swedish exports to the then EEC had increased due to an FTA signed between Sweden and the EEC and the US industry had considerably improved.[222] In line with that, *EC – Tube or Pipe Fittings* demonstrates which changes in market conditions warrant the initiation of an interim review. A serious currency devaluation in Brazil impacted the normal value and the export price of an anti-dumping calculation. The relevant factors that led the Panel in that case to, nevertheless, conclude that the initiation of an interim review was not warranted, were that it was not clear whether and to what extent such a devaluation would continue and what effects such a devaluation had on the pricing decisions of the exporters.[223]

---

[215] Interested party refers to Art. 6.11 ADA; *US - Shrimp II (Viet Nam)* (n 214) para 7.379.

[216] The ADA does not define a reasonable period of time, giving WTO Members the space to do so ibid 7.380. Implicitly there is a time limitation to a "reasonable period of time prior" (Art. 11.3 ADA) to the five year limitation, as in that case an expiry review will take place, see this argument in relation to EU law: Scharf, 'AD-GVO Art. 11 Geltungsdauer, Überprüfung und Erstattung' (2018) para. 17. If the measure has not been in force for a reasonable period of time yet, the investigating authority may self-initiate a review nevertheless: Müller et al. (2009) para 11.53.

[217] Art. 11.2 ADA.

[218] *United States - Anti-Dumping Duty on Dynamic Random Access Memory Semiconductors (DRAMS) of One Megabit or Above from Korea* [1999] WTO Panel Report WT/DS99/R [6.26–6.29].

[219] ibid 6.48.

[220] Also pointing to Art. 11.3 ADA which includes a possible determination that dumping can "recur" and Footnote 22, which would both be meaningless if a duty existed to terminate the measures ibid 6.30–6.32. See also: *EC - Tube or Pipe Fittings* (n 211) para 7.116; Mavroidis, *Trade in Goods* (Chap. 2, n 10), p. 475.

[221] *US - DRAMS* (n 218) para 6.48.

[222] *United States - Anti-Dumping Duties on Imports of Stainless Steel Plate from Sweden* [1994] GATT 1947 Panel Report ADP/117, and Corr. 1 [246].

[223] *EC - Tube or Pipe Fittings* (n 211) para 7.116. This case cannot apply directly, as the circumstances changed in the country under investigation and not the investigating country. Nevertheless, the same principles may apply.

A review is thus only warranted due to changes in the market conditions if those changes specifically relate to the conditions to impose the anti-dumping measure and have changed lastingly.

Above that, the review procedure is different from the initial investigation and certain circumstances are not considered in the review proceedings.[224] Changes in these circumstances will not warrant the initiation of a review either. Specifically, the following differences exist:

- According to Art. 11.4 ADA the provisions of the initial investigation concerning the procedure and the evidence in Art. 6 ADA apply. Importantly, this does not refer to Art. 5 ADA, which is why particularly the standing requirement[225] and the *de minimis* threshold[226] do not apply, except if WTO members specifically legislate to the contrary.[227]
- Concerning the dumping calculation, the investigating authority does not need to establish which dumping margins would result if the duties were removed.[228] If a member goes ahead and calculates dumping margins, it should do so in accordance with Art. 2 ADA, however.[229] The investigating authority is thereby not bound by the methodology used in the initial investigation, as long as the determination rests on a sufficient factual basis that allows to draw reasoned and adequate conclusions.[230] Despite the reference in Art. 11.4 ADA to Art. 6 ADA, this does not include a reference to the obligation to determine individual

---

[224] *United States - Countervailing Duties on Certain Corrosion-Resistant Carbon Steel Flat Products from Germany* [2002] WTO Appellate Body Report WT/DS213/AB/R [87]. This case relates to an SCM proceeding, but also applies in the context of the ADA, *US - Corrosion-Resistant Steel Sunset Review* (Chap. 5, n 82) para 107.

[225] *United States - Sunset Review of Anti-Dumping Duties on Corrosion-Resistant Carbon Steel Flat Products from Japan* [2003] WTO Panel Report WT/DS244/R [7.68].

[226] Art. 5.8 ADA. *US - Carbon Steel* (n 225) para 89 (In relation to the SCM Agreement. The same considerations apply in the context of the ADA. Concerning expiry reviews, Art. 11.3 ADA: *United States - Sunset Reviews of Anti-Dumping Measures on Oil Country Tubular Goods from Argentina* [2004] WTO Appellate Body Report WT/DS268/AB/R [346]; *US - Corrosion-Resistant Steel Sunset Review* (n 225) 7.70. Concerning a duty assessment procedure, Art. 9.3 ADA: *US - DRAMS* (n 218) para 6.89. The arguments presented in these cases also apply to Art. 11.2 ADA proceedings, which is why the conclusions can also apply.

[227] Which they could, as these requirements are to the advantage of exporters and producers.

[228] *US - Corrosion-Resistant Steel Sunset Review* (n 225) para 7.162–7.180; *US - Corrosion-Resistant Steel Sunset Review* (Chap. 5, n 82) paras 123, 124.

[229] *US - Corrosion-Resistant Steel Sunset Review* (Chap. 5, n 82) paras 127, 128.

[230] *US - Shrimp II (Viet Nam)* (n 214) para 7.367, 7.375. For this interpretation in cases of sunset reviews, see: *US - Oil Country Tubular Goods Sunset Review* (n 226) para 234; *US - Corrosion-Resistant Steel Sunset Review* (n 225) para 7.166, 7.271. See also: *Ukraine - Anti-Dumping Measures on Ammonium Nitrate* [2018] WTO Panel Report WT/DS493/R [7.165]. If the investigating authority relies on a specific methodology, however, it must act in accordance with the provisions on the dumping margin: *US - Shrimp II (Viet Nam)* (n 214) para 7.393. With relation to Art. 2.4 ADA: *US - Corrosion-Resistant Steel Sunset Review* (Chap. 5, n 82) para 127.

dumping margins, contained in Art. 6.10 ADA, as an investigating authority is not required in a review to calculate dumping margins in the first place.[231]

- In relation to the injury investigation, the circumstances must demonstrate that the injury would be likely to continue or recur. To do that, the investigating authority does not have to conduct an injury determination following Art. 3 ADA, but if it does so any mistakes therein will taint the determinations made.[232]
- A causal link between dumping and the injury will not have to be established anew, as otherwise the review investigation would turn into an original investigation.[233]

Above these differences, an interim review can also be partial.[234] It can be limited to the examination of the continuation or recurrence of either dumping or injury[235] or a re-examination of the product scope, or other modalities of the anti-dumping measure.[236]

This section takes the approach that an interim review is warranted if a hypothetical investigation limited to those considerations that can become relevant in a review leads to a different outcome and the difference in outcome is of a lasting nature. This is the case if upon repetition of an investigation limited to a dumping and injury determination, the results would differ. Above that, states or customs unions may also initiate interim reviews below that threshold. Where the reason for these changes is apparent, investigating authorities must self-initiate reviews. Otherwise, additional information that supports these circumstances must be provided in the request to initiate such review.

---

[231] *US - Corrosion-Resistant Steel Sunset Review* (Chap. 5, n 82) para 155. For criticism of the methodology used to establish dumping in sunset reviews, see: Howse and Staiger (2006), pp. 471, 480–487.

[232] *Ukraine - Ammonium Nitrate (Russia)* (n 230) para 7.166, 7.168, 7.175, 7.179, 7.181, 7.182. This is because there is no cross-reference to Art. 3 ADA in Art. 11.2 ADA. This also makes sense in light of the different nature and purpose of original investigations and reviews. For the same reasoning on an Art. 11.3 ADA review, see: *US - Oil Country Tubular Goods Sunset Review* (n 226) para 280; *EU — Footwear (China)* (Chap. 4, n 33) para 7.337. Yet, see the caveat in *United States - Sunset Reviews of Anti-Dumping Measures on Oil Country Tubular Goods from Argentina* [2004] WTO Panel Report WT/DS268/R [7.276] that the claims under Art. 3 ADA will only be addressed insofar as the investigating authority has made an injury determination instead of a likelihood-of-injury determination.

[233] *US - Oil Country Tubular Goods Sunset Review* (n 226) paras 123–124. See critical comments by Mavroidis, *Trade in Goods* (Chap. 2, n 10), p. 486; Mavroidis (2016), p. 134.

[234] Wolfrum and Stoll (2008), p. 152. Also referred to as "narrow" review in Mavroidis, *Trade in Goods* (Chap. 2, n 10), p. 475.

[235] Mavroidis, *Trade in Goods* (Chap. 2, n 10), p. 475; Müller et al. (2009) para 11.46.

[236] Wolfrum and Stoll (2008), p. 152.

6.3.4.2   Are Reviews Warranted Following Economic (Dis-) Integration?

To calculate an anti-dumping duty, the product under investigation must be defined and data must be gathered to determine whether there is dumping that causes injury. An anti-dumping duty then takes the form of an *ad valorem,* a fixed or a variable duty.[237] Alternatively, a price undertaking can be agreed between an exporter and the investigating WTO member.[238] The exporter may be required to raise its prices but quantitative restrictions are also possible. The quantitative element may be calculated using data relating to the customs union such as its absolute market size. As the market size probably changes following instances of economic integration and disintegration, an interim review will be warranted. This situation occurred in the 2004 EC enlargement which warranted reviews of certain undertakings. Moreover, it is possible that the product scope of a measure must be adapted if the sold products differ depending on geographical location within the customs union. Additional information will have to be provided to warrant a review.

More generally, it is possible that the data used for the calculation of dumping and injury has changed lastingly due to the economic integration or disintegration.

Data that is used in the relevant calculations either relates to the market under investigation on the one hand or to the market of the investigating state or customs territory on the other hand. Data relating to transactions between exporters and importers is data that relates to the investigating customs union, as the purpose of it is to calculate the price upon entry to the customs union.

Economic integration and disintegration must impact that data to such an extent that the results differ from the initial investigation, were they repeated. With regards to data relating to the country under investigation, only indirect effects are possible. With regards to data relating to the customs union, new data must possibly be considered in cases of economic integration and certain data can no longer be considered in cases of economic disintegration. Having to consider new data or not being able to consider data any longer may lastingly lead to a different outcome.

Data Relating to the Country Under Investigation

The determination of the normal value usually depends solely on data relating to exporters or other data originating in the country under investigation.[239] Even if the normal value is calculated using third country information, this data could only change indirectly through economic integration.[240]

---

[237]*Argentina - Definitive Anti-Dumping Duties on Poultry from Brazil* [2003] WTO Panel Report WT/DS241/R [7.364].

[238] Art. 8 ADA.

[239] That is if normal value is calculated following Art. 2.1, 2.2 ADA. For the exceptions, see below.

[240] Certain customs unions allow for this possibility: e.g. Art. 2 (7) Reg. (EU) 2016/1036 in the EU.

Economic integration and disintegration impact this data only insofar it leads to changes in the supply-chain or the global market generally. Although such an argument is possible, evidence would need to prove that the changes do not merely come from an economic shock but are of a lasting nature.[241]

Data Relating to the Customs Union

Data relating to the customs union is used in certain circumstances in the calculation of the normal value,[242] the export price,[243] and for the injury determination.

All data may change because of the indirect effects that economic integration and disintegration may have on the economy of the customs union and its (former) members. As these changes stem from other events in the causality chain, these changes will need to be proven separately to warrant a review.

Economic integration and disintegration may also have a direct effect on the calculation of dumping and injury. In cases of economic integration, the market size of the customs union increases, and new importers or producers may have to be considered. In cases of economic disintegration, the market size of the customs union decreases, and producers or importers are no longer part of the union market.

Whether these changes in data lead to a different outcome of an investigation depends on the following questions:

1. Must the changed data be considered? If not, the new data will not have an impact on the result of the investigation.
2. Does the new data lead to a change in the methodology of the dumping or injury determination? If the methodology changes, this could lead to a different result.
3. Is the new data different from the old data? If it is not different, the result will not change either.
4. Do the results of the investigation change? Despite the data being different, it is possible that the data must be adjusted so that in effect the result remains the same.

Must the Changed Data Be Considered?

The first step is that the data that is affected by economic integration or disintegration must be considered in a review proceeding.

---

[241] The threshold in *EC – Tube or Pipe Fittings* applies, see: Sect. 6.3.4.1.

[242] In rare cases the costs of production (Art. 2.2, 2.2.1.1 ADA) and SGA costs and profits (Art. 2.2.2.(iii) ADA) may have been calculated using "any other reasonable method" which may include data relating to the customs union.

[243] In all possible methods to calculate the export price: using the prices between the exporter and importer in the customs union, using the first resale to an independent buyer in the customs union, or "any other reasonable basis", Art. 2.3 ADA.

If the investigating authority has calculated individual dumping margins,[244] the data of all importers has been considered. Consequently, if new importers emerge, their data must be considered and if importers are no longer domestic importers, their data can no longer be considered. If the investigating authority sampled data for the calculation of the dumping margins,[245] the investigating authority has only considered data of some importers. The investigating authority must only consider the new data if it concerns a sampled importer or if it can be used to demonstrate that the samples are no longer statistically valid.[246]

Data relating to the domestic industry has been used to establish the injury analysis in the initial investigation.[247] The domestic industry refers either to all domestic producers or to those producers whose collective output of the products constitutes a major proportion of the total domestic production of those products.[248] Economic integration will have the effect that there are more union producers. They must only be considered, however, if the addition of new producers has the consequence that the producers in the initial investigation no longer constitute a major proportion of the total union production. Moreover, the investigating authority is also not under an obligation to use data from all those producers that make up the domestic producers.[249] In cases of economic disintegration it is possible that data has been used in the initial investigation that can no longer be used as the union producer is no longer a union producer. Overall, additional evidence will need to be provided to substantiate this.

---

[244] Art. 9.2 ADA.

[245] Art. 9.4, 6.10 ADA.

[246] Art. 6.10 ADA.

[247] This is different than ensuring that the standing requirement in Art. 5.2 ADA has been met. On the relationship of the two, see: *EC — Fasteners (China)* (Chap. 4, n 15) paras 417–419.

[248] Art. 4.1 ADA. If the initial investigation was geographically limited to some parts of the customs union according to Art. 4.1.(ii) ADA, the producers not within that part, i.e. the new producers following enlargement, will not be considered.

[249] Concerning EU law: In special circumstances, prices of individual producers (e.g. with regards to EU law: Council Regulation (EC) No 92/2002 of 17 January 2002 imposing definitive anti-dumping duty and collecting definitively the provisional anti-dumping duty imposed on imports of urea originating in Belarus, Bulgaria, Croatia, Estonia, Libya, Lithuania, Romania and the Ukraine, OJ. L 17/1, 19.1.2002, Rec. 93–97: The special circumstances were that the price undercutting varied from 0% to 56%, a significant volume of exports were made at prices below those of the Community industry and that the urea market is highly transparent and price sensitive) or a selection of sales (E.g. with regards to EU law: Council Regulation (EC) No 1965/98 of 9 September 1998 imposing a definitive anti-dumping duty on imports of polysulphide polymers originating in the United States of America and collecting definitively the provisional duty imposed, OJ. L 255/1, 17.9.1998, Rec. 18, 19: In that case, a price comparison was made on a per member state basis. This was mainly due to the fact that the community industry consisted of one producer and that producer did not export to every country in the EC) can be used.

Does the New Data Lead to a Change in the Methodology of the Dumping or Injury Determination?

The methodology to collect data depends on the fulfilment of certain conditions. Economic integration and disintegration could impact the conditions that determine how the normal value or export price are calculated. Having to employ a different method of calculation could then impact the dumping margin, irrespective of whether the data has materially changed.[250]

The calculation of the normal value as well as the export price follow the same structure: a principle method of calculation exists and if certain conditions are met, another form of calculation applies.

When establishing normal value, the only condition that depends on data relating to the customs union is the determination whether sufficient domestic sales have occurred. There are sufficient domestic sales, if the sales of the like product destined for consumption in the domestic market of the country under investigation constitute at least 5% or more of the sales of the product under consideration to the customs union.[251] It is possible that large quantities of exports were made to the acceding members so that there are fewer than 5% domestic sales compared to these exports combined with the exports to the customs union. As domestic sales were sufficient in the initial investigation, the investigating authority will probably find that domestic sales are nevertheless of "sufficient magnitude to provide for a proper comparison."[252] Unlike in cases of economic integration, the percentage of sales made in the domestic market compared to the sales of the product to the customs union[253] can only remain the same or rise in cases of economic disintegration as certain exports are disregarded from that calculation.

The export price is usually the price of the product when sold for export from the exporting country to the customs union.[254] A deviation of this method of establishing the export price is possible if there is no export price or the export price is unreliable.[255] In the case that there is no export price, no individual dumping margin can be calculated, and the weighted average dumping duty applies to that

---

[250] E.g. relating to EU law: Commission Implementing Regulation (EU) 2017/220 of 8 February 2017 amending Council Implementing Regulation (EU) No 1106/2013 imposing a definitive anti-dumping duty on imports of certain stainless steel wires originating in India following a partial interim review under Article 11(3) of Regulation (EU) 2016/1036 of the European Parliament and of the Council, OJ. 9.2.2017, L 34/23, para. 21. In this case one exporter successfully argued that a related importer did not exist anymore, which is why the export price should no longer be constructed following Art. 2 (9) Reg. (EU) 2016/1036 and this would entail a significant change in dumping margins.

[251] Fn. 2 ADA.

[252] Fn. 2 ADA.

[253] Fn. 2 ADA.

[254] Art. 2.3 ADA.

[255] Art. 2.3 ADA.

exporter.[256] In cases of economic integration additional data may arise. The situation may arise that for those exporters where initially the calculation of an individual dumping margin has failed, this could now be possible. If an exporter has only exported to acceding members that exporter can request a newcomer review.[257] If an exporter has only traded with unreliable prices, due to association with the importer but also trades with unrelated parties in the acceding members, those exports to unrelated importers can now be used to establish the export price. Economic disintegration may have the effect that the number of exports to the customs union decreases. Consequently, the export price may be unreliable because too few exports are made.[258] Additional data is required to prove these effects, however.

The injury determination does not follow the same structure and these considerations cannot apply in that regard.

Is the New Data Different to the Data Used in the Initial Investigation?

If it cannot be proven that the employed methodology changes, it is not sufficient to prove that different data to the initial investigation will have to be considered. The data must also be materially different to the data used in the initial investigation.

Different kind of data is used in the investigation: there is price data as well as relative and absolute market information data. Whether the data is different depends on the type of data used. Price data may be different, but there is a factual presumption that this is not the case, absolute market data is different and relative market data is potentially different.

Price Data

Price data refers to all prices between parties or the data that is used to calculate such prices. It is used to establish the normal value and export price in the dumping determination as well as the domestic market price in the injury determination.

Some have argued in relation to the UK's withdrawal from the EU that where any EU price data has been used, the dumping margin would "necessarily" change post Brexit.[259] However, it is difficult to support why this is necessarily the case. In cases

---

[256]E.g. in the EU: Council Regulation (EC) No 2744/2000 of 14 December 2000 amending Regulation (EC) No 1950/97 imposing a definitive anti-dumping duty on imports of sacks and bags made of polyethylene or polypropylene originating, inter alia, in India, OJ L 316/67, 15.12.2000, Rec. 14. For such an exporter a Newcomer Review is available and refund requests may be made: Müller et al. (2009) para 2.184.

[257]Art. 9.5 ADA.

[258]E.g. in the EU: Reg. (EC) 2744/2000, Rec. 12, 14.

[259]Kim et al. (2021), pp. 61–62. Arguing that the export price will always be different: Yves Melin and Danyal Arnold, 'Brexit Briefing: The Impact of Brexit on Trade Remedies (Anti-Dumping, Anti-Subsidy, Safeguard) in the UK' (*International Law @ UEA*) <https://www.uea.ac.uk/law/research/international-law-blog/> accessed 5 July 2021. To support their argument, they refer to Commission Implementing Regulation (EU) 2015/1953 of 29 October 2015 imposing a definitive

of economic disintegration certain producers, users, importers or customers will no longer operate on the market. Nevertheless, changes to the market structure are not by themselves proof of changed prices.[260] In the same way as mergers, acquisitions or insolvencies change the market structure but do not mean that this will always impact prices. Additional evidence that demonstrates the effects on the prices is necessary.

Moreover, if prices differ, these differences must also be of a lasting nature. In this regard cases of economic integration and disintegration are different.

In cases of economic integration, typically the market conditions between the acceding member and the customs union are different, so that a difference in prices may exist as a starting point. These differences are, however, not lasting after accession. With regards to the export price, the risk of arbitrage will prevent exporters to discriminate their export prices into the customs union. Conversely, if union producers engage in price discrimination in the customs union, the cheapest buyer can export them to the entire customs union. Prices should therefore align. That alignment of prices will occur can also be presumed as customs unions will only be competent to impose anti-dumping measures if dumping does not occur within the customs union. This is the case if arbitrage is not possible within the customs union.[261] Evidence of that presumption can be found in EU regulation, according to which the Commission must establish the "prices in the Union *market*"[262] (emphasis added) and not the union markets. Only after determining that vast price differences between member states exist, will the Commission compare the export prices to member state prices[263] or even limit the investigation to specific regional markets.[264]

---

anti-dumping duty on imports of certain grain-oriented flat-rolled products of silicon-electrical steel originating in the People's Republic of China, Japan, the Republic of Korea, the Russian Federation and the United States of America, OJ L 284/109, 30.10.2015 and Council Implementing Regulation (EU) No 157/2013 of 18 February 2013 imposing a definitive anti-dumping duty on imports of bioethanol originating in the United States of America, OJ L 49/10, 22.2.2013. They claim that EU price data has been used to construct normal value (at pp. 61, 62). This must be rejected, as in Reg. (EU) 2015/1953, Rec. 56, the costs of production and SGA costs and profits by cooperating exporters were used and in Reg. (EU) 2013/157, Rec. 13 data by US traders/blenders was used. More fundamentally, they never explain what changes specifically.

[260] E.g. Commission Implementing Regulation (EU) 2018/1722 of 14 November 2018 amending Implementing Regulation (EU) No 999/2014 imposing a definitive anti-dumping duty on imports of ammonium nitrate originating in Russia following an interim review pursuant to Article 11(3) of Regulation (EU) 2016/1036 of the European Parliament and of the Council, OJ L 287/3, 15.11.2018, para. 47–61. Between the initial investigation and the interim review, the market has concentrated significantly due to several mergers and acquisitions yet this was not sufficient to evidence changes in prices.

[261] See above at: Sect. 2.3.3.

[262] Art. 3 (2) (a) Reg. (EU) 2016/1036.

[263] Reg. (EC) 1965/98, Rec. 18, 19.

[264] Art. 4 (1) (b) Reg. (EU) 2016/1036.

In cases of economic disintegration, the reverse can be presumed. Prices will have been aligned but the economic disintegration may impact the market structure such as to have a lasting effect on prices. If changes in prices can be demonstrated, these changes will also be of a lasting nature. The magnitude of this effect depends on the relative consequences of the economic disintegration. As the UK loses at least to some degree access to the entire EU market consisting of 27 states but those 27 states only lose access to one state—the UK—, Brexit will lead to more changes in the market structure of the UK than the EU, raising the likelihood that the requirements to conduct a review are higher in the UK than the EU27. This is probably why the UK has announced that it would review all transposed measures. To warrant a review in the individual case, these effects will have to be proven, however.

Market Information Data

Market information data is relevant in the injury calculation when establishing the volume of dumped imports and the effects of the imports on the domestic customs union industry.[265]

In absolute terms, the import volumes either stay the same or will increase after economic integration and stay the same or decrease after economic disintegration. The relative volume of imports can either increase or decrease in cases of economic integration and disintegration.

Art. 3.4 ADA provides a list of economic factors that can be considered when determining the effects of dumping upon the domestic industry. Certain factors are directly affected by the absolute market size, such as production, sales, union consumption,[266] growth, and investments.

They will change due to economic integration: the volume of production, sales, and domestic consumption will increase, because of the increase in production, there will be a positive growth rate of the domestic industry, and because of there being more domestic producers, there will be more investments in absolute terms. The reverse will be the case in cases of economic disintegration.

Other indicators relate to the domestic industry but are independent of total market size: capacity utilization, accumulation of stocks, market share, productivity, return on investment, actual or potential effects on cash flow, ability to raise capital, prices, and profitability. These factors may change as production conditions may be different but such changes will need to be proven to warrant a review.

Do the Results Change?

Lastly, it is also necessary that the results of the investigation change.

---

[265] Art. 3.1 ADA.

[266] Van Bael and Bellis (2011), p. 306.

Typically, using different data will result in a different outcome. This is, however, not the case if the data must be adjusted so that no difference exists to the initial data or the data alone cannot justify a different outcome.

Where price data relating to the customs union has been used to construct the cost of production in the normal value determination, those costs must have been adjusted to reflect the market conditions in the country under investigation,[267] as the result of the construction must be to determine the "cost of production in the country of origin".[268,269] The same considerations also apply when calculating SGA costs and profits according to Art. 2.2.2.(iii) ADA.[270] In general, the normal value determination will not change due to economic integration and disintegration.

These adjustments are distinct from the ones required under Art. 2.4 ADA. The purpose of adjustments according to Art. 2.4 ADA is to compare the normal value with the export price at the ex-factory level. Although it is possible that the adjustments change due to economic integration,[271] these adjustments—unlike the adjustments under Art. 2.2.2.(iii) ADA—will not nullify the differences in the data.

Where the export price is different, this may have an impact on the dumping margin. In such a case the individual dumping margins will change. This may also change the residual anti-dumping margin, if it the new dumping margin is the highest.[272] Finally, this can also have an impact on the weighted average dumping margin of cooperating exporters.[273,274]

Data relating to market size in absolute terms will change after enlargement. The fact that the absolute market size changes without any additional information cannot, however, justify a review. This is because the purpose of Art. 11.2 ADA is not to react to any change in the market but only to those changes that make the imposition of the anti-dumping measure no longer necessary. Variations in the market size and the direct effect this has on the markers used in the injury determination do not prove that anti-dumping measures are no longer necessary. The result will therefore only change if additional data relating to the injury determination is provided.

---

[267] *EU - Biodiesel* (Chap. 2, n 1) para 6.81. Akritidis and Sneij (2018), p. 135; Bossche and Zdouc (2017), p. 709.

[268] Art. VI.1(a)(ii) GATT, Art. 2.2 ADA.

[269] *EU - Biodiesel* (Chap. 2, n 1) para 6.76–6.81.

[270] Although Art. 2.2.2.(iii) ADA only requires that the profits be adjusted to the situation in the country of origin, the comparison with Art. 2.2.2.(ii), 2.2.2. (i) ADA and Art. 2.2.1.1. ADA shows that the SGA costs should also be adjusted to the level in the country of origin.

[271] E.g. exporters may choose different transport routes.

[272] Van Bael and Bellis (2011), p. 411.

[273] Müller et al. (2009) para 17.29.

[274] The changes on the residual dumping margin and the average dumping margin of cooperating exporters can also occur following a newcomer review, Art. 9.5 ADA.

6.3.4.3   Conclusions

This section has argued that an interim review according to Art. 11.2 ADA is warranted where a hypothetical investigation limited to those considerations that can become relevant in a review leads to a different outcome following a case of economic integration or disintegration and the difference in outcome is of a lasting nature. Where this is apparent, an investigating authority must self-initiate a review and where this may be the case, a review is warranted if the additional evidence is provided in the request.

Anti-dumping investigations evaluate different data, which may have changed, and these changes may lead to different outcomes of the investigation. Data that relates to the country under investigation will only have changed indirectly. The effects for the data that relates to the customs union is different. Insofar as it must be considered, it is possible that arising new data or the fact that certain data can no longer be used leads to a change in the methodology. It is also possible that the data differs due to economic integration or disintegration and this also changes the outcome of the investigation. This will have to be proven separately.

Overall, although cases of economic integration and disintegration may warrant interim reviews, the evidentiary burden that such a review is warranted is high. This explains why relatively few reviews have been initiated in the EU's recent enlargements. The UK's offer to review all transposed anti-dumping measures is thus better understood as a political tool to mediate between the different views of whether it is allowed to transpose the EU's anti-dumping measures rather than fulfilling its legal obligations under the ADA.

6.4   Conclusions

This chapter has focussed on the consequences of economic integration and disintegration on the anti-dumping measures in force at the time at which the customs union integrates or disintegrates. No problems arise if the competence to investigate and impose anti-dumping measures remains unchanged and relates to the same territory. The situation is less straightforward, where either the competences change or the territory of the customs union changes. This chapter has analysed how customs unions have dealt with this and has offered an analysis of the limits WTO law imposes.

The consequences that may happen are that certain measures apply to imports into a different territory, i.e. that their territorial scope changes or that certain measures must be reviewed.

First, WTO law allows changes in the territorial scope of measures as long as the investigation remains attributable to the entity imposing the measure and the measure does not get limited to only parts of the territory. Second, although circumstances change, usually additional information must be provided to warrant a review. Economic integration or disintegration does not justify a review in and of itself.

References

Akritidis V, Sneij F (2018) The shake-up of the EU institutions' dumping calculation methodology and the compatibility of a market-oriented concept of normal value with WTO law. Global Trade Customs J 13:129

Aurich B (2018) Harter Brexit – Harte Folgen. Gesellschafts- und Wirtschaftsrecht 443

Azevêdo R (2016) Azevêdo addresses world trade symposium in London on the state of global trade. World Trade Organization, 7 June 2016. <https://www.wto.org/english/news_e/spra_e/spra126_e.htm>. Accessed 5 July 2021

Bacchus J (2017) Making room for Britain at the world trade organization. Wall Street Journal (6 February 2017). <https://www.wsj.com/articles/making-room-for-britain-at-the-world-trade-organization-1486407601>. Accessed 5 July 2021

Baetens F (2018) "No deal is better than a bad deal"? The fallacy of the WTO fall-back option as a post-Brexit safety net. Common Market Law Rev 55:133, 139

Bickel F (2021) Brexit and trade defence: effects of a changed territory. J Int Econ Law 24:5, 9

Boonekamp C (2017) Alternative thinking: out of the box for Brexit — and radically. Trade β Blog, 12 February 2017. <https://tradebetablog.wordpress.com/2017/02/12/alternative-thinking-out-of-box/>. Accessed 5 July 2021

Bordin FL (2019) The analogy between states and international organizations. Cambridge University Press, pp 49–86

Bossche P, Zdouc W (2017) The law and policy of the world trade organization: text, cases and materials, 4th edn. Cambridge University Press, pp 692–693

Bühler KG (2001) State succession and membership in international organizations: legal theories versus political pragmatism. Martinus Nijhoff Publishers, pp 14–18

Cabinet Office (2020) The UK's approach to the Northern Ireland Protocol. GOV.UK, 20 May 2020. <https://www.gov.uk/government/publications/the-uks-approach-to-the-northern-ireland-protocol>. Accessed 5 July 2021

Cheng T-H (2006) State succession and commercial obligations. Brill Nijhoff

Connolly E, Doyle J (2019) Brexit and the Irish border. Eur J Leg Stud 11:153

Crowley M et al (2018) How damaging would a "no-deal" Brexit be? LSE BREXIT, 24 January 2018. <http://blogs.lse.ac.uk/brexit/2018/01/24/how-damaging-would-a-no-deal-brexit-be/>. Accessed 5 July 2021 January 2018

De Baere P (2017) Building a trade defence system in the UK. UCL London

Denman D (2016) The EU's external relations: a questions of competence. In: Birkinshaw PJ, Biondi A (eds) Britain Alone!: The implications and consequences of United Kingdom exit from the EU, 1st edn. Wolters Kluwer Law & Business

Dolle T, Leys D (2017) The trade and customs law consequences of Brexit. Global Trade Customs J 12:117

Downes C (2017) The post-Brexit management of EU agricultural tariff rate quotas. J World Trade 51:741

Dunt I (2019) The trade remedies problem: Brexit no-deal plan in disarray. politics.co.uk (16 July 2019). <http://www.politics.co.uk/blogs/2019/07/16/the-trade-remedy-problem-brexit-no-deal-plan-in-disarray>. Accessed 5 July 2021

Eeckhout P (2018) Future trade relations between the EU and the UK: options after Brexit. European Parliament - Directorate-General for External Policies, Policy Department 2018. PE 603.866

European Commission (2013) Enlargement: impact on trade defence. Trade - European Commission, 20 March 2013. <http://trade.ec.europa.eu/doclib/press/index.cfm?id=880>. Accessed 5 July 2021

Fox L (2016) UK's commitments at the world trade organization. House of Commons 2016. Written Statement HCWS316. <https://www.parliament.uk/business/publications/written-questions-answers-statements/written-statement/Commons/2016-12-05/HCWS316/>. Accessed 5 July 2021

Gehring M (2016) Brexit and EU-UK trade relations with third states. EU Law Analysis, 6 March 2016. <http://eulawanalysis.blogspot.com/2016/03/brexit-and-eu-uk-trade-relations-with.html>. Accessed 5 July 2021

Häberli C (2017) Brexit without WTO-problems: for the UK? The EU? Global Business? Global Trade Customs J 12:87

Henderson J, Pils E (2016) The impact of Brexit on relations with Russia and China. King's Law J 27:473

Herrmann C (2017a) Brexit and the WTO: challenges and solutions for the United Kingdom (and the European Union). In: Shaping a new legal order for Europe: a tale of crises and opportunities

Herrmann C (2017b) Brexit, WTO und EU-Handelspolitik. Europäische Zeitschrift für Wirtschaftsrecht 28:961

Hestermeyer H, Ortino F (2016) Towards a UK trade policy post-Brexit: the beginning of a complex journey. King's Law J 27:452

Hillman JA, Horlick G, Fressynet I (2017) The legal impact of Brexit on the Comprehensive Economic Trade Agreement (CETA) between the European Union and Canada. In: Legal aspects of Brexit: implications of the United Kingdom's decision to withdraw from the European Union, 1st edn. Institute of International Economic Law

Howse R, Staiger RW (2006) United States-sunset review of anti-dumping duties on corrosion-resistant carbon steel flat products from Japan, AB-2003-5, WT/DS244/AB/R. World Trade Rev 5:471, 480–487

Kembayev Z (2009) Legal aspects of the regional integration processes in the post-soviet area. Springer-Verlag

Khalfaoui A, Gehring M (2018) What role for TDIs between the EU and the UK after Brexit: a trade or competition solution to a future problem? In: Bungenberg M, Herrmann C, Müller-Ibold T (eds) The future of trade defence instruments: global policy trends and legal challenges, vol 1. Springer, pp 17–19

Kikarea E (2019) Brexit and preferential trade agreements: issues of termination and survival clauses. Leg Issues Econ Integrat 46:53

Kim JW (2017) Is the United Kingdom still a party to the EU - Korea FTA after Brexit? In: Hillman JA, Horlick G (eds) Legal aspects of Brexit: implications of the United Kingdom's decision to withdraw from the European Union, 1st edn. Institute of International Economic Law

Kim JW (2019) Lack of certification of the WTO schedules of the United Kingdom: a way for frictionless trade under a no-deal Brexit scenario? EJIL: Talk!, 7 March 2019. <https://www.ejiltalk.org/lack-of-certification-of-the-wto-schedules-of-the-united-kingdom-a-way-for-frictionless-trade-under-a-no-deal-brexit-scenario/>. Accessed 5 July 2021

Kim JW, Kuelzow J, Strong T (2021) The US response to Brexit: implications for international trade rights and obligations under the WTO system. tradelab.legal.io, 5 July 2021, pp 61–62. <https://georgetown.app.box.com/s/hrpz0wsi1rrbr3tyssc1if79c58ktg0q>. Accessed 5 July 2021

Kozyrin AN, Yalbulganov AA (2015) Anti-dumping procedures in the EurAsEC customs union. Liverpool Law Rev 36:183

Larik J (2017) Sincere cooperation in the common commercial policy: Lisbon, a "Joined-Up" Union, and "Brexit". In: Bungenberg M et al (eds) European Yearbook of International Economic Law 2017. Springer International Publishing, p 102. <https://www.springer.com/de/book/9783319588315>. Accessed 5 July 2021

Łazowksi A, Wessels R (2016) The external dimension of withdrawal from the European Union. Revue des affaires européennes 623, 523

Luca G (2017) The impact of Brexit on the UK's membership in the WTO. J Int Bank Law Regul 32:479

Lux M, Pickett E (2017) The Brexit: implications for the WTO, free trade models and customs procedures. Global Trade Customs J 3:12, at 92, at 110

Mandal S (2017) Post Brexit Uk- EU trade under WTO. Social Science Research Network 2017. SSRN Scholarly Paper ID 3025413 <https://papers.ssrn.com/abstract=3025413>. Accessed 5 July 2021

Mariani P, Sacerdoti G (2019) Brexit and trade issues. Eur J Leg Stud 11:187

Matthews A (2016) WTO dimensions of a UK "Brexit" and agricultural trade. CAP Reform.eu, 5 January 2016. <http://capreform.eu/wto-dimensions-of-a-uk-brexit-and-agricultural-trade/>. Accessed 5 July 2021

Mavroidis PC (2016) The regulation of international trade: the WTO agreements on trade in goods, vol 2, 1st edn. The MIT Press, p 134

Meinen L (2018) A "frictionless" border for Gibraltar: stumbling blocks and solutions following Brexit. Leg Issues Econ Integrat 45:397

Müller W, Khan N, Scharf T (2009) EC and WTO anti-dumping law: a handbook, 2nd edn. Oxford University Press

Ni S (2018) EU trade remedy policy in the wake of Brexit: a case study of the steel industry. In: Getting to Brexit: legal aspects of the process of the UK's withdrawal from the EU. Institute of International Economic Law, pp 277–294

O'Connell DP (1967a) State succession in municipal law and international law, vol international relations. Cambridge University Press, pp 88, 91–112, 164

O'Connell DP (1967b) State succession in municipal law and international law, vol internal relations. Cambridge University Press, p 3

Odermatt J (2017) Brexit and international law: disentangling legal orders. Emory Int Law Rev 31:1051, 1056

Peers S (2020) EU law analysis: the protocol on Ireland/ Northern Ireland: what it says is not what it does. EU Law Analysis, 17 March 2020. <http://eulawanalysis.blogspot.com/2020/03/the-protocol-on-ireland-northern.html>. Accessed 5 July 2021

Peretz G (2018) Briefing paper: the government's proposed legislation for trade remedies. UK Trade Forum, 22 January 2018. <https://uktradeforum.net/2018/01/22/418/>. Accessed 5 July 2021

Piris J-C (2015) Which options would be available to the United Kingdom in case of a withdrawal from the EU? CSF - SSSUP Working Paper Series 25

Sacerdoti G (2017) The United Kingdom's post-Brexit trade regime with the European Union and the rest of the world: perspectives and constraints. J Int Econ Law 20:905, 212

Sagara N (2002) Provisions for trade remedy measures (anti-dumping, countervailing and safeguard measures) in preferential trade agreements. Research Institute of Economy, Trade and Industry, 02-E-013

Sosnow C, Logvin A, Massicotte K (2017) The Brexit vote: its impact on the Canada-EU comprehensive economic and trade agreement and UK's obligations under comprehensive trade and economic trade agreement. Global Trade Customs J 12:125

Stojanovic A (2020) Brexit Deal: The Northern Ireland Protocol. The Institute for Government, 5 February 2020. <https://www.instituteforgovernment.org.uk/explainers/brexit-deal-northern-ireland-protocol>. Accessed 5 July 2021

Swinbank A (2017) World trade rules and the policy options for British Agriculture Post-Brexit. UK Trade Policy Observatory, p 12

Terhechte JP (2020) Brexit-Vertrag Vertragstext/Protokolle/Politische Erklärung, 1st edn. Nomos Verlagsgesellschaft Mbh & Co, pp 20–21

Townsend M, Renard F, Benson J (2018) The UK's new trade remedies regime. In: Brexit law - your business, the EU and the way ahead, September 2018

Ungphakorn P (2016) Second bite — how simple is the UK-WTO relationship post-Brexit? Trade ß Blog, 17 August 2016. <https://tradebetablog.wordpress.com/2016/08/17/2nd-bite-how-simple-uk-eu-wto/>. Accessed 5 July 2021

Ungphakorn P (2019) Text of the UK-South Korea Free Trade Agreement. Trade β Blog, 3 September 2019. <https://tradebetablog.wordpress.com/2019/09/03/text-of-the-uk-south-korea-free-trade-agreement/>. Accessed 5 July 2021

Ungphakorn P (2020a) Summary: "WTO terms" apply in any future UK-EU trade relationship. But how much? Trade β Blog, 27 May 2020. <https://tradebetablog.wordpress.com/2020/05/27/summary-wto-terms-brexit/>. Accessed 5 July 2021

Ungphakorn P (2020b) "WTO terms" apply in any future UK-EU trade relationship. But how much? Part 1 "WTO terms". Trade β Blog, 27 May 2020. <https://tradebetablog.wordpress.com/2020/05/27/wto-terms-part-1-meaning/>. Accessed 5 July 2021

Ungphakorn P (2020c) "WTO terms" apply in any future UK-EU trade relationship. But how much? Part 2 Goods. Trade β Blog, 27 May 2020. <https://tradebetablog.wordpress.com/2020/05/27/wto-terms-part-2-goods/>. Accessed 5 July 2021

Ungphakorn P (2020d) "WTO terms" apply in any future UK-EU trade relationship. But how much? Part 3 Services and more. Trade β Blog, 27 May 2020. <https://tradebetablog.wordpress.com/2020/05/27/wto-terms-part-3-services/>. Accessed 5 July 2021

Van Bael I, Bellis J-F (2011) EU anti-dumping and other trade defence instruments, 5th edn. Kluwer Law International, p 306

Volterra R (2017) Brexit negotiations series: "The Impact of Brexit on the UK's Trade with Non-EU Member States Under the EU's Mixed Free Trade Agreements". Oxford Business Law Blog, 17 May 2017. <https://www.law.ox.ac.uk/business-law-blog/blog/2017/05/brexit-negotiations-series-impact-brexit-uk%E2%80%99s-trade-non-eu-member>. Accessed 5 July 2021

Vroom M, de Wit W (2018) Brexit: the road ahead for EU-UK trade. EC Tax Rev 27:196

Wang P (2018) The United Kingdom's application to accede to the WTO Agreement on Government Procurement (GPA) in its own right. Public Procurement Law Review 143

Wessel R (2016) You can check out any time you like, but can you really leave?: On "Brexit" and leaving international organizations. Int Organ Law Rev 13:197

Wessel R (2018) Consequences of BREXIT for international agreements concluded by the EU and its member states. Common Market Law Rev 55:101

Willemyns I, Koekkoek M (2017) The legal consequences of Brexit from an international economic law perspective. KU Leuven 2017. Working Paper 188

Wolfrum R, Stoll P-T (eds) (2008) WTO - trade remedies, vol 4, 1st edn. Nijhoff, p 152

Zhuang W (2019) EU anti-dumping duties after Brexit – UK's duty to dump? TradeLinks, 6 January 2019. <https://www.linklaters.com/en/insights/blogs/tradelinks/eu-anti-dumping-duties-after-brexit-uks-duty-to-dump>. Accessed 5 July 2021

Zimmermann A (2000) Staatennachfolge in völkerrechtliche Verträge. Springer, pp 11–15

Chapter 7
Anti-Dumping Measures Against Customs Unions

The previous chapters have only considered the perspective of the customs unions and their member states. They have considered why customs unions modify anti-dumping legislation, how they do so and what limits WTO law imposes on them in doing so. Previous chapters have also considered the effects of these modifications, focussing on the effects on notions of responsibility and attribution and instances of economic integration and disintegration.

This chapter deals with the perspective of third parties and answers what consequences the above has for third states or customs unions that wish to impose anti-dumping measures against a customs union or members thereof. More specifically, it deals with two different perspectives. First, generally the fact that certain WTO members are in a customs union could warrant that anti-dumping measures are imposed against the entire customs union instead of against some members of the customs union (under Sect. 7.1). Second, in cases of economic integration and disintegration the same questions arise as with relation to the customs union: which measures continue to apply, and must those measures be reviewed in some way (under Sect. 7.2)?

Overall, some work exists generally on the question against which territory anti-dumping measures apply. This study adds to that literature by arguing that anti-dumping measures can also be imposed against customs unions and not just their member states, if they have a centralized anti-dumping and are WTO members. Moreover, this study considers how instances of economic integration and disintegration impact anti-dumping measures imposed against customs unions.

As a preliminary note, this chapter also deals with the territorial scope of anti-dumping measures. The territorial scope of an anti-dumping measure is relevant in two relations. First, territory is relevant to define imports into which territory may be subject to anti-dumping measures. This is the territory of the state or customs union that imposes the measure, and this is the perspective that has been considered in the previous chapter. Second, territory is also relevant to define goods originating in which territory are subject to the anti-dumping measure, which is the perspective of this chapter.

© The Author(s), under exclusive license to Springer Nature Switzerland AG 2021
F. Bickel, *Customs Unions in the WTO*, European Yearbook of International
Economic Law 20, https://doi.org/10.1007/978-3-030-86312-8_7

The territorial scope is relevant during the investigation and to identify the scope of the measure. Anti-dumping investigations focus on the producers and exporters of a certain geographical territory. Defining that territory is relevant for the investigation as all producers or exporters of the like product within that territory are interested parties in the investigation[1] and they may be requested to participate by filling out questionnaires[2] and may thus gain certain procedural rights such as the right to defend their interests.[3]

Usually, an individual dumping margin is then calculated[4] resulting in an individual anti-dumping duty for each exporter or producer.[5] If the number of exporters is so large that it would be impracticable to determine individual dumping margins, an investigating authority may sample exporters.[6] Individual anti-dumping duties are calculated for the sampled exporters and the weighted average dumping margin is applied against non-sampled exporters.[7]

Beyond that, there may be exporters or producers that have not taken part in the investigation but fall within the scope of the measure, nevertheless. These are either producers or exporters that have started exports after the period of investigation (newcomer exporters), exporters that were unknown to the investigating authority (unknown exporters) or exporters that did not cooperate with the investigating authority. An anti-dumping duty based on the available facts can be levied from those exporters that did not cooperate.[8] The ADA provides that newcomer exporters may request an expedited newcomer review that determines their individual dumping margin.[9] The ADA does not regulate the applicable duty for unknown exporters or newcomer exporters that have not (yet) requested a newcomer review. In practice a residual amount applies. The calculation of the residual amount varies, however. Whereas in the US the residual amount is usually the weighted average of the individually calculated dumping margins, the EU applies the highest identified individual dumping margin.[10]

---

[1] Art. 6.11 (i) ADA.

[2] Art. 6.1.1 ADA.

[3] Art. 6.2 ADA.

[4] Art. 6.10 ADA.

[5] Saying that there is a close link between the two: *EC — Fasteners (China)* (Chap. 4, n 15) n 300.

[6] Art. 6.10 ADA.

[7] Art. 9.4 (i) ADA. In a retroactive system of duty assessment, the weighted average dumping margin of the applicable final duty applies, Art. 9.4 (ii) ADA. Moreover, in a sampling scenario, where an exporter has requested individual treatment, according to Art. 6.10.2 ADA and that individual treatment has been granted, the individual dumping margin applies, Art. 9.4 ADA.

[8] Art. 6.8 ADA, Annex II ADA.

[9] Art. 9.5 ADA.

[10] Mavroidis (2016), pp. 120, 121.

Table 7.1 Anti-dumping measures against customs unions or their member states

Customs union	Definitive measures against customs union	Definitive measures against at least one member of a customs union
CAN	–	22
CARICOM	–	3
CACM	–	2
COMESA	–	13
EAC	–	1
CEMAC	–	–
ECOWAS	–	1
EU - Andorra[a]	–	–
EU – San Marino[b]	–	–
EU - Turkey[c]	–	149
EU	454	91
EAEU	–	42
GCC	–	12
SACU	–	55
MERCOSUR	–	138
WAEMU	–	–

[a] To avoid duplication, this excludes measures imposed against the EU
[b] To avoid duplication, this excludes measures imposed against the EU
[c] To avoid duplication, this excludes measures imposed against the EU

7.1 Scope of Anti-Dumping Measures Applied Against a Customs Union or a Member Thereof

It is possible that anti-dumping measures apply against all producers or exporters of a certain product from a state or from a customs union. Member practice will be examined (under Sect. 7.1.1), before considering legality of imposing anti-dumping measures against states (under Sect. 7.1.2) and customs unions (under Sect. 7.1.3).

7.1.1 Member Practice

Table 7.1 shows the number of anti-dumping measures imposed against customs unions or their members between 1995 and 2020.[11]

Strikingly, the only customs union against which anti-dumping measures have been imposed on a union wide level is the EU. Interestingly, this has not happened

---

[11] Source: WTO, Anti-Dumping Gateway (https://www.wto.org/english/tratop_e/adp_e/adp_e. htm), last accessed: 5 July 2021.

consistently, however. Some WTO members even impose anti-dumping measures against the EU or its members interchangeably.[12] A reason for this may be that often anti-dumping investigations are initiated due following an application of the domestic industry.[13] The scope of the investigation and the measure will then usually follow that application. Conversely, the domestic industry will chose strategically whether to request initiation of an anti-dumping investigation against the EU or some of its members depending on which is more likely to result in a positive outcome for them. Factors that will influence this are whether within the EU there are harmonious price levels or whether the EU industry is centred in specific countries.

Applying anti-dumping measures only against states of a tightly integrated customs union or applying them interchangeable against the customs union or only some of its members raises questions on how that works in practice. If goods circulate freely within the EU but anti-dumping measures are national, which goods fall under the measures specifically? Similarly, India has imposed anti-dumping measures against the EU and some of its member states, how do Indian authorities detect which goods fall into the respective anti-dumping measures?

Unfortunately, it is difficult to explain generally how these anti-dumping measures are employed as the WTO has not yet harmonized non-preferential rules of origin and many countries, like India, have not notified the WTO of even applying non-preferential rules of origin. Ultimately, how each country detects which goods fall within the relevant measures will depend on their national legislation on non-preferential rules of origin, which will not be assessed in this study.

7.1.2 Anti-Dumping Measures Imposed Against Member States of a Customs Union

In most cases anti-dumping measures have been imposed against the member states of customs unions. This does not violate WTO obligations.

Even though the ADA provides in detail the conditions that must be satisfied to initiate an investigation in Art. 5 ADA and how that investigation should be conducted (Art. 6 ADA), it remains vague as to dumping originating in which territory is subject to the investigation. A request to initiate an investigation should include a list of the "names of the country or countries of origin or export in question",[14] the exporting member should be informed of an investigation that has

---

[12] E.g. in 2016 Brazil imposed one Anti-Dumping measures against the entire EU and two against Germany: Committee on Anti-Dumping Practices, 'Semi-Annual Report under Article 16.4 of the Agreement, Brazil', G/ADP/N/280/BRA, 25.2.2016, p. 4; Committee on Anti-Dumping Practices, 'Semi-Annual Report under Article 16.4 of the Agreement, Brazil', G/ADP/N/286/BRA, 30.8.2016, p. 4.

[13] Art. 5.1 ADA.

[14] Art. 5.2.(ii) ADA.

been opened[15] and the government of the exporting member is an interested party in the investigation.[16] This applies in a straight-forward way if anti-dumping investigations are initiated against member states of customs unions.

When defining who an anti-dumping measure is imposed against, Art. 9.2 ADA mandates that the measure should in principle name the suppliers of the product concerned. Only insofar as it is impracticable to name all the suppliers that reside in the same country is it possible to name the supplying country instead. Finally, if the suppliers reside in more than one country and it is impracticable to name all suppliers, the measure can be imposed against all supplying countries. Again, this applies straight-forward if anti-dumping measures are imposed against member states of customs unions.

7.1.3 Anti-Dumping Measures Imposed Against Customs Unions

The more problematic question is whether anti-dumping measures can also be imposed against customs unions. The only anti-dumping measures that have been imposed against an entire customs union are the ones imposed against the EU so that this is a hypothetical question for the other customs unions.

Problems may arise because even though the requirements may be met cumulatively between all member states to justify imposition against the entire EU, they may not be met with respect to every member state. It is possible that producers or exporters of certain EU member states were not even part of the investigation, or that the requirements are not fulfilled with respect to certain EU member states because producers and exporters do not dump. Nevertheless, anti-dumping measures still apply against them.[17]

This could violate Art. 9.2 ADA as an anti-dumping measure is imposed against all producers and exporters of a supplying country even though no investigation has been conducted against that country or no dumping has been determined by producers or exporters originating in that country. The approach could, however, be justified if the term "supplying country" in Art. 9.2 ADA, "country or countries" in Art. 5.2.(ii) ADA, and "exporting member" in Art. 6.1.3 ADA can be interpreted in a way that allows investigations to be conducted against an entire customs union and that allows measures to apply against entire customs unions as well.

---

[15] Art. 6.1.3 ADA.

[16] Art. 6.11.(ii) ADA.

[17] E.g. Government of India, Ministry of Finance, Notification No. 17/2018, 27.3.2018 concerning Anti-Dumping measures of Veneered Engineered Wooden Flooring from China, Malaysia, Indonesia and the EU. The investigating authority sent questionnaires to known producers and exporters from Austria, Belgium, Germany, Sweden and the UK. See: Government of India, Ministry of Commerce & Industry, Department of Commerce, Directorate General of Anti-Dumping & Allied Duties, Notification Final Findings, Case No. O.I./08/2017, 13.2.2018.

The fact that the term "country" and WTO "member" is used interchangeably indicates that at least customs unions that are WTO members themselves and behave in their anti-dumping action like states by having a unified external anti-dumping regime—which means only the EU currently—fall within the interpretation of the term "country". Customs unions that are not WTO members are neither "countries" nor "members". For an interpretation of these terms to include them, that interpretation would have to contradict the wording of the ADA and is therefore not possible.[18]

Further points speak in favour of allowing anti-dumping measures against the entire EU and other potential customs unions that are WTO members and have a unified anti-dumping practice.

During the negotiating history of the ADA in the Uruguay Round Japan proposed that where a customs union imposes anti-dumping measures on a union wide basis and bases its domestic industry on all union producers according to Art. 4.3 ADA, it should be possible to impose anti-dumping measures against the entire customs union as well.[19] In the following meeting of the Negotiating Group on MTN Agreements and Arrangements, this proposal has been recalled but not discussed.[20] Future meetings did not mention this proposal again. This could of course indicate that the members of the negotiating group either felt that this was not a necessary clarification or that anti-dumping measures should not be imposed against a customs territory.

Further clarification may be drawn from the object and purpose of why anti-dumping measures apply against products originating in a certain territory or exports from a specific territory. Mavroidis and Sapir argue that the ADA is inconsistent in this regard: On the one hand the ADA recognizes that dumping is a private business practice, by principally requiring the calculation of individual dumping margins on the other hand it presumes that all exporters and producers within a geographic location that happen to export the same product to the same country dump, as anti-dumping duties can be levied against newcomer, unknown, and non-sampled producers or exporters. Yet, there is no economic reason why different exporters or producers from one country will employ the same pricing strategy in its exports.[21]

The lack of a clear rationale why anti-dumping measures can be imposed against an entire country instead of just against private exporters or producers could be used in support of a restrictive interpretation of the terms, i.e. limiting it to states. If it is not economically justified to impose an anti-dumping measure against an entire country and that possibility is best understood as a historic accident, it is not justified

---

[18] See: *US - Gasoline* (Chap. 4, n 24) 17; *Japan - Alcoholic Beverages II* (Chap. 4, n 24) 10; *Peru - Agricultural Products* (Chap. 4, n 26) para 5.94.

[19] Negotiating Group on MTN Agreements and Arrangements, 'Submission of Japan on the Amendments of the Anti-Dumping Code', MTN.GNG/NG8/W/48/Add.1, 29.1.1990, p. 7.

[20] Negotiating Group on MTN Agreements and Arrangements, 'Meetings of 31 January-2 February and 19-20 February 1990', MTN.GNG/NG8/15, 19.3.1990, p. 12.

[21] Mavroidis and Sapir (2008), pp. 319–322.

to impose it against an entire customs union, i.e. potentially even against states that have not participated in the investigation at all.

However, the rationale of the ADA's approach can be defended based on the reason why anti-dumping measures are justified. One justification of anti-dumping measures is to prevent injury arising from dumping enabled by market segregation between two countries.[22] Every producer or exporter in a country is in the same situation to benefit from the market segregation through dumping. The risk that dumping is possible combined with the fact that some exporters and producers in a similar situation have acted in that way could justify that all exporters and producers of one country are presumed to dump. This presumption is then justified because producers and exporters that do not dump may be excluded from the measure, which is why the ADA requires that principally individual dumping margins are calculated, makes newcomer and interim reviews available and foresees refunds.

If the lack of market segregation justifies this presumption with regards to all producers and exporters of a state, it can also justify an anti-dumping measure against territories which have the same asymmetric market access. The presumption that justifies why anti-dumping measures apply against all producers and exporters of a state is that within a state similar market conditions apply. If two states share the same market conditions, this presumption may also apply to the other state. The problem is, of course, that the abstract concept of asymmetric market access is difficult to judge.

A good indication of whether two states share the same level of market segregation with third countries is if they judge so for themselves. Where a customs union has harmonized its anti-dumping regime and applies the same anti-dumping measures against imports into the entire customs union, it has assessed that between its member states internal market segregation is so minimal that dumping is unlikely.[23] Customs unions will only harmonize external anti-dumping measures if they assess that usually the entire union industry will be injured by third party dumping. In that case, customs unions apply the same tariffs externally and consider their internal markets to be integrated. This justifies that third parties also rely on that judgment. In such a case, it could be justified to impose an anti-dumping measure against an entire customs union.

Finally, as the ADA is vague concerning its requirements on the scope of an investigation, thereby using the terms "country" and WTO "member" interchangeably, this leaves sufficient freedom to justify that anti-dumping investigations and measures can not only apply against countries but against customs unions that are a WTO member themselves and that have a harmonised external anti-dumping regime.

---

[22] See above: Sect. 2.1.3.

[23] See above at: Sect. 2.4.1.

7.2   Effects of Economic Integration and Disintegration

Third parties that wish to impose anti-dumping measures can impose them against WTO members. Only if a WTO member is a customs union may measures be imposed against states or the entire customs union.

Who anti-dumping measures are imposed against becomes particularly relevant in cases of economic integration and disintegration. Insofar as anti-dumping measures have been imposed against states, no specific problems apply. Their scope cannot change regardless of whether that state joins or leaves a customs union. Membership in a customs union is distinct from statehood and therefore does not influence the scope of the measure. Similarly, if a customs union is formed, measures that were imposed against states cannot automatically apply against the entire customs union, as the investigation only justifies that anti-dumping measures are imposed against certain states.

The more problematic question is what happens to the measures that have been imposed against an entire customs union. The same arguments that have been developed for customs unions and their anti-dumping measures may apply in reverse. The relevant questions are (1) whether measures can apply against an enlarged or reduced customs union and (2) whether the measures continue to apply against the withdrawing state or the individual states after dissolution.

7.2.1   Anti-Dumping Measures Against an Enlarging Customs Union

Where anti-dumping measures have been imposed against a customs union and that customs union enlarges, the imposing WTO member may extend the measure to exports from the joining state or may not do so. As there is no obligation to impose anti-dumping measures, there is no obligation to extent their scope either.

Customs unions may extend the measures to also apply against the joining member. The same two steps of argumentation apply as regards the reverse situation.[24] First, the time at which legality of an investigation is determined is the time at which the investigation takes place. Second, there may be an exception to this based on Art. 1 ADA. The scope of the investigation and the final measure must coincide. Were it possible to change the scope of the measure after its imposition to a reduced territory, this requirement could be circumvented. This exception does not apply here because the entire territory of the customs union against which the measure is imposed changes.[25] The situation should be treated in the same way as if new producers or exporters arise in the country of origin. This result is also justified as

---

[24] See above at: Sect. 6.3.3.

[25] This is the same reason as why Art. 4.1.(ii) ADA is not an exception in the reverse situation.

the producers and exporters have the same advantage of asymmetric market access as the other producers or exporters of the customs union, are therefore in a similar position to dump and should therefore be treated in the same way.

The extended measures must, however, possibly be reviewed. The same principles apply as above.[26] In general additional information that proves that a review is warranted will have to be provided. Because of the similarities to the situation in which a new producer or exporter arises, the provisions on newcomer reviews in Art. 9.5 ADA may apply by way of analogy as well.

7.2.2 Anti-Dumping Measures Following Withdrawal

Following withdrawal from a customs union the two constellations that are of interest are whether anti-dumping measures can be imposed against the reduced territory of the customs union and whether they can be imposed against the withdrawing state.

Relating to the question whether anti-dumping measures may apply against the reduced customs union territory, the same argumentation as in the cases of enlargement may apply. Changed circumstances can in principle only warrant a review. An exception may stem from Art. 1 ADA. This exception does, however, not apply as the situation is not that the scope of an anti-dumping measure changes its scope arbitrarily but the territory of the entire customs union against which it is imposed changes. It is therefore possible to apply the measure against the reduced territory.

Relating to the question whether anti-dumping measures may apply against the withdrawing state, practice relating to state succession exists. The issue arose in *Belgian State v. Banque Indosuez.* Although this case concerned the ECJ's interpretation of EU law, the arguments of the case can also be made in relation to WTO Law.

In 1984, the Commission issued decisions protecting EC manufacturers from dumped or subsidized steel and iron originating from the Socialist Federal Republic of Yugoslavia (SFRY).[27] Following the Former Yugoslav Republic of Macedonia's (FYROM—now: North Macedonia) declaration of independence on 17 September 1991, Belgium continued to levy anti-dumping duties on importers of steel from the territory of FYROM. Legality of this was at issue in the case.

The Advocate-General[28] presented several arguments, defending why the EC can apply the anti-dumping duties against FYROM: (1) The purpose of anti-dumping

---

[26] See above at: Sect. 6.3.4.

[27] Commission Decision No 2131/88/ECSC of 18 July 1988 imposing a definitive anti-dumping duty on imports of certain sheets and plates, of iron or steel, originating in Yugoslavia and definitively collecting the provisional anti-dumping duty imposed on those imports, OJ L 188/14, 19.7.1988.

[28] *Belgian State v Banque Indosuez and Other* [1997] CJEU, Opinion of Advocate General Jacobs ECLI:EU:C:1997:342.

measures is to protect an industry from injury. This purpose would be undermined if a producer could avoid those duties solely because the authorities of the territory in which it was situated had declared independence.[29] (2) Measures are imposed against products from a specific geographical location upon an investigation that proves that the imports from that specific geographical location leads to injury to certain producers. A change of political boundaries is in itself of no relevance to the economic purpose of anti-dumping duties.[30] (3) This is also expressed by the fact that anti-dumping duties usually name the specific producers of goods and only if that is not practicable as a geographic shorthand all the producers of a country are named.[31] The reference to Yugoslavia is thus merely used as a descriptive term to identify the products of which geographic location are within the scope of the anti-dumping measure.[32]

The ECJ concurred with these arguments, highlighting the purpose of anti-dumping measures to protect an industry from injury and that anti-dumping duties are imposed on imports from a specific geographical area irrespective of the political boundaries.[33]

This view can also be justified in the context of the WTO borrowing similar arguments as in the previous chapter.[34] Anti-dumping measures are imposed prospectively based on a retrospective investigation. At the time at which the measure was imposed, the investigation justified that all producers and exporters of that customs union should be subject to the anti-dumping measure. Future changes in the territory do not impact this assessment. This means that upon withdrawal from a customs union, the anti-dumping measures can still apply against the withdrawing state.

Finally, economic integration and disintegration may constitute changed circumstances that warrant interim reviews. The same principles as laid down in the previous chapter apply.[35]

7.3   Conclusions

This chapter has focussed on the effects that forming a customs union has on third parties that wish to impose anti-dumping measures against customs unions or member states thereof.

---

[29] ibid 23.

[30] ibid 25.

[31] ibid 26.

[32] ibid 25–26.

[33] *Belgian State v. Banque Indosuez and Other* (Chap. 6, n 227) paras 19–21.

[34] See above: Sect. 6.3.3.

[35] See above: Sect. 6.3.4.

In practice, most anti-dumping measures are imposed against states. The only exception is the EU, whereby anti-dumping measures are sometimes imposed against the entire union and sometimes against certain member states. It is always justified to impose anti-dumping measures against states. However, it is only possible to apply anti-dumping measures against a customs union where that customs union applies a harmonious external anti-dumping regime and is a WTO member.

This chapter has also considered the effects economic integration and disintegration have on existing anti-dumping measures. Problems only arise if anti-dumping measures have been imposed against a customs union and new states join or withdraw from that customs union or the customs union dissolves. The measures will not change their scope of application but may have to be reviewed.

References

Mavroidis PC (2016) The regulation of international trade: the WTO agreements on trade in goods, vol 2, 1st edn. The MIT Press

Mavroidis PC, Sapir A (2008) Mexico – antidumping measures on rice: "Don't Ask Me No Questions and I Won't Tell You No Lies". World Trade Rev 7:305

Chapter 8
Conclusions

This study has analysed problems that arise with anti-dumping measures in the context of WTO law. In particular, the different chapters have developed the following arguments.

Chapter 2

- There are three reasons why the imposition of anti-dumping measures is legal. First, to prevent harmful predatory pricing, second as a political tool that is either purely protectionist or a necessary pressure valve to achieve greater trade liberalization or third, because exploiting asymmetric market access at the expense of domestic producers is unfair. There are several reasons why regional integration occurs but an institutional analysis focussing on transaction gains, losses, costs, and transition costs explains why the institutional setup of the customs unions differs so vastly.

- Combining the reason why anti-dumping measures are imposed and why customs unions are entered into explains why customs unions modify anti-dumping regulation internally. If the only purpose of anti-dumping measures is to prevent predatory pricing, an effective competition law system will replace them. If they are necessary as a pressure valve to achieve economic integration, some additional procedural requirements to minimise the risks of protectionist abuse are justified. Finally, if they are justified to counteract the injurious exploitation of asymmetric market access, they will not be necessary internally if the customs union has economically integrated sufficiently.

- Combining the reasons why anti-dumping measures are justified and why customs unions are entered into also justifies the external modifications. The anti-dumping regime will be harmonized if it is effective to do so. It is effective to do so if the risk that dumping injures the union production outweighs the risk that dumping injures only the production of some members. This depends on the overall market integration. If that is the case, transaction costs will be sufficiently low so that they do not outweigh the transaction gains. Especially if there is a power asymmetry between the parties, exceptions to this may exist as the stronger

F. Bickel, *Customs Unions in the WTO*, European Yearbook of International Economic Law 20, https://doi.org/10.1007/978-3-030-86312-8_8

party's preferences may be to retain the competences to impose anti-dumping measures.

Chapter 3

- Internally, modifications happen to disincentivize the imposition of anti-dumping measures or to integrate the anti-dumping procedures to avoid protectionist abuse of these measures. The strongest form in which this can happen is by prohibiting internal anti-dumping measures. The 16 customs unions are centred around the extremes of either prohibiting anti-dumping measures or not modifying them at all. Only few customs unions make full use of the possibility to modify anti-dumping legislation extensively.
- Externally, modifications happen to harmonize external trade. The anti-dumping regime is harmonized if the same anti-dumping measures apply to imports into the entire customs union. Again, customs unions are centred around the extremes of either harmonizing anti-dumping measures or not modifying them at all.
- If a state is in a customs union, certain limitations exist on its ability to conclude further RTAs. In general, it is possible to conclude further FTAs. Further customs unions are only possible if they do not lead to conflicts between their CET.

Chapter 4

- Most modifications do not violate Art. VI GATT and the ADA, as they leave sufficient flexibilities. Importantly, Art. VI GATT and the ADA only form minimum requirements and Art. 4.3 ADA allows having a harmonized external anti-dumping system. Art. 1 ADA is violated if the scope of the investigation and the scope of the measure do not align.
- Even though the MFN principle applies, its scope is severely limited by Art. 4.3 ADA. As Art. 4.3 ADA must be interpreted to allow having a harmonized external anti-dumping regime, the different treatment that stems from having a harmonized external anti-dumping regime does not violate the MFN principle. Customs unions that operate a harmonized external anti-dumping system and have prohibited internal anti-dumping measures therefore do not violate Art. VI GATT and the ADA and therefore need no justification.
- Art. XXIV:5 GATT may justify any violation. Its requirements relate to the entire customs union and are measure specific. Nothing definitive with regards to anti-dumping measures can be said about those requirements that relate to the entire customs union. The measure specific requirements as developed by the Appellate Body in *Turkey – Textiles* should be rejected. Instead, a list of negative requirements should apply, one them being that Art. XXIV:5 GATT may not be used as a defence for a broad roll-back on members rights. This study argues that the relatively recent *Peru – Agricultural Products* decision supports such an approach.
- The Enabling Clause may justify a violation of the MFN principle only. This study argues that the Enabling Clause applies to customs unions and also to RTAs that have eliminated non-tariff measures. No specific requirements relating to anti-dumping emerge.

- RTAs between WTO members and non-WTO members are special in that only WTO members are bound by WTO law. No WTO problems arise, if only the non-WTO member violates WTO law.

Chapter 5

- Attribution in the context of anti-dumping is relevant for two reasons. First, for anti-dumping measures to be legal the investigation and the decision to impose the measure mut be attributable to a WTO member. Second, attribution is relevant in the context of responsibility. Where a WTO obligation related to anti-dumping is violated, that violation must be attributable to a WTO member.
- ARIO and ARSIWA apply in the WTO for questions of attribution. The WTO does not contain *lex specialis* and rules of competences do not answer questions of attribution.
- Art. 6 ARIO, according to which acts of agents or organs of an international organization are attributable to it, is the central norm of attribution in the context of anti-dumping. WTO practice supports an extensive definition of the term organ. Accordingly, an organ is either an entity that carries out the functions of an international organization or an entity under the normative control of an international organization. The WTO practice also corresponds with broader international customary law practice. The other grounds of attribution do not focus on the institutional setup of a customs union and should therefore not apply in the context of attributing anti-dumping measures.
- The parallel provision to Art. 6 ARIO – Art. 4 ARSIWA, is used to explain attribution to member states. Using a functional integration definition of the term organ, insofar as the customs union fulfils functions that are typically state functions, they are an organ of the state. WTO practice supports such an extensive reading of the term organ. Other grounds of attribution should be disregarded, as they do not focus on the institutional setup of customs unions.
- Attribution is not exclusive. It is possible that an act can be attributed to the customs union as well as their members.

Chapter 6

- There is only limited WTO practice on the effects of economic integration and disintegration on existing anti-dumping measures. The formation of the Belarus, Kazakhstan and Russia customs union provides practice that measures that were imposed on a member state wide basis were extended to a customs union wide basis following review. The 2004 EC enlargement provides practice that measures of joining members and measures by the EC against the joining members drop. The 2007 EC also provides practice that measures against the joining members drop. Above that all recent EU and EAEU enlargements provide evidence that the scope of the customs union measures is extended to include the joining members. Only the 2004 EC enlargement provides some limited evidence that the measures were then reviewed following enlargement.
- The only WTO practice concerning economic disintegration is Brexit. Following the transition period the EU will continue to apply its anti-dumping measures to

the reduced EU27 territory and the UK will transition some EU measures into national law.

- In general WTO law leaves its members great flexibilities when defining the effects of economic integration and disintegration on anti-dumping measures. The two questions that arise following cases of economic integration and disintegration are which measures apply and whether the applicable measures must be reviewed.
- WTO law is flexible as to which measures apply. Customs unions and their members can define which measures apply and no problems arise except if the territorial scope of the measure changes. In principle this is not problematic, as changing circumstances only warrant a review but do not invalidate an anti-dumping measure. A change in the territorial scope cannot undermine Art. 4.1 (ii) ADA, however, and the investigation must remain attributable to the entity imposing the measure. If this is the case, customs unions or member states may change the scope of anti-dumping measures.
- The threshold to warrant an interim review is rather high. In general, cases of economic integration and disintegration will not *per se* warrant an interim review. Additional information will have to be provided. The likelihood that an interim review is warranted increases relative to the economic significance of the economic integration or disintegration, however.

Chapter 7
- Usually anti-dumping measures are imposed against states. The only exception is that some anti-dumping measures are imposed against the EU.
- It is questionable whether it is possible to impose anti-dumping measures against customs unions and not only against some of its member states. The principle problem is that although the requirements to impose measures against a customs union may be fulfilled cumulatively, an investigation against the entire customs union may not prove that the conditions have been met with respect to every member state. Where a customs union is a WTO member and has a harmonized anti-dumping regime, it is possible to impose anti-dumping measures against that customs union. Beyond that, this is not possible.
- Cases of economic integration and disintegration are only relevant if measures are imposed against an entire customs union. WTO law does not limit the members' freedom to change the scope of anti-dumping measures either to extend it to joining members or to reduce it to a reduced territory of the customs union or member state. Reviews may have to be conducted, but the thresholds developed in Chap. 6 will need to be considered.

Cited Treaties and Legislation

General International Law

Articles on the Responsibility of International Organizations (ARIO), ILC Report on the Work of its Sixty-third Session, UNGAOR 66th Sess, Supp. No. 10, UN Doc. A/66/10 (2011)

Articles on Responsibility of States for Internationally Wrongful Acts (ARSIWA), ILC Yearbook 2001/II(2)

Statute of the International Court of Justice (ICJ Statute), 18.04.1946

Vienna Convention on Succession of States in respect of Treaties, 23.08.1978

Vienna Convention on Succession of States in respect of State Property, Archives and Debts, 08.04.1983

Vienna Convention on the Law of Treaties (VCLT), 23.05.1969

Vienna Convention on the Law of Treaties between States and International Organizations or between International Organizations (VCLTIO), 21.03.1986

WTO Law

Agreement on Implementation of Article VI of the General Agreement on Tariffs and Trade 1994

General Agreement on Tariffs and Trade (GATT)

Differential and More Favourable Treatment Reciprocity and Fuller Participation of Developing Countries ("Enabling Clause")

Agreement on Rules of Origin (RoO Agreement)

General interpretative note to Annex 1A

Understanding on the Interpretation of Article XXIV of the General Agreement of Tariffs and Trade 1994 (RTA Understanding)

© The Author(s), under exclusive license to Springer Nature Switzerland AG 2021   277
F. Bickel, *Customs Unions in the WTO*, European Yearbook of International
Economic Law 20, https://doi.org/10.1007/978-3-030-86312-8

Understanding on Rules and Procedures Governing the Settlement of Disputes (DSU)

Trade Negotiations Committee, Decision on anti-circumvention, 15.12.1993, 14.4.1994

Regional Agreements & Customs Union Law

CACM

Convenio sobre el Regimen Arancelario y aduanero Centroamericano (Central American Tariff and Custom Regime), 27.12.1984

Protocolo al Tratado General de Integración Económice Controamericana (Guatemala Protocol), 29.10.1993

Resolucion 193/2007 (COMIECO-XLIV) (Resolucion 193/2007), 24.04.2007

CAN

Acuerdo de Integracion Subregional Andino (Cartagana Agreement), 12.5.1987, entered into force: 25.5.1988, last amended by the Decisión 583, 26.6.2003

Decision 283, Normas para prevenir o corregir las distorsiones en la competencia generadas por prácticas de dumping o subsidios (Decision 283), 31.03.1991

Decision 425, Reglamento de Procedimientos Administrativos de la Secretaría General de la Comunidad Andina, 11.12.1997

Decision 456, Normas para prevenir o corregir las distorsiones en la competencia generadas por prácticas de dumping en importaciones de productos originarios de Países Miembros de la Comunidad Andina, 04.05.1999

CARICOM

Revised Treaty of Chaguaramas establishing the Caribbean Community including the CARICOM Single market and Economy, 05.07.2001

CEMAC

Convention Régissant l'Union Économique de l'Afrique Centrale (UEAC), 16.3.1994.

Traité Instituant la Communauté Économique et monétaire de l'afrique centrale (CEMAC Agreement), 16.3.1994, entered into force: 24.6.1999

COMESA

COMESA Regulations on Trade Remedy Measures, 1.10.2002
Council Regulations Governing the COMESA Customs Union, 9.6.2009, OJ. Vol. 15 No. 1
Revised COMESA Treaty amended by Council Meeting 2009 (COMESA Treaty), 12.09.2012

EAC

East African Community Customs (Anti-Dumping Measures) Regulations, Annex IV to Treaty for the Establishment of the East African Community (EAC Customs Union (Anti-Dumping Measures) Regulations), 30.11.1991
Protocol on the Establishment of the East African Customs Union, 02.03.2004

EAEU and Predecessor

Agreement on Customs Union and Common Economic Zone, 26.02.1999
Agreement on the Application of Special Protective, Anti-dumping and Countervailing Measures against Third Parties, 25.01.2008
Agreement on the Application of Special Protective, Anti-dumping and Countervailing Measures during the Transitional Period of November 19, 2010, 19.11.2010
Agreement on the Customs Union of 20.1.1995 between Belarus, Kazakhstan and Russia, 20.01.1995
Anti-Dumping Measures against China on Rolling-element bearings (excluding needle roller bearings), No. 868, 13.12.2007, published in Российская газета on 21.12.2007
Anti-Dumping Measures against China on Rolling-element bearings (excluding needle roller bearings), Decision of the Commission of the Customs Union No. 705, 22.06.2011
Anti-Dumping measures against Ukraine on Certain steel pipes and tubes, No. 297, 31.1.2006, published in Российская газета on 31.12.2005
College of the Eurasian Economic Commission Decision, On the Advisory Committee on Trade (Decision No. 6), 7.3.2012 N. 6, as amended on 24.1.2017

Decision by the Customs Union Commission on the Use of Veterinary-Sanitary Measures in the Customs Union, No. 317, 18.6.2010 (Customs Union Decision No. 317)

Decision of the Commission of the Customs Union No. 191 of 26.2.2010 on the Application of Safeguard, Antidumping and Countervailing Measures in the Territory of the Customs Union of Belarus, Kazakhstan and the Russian Federation, 26.02.2010

Decision of the Commission of the Customs Union No. 702, 22.06.2011

Decision of the Customs Union Commission No. 339 of August 17, 2010, 17.08.2010

Definitive Anti-Dumping duties on Rolling-element bearings (excl. needle roller bearings) against China No. 287, published in Российская газета on 21.12.2007

Definitive Anti-Dumping duties on Rolling-element bearings (excl. needle roller bearings) against China, Decision of the EEC No. 197, 17.09.2013

On Some Issues of Special Protective, Anti-dumping and Countervailing Measures within the Common Customs Territory of the Customs Unions, Decision 802 of the Customs Union Commission, 23.09.2011

Protocol on Rules on Entry into Force of International Treaties aimed at the Formation of the Legal Basis of the Customs Union, Withdrawal from them, and Accession to them, 06.10.2007

Some issues of safeguard, antidumping and countervailing measures in the common customs territory of the customs union, Decision of the Eurasian Economic Commission, No. 1, 07.03.2012

Treaty on Setting up the Economic Union of 24.9.1993, between Belarus, Kazakhstan and Russia, 24.09.1993

Treaty on the Establishment of the Common Customs Territory and the Formation of the Customs Union, 06.10.2007

Treaty on the Eurasian Economic Union (EAEU Treaty), 29.5.2014, entered into force: 1.1.2015

ECOWAS

Economic Community of East African States (ECOWAS) Revised Treaty (ECOWAS Treaty), 06.07.2005

Regulation C/Reg.6/06/13 Relative to Defense Measures to be Imposed on Imports Which are Dumped from Non-Member States of the Economic Community of West African States (Regulation C/Reg.6/06/13), 21.06.2013

EU and Predecessor

2004/498/EC: Commission Decision of 18 May 2004 accepting undertakings offered in connection with the anti-dumping proceeding concerning imports of silicon carbide originating, inter alia, in Ukraine, OJ L 267M/3, 12.10.2005

2004/782/EC: Commission Decision of 19 November 2004 accepting an undertaking offered in connection with the anti-dumping proceeding concerning imports of silicon carbide originating, inter alia, in Ukraine, OJ L 344/37, 20.11.2004

2006/22/EC: Commission Decision of 20 January 2006 granting certain parties an exemption from the extension to certain bicycle parts of the anti-dumping duty on bicycles originating in the People's Republic of China imposed by Council Regulation (EEC) No 2474/93, last maintained and amended by Regulation (EC) No 1095/2005, and lifting the suspension of the payment of the anti-dumping duty extended to certain bicycle parts originating in the People's Republic of China granted to certain parties pursuant to Regulation (EC) No 88/97, OJ L 17/16, 21.1.2006

Agreement establishing an Association between the EU and its Member States, on the one hand, and Central America on the other, OJ L 2012 346, 15.12.2012

Annex to the Council Decision authorising the opening of negotiations with the United Kingdom of Great Britain and Northern Ireland for a new partnership agreement, 5870/20 Add 1 Rev 3 25.2.2020

Commission Decision No 2131/88/ECSC of 18 July 1988 imposing a definitive anti-dumping duty on imports of certain sheets and plates, of iron or steel, originating in Yugoslavia and definitively collecting the provisional anti-dumping duty imposed on those imports, OJ L 188/14, 19.7.1988

Commission Implementing Regulation (EU) 2015/1953 of 29 October 2015 imposing a definitive anti-dumping duty on imports of certain grain-oriented flat-rolled products of silicon-electrical steel originating in the People's Republic of China, Japan, the Republic of Korea, the Russian Federation and the United States of America, OJ L 284/109, 30.10.2015

Commission Implementing Regulation (EU) 2016/1246 of 28 July 2016 imposing a definitive anti-dumping duty on imports of high fatigue performance steel concrete reinforcement bars originating in the People's Republic of China, OJ L 204/70, 29.7.2016

Commission Implementing Regulation (EU) 2017/220 of 8 February 2017 amending Council Implementing Regulation (EU) No 1106/2013 imposing a definitive anti-dumping duty on imports of certain stainless steel wires originating in India following a partial interim review under Article 11(3) of Regulation (EU) 2016/1036 of the European Parliament and of the Council, OJ. 9.2.2017, L 34/23

Commission Implementing Regulation (EU) 2018/1722 of 14 November 2018 amending Implementing Regulation (EU) No 999/2014 imposing a definitive anti-dumping duty on imports of ammonium nitrate originating in Russia

following an interim review pursuant to Article 11(3) of Regulation (EU) 2016/
1036 of the European Parliament and of the Council, OJ L 287/3, 15.11.2018
Commission Regulation (EC) No 1000/2004 of 18 May 2004 accepting undertakings offered in connection with the anti-dumping proceeding concerning imports
of certain grain oriented electrical sheets and strips of silicon-electrical steel with
a width of more than 500 mm originating in the Russian Federation and making
imports of certain grain oriented electrical sheets originating in the Russian
Federation subject to registration, OJ L 183/10, 20.5.2004
Commission Regulation (EC) No 1001/2004 of 18 May 2004 accepting undertakings offered in connection with the anti-dumping proceeding concerning imports
of ammonium nitrate originating in the Russian Federation and Ukraine and
making imports of ammonium nitrate originating in the Russian Federation or
Ukraine subject to registration, OJ L 183/13, 20.5.2004
Commission Regulation (EC) No 1002/2004 of 18 May 2004 accepting undertakings offered in connection with the anti-dumping proceeding concerning imports
of potassium chloride originating in the Republic of Belarus, the Russian Federation or Ukraine and making imports of potassium chloride originating in the
Republic of Belarus and the Russian Federation subject to registration, OJ L
183/16, 20.5.2004
Commission Regulation (EC) No 498/2004 of 17 March 2004 adapting several
regulations concerning the market of products processed from fruit and vegetables by reason of the accession of the Czech Republic, Estonia, Cyprus, Latvia,
Lithuania, Hungary, Malta, Poland, Slovenia and Slovakia to the European
Union, OJ L 80/20, 18.3.2004
Commission Regulation (EC) No 858/2005 of 6 June 2005 accepting undertakings
offered in connection with the anti-dumping proceeding concerning imports of
potassium chloride originating in the Republic of Belarus or the Russian Federation and making imports of potassium chloride originating in the Republic of
Belarus and the Russian Federation subject to registration, OJ L 143/11, 7.6.2005
Commission Regulation (EU) 2016/113 of 28 January 2016 imposing a provisional
anti-dumping duty on imports of high fatigue performance steel concrete reinforcement bars originating in the People's Republic of China, OJ L 23/16,
29.1.2016
Council Decision authorising the opening of negotiations with the United Kingdom
of Great Britain and Northern Ireland for a new partnership agreement, 5870/20,
13.2.2020
Council Implementing Regulation (EU) No 1294/2009 of 22 December 2009
imposing a definitive anti-dumping duty on imports of certain footwear with
uppers of leather originating in Vietnam and originating in the People's Republic
of China, as extended to imports of certain footwear with uppers of leather
consigned from the Macao SAR, whether declared as originating in the Macao
SAR or not, following an expiry review pursuant to Article 11(2) of Council
Regulation (EC) No 384/96, OJ L 352/1, 30.12.2009
Council Reg. (EU) 502/2013 of 29 May 2013 amending Implementing Regulation
(EU) No 990/2011 imposing a definitive anti-dumping duty on imports of

bicycles originating in the People's Republic of China following an interim review pursuant to Article 11(3) of Regulation (EC) No 1225/2009, OJ L 153/17, 5.6.2013

Council Regulation (EC) No 1095/2005 of 12 July 2005 imposing a definitive anti-dumping duty on imports of bicycles originating in Vietnam, and amending Regulation (EC) No 1524/2000 imposing a definitive anti-dumping duty on imports of bicycles originating in the People's Republic of China, OJ L 183/1, 14.7.2005

Council Regulation (EC) No 1100/2000 of 22 May 2000 imposing definitive anti-dumping duties on imports of silicon carbide originating in the People's Republic of China, the Russian Federation and the Ukraine and prolonging the undertaking accepted by Commission Decision 94/202/EC, OJ L 125/3, 26.5.2000

Council Regulation (EC) No 1225/2009 of 30 November 2009 on protection against dumped imports from countries not members of the European Communities (Reg. (EC) 1225/2009)., OJ L 343/51, 22.12.2009

Council Regulation (EC) No 132/2001 of 22 January 2001 imposing a definitive anti-dumping duty and collecting definitively the provisional duty imposed on imports of ammonium nitrate originating in Poland and Ukraine, and terminating the anti-dumping proceeding in respect of imports originating in Lithuania, OJ L 23/1, 25.1.2001

Council Regulation (EC) No 132/2001 of 22 January 2001 imposing a definitive anti-dumping duty and collecting definitively the provisional duty imposed on imports of ammonium nitrate originating in Poland and Ukraine, and terminating the anti-dumping proceeding in respect of imports originating in Lithuania, OJ L 23/1, 25.1.2001

Council Regulation (EC) No 151/2003 of 27 January 2003 imposing a definitive anti-dumping duty on imports of certain grain oriented electrical sheets originating in Russia, OJ L 25/7, 30.1.2003

Council Regulation (EC) No 1965/98 of 9 September 1998 imposing a definitive anti-dumping duty on imports of polysulphide polymers originating in the United States of America and collecting definitively the provisional duty imposed, OJ. L 255/1, 17.9.1998

Council Regulation (EC) No 2744/2000 of 14 December 2000 amending Regulation (EC) No 1950/97 imposing a definitive anti-dumping duty on imports of sacks and bags made of polyethylene or polypropylene originating, inter alia, in India, OJ L 316/67, 15.12.2000

Council Regulation (EC) No 3283/94 of 22 December 1994 on protection against dumped imports from countries not members of the European Communities, OJ L 349/1, 31.12.1994

Council Regulation (EC) No 384/96 of 22 December 1995 on protection against dumped imports from countries not members of the European Communities (Reg. (EC) 384/96), OJ L 056/1, 6.3.1996

Council Regulation (EC) No 398/2004 of 2 March 2004 imposing a definitive anti-dumping duty on imports of silicon originating in the People's Republic of China, OJ L 66/15, 4.3.2004

Council Regulation (EC) No 658/2002 of 15 April 2002 imposing a definitive anti-dumping duty on imports of ammonium nitrate originating in Russia, OJ L 102/1, 18.4.2002

Council Regulation (EC) No 661/2008 of 8 July 2008 imposing a definitive anti-dumping duty on imports of ammonium nitrate originating in Russia following an expiry review pursuant to Article 11(2) and a partial interim review pursuant to Article 11(3) of Regulation (EC) No 384/96, OJ L 185/1, 12.7.2008

Council Regulation (EC) No 785/2005 of 23 May 2005 terminating the partial interim review of the anti-dumping measures applicable to imports of silicon originating in the People's Republic of China, OJ L 132/1, 26.5.2004

Council Regulation (EC) No 866/2005 of 6 June 2005 extending the definitive anti-dumping measures imposed by Regulation (EC) No 1470/2001 on imports of integrated electronic compact fluorescent lamps (CFL-i) originating in the People's Republic of China to imports of the same product consigned from the Socialist Republic of Vietnam, the Islamic Republic of Pakistan and the Republic of the Philippines, OJ L 145/1, 9.6.2005

Council Regulation (EC) No 92/2002 of 17 January 2002 imposing definitive anti-dumping duty and collecting definitively the provisional anti-dumping duty imposed on imports of urea originating in Belarus, Bulgaria, Croatia, Estonia, Libya, Lithuania, Romania and the Ukraine, OJ. L 17/1, 19.1.2002

Council Regulation (EC) No 945/2005 of 21 June 2005 amending Regulation (EC) No 658/2002 imposing a definitive anti-dumping duty on imports of ammonium nitrate originating in Russia and Regulation (EC) No 132/2001 imposing a definitive anti-dumping duty on imports of ammonium nitrate originating in, inter alia, Ukraine, following a partial interim review pursuant to Article 11(3) of Regulation (EC) No 384/96, OJ L 160/1, 23.6.2005

Council Regulation (EC) No 954/2006 of 27 June 2006 imposing definitive anti-dumping duty on imports of certain seamless pipes and tubes, of iron or steel originating in Croatia, Romania, Russia and Ukraine, repealing Council Regulations (EC) No 2320/97 and (EC) No 348/2000, terminating the interim and expiry reviews of the anti-dumping duties on imports of certain seamless pipes and tubes of iron or non-alloy steel originating, inter alia, in Russia and Romania and terminating the interim reviews of the anti-dumping duties on imports of certain seamless pipes and tubes of iron or non-alloy steel originating, inter alia, in Russia and Romania and in Croatia and Ukraine, OJ L 175/4, 29.6.2006

Council Regulation (EC) No 969/2000 of 8 May 2000 imposing a definitive anti-dumping duty on imports of potassium chloride originating in Belarus, Russia and Ukraine, OJ L 112/4, 11.5.2000

Council Regulation (EC) No 989/2004 of 17 May 2004 amending Regulation (EC) No 151/2003 imposing a definitive anti-dumping duty on imports of certain grain oriented electrical sheets originating in Russia, OJ L 182/1, 19.5.2004

Council Regulation (EC) No 990/2004 of 17 May 2004 amending Regulation (EC) No 151/2003 imposing a definitive anti-dumping duty on imports of certain grain oriented electrical sheets originating in Russia, OJ L 182, 19.5.2004

Council Regulation (EC) No 991/2004 of 17 May 2004 amending Regulation (EC) No 1100/2000 imposing definitive anti-dumping duties on imports of silicon carbide originating in the People's Republic of China, the Russian Federation and the Ukraine and prolonging the undertaking accepted by Commission Decision 94/202/EC, OJ L 182/18, 19.5.2004

Council Regulation (EC) No 992/2004 of 17 May 2004 amending Regulation (EEC) No 3068/92 imposing a definitive anti-dumping duty on imports of potassium chloride originating in Belarus, Russia or Ukraine, OJ L 182/23, 19.5.2004

Council Regulation (EC) No 993/2004 of 17 May 2004 amending Regulation (EC) No 658/2002 imposing a definitive anti-dumping duty on imports of ammonium nitrate originating in Russia and Regulation (EC) No 132/2001 imposing a definitive anti-dumping duty and collecting definitively the provisional duty imposed on imports of ammonium nitrate originating in Poland and Ukraine, and terminating the anti-dumping proceeding in respect of imports originating in Lithuania, OJ L 182/28, 19.5.2004

Council Regulation (EC) No 998/2004 of 17 May 2004 amending Regulation (EC) No 950/2001 imposing a definitive anti-dumping duty on imports of certain aluminium foil originating in the People's Republic of China and Russia, OJ L 183/4, 20.5.2004

Council Regulation (EC) No 999/2004 of 17 May 2004 on the application of Regulation (EC) No 1531/2002 imposing a definitive anti-dumping duty on imports of colour television receivers originating in the People's Republic of China, the Republic of Korea, Malaysia and Thailand and terminating the proceeding regarding imports of colour television receivers originating in Singapore, OJ L 183/7, 20.5.2004

Documents concerning the accession of the Czech Republic, the Republic of Estonia, the Republic of Cyprus, the Republic of Latvia, the Republic of Lithuania, the Republic of Hungary, the Republic of Malta, the Republic of Poland, the Republic of Slovenia and the Slovak Republic to the European Union, OJ L 236, 23.9.2003

Documents concerning the accession of the Republic of Bulgaria and Romania to the European Union, OJ L 157, 21.6.2005

Documents concerning the accession of the Republic of Croatia to the European Union, OJ L 112, 24.4.2012

Regulation (EU) 2016/1036 of the European Parliament and of the Council of 8 June 2016 on protection against dumped imports from countries not members of the European Union (Reg. (EU) 2016/1036 or Basic Anti-Dumping Regulation), OJ L 176/21, 30.6.2016

Regulation (EU) No 182/2011 of the European Parliament and of the Council of 16 February 2011 laying down the rules and general principles concerning mechanisms for control by Member States of the Commission's exercise of implementing powers (Reg. (EU) 2011/182), OJ L 55/13, 28.2.2011

Regulation (EU) No 952/2013 of the European Parliament and of the Council of 9 October 2013 laying down the Union Customs Code (Reg. (EU) 952/2013 or Union Customs Code), OJ L 269/1, 10.10.2013

Treaty on European Union (TEU), Consolidated Version, OJ C 326/13, 26.10.2012
Treaty on the Functioning of the European Union (TFEU), Consolidated Version, OJ
    2012/C 326/01, 26.10.2012

EU – Andorra

Agreement between the EEC and Andorra (EU – Andorra Agreement), 28.06.1990

EU – San Marino

Agreement between the EEC and San Marino (EU – San Marino Agreement),
    28.03.2002

EU – Turkey

Additional Protocol to the Agreement establishing the Association be-tween the
    EEC and Turkey (Additional Protocol), 23.11.1970
Council Decision No 1/95 of the EC-Turkey Association Council of 22.12.1995 on
    implementing the final phase of the Customs Union (Decision 1/95), 96/142/EC

GCC

The Economic Agreement Between the GCC States (GCC Agreement), 31.12.2001
The GCC Common Law on Antidumping, Countervailing Measures and Safeguard
    Measures and Its Rules of Implementation (GCC Antidumping law), 2011-1432

MERCOSUR

Acuerdo Antidumping de le Organización Mundial de Comercia, MERCOSUR/
    CMC/Dec. N 13/02
Additional Protocol to the Treaty of Asunción on the Institutional Structure of
    MERCOSUR (Ouro Preto Protocol), 17.12.1994
Defensa Comercial Intrazone, MERCOSUR/CMC/Dec. N 22/02

Marco Normativo del Reglamento común relative a la defensa contra las importaciones objeto de dumping provenientes de países no miembros del Mercado común del sur (Dec. N. 11/97), MERCOSUR/CMC/DEC N 11/97

Treaty Establishing a Common Market between the Argentine Republic, the Federal Republic of Brazil, the Republic of Paraguay and the Eastern Republic of Uruguay (MERCUSOR Treaty), 26.03.1991

SACU

Customs Union Agreement between the Governments of the Republic of South Africa, the Republic of Botswana, the Kingdom of Lesotho and the Kingdom of Swaziland (1969 SACU Agreement), 11.12.1969, entered into force: 1.3.1970

Southern African Customs Union Agreement 2002 (SACU Agreement), 21.10.2002, as amended on 12.4.2013

WAEMU

Règlement N° 09/2003/CM/UEMOA portant Code Communautaire Antidumping (Reg. N. 09/2003), 23.05.2003

Traité modifié de l'Union Economique et Monetaire Ouest Africaine (WAEMU Treaty), 29.01.2003

Other

Agreement Establishing the African Continental Free Trade Area, 21.3.2018, entry into force: 30.5.2019

Comprehensive and Progressive Trans-Pacific Partnership (CPTPP), entry into force: 30.12.2018

Comprehensive Economic and Trade Agreement (CETA) between Canada, of the one part, and the European Union and its Member States, entry into force: 21.9.2017

Customs Convention between France and Monaco, 18.5.1963 (Journal officiel de la République Française of 27.9.1963, p. 8679)

Free Trade Agreement between the European Union and its Member States, on the one part, and the Republic of Korea, of the other part entry into force, 1.12.2015.

Treaty Establishing the African Economic Community (Treaty of Abuja), 3.6.1991, entry into force: 12.5.1994

North American Free Trade Agreement, 17.12.1992, entered into force: 1.1.1994

The Treaty of the Southern African Development Community, 17.08.1992

Agreement between the United States of America, the United Mexican State, and Canada, 13.12.2019

Agreement of the Withdrawal of the United Kingdom of Great Britain and Northern Ireland from the European Union and the European Atomic Energy Community (Withdrawal Agreement), 19.10.2019

Decision No3/2020 of the Joint Committee established by the Agreement on the withdrawal of the United Kingdom of Great Britain and Northern Ireland from the European Union and the European Atomic Energy Community of 17 of December 2020amending the Protocol on Ireland and Northern Ireland to the Agreement on the withdrawal of the United Kingdom of Great Britain and Northern Ireland from the European Union and the European Atomic Energy Community.

Trade and Cooperation Agreement between the United Kingdom of Great Britain and Northern Ireland, of the one part, and the European Union and the European Atomic Energy Community, of the other part, 30. December 2020.

United Nations, Charter of the United Nations, 24 October 1945, 1 UNTS XVI

Australia – New Zealand Closer Economic Relations Trade Agreement, date of signature December 14, 1982, the Protocol to the Australia New Zealand Closer Economic Relations – Trade Agreement on Acceleration of Free Trade in Goods, date of signature August 18, 1988 ("ANZCERTA")

Free Trade Agreement between the EFTA States and The Republic of Chile, date of signature June 26, 2003 ("EFTA – Chile")

Agreement between the EFTA States and Singapore, date of signature June 26, 2002 ("EFTA – Singapore")

Free Trade Agreement be-tween Armenia and Kazakhstan, date of signature September 2, 1999 ("Armenia – Kazakhstan").

National Law

Argentina, Definitive Anti-Dumping Measures on Ceramic, marble, travertine or glass tiles against Brazil and China, 2.7.2014, Official Journal of Argentina No. 32941 (Resolución N 309/2014)

Costa Rica, Anti-Dumping Measure on Water-based latex paint from the United States, Final Resolution of 18.1.2007, published in Official Journal La Gaceta No. 21 of 30.1.2007, extended by Resolution of 21.11.2011, published in Official Journal La Gaceta, No. 3 of 5.1.2012

Germany, German Civil Code – Bürgerliches Gesetzbuch (BGB), Civil Code in the version promulgated on 2.1.2002 (Federal Law Gazette [Bundesgesetzblatt] I page 42, 2909; 2003 I page 738

Germany, German Commercial Code – Handelsgesetzbuch (HGB), Commercial Code in the version promulgated on 22.12.2015 (Federal Law Gazette [Bundesgesetzblatt] I page 2567, 2015

South Africa, International Trade Administration Act, No. 71 of 2002

South Africa, The International Trade Administration Commission, Anti-Dumping Regulations (Anti-Dumping Regulations), N. 3197 of 2003, 14.11.2003

South Africa, Definitive Anti-Dumping Measures on Soda Ash against the United States, GG37756, 19.6.14

Trinidad and Tobago, Final Determination by the Minister of Trade and Industry Arising out of an Investigation into the Allegation of The Dumping of Imports of Aluminium Extrusions Originating in the People's Republic of China, Legal Supplement Part B – Vol. 55, No. 30, 3.3.2016.

UK, Taxation (Cross-border Trade) Act 2018, 13.09.2018

UK, The Trade Remedies (Dumping and Subsidisation) (EU Exit) Regulations 2019 (Dumping Regulation), 04.03.2019

UK, The Trade Remedies (Amendment) (EU Exit) Regulations 2019, 02.07.2019

UK, European Union (Withdrawal) (No. 2) Act 2019, 9.9.2019

Cited Cases

WTO & GATT Panels

Argentina – Definitive Anti-Dumping Duties on Poultry from Brazil [2003] WTO Panel Report WT/DS241/R

Argentina – Safeguard Measures on Imports of Footwear [1999] WTO Panel Report WT/DS121/R

Argentina – Safeguard Measures on Imports of Footwear [1999] WTO Appellate Body Report WT/DS121/ABRR

Australia – Measures Affecting Importation of Salmon – Recourse to Article 215 by Canada [2000] WTO Panel Report WT/DS18/RW

Brazil – Certain Measures Concerning Taxation and Charges [2018] WTO Appellate Body Report WT/DS472/AB/R; WT/DS497/AB/R

Brazil – Measures Affecting Desiccated Coconut [1996] WTO Panel Report WT/DS22/R

Brazil – Measures Affecting Desiccated Coconut [1997] WTO Appellate Body Report WT/DS22/AB/R

Brazil – Measures Affecting Imports of Retreaded Tyres [2007] WTO Panel Report WT/DS332/R

Canada – Certain Measures Affecting the Automotive Industry [2000] WTO Panel Report WT/DS139/R; WT/DS142/R

Canada – Certain Measures Affecting the Automotive Industry [2000] WTO Appellate Body Report WT/DS139/AB/R; WT/DS142/AB/R

EC – Measures Concerning Meat and Meat Products (Hormones) [1998] WTO Appellate Body WT/DS26/AB/R; WT/DS48/AB/R

European Communities – Anti-Dumping Duties on Malleable Cast Iron Tube or Pipe Fittings from Brazil [2003] WTO Panel Report WT/DS219/R

European Communities – Conditions for the Granting of Tariff Preferences to Developing Countries [2004] WTO Appellate Body Report WT/DS246/AB/R

F. Bickel, *Customs Unions in the WTO*, European Yearbook of International Economic Law 20, https://doi.org/10.1007/978-3-030-86312-8

European Communities – Customs Classification of Certain Computer Equipment
[1998] WTO Panel Report WT/DS62/R; WT/DS67/R; WT/DS68/R

European Communities – Customs Classification of Frozen Boneless Chicken Cuts
[2005] WT/DS269/AB/R

European Communities – Definitive Anti-Dumping Measures on Certain Iron or Steel Fasteners from China [2010] WTO Panel Report WT/DS397/R

European Communities – Definitive Anti-Dumping Measures on Certain Iron or Steel Fasteners from China [2011] WTO Appellate Body Report WT/DS397/AB/R

European Communities – Measures Affecting the Approval and Marketing of Biotech Products [2006] WTO Panel Report WT/DS291/R; WT/DS292/R; WT/DS293/R

European Communities – Measures Prohibiting the Importation and Marketing of Seal Products [2014] WTO Appellate Body Report WT/DS400/AB/R; WT/DS401/AB/R

European Communities – Protection of Trademarks and Geographical Indications for Agricultural Products and Foodstuffs [2005] WTO Panel Report DT/DS174/R

European Communities – Regime for the Importation, Sale and Distribution of Bananas [1997] WTO Panel Report WT/DS27/R/USA

European Communities – Selected Customs Matters [2006] WTO Panel Report WT/DS315/R

European Communities – Trade Description of Sardines [2002] WTO Appellate Body Report WT/DS231/AB/R

European Communities and its Member States – Tariff Treatment of Certain Information Technology Products: Report of the Panel [2010] WTO Panel Report WT/DS375/R; WT/DS376/R; WT/DS377/R

European Union – Anti-Dumping Measures on Biodiesel from Argentina [2016] WTO Panel Report WT/DS473/R

European Union – Anti-Dumping Measures on Biodiesel from Argentina [2016] WTO Appellate Body Report WT/DS473/AB/R

European Union – Anti-Dumping Measures on Certain Footwear from China [2011] WTO Panel Report WT/DS405/R

India – Patent Protection for Pharmaceutical and Agricultural Chemical Products [1998] WTO Panel Report WT/DS79/R

India – Quantitative Restrictions on Imports of Agricultural, Textile and Industrial Products [1999] WTO Appellate Body WT/DS90/AB/R

Indonesia – Certain Measures Affecting the Automobile Industry [1998] WTO Panel Report WT/DS54/R; WT/DS55/R; WT/DS59/R; WT/DS64/R

Japan – Taxes on Alcoholic Beverages [1996] WTO Appellate Body Report WT/DS8/AB/R; WT/DS10/AB/R; WT/DS11/AB/R

Korea – Measures Affecting Government Procurement [2000] WTO Panel Report WT/DS163/R

Korea – Measures Affecting Imports of Fresh, Chilled and Frozen Beef [2000] WTO
   Appellate Body Report WT/DS161/AB/R; WT/DS169/AB/R
Mexico – Tax Measures on Soft Drinks and Other Beverages [2006] WTO Appellate
   Body Report WT/DS308/AB/R
Peru – Additional Duty on Imports of Certain Agricultural Products [2015] WTO
   Appellate Body Report WT/DS457/AB/R; WT/DS457/AB/R/Add.1
*Russia – Anti-Dumping Duties on Light Commercial Vehicles from Germany and
   Italy* [2017] WTO Panel Report WT/DS479/R
*Russia – Anti-Dumping Duties on Light Commercial Vehicles from Germany and
   Italy* [2018] WTO Appellate Body Report WT/DS479/AB/R
*Russia – Measures Affecting the Importation of Railway Equipment and Parts
   thereof* [2018] WTO Panel Report WT/DS499/R, WT/DS485/R/Corr.1,
   WT/DS485/R/Corr.2
Russia – Measures Concerning Traffic in Transit [2019] WTO Panel Report
   WT/DS512/R
*Russia – Tariff Treatment of Certain Agricultural and Manufacturing Products:
   Report of the Panel* [2016] WTO Panel Report WT/DS485/R
*Russian Federation – Measures on the Importation of Live Pigs, Pork and other Pig
   Products from the European Union* [2016] WTO Panel Report WT/DS475/R
*Russian Federation – Measures on the Importation of Live Pigs, Pork and other Pig
   Products from the European Union* [2017] WTO Appellate Body WT/DS475/
   AB/R
Spain – Tariff Treatment of Unroasted Coffee [1981] GATT 1947 Panel Report
   L/5135
Thailand – Customs and Fiscal Measures on Cigarettes from the Philippines [2010]
   WTO Panel Report WT/DS371/R
Turkey – Restrictions on Imports of Textile and Clothing Products [1999] WTO
   Panel Report WT/DS34/R
Turkey – Restrictions on Imports of Textile and Clothing Products [1999] WTO
   Appellate Body Report WT/DS34/AB/R
Ukraine – Anti-Dumping Measures on Ammonium Nitrate [2018] WTO Panel
   Report WT/DS493/R
United States – Anti-Dumping Act of 1916 [2000] WTO Appellate Body Report
   WT/DS136/AB/R; WT/DS162/AB/R
*United States – Anti-Dumping Duties on Imports of Stainless Steel Plate from
   Sweden* [1994] GATT 1947 Panel Report ADP/117, and Corr. 1
*United States – Anti-Dumping Duty on Dynamic Random Access Memory Semi-
   conductors (DRAMS) of One Megabit or Above from Korea* [1999] WTO Panel
   Report WT/DS99/R
*United States – Anti-Dumping Measures on Certain Hot-Rolled Steel Products from
   Japan* [2001] WTO Appellate Body Report WT/DS184/AB/R
United States – Anti-Dumping Measures on Certain Shrimp from Viet Nam [2014]
   WTO Panel Report WT/DS429/R

United States – Countervailing Duties on Certain Corrosion-Resistant Carbon Steel Flat Products from Germany [2002] WTO Appellate Body Report WT/DS213/AB/R

United States – Definitive Safeguard Measures on Imports of Certain Steel Products [2003] WTO Panel Report WT/DS248/R; WT/DS249/R; WT/DS251/R; WT/DS252/R; WT/DS253/R; WT/DS254/R; WT/DS258/R; WT/DS259/R

United States – Definitive Safeguard Measures on Imports of Certain Steel Products [2003] WTO Appellate Body Report WT/DS248/AB/R; WT/DS249/AB/R; WT/DS251/AB/R; WT/DS252/AB/R; WT/DS253/AB/R; WT/DS254/AB/R; WT/DS258/AB/R; WT/DS259/AB/R

United States – Definitive Safeguard Measures on Imports of Circular Welded Carbon Quality Line Pipe from Korea [2001] WTO Panel Report WT/DS202/R

United States – Definitive Safeguard Measures on Imports of Circular Welded Carbon Quality Line Pipe from Korea [2002] WTO Appellate Body Report WT/DS202/AB/R

United States – Definitive Safeguard Measures on Imports of Wheat Gluten from the European Communities [2000] WTO Panel Report WT/DS166/R

United States – Denial of Most-Favoured Nation Treatment as to Non-Rubber Footwear from Brazil [1992] GATT 1994 Panel Report DS18/R-39S/128

United States – Measures Affecting the Cross-Border Supply of Gambling and Betting Services, [2005] WTO Appellate Body Report DS285/AB/R

United States – Import Prohibition of Certain Shrimp and Shrimp Products [2001] WTO Art 215 DSU Appellate Body Report WT/DS58/AB/RW

United States – Measures Concerning the Importation, Marketing and Sale of Tuna and Tuna Products [2015] WTO Art 215 DSU Appellate Body Report (Mexico) WT/DS381/AB/RW

United States – Standards for Reformulated and Conventional Gasoline [1996] WTO Appellate Body Report WT/D2/AB/R

United States – Sunset Review of Anti-Dumping Duties on Corrosion-Resistant Carbon Steel Flat Products from Japan [2003] WTO Panel Report WT/DS244/R

United States – Sunset Review of Anti-Dumping Duties on Corrosion-Resistant Carbon Steel Flat Products from Japan [2003] WTO Appellate Body Report WT/DS244/AB/R

United States – Sunset Reviews of Anti-Dumping Measures on Oil Country Tubular Goods from Argentina [2004] WTO Appellate Body Report WT/DS268/AB/R

United States – Sunset Reviews of Anti-Dumping Measures on Oil Country Tubular Goods from Argentina [2004] WTO Panel Report WT/DS268/R

Other

Al-Jedda v The United Kingdom [2011] Judgment of the ECtHR Application no. 27021/08

Applicability of Article VI, Section 22, of the Convention on the Privileges and Immunities of the United Nations (1989) 1989 ICJ Rep 177 (ICJ Advisory Opinion)

Belgian State v Banque Indosuez and Other [1997] CJEU, Opinion of Advocate General Jacobs ECLI:EU:C:1997:342

Belgian State v Banque Indosuez and Other [1997] Judgment of the CJEU ECLI:EU:C:1997:494

Bosphorus Hava Yolları Turizm ve Ticaret Anonim Şirketi v Ireland [2005] ECtHR Application no. 45036/98

Kadi and Al Barakaat International Foundation v Council and Commission [2008] Judgment of the CJEU ECLI:EU:C:2008:461

Reparation for Injuries Suffered in the Service of the United Nations (1949) 1949 ICJ Rep 174 (ICJ Advisory Opinion)

[1998] BVerfG, Order of the Second Senate 2 BvR 1877/97 and 2 BvR 50/98

Official Documents

WTO & GATT Documents

Committee on Anti-Dumping Practices, Minutes of the Regular Meeting held on 1–2 May 2003, G/ADP/M/24, 17.10.2003

Committee on Anti-Dumping Practices, Minutes of the Regular Meeting held on 23–24 October 2003, G/ADP/M/25, 9.3.2004

Committee on Anti-Dumping Practices, Notification of Laws and Regulations under Articles 18.5, 32.6 and 12.6 of the Agreements, Cameroon, G/ADP/N/1/CMR/1, 4.7.2013

Committee on Anti-Dumping Practices, Notification of Laws and Regulations under Articles 18.5, 32.6 and 12.6 of the Agreements, Cameroon, Corrigendum, G/ADP/N/1/Corr.1, 13.6.2014

Committee on Anti-Dumping Practices, Notification of Laws and Regulations under Articles 18.5, 32.6 and 12.6 of the Agreements, Cameroon, Supplement, G/ADP/N/1/CMR/1/Suppl.1, 27.5.2014

Committee on Anti-Dumping Practices, Notification of Laws and Regulations under Articles 18.5, 32.6 and 12.6 of the Agreements, Russian Federation, G/ADP/N/1/RUS/1, 3.10.2012

Committee on Anti-Dumping Practices, Recommendation Concerning the Period of Data Collection for Anti-Dumping Investigations, G/ADP/6, 16.5.2000

Committee on Anti-Dumping Practices, Report (2003) of the Committee on Anti-Dumping Practices, G/L/653, 28.10.2003

Committee on Anti-Dumping Practices, Report (2007) of the Committee on Anti-Dumping Practices, G/L/830, 26.10.2007

Committee on Anti-Dumping Practices, Report (2010) of the Committee on Anti-Dumping Practices, G/L/935, 28.10.2010

Committee on Anti-Dumping Practices, Report (2011) of the Committee on Anti-Dumping Practices, G/L/966, 26.20.2011

© The Author(s), under exclusive license to Springer Nature Switzerland AG 2021
F. Bickel, *Customs Unions in the WTO*, European Yearbook of International
Economic Law 20, https://doi.org/10.1007/978-3-030-86312-8

Committee on Anti-Dumping Practices, Report (2012) of the Committee on Anti-Dumping Practices, G/L/1006, 25.10.2012

Committee on Anti-Dumping Practices, Report (2013) of the Committee on Anti-Dumping Practices, G/L/1053, 29.10.2013

Committee on Anti-Dumping Practices, Report (2014) of the Committee on Anti-Dumping Practices, G/L/1079, 31.10.2014

Committee on Anti-Dumping Practices, Report (2015) of the Committee on Anti-Dumping Practices, G/L/1134, G/ADP/22, 30.10.2015

Committee on Anti-Dumping Practices, Report (2016) of the Committee on Anti-Dumping Practices, G/L/1158, G/ADP/23, 1.11.2016

Committee on Anti-Dumping Practices, Report (2017) of the Committee on Anti-Dumping Practices, G/L/1193, G/ADP/24, 30.10.2017

Committee on Anti-Dumping Practices, Report (2018) of the Committee on Anti-Dumping Practices, G/L/1270, G/ADP/25, 29.10.2018

Committee on Anti-Dumping Practices, Report (2019) of the Committee on Anti-Dumping Practices, G/L/1344, G/ADP/26, 21.11.2019

Committee on Anti-Dumping Practices, Report (2020) of the Committee on Anti-Dumping Practices, G/L/1366, G/ADP/27, 30.10.2020

Committee on Anti-Dumping Practices, Semi-Annual Report under Article 16.4 of the Agreement, Armenia, G/ADP/N/272/ARM, 3.10.2016

Committee on Anti-Dumping Practices, Semi-Annual Report under Article 16.4 of the Agreement, Brazil, G/ADP/N/280/BRA, 25.2.2016

Committee on Anti-Dumping Practices, Semi-Annual Report under Article 16.4 of the Agreement, Brazil, G/ADP/N/286/BRA, 30.8.2016

Committee on Anti-Dumping Practices, Semi-Annual Report under Article 16.4 of the Agreement, Costa Rica, G/ADP/N/237/CRI, 18.2.2013

Committee on Anti-Dumping Practices, Semi-Annual Report under Article 16.4 of the Agreement, Costa Rica, G/ADP/N/244/CRI, 24.9.2013

Committee on Anti-Dumping Practices, Semi-Annual Report under Article 16.4 of the Agreement, European Communities, G/ADP/N/158/EEC, 29.8.2007

Committee on Anti-Dumping Practices, Semi-Annual Report under Article 16.4 of the Agreement, European Communities, G/ADP/N/112/EEC, 8.3.2004

Committee on Anti-Dumping Practices, Semi-Annual Report under Article 16.4 of the Agreement, European Communities, Addendum, G/ADP/N/119/EEC/Add. 1, 14.9.2004

Committee on Anti-Dumping Practices, Semi-Annual Report under Article 16.4 of the Agreement, European Union, G/ADP/N/244/EU, 20.9.2013

Committee on Anti-Dumping Practices, Semi-Annual Report under Article 16.4 of the Agreement, Kyrgyz Republic, G/ADP/N/280/KGZ, 3.10.2016

Committee on Anti-Dumping Practices, Semi-Annual Report under Article 16.4 of the Agreement, Russian Federation, G/ADP/N/265/RUS, 20.3.2015

Committee on Anti-Dumping Practices, Semi-Annual Report under Article 16.4 of the Agreement, Russian Federation, G/ADP/N/280/RUS, 16.3.2016

Committee on Anti-Dumping Practices, Semi-Annual Report under Article 16.4 of the Agreement, Russian Federation, G/ADP/N/237/RUS, 5.3.2013

Committee on Anti-Dumping Practices, Semi-Annual Report under Article 16.4 of the Agreement, Russian Federation, G/ADP/N/272/RUS, 17.9.2015

Committee on Government Procurement, Minutes of the Formal Meeting of 27 February 2019, GPA/M/75, 28.5.2019

Committee on Government Procurement, Accession of the United Kingdom to the Agreement on Government Procurement in its own right, GPA/ACC/GBR/20/Rev.1, 6.2.2019

Committee on Government Procurement, Accession of the United Kingdom to the Agreement on Government Procurement in its own right, GPA/CD/2/Add.1, 26.6.2019

Committee on Regional Trade Agreements, Customs Union Between the European Community and the Principality of Andorra, WT/REG53/3, 12.11.1998

Committee on Regional Trade Agreements, Gulf Cooperation Council Customs Union, Notification from Saudi Arabia, WT/REG222/N/1, 20.11.2006

Committee on Regional Trade Agreements, Gulf Cooperation Council Customs Union, Notification from Saudi Arabia, Corrigendum, WT/REG222/N/1/Corr.1, 31.3.2008

Committee on Regional Trade Agreements, Note on the Meeting of 19–20 June 2018, WT/REG/M/89, 25.6.2018

Committee on Regional Trade Agreements, Note on the Meeting of 27 June 2016, WT/REG/M/81, 12.7.2016

Committee on Regional Trade Agreements, Note on the Meeting of 27 September 2016, WT/REG/M/82, 4.11.2016

Committee on Regional Trade Agreements, Note on the Meeting of 7–8 November 2016, WT/REG/M/83, 7.12.2016

Committee on Regional Trade Agreements, Note on the Meeting of 9–10 November 2017, WT/REG/M/87, 5.12.2017

Committee on Regional Trade Agreements, Notification of Regional Trade Agreement, Gulf Cooperation Council, Revision, WT/REG276/N/1/Rev.1, 17.11.2009

Committee on Regional Trade Agreements, Rules of Procedure for Meetings of the Committee on Regional Trade Agreements, Adopted by the Committee on Regional Trade Agreements on 2 July 1996, WT/REG/1, 14.8.1996

Committee on Regional Trade Agreements, Systemic Issues Related to "Other Regulations of Commerce", Background Note by the Secretariat (Revision), WT/REG/W/17/Rev. 1, 5.2.1998

Committee on Rules of Origin, Report (2013) of the Committee on Rules of Origin to the Council for Trade in Goods, G/L/1047, 10.10.2013

Committee on Rules of Origin, Report (2018) of the Committee on Rules of Origin to the Council for Trade in Goods, G/L/1266, 18.10.2018

Committee on Rules of Origin, Notification under Article 5.1 and Paragraph 4 of Annex II of the Agreement of Rules of Origin, G/RO/N/1, 9.5.1995

Committee on Market Access, Rectification and modification of Schedules, Schedule CLXXV – European Union, G/MA/TAR/RS/506, 17.10.2017

Committee on Market Access, Rectification and modification of Schedules – Schedule XIX – United Kingdom, G/MA/TAR/RS/570, 24.7.2018

Council for Trade in Services, European Communities and their Member States, Schedule of Specific Commitments, GATS/SC/31, 15.04.1994

Council for Trade in Services, Communication from the United Kingdom of Great Britain and Northern Ireland, Certification of schedule of specific commitments, S/C/W/380, 3.12.2018

Council for Trade in Services, Communication from the United Kingdom of Great Britain and Northern Ireland, Certification of list of article II (MFN) exemptions, S/C/W/381, 3.12.2018

Committee on Trade and Development, Dedicated Session on Regional Trade Agreements, Preferential Trade Agreement Between Chile and India (Goods), Questions and Replies, WT/COMTD/RTA/4/2, 4.5.2010

Committee on Trade and Development, Dedicated Session on Regional Trade Agreements, Preferential Trade Agreement Between Chile and India (Goods), Questions and Replies, WT/COMTD/RTA/4/3, 26.7.2010

Committee on Trade and Development, Gulf Cooperation Council Customs Union – Saudi Arabia's Notification (WT/COMTD/N/25), Communication from Bahrain, the United Arab Emirates, Saudi Arabia, Oman, Qatar and Kuwait, Addendum, WT/COMTD/66/Add.3, 5.12.2008

Committee on Trade and Development, Gulf Cooperation Council Customs Union – Saudi Arabia's Notification (WT/COMTD/N/25), Communication from the European Communities, Addendum, WT/COMTD/66/Add.2, 25.11.2008

Committee on Trade and Development, Gulf Cooperation Council Customs Union – Saudi Arabia's Notification (WT/COMTD/N/25), Communication from the United States, Addendum, WT/COMTD/66/Add.1, 24.11.2008

Committee on Trade and Development, Legal Note on Regional Trade Arrangements under the Enabling Clause, Note by the Secretariat, WT/COMTD/W/114, 13.5.2003

Committee on Trade and Development, Note on the Meeting of 15 November 2017, WT/COMTD/M/104, 19.3.2018

Committee on Trade and Development, Note on the Meeting of 28 June 2019, WT/COMTD/M/109, 8.11.2019

Committee on Trade and Development, Note on the Meeting of 5 April 2019, WT/COMTD/M/108, 21.6.2019

Committee on Trade and Development, Notification of Regional Trade Agreement, Gulf Cooperation Council, WT/COMTD/N/25, 31.3.2008

Committee on Trade and Development, Systematic and Specific Issues Arising out of the Dual Notification of the Gulf Cooperation Council Customs Union, Communication from China, Egypt and India, WT/COMTD/W/175, 30.9.2010

Committee on Trade and Development, Third (Special) Session, Note of the Meeting of 14 September 1995, WT/COMTD/M/3, 23.10.1995

Committee on Trade and Development, Committee on Regional Trade Agreements, Factual Presentation, Gulf Cooperation Council Customs Union (Goods), WT/REG276/1, 21.3.2018

CRTA, The Cooperation and Customs Union Agreement between the European Union and the Republic of San Marino (Goods), WT/REG280/1, 9.2.2018

Dispute Settlement Body, Minutes of the Meeting, Held in the Centre William Rappard on 10 January 2001, WT/DSB/M/96, 22.2.2001

Director General, Communication from the European Union, WLI/100, 29.2.2020

General Council, Decision of 14 December 2006, Transparency for Preferential Trade Arrangements, WT/L/672, 14.12.2006

General Council, Decision of 14 December 2010, Transparency Mechanism for Preferential Trade Arrangements, WT/L/806, 16.12.2010

General Council, Transparency Mechanism for Regional Trade Agreements, WT/L/ 671, 14.12.2006

General Council, The United Kingdom's Withdrawal From the European Union, Communication from the United Kingdom, WT/GC/2016, 1.2.2020

Ministerial Conference, Accession of the Russian Federation, Decision of 16 December 2011, WT/MIN(11)/24, WT/L/839, 17.12.2011

Ministerial Conference, Eleventh Session, Buenos Aires, 10–13 December 2017, Draft Ministerial Decision on Improvement of Transparency for Regional Trade Agreements, Communication from the Russian Federation, WT/MIN(17)/28, 8.12.2017

Ministerial Conference, Tenth Session, Nairobi, 15–18 December 2015, Nairobi Ministerial Declaration, Adopted on 19. December 2015, WT/MIN(15)/DEC, 21.12.2015

Negotiating Group on MTN Agreements and Arrangements, Meeting of 18 October 1990, MTN.GNG/NG8/21, 29.10.1990

Negotiating Group on MTN Agreements and Arrangements, Meeting of 18 October 1990, MTN.GNG/NG8/21, 29.10.1990

Negotiating Group on MTN Agreements and Arrangements, Meetings of 31 January-2 February and 19–20 February 1990, MTN.GNG/NG8/15, 19.3.1990

Negotiating Group on MTN Agreements and Arrangements, Report of the Acting Chairman of the Informal Group on Anti-Dumping, MTN.GNG/NG8/W/83/ Add.5, 23.7.1990

Negotiating Group on MTN Agreements and Arrangements, Report of the acting Chairman of the Informal Group on Anti-Dumping, MTN/GNG/NG8/W/83/ Add5, 23.7.1990

Negotiating Group on MTN Agreements and Arrangements, Report of the Negotiating Group on MTN Agreements and Arrangements to the Group of Negotiations on Goods, MTN.GNG/NG8/W/85, 30.10.1990

Negotiating Group on MTN Agreements and Arrangements, Report of the Negotiating Group on MTN Agreements and Arrangements to the Group of Negotiations on Goods, MTN.GNG/NG8/W/85, 30.10.1990

Negotiating Group on MTN Agreements and Arrangements, Submission of Japan on the Amendments of the Anti-Dumping Code, MTN.GNG/NG8/W/48/Add.1, 29.1.1990

Negotiating Group on Rules, Compendium of Issues Related to Regional Trade Agreements, Background Note by the Secretariat, Revision, TN/RL/W/8/Rev.1, 1.8.2002

Sub-Committee on Non-Tariff Barriers, Group on Anti-Dumping Policies, Draft Report on the Group on Anti-Dumping Policies, TN.64/NTB/W/19, 24.4.1967

Trade Policy Review Body, Trade Policy Review, Report by the Secretariat, Armenia, WT/TPR/S/379, 25.9.2018

Trade Policy Review Body, Trade Policy Review, Report by the Secretariat, Countries of the Central African Economic and Monetary Community, WT/TPR/S/285, 24.6.2013

Trade Policy Review Body, Trade Policy Review, Report by the Secretariat, Countries of the Central African Economic and Monetary Community (CEMAC), WT/TPR/S/285, 24.6.2013

Trade Policy Review Body, Trade Policy Review, Report by the Secretariat, East African Community, WT/TPR/S/384, 13.2.2019

Trade Policy Review Body, Trade Policy Review, Report by the Secretariat, Egypt, WT/TPR/S/367, 16.1.2018

Trade Policy Review Body, Trade Policy Review, Report by the Secretariat, European Union, WT/TPR/S/395, 10.12.2019

Trade Policy Review Body, Trade Policy Review, Report by the Secretariat, Guinea, WT/TPR/S/370, 24.4.2018

Trade Policy Review Body, Trade Policy Review, Report by the Secretariat, Peru, WT/TPR/S/393, 27.8.2019

Trade Policy Review Body, Trade Policy Review, Report by the Secretariat, South African Customs Union, WT/TPR/S/324, 30.9.2015

Trade Policy Review Body, Trade Policy Review, Report by the Secretariat, Southern African Customs Union, WT/TPR/S/324, 30.9.2015

Trade Policy Review Body, Trade Policy Review, Report by the Secretariat, The Kingdom of Saudi Arabia, WT/TPR/S/333, 29.2.2016

Trade Policy Review Body, Trade Policy Review, Report by the Secretariat, The Member Countries of the West African Economic and Monetary Union, WT/TPR/S/362, 14.9.2017

Trade Policy Review Body, Trade Policy Review, Report by the Secretariat, The Member Countries of the West African Economic and Monetary Union (WAEMU), WT/TPR/S/362, 14.9.2017

Trade Policy Review Body, Trade Policy Review, Report by the Secretariat, Trinidad and Tobago, WT/TPR/S/388, 27.3.2019

Trade Policy Review Body, Trade Policy Review, Report by the Secretariat, Turkey, WT/TPR/S/331, 9.2.2016

Trade Policy Review Body, Trade Policy Review, Report by the Secretariat, Uruguay, WT/TPR/S/374, 23.5.2018

Trade Policy Review Body, Trade Policy Review, Report by the Secretariat, The Member Countries of the West African Economic and Monetary Union (WAEMU), WT/TPR/S/362, 14.9.2017

Working Party on the Accession of the Russian Federation, Report of the Working
Party on the Accession of the Russian Federation to the World Trade Organiza-
tion (Russia Accession Protocol), WT/ACC/RUS/70, WT/MIN(11)/2,
17.11.2011
GATT Analytical Index (pre1995), Article VI Anti-Dumping and Countervailing
Duties, (https://www.wto.org/english/res_e/publications_e/ai17_e/gatt1994_
art6_gatt47.pdf) last accessed: 11.10.2020.
RTA Database, https://rtais.wto.org/, last accessed 11.10.2020

Other

Communauté Économique et Monétaire de l'Afrique Centrale, Rapport
Intermimaire de Surveillance Multilatérale 2017 et Perspective Port 2018, 34th
Edition, 03.2018
Eurasian Economic Commission, The Eurasian Economic Union – Facts and Figures, Library of Eurasian Integration 2018
European Commission, Notice regarding the application of anti-dumping, anti-
subsidy and safeguard measures in force in the Community following enlarge-
ment to include the Republic of Bulgaria and Romania and the possibility of
review (2007 Enlargement Notice), OJ C 297/12, 7.12.2006
European Commission, Notice regarding the application of anti-dumping and anti-
subsidy measures in force in the Community following enlargement to include
the Czech Republic, the Republic of Estonia, the Republic of Cyprus, the
Republic of Latvia, the Republic of Lithuania, the Republic of Hungary, the
Republic of Malta, the Republic of Poland, the Republic of Slovenia and the
Slovak Republic and the possibility of review (2004 Enlargement Notice)., OJ C
91/2, 15.4.2004
European Commission, Notice regarding the application of anti-dumping and anti-
subsidy measures in force in the Union following enlargement to include the
Republic of Croatia and the possibility of review (2013 Enlargement Notice), OJ
C 137/09, 16.5.2013
European Commission, Notice of initiation of a partial interim review of the
antidumping measures applicable to imports of certain products originating in
the People's Republic of China, Russian Federation, Ukraine and the Republic of
Belarus, OJ C 70/15, 20.3.2004
European Commission, Notice of initiation of an anti-dumping proceeding
concerning imports of high fatigue performance steel concrete reinforcement
bars originating in the People's Republic of China, OJ C 143/12, 30.4.2015
European Commission, Notice regarding the application of anti-dumping and anti-
subsidy measures in force in the Union following the withdrawal of the United
Kingdom and the possibility of a review, OJ C 18/41, 18.1.2021.

European Commission, Notice on the application of the trade defence legislation and measures of the European Union in Northern Ireland from 1 January 2021, OJ C 248/3, 25.6.2021.

European Commission, Task Force for Relations with the United Kingdom, Draft text of the Agreement on the New Partnership with the United Kingdom, 18.3.2020, UKTF (2020)

European Commission, Getting ready for changes, Communication on readiness at the end of the transition period between the European Union and the United Kingdom, 09.07.2020

Government of India, Ministry of Commerce & Industry, Department of Commerce, Directorate General of Anti-Dumping & Allied Duties, Notification Final Findings, Case No. O.I./08/2017, 13.2.2018.

HM Government, The Future Relationship with the EU, The UK's Approach to Negotiations, CP211, 2.2020

HM Government, Draft UK Negotiating Document, Draft Working Text for a Comprehensive Free Trade Agreement Between the United Kingdom and the European Union, 19.5.2020.

House of Commons, Oral evidence taken before the International Trade Committee on 29.11.2017, HC (2017–19) 603i

House of Commons, Oral evidence taken before the International Trade Committee on 14.3.2018, HC (2018–19) 743ii

International Law Commission, Commentary to the Articles on Responsibility of States for Internationally Wrongful Acts (ARSIWA Commentary), ILC Yearbook 2001/II(2)

International Law Commission, Commentary to the Articles on the Responsibility of International Organizations (ARIO Commentary), ILC Report on the Work of its Sixty-third Session, UNGAOR 66th Sess, Supp. No. 10, UN Doc. A/66/10 (2011)

International Law Commission, Comments and observations received from international organizations, 2004, Doc A/CN.4/545

International Law Commission, Responsibility of International Organizations, Second report on responsibility of international organizations, by Mr. Giorgio Gaja, Special Rapporteur, Doc A/CN.4/541, 2.4.2004

International Law Commission, Report of the International Law Commission on the work of its sixty-first session, Responsibility of International Organizations, Doc A/64/10, 2009

International Law Commission, Responsibility of International Organizations, Comments and observations received from international organizations, 2004, A/CN.4/545

International Law Commission, Responsibility of International Organizations, Seventh report on responsibility of international organizations, by Mr. Giorgio Gaja, Special Rapporteur, Doc A/CN.4/610, 29.3.2009

International Law Commission, Responsibility of International Organizations, Third report on responsibility of international organizations, by Mr. Giorgio Gaja, Special Rapporteur, Doc. A/CN.4/553, 13.5.2005

International Trade Administration Commission, Investigation Into the Alleged Dumping of Clear Float Glass Originating in or Imported from Saudi Arabia and the United Arab Emirates: Final Determinations, Report No. 615, 18.10.2019

United States Trade Representative, Report on the Appellate Body of the World Trade Organization, 02.2020

Political Declaration setting out the framework for the future relationship between the European Union and the United Kingdom (Revised Political Declaration), 19.10.2019

Political Declaration setting out the framework for the future relationship between the European Union and the United Kingdom (Initial Political Declaration), 25.11.2018